Jacques
Cousteau

# WHALES

By Jacques-Yves Cousteau and Yves Paccalet

Translated by I. Mark Paris

Harry N. Abrams, Inc., Publishers, New York

Jacques Cousteau
WHALES

# Contents

This book is dedicated to the biggest and
most beautiful cetaceans of them all;
the ones that whalers have hunted relentlessly
and nearly to extinction.

To all the baleen whales:
Right whale (*Balaena glacialis*),
Bowhead whale (*Balaena mysticetus*),
Pygmy right whale (*Caperea marginata*),
Gray whale (*Eschrichtius robustus*),
Blue whale (*Balaenoptera musculus*),
Fin whale (*Balaenoptera physalus*),
Sei whale (*Balaenoptera borealis*),
Bryde's whale (*Balaenoptera edeni*),
Minke whale (*Balaenoptera acutorostrata*),
Humpback whale (*Megaptera novaeangliae*);
and the largest of all toothed cetaceans,
the sperm whale (*Physeter macrocephalus*).

Project Director: Robert Morton
Editor: Ann Whitman
Typography: Maria Miller

Library of Congress Cataloging-in-Publication Data

Cousteau, Jacques Yves.
Jacques Cousteau—whales.

Translation of: La planète des baleines.
Bibliography: p. Includes index.
1. Whales. I. Paccalet, Yves. II. Title.
QL737.C4C69313 1988 599.5′1 88–3426
ISBN 0–8109–1046–2



Published in 1988 by Harry N. Abrams, Incorporated, New York


A Times Mirror Company

Printed and bound in Italy

The Cousteau Society is a nonprofit membership-supported organization
dedicated to the protection and improvement of the quality of life
for present and future generations.

The Cousteau Society, 930 West 21st Street, Norfolk, Va. 23517

*Let our imagination transport us high above our planet. Earth spins below us; only the vast oceans that gird the continents and islands seem to be alive. From our lofty vantage point, the living creatures that dwell on the dry surface of the globe are no longer visible; we can no longer make out rhinoceroses or elephants or crocodiles or huge snakes. But on the surface of the seas we can still see large herds of animals swiftly plying measureless expanses of water, cavorting with mountainous, storm-tossed waves. These creatures—which from our imaginary perch in space we might well think the only living things on earth—are the cetaceans.*

Lacépède (1804)

## INTRODUCTION

*"Rising with his utmost velocity from the furthest depths, the Sperm Whale thus booms his entire bulk into the pure element of air. . . . In those moments, the torn, enraged waves he shakes off, seem his mane." In* Moby-Dick *(1851), Herman Melville tried to convey the incredible beauty of a whale as it breaks the surface and seems to vault over the moon.*

*Overleaf: The huge, spectacular body of the humpback whale—shaped and smoothed by evolution for maximum swimming efficiency —was millions of years in the making.*

The whale is the most astonishing animal the earth has ever known. It does not merely inspire superlatives—it is a living superlative. Some whales are much larger than the gigantic dinosaurs of the Mesozoic. It would take 25 elephants, or 2,000 human beings, to equal the weight of a single blue whale; its tongue alone weighs as much as an elephant. The blue whale is as long as four buses placed end to end. Its skeleton weighs 18 tons, its blubber 30, its meat 44. When it blows at the ocean's surface, the spout looks for all the world like a new cloud in the sky.

When it swims, however, this mountain of muscle and fat is as fluid as the element it calls home. The whale can be a gregarious, intelligent, peaceable creature that coaxes and cajoles its young, comes to the defense of its fellow whales, converses with them in an enigmatic language, and sings with all its might in raging storms.

So: what has mankind made of these creatures? We've made them into oil for our lamps, stays for our corsets, meat for our pets. We have made them into lipstick for our makeup kits and lubricants to keep our engines of war running smoothly. While *Homo sapiens* probes outer space for life on other planets, certain members of our species are eradicating wondrous forms of life right here on earth!

As recently as thirty years ago, this slaughter did not strike everyone as unusual or illogical. "It is extraordinary how few people realize that a whale secretes a prodigious amount of oil, that greasy substance coveted by the entire world," wrote Georges Blond in 1953. "The modern demand for oil for machinery, war industries, and the armies they supply rises day by day. Modern chemistry extracts from whale oil not only lubricants but glycerine, margarine, soap, skin-foods, and cosmetics. . . ."

More than fifty million years of peace in the oceans came to an end when man started butchering whales by the thousands. The carnage went from bad to worse. More whales have been wiped out in the last fifty years than in the four centuries previous: between 1929 and 1979, more than 2 million were caught and flensed, for an annual average of 40,000. Every whaling season, whales collectively shed as much blood as the *Amoco Cadiz* lost oil during its disastrous spill. But this slick turns the seas red.

Today there is not a single whale product or by-product that chemists cannot produce synthetically or extract from plant or mineral substances, and at competitive prices; yet we go right on taking whales. There is no longer any economic justification for keeping whaling fleets in operation. To be sure, it can still pay to whale: a harpooned whale can be worth between $15,000 and $25,000, depending on its size. But the profit margin is growing smaller and smaller; whale stocks are dwindling, while the cost of fuel and manpower is going up. The absurd result? Subsidies. Thus an activity that deprives the citizens of the world of a fabulous sight is supported at taxpayer expense! The titans of the animal kingdom are vanishing, and our planet is that much poorer for it. This massacre not only upsets the balance of the marine ecosystem, but also deprives our dreams and musings of creatures beyond belief—all to line the pockets of a handful of shipowners and fishing magnates.

Whaling advocates usually fall back on two arguments, and we might just as well dispose of them right away. First, they say, suspending operations would be unfair to all the people on factory ships or shore stations, who would be thrown out of work. Second, mankind is in dire need of every possible source of protein.

We have all heard the unemployment argument before; it is the refuge of those too lazy to come up with a better rationale. Out it pops at us like a jack-in-the-box every time a commercial venture stands accused of despoiling nature. Applied to whales, the argument is less convincing than ever. The number of people whose livelihood depends on factory vessels, shore stations, and whaling-related industries does not exceed a few thousand worldwide. In Japan and the Soviet Union—the only two countries where this sector of the population is of any consequence—whalers account for 2 to 3 percent of all fishery employees. The Soviet and Japanese fisheries derive no more than 4 percent of their total income from whaling. In 1973, whaling operations accounted for a scant 0.024 percent of Japan's gross national product; by now, this figure is probably one-tenth of what it was—hardly worth considering. We might point out that substituting plant or mineral derivatives for whale products generates new jobs. Moreover, the recovery of whale populations has opened up another important source of revenue: tourism.

The animal protein argument is not worth a single yen or ruble more. The Soviet Union feeds its whale meat to animals (primarily on fur farms) or exports it to Japan. Whale meat is an important part of the diet of Eskimos and a few other aboriginal hunters, but their dependence on it is decreasing.

Only in Japan is whale meat eaten with any regularity; it accounts for exactly 0.9 percent of total protein intake, 2.1 percent of all animal-derived protein, and 4 percent of protein from seafood (according to a 1976 report by the Food and Agricultural Organization's Advisory Committee on Marine Resources Research). These minuscule proportions cannot possibly justify a continuation of the butchery. As a leading economic power, Japan wins no respect by marshaling its vast industrial and technological resources for an activity that is nothing more than plunder. No one denies that whaling is a centuries-old tradition in Japan, but the past does not excuse the present.

Can nations be persuaded to stop shedding the blood of whales? Many countries have already done so, but a few are determined not to give in. The ideology of state doctrine is not easily swayed. Soviet officials tell us that whaling is consistent with the Marxist-Leninist concept of man's relationship with nature. But the Soviet people are not unmoved by the wonders of our planet, and the champions of the whale are gaining ground in Moscow and Leningrad.

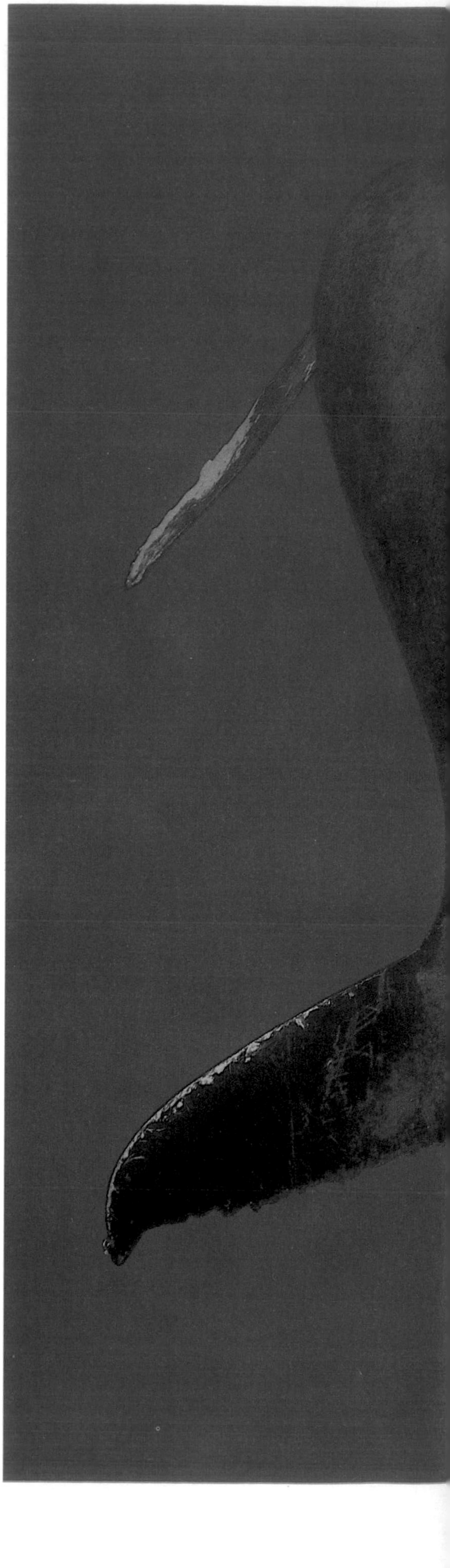

With regard to Japan (and the countries it has enlisted to carry on its whaling operations by proxy—South Korea, Taiwan, Brazil, and Chile), the problem is different. Here we are dealing with a situation that is analogous to the illicit trade in fur or ivory: a handful of clever, greedy individuals versed in the ins-and-outs of manipulating officials and markets, and forming pressure groups. The whaling lobby is a fact of life; it puts up a good fight, and nowhere better than in the halls of the International Whaling Commission, where it battles a worldwide movement that asks that whales be left in peace.

Nevertheless, the picture is changing, because the laws of economics are working in favor of the whales. The animals cannot breed fast enough for capitalist fleets to turn a profit. Whales have become a scarce commodity, and tracking them down across vast ocean expanses uses up equally vast amounts of costly fuel. In this respect, it may be said that OPEC has been more effective in safeguarding whales than have all the preservationist societies put together.

In addition, a growing number of citizens now understand that economic arguments become unacceptable as soon as they threaten the survival of even a single species. We live in an age of sweeping change; things once reserved for a privileged few—manufactured consumer goods—are becoming commonplace, while commodities once plentiful and free—clean air and water, nature in all its exuberance—are growing scarce. If we gauge things this way, a single sperm whale could be reckoned more valuable than a whole fleet of whaling ships.

There is still hope, but time is of the essence. For some local stocks, the drop in population is so severe that, even if all whaling were to cease overnight, there is no guarantee that the animals could ever recover.

Furthermore, whales (like all marine life) are reeling from the effects of overdevelopment and pollution. They suffer from oil spills and the discharge of toxic waste from homes, farms, and factories; demolitions at sea, the building of seawalls, and the intrusion of overzealous tourists.

Compared with other endangered species, whales are at a special disadvantage: because of their enormous size, they are presumed indestructible. After all, people reason, the whales roam vast expanses of water; surely they can manage to give harpoon gunners the slip. But anyone who believes this rationale is deluding himself: man is everywhere.

It is time we gave these animals a fighting chance. We owe it to ourselves, to our children, and to generations yet unborn. If we do not, we shall have to use the past tense when we talk about the right whale and its bonnet of barnacles, the fabulously large blue whale, the swift, streamlined rorquals, the singing humpbacks, the gray whales that migrate through the waters off the California coast, and the brawny, once dreaded sperm whale.

This book is a labor of love—and of anger. It is an indignant outcry against pointless slaughter and a solemn declaration of unswerving friendship for the nation of the whales. If we lose the whales, we lose something of incalculable value from our dreams, our myths, our finest poetry—from all the things that made us human before we defined ourselves in terms of heavy industry. In *Whales*, we endeavor to explain that mankind is annihilating species that may have countless wonderful secrets to share with us. Whales may yet guide us to the ocean depths or open our ears to the pulse of the seas.

This is our hope: that the children born today may still have, twenty years hence, a bit of green grass under their bare feet, a breath of clean air to breathe, a patch of blue water to sail upon, and a whale on the horizon to set them dreaming.

CHAPTER 1

# A Crimson Mantle Floating on the Sea

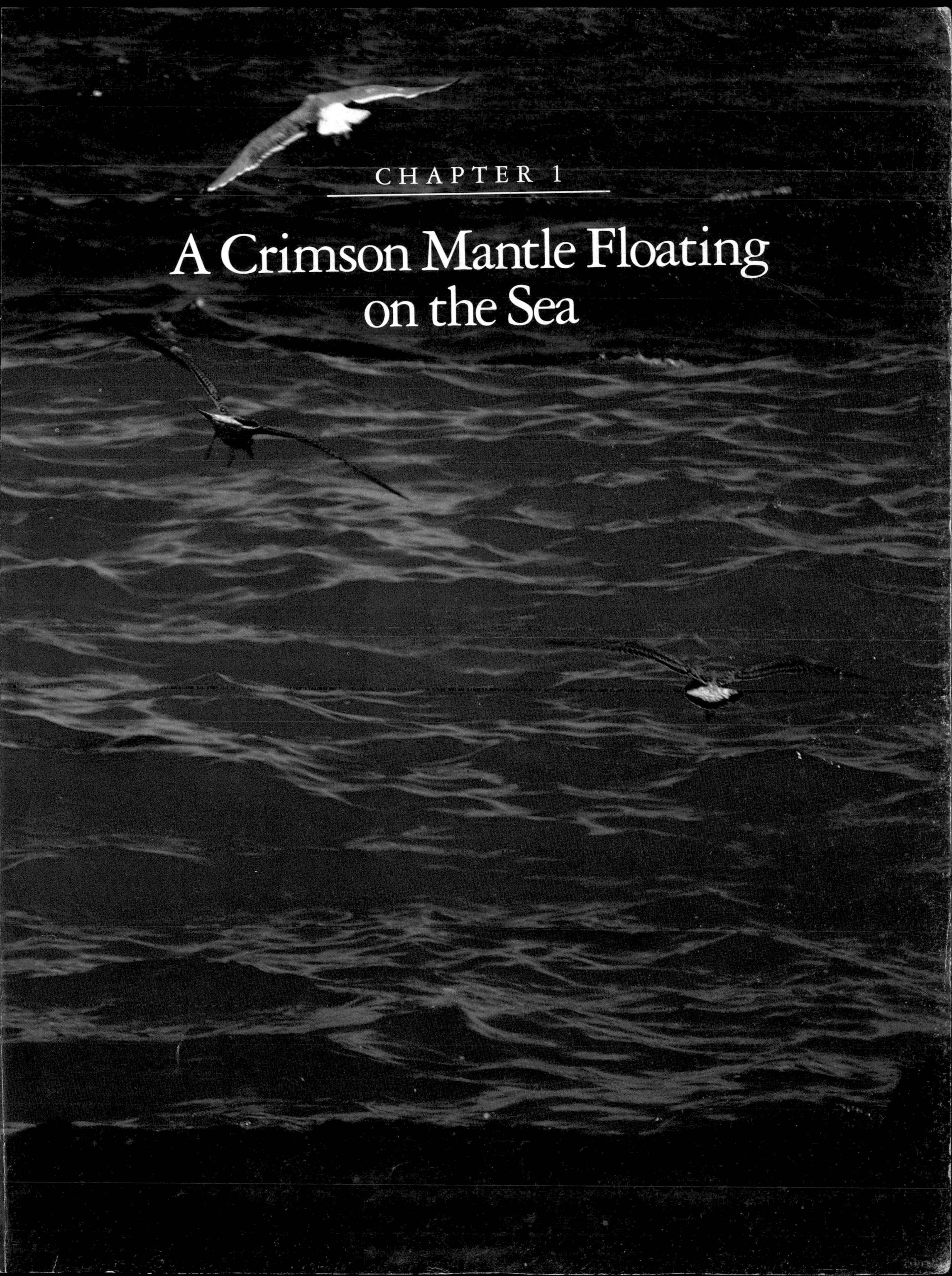

CETVS INGENS, QVEM INCOLÆ FARÆ INSVLÆ ICH-
*thyophagi tempestatibus appulsum, unco comprehensum ferreo securibus dissecant & partiuntur inter se.*

NAVTÆ IN DORSA CETORVM, QVAE INSVLAS PVTANT,
*anchoras figentes sæpe periclitantur. Hos cetos Trolual sua lingua appellant, Germani e Teuffeluual.*

SIMILIS EST ET ILLORVM ICON APVD EVNDEM, CAPITE,
*rostro, dentibus, fistulis, quos montium instar grandes esse scribit, & naues euertere, nisi sono tubarum aut missis in mare rotundis & vacuis vasis absterreantur: quod & in Balthico mari circa balenam Brunfisch dictam fieri diximus.*

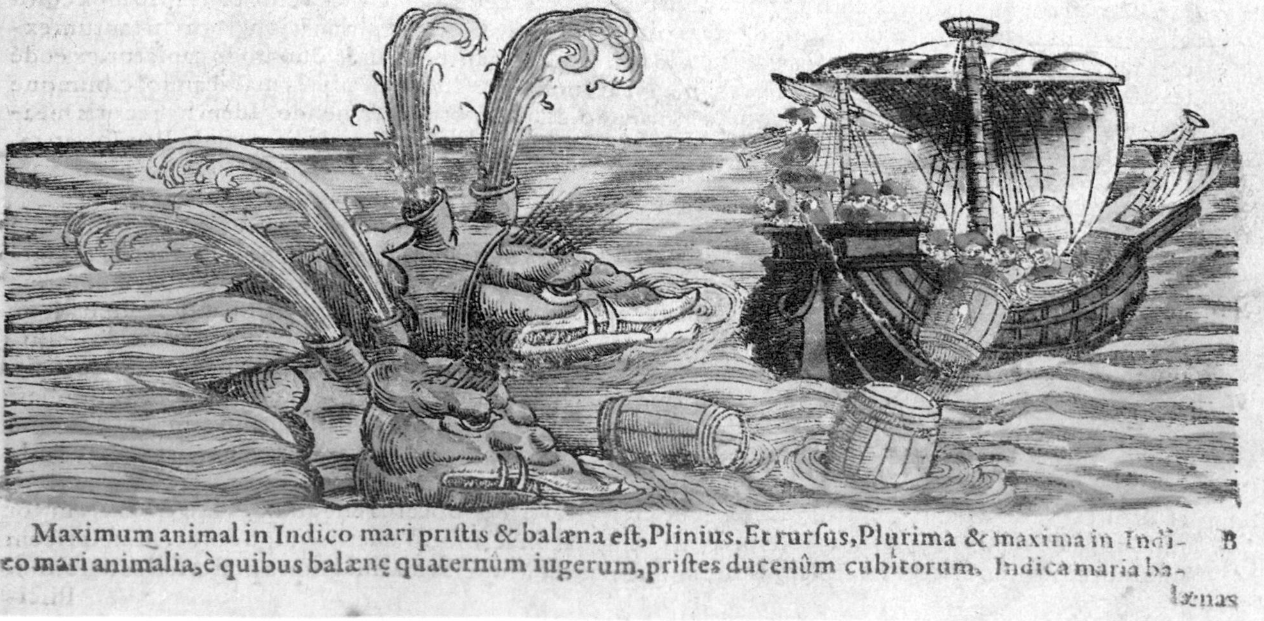

Maximum animal in Indico mari pristis & balæna est, Plinius. Et rursus, Plurima & maxima in Indi- B
co mari animalia, è quibus balænę quaternûm iugerum, pristes ducenûm cubitorum. Indica maria ba-

lænas

*Enticed by the riches that would come from vanquishing the whales, man disturbed the peace of their vast wilderness, violated their haven, wiped out all those unable to steal away to the inaccessible wasteland of icy polar seas. . . . And so, the giant of giants fell prey to his weaponry. Since man shall never change, only when they cease to exist shall these enormous species cease to be the victims of his self-interest. They flee before him, but it is no use; man's resourcefulness transports him to the ends of the earth. Death is their only refuge now.*

Lacépède (1804)

IV.

QVA INDVSTRIA BARBARI IN S. MARIÆ INSVLA CETOS capiant.

*INDI S. Mariæ insulæ accolæ, cetos hoc ferè modo captant. Vbi morentur, prius attendunt. Ad proditum vnum scaphis suis applicant: & vnius lapidis iactu absistentes, hamum seu vncum ferreum, oblongo ex arborum corticibus fune religatum, in corpus eius eiaculantur. Altera ergò funis extremitate in scaphis retenta, piscem tamdiu attrahunt, dum & penitus longo exercitio ille fatigetur, & renisu valentiore vulnus augeatur grandescatq́ue, isque adeò cruoris copiosioris emanatione infirmetur & q. emoriatur. Hoc impetrato, in vadum eum extrahunt: extractum laniant: & suam quilibet portionem auferunt.*

*b*

*The relationship between men and whales over the centuries has been ambivalent and intensely emotional. Above: An eighteenth-century engraving of primitives shore-whaling in the Indian Ocean. Left: An engraving from Conrad Gesner's* Historiae Animalium *(Zurich, 1551–1587): The top illustration shows the flensing of a whale in the Faeroe Islands. At center is a whale so big that sailors have mistaken it for an island. The bottom scene shows sailors flinging out empty barrels in hopes of diverting whales from their ship; legend held that music would soothe an angry whale, so the sailor on the poop deck is leaving nothing to chance.*

"Strike the whale, bully whaler!" the sea chantey goes. The cheeriness of the chantey belies its grim import. The "bully" whaleman brandished a fearsome weapon, and a refrain of "Bleed 'em pale!" would have been more in keeping with his grisly task.

A centuries-old style of seafaring adventure is more aptly described as an unrelenting slaughter that turned the seas red with the blood of whales. What words can convey the terror a whale experiences as a harpoon rips into its sensitive pulmonary tissue? The panic this creature must feel as its ruptured alveoli become choked with blood, as its spout finally turns crimson, and it knows that the end is near? The last hopeless dive, the writhing "flurry" as its blowholes spurt scarlet gore, the gurgling death throes? All that butchery, all that torment—for what? Some oil, some meat, some baleen!

The strangest part of all is that people have characterized this spectacle as "stirring"; they have extolled its "rugged poetry" and waxed rhapsodic over its "sublime grandeur." Then again, man has never been shy about dignifying his cruelty.

## THE EARLIEST WHALERS

Man has been chopping whales to pieces for a long, long time indeed. Sometimes it was for their oil, but Guillaume Rondelet (1568) reported that ancient seafaring peoples ate the tongue. Meling, Norway, is the site of the oldest known representation of whaling—cave engravings from about 1800 B.C. showing men in boats giving chase to a spouting animal. In his *Geography* (first century A.D.), Strabo tells us that primitive fish-eating peoples used whale jaws for door jambs and whale ribs for house frames.

At first, only stranded animals were taken; if not already dead when washed ashore, they were finished off with spears. Such was the fate that awaited the famous *"orca"* (possibly a sperm whale) that strayed into the harbor at Ostia in the first century A.D., during the reign of the emperor Claudius. Pliny the Elder recounts the memorable incident in his *Naturalis Historia* (IX, 5): "The emperor ordered several nets spread out to block the harbor channels and thither repaired with his Praetorian cohorts. The Roman people were then treated to a spectacular sight: soldiers hurling spears from the attacking vessels, one of which we saw fill up with water the creature spouted, and sink."

## DEATH BY SUFFOCATION

*According to some accounts, Indians used to catch whales off the coast of Florida by plugging their blowholes with wooden chocks. This implausible technique was also ascribed to "Africans along the east coast of Madagascar" in an anonymous engraving from 1780. Here is how P.-J. van Beneden (1867–92) described this primitive fishery: "Savages . . . caught right whales by jumping onto their snouts and driving a long wooden cone into one of their blowholes, after which they clung to the animal as it went underwater; when they surfaced together, another plug would be rammed into the other blowhole. . . . This forced [the whales] to swim towards the coast."*

*Louis Thiercelin (1866), for one, found this* tour de force *hard to believe. "How do you suppose a man with a stopper in each hand could have managed to swim right up to a whale, clamber onto its back . . . drive a plug into a blowhole powerful enough to pop all the corks on earth with a single contraction, dive with the animal into the ocean depths for fifteen or twenty minutes, and then drive in the other plug?"*

Some primitive peoples caught whales in astonishingly resourceful ways. The Eskimos of Greenland, for example, hunted the huge, guileless bowhead, or Greenland right whale, by inflating sealskin bags with air and lashing them to their harpoons; their stricken quarry was, thus, easier to track and would not sink after they died.

The Eskimos of Alaska, the Siberians of the Bering Strait, and the Ainu of Japan were partial to the California gray whale and the North Pacific right whale. "Throughout the fall," according to Lacépède (1804), "the inhabitants of several islands near Kamchatka set out in search of whales, which are plentiful just offshore at that time of year. When they come across any that are asleep, they silently steal upon them and stab them with poisoned spears." In 1802, M. Sauer suggested that the active ingredient in the lethal dose might be an extract of the Eurasian herb monkshood (aconite) and that the concoction further included rendered fat from human corpses.

Every migration season, Indians living on Vancouver and Queen Charlotte islands would stealthily put to sea and lie in wait just offshore for California gray whales and smaller rorquals. As Charles Scammon noted in 1874, they added a touch of panache to their toil. "Like enemies in ambush, [they] glide in canoes . . . , launching their instruments of torture, and like hounds worrying the last life-blood from their vitals. . . . Those among them who could boast of killing a whale formerly had the most exalted mark of honor conferred upon them by a cut across the nose."

The first people to go whaling on the high seas were the Norwegians. Although this activity probably began in the Bronze Age, the first historical reference dates from the ninth century A.D. King Alfred's Anglo-Saxon translation of Orosius'

*The Basques were the first to turn whaling into a full-blown industry; they started scouring the North Atlantic for right whales as far back as the late ninth century. Basque sailors landed in the New World a century before Columbus and trained seamen from other European nations in the art of whaling. Opposite, top: The seal of the town of Biarritz. A number of municipalities in the Basque country gave whales a place of honor on their armorial bearings. Opposite, below: A map of the Biscayan coast, as seen by a Dutch geographer in 1585.*

*Seven Books of History Against the Pagans* tells of Ohthere, a Norse explorer who ventured into the White Sea and, in a feat reminiscent of the Miraculous Draught of Fishes, boasted of capturing "sixty whales in two days," single-handed.

## THE BASQUES IN TERRANOVA

The modern age of systematic commercial whaling began with the Basques. From the ninth century to the sixteenth, they had a virtual monopoly on this lucrative fishery; they passed on what they knew to other seafaring Europeans and, through them, to the rest of the world. The primary target of Basque exploitation was the northern right whale, a species with which they were so closely associated that it came to be known as the Biscayan right whale.

Initially, Basque whaling was a sporadic, small-scale operation: a few signal towers perched on clifftops overlooking the bay, primitive boats shoved into the water when the signal was given, and some try-pots on the beach to render blubber into whale oil. Guillaume Rondelet (1568) paints the following winter scene:

> The seamen and fishermen watch for the whales from lookouts high up. As soon as they spot any, they signal by beating on a drum. Then everyone comes running with all the necessary equipment. They have several dinghies, each with ten brawny rowers and several other men with harpoons . . . which they hurl at the whale with all their might. They let the lines fastened thereto spin out until the lifeblood has gone out of the whale. Then they haul the whale back to shore and divvy it up; since the harpoons have identifying marks, each man is allotted his share according to the number he has thrown.

The earliest written reference to Basque whaling occurs in a work entitled *Translation and Miracles of Saint Waast* (A.D. 875). Records of whale catches go back as far as 1381, for it was customary at the time to present the sovereign with

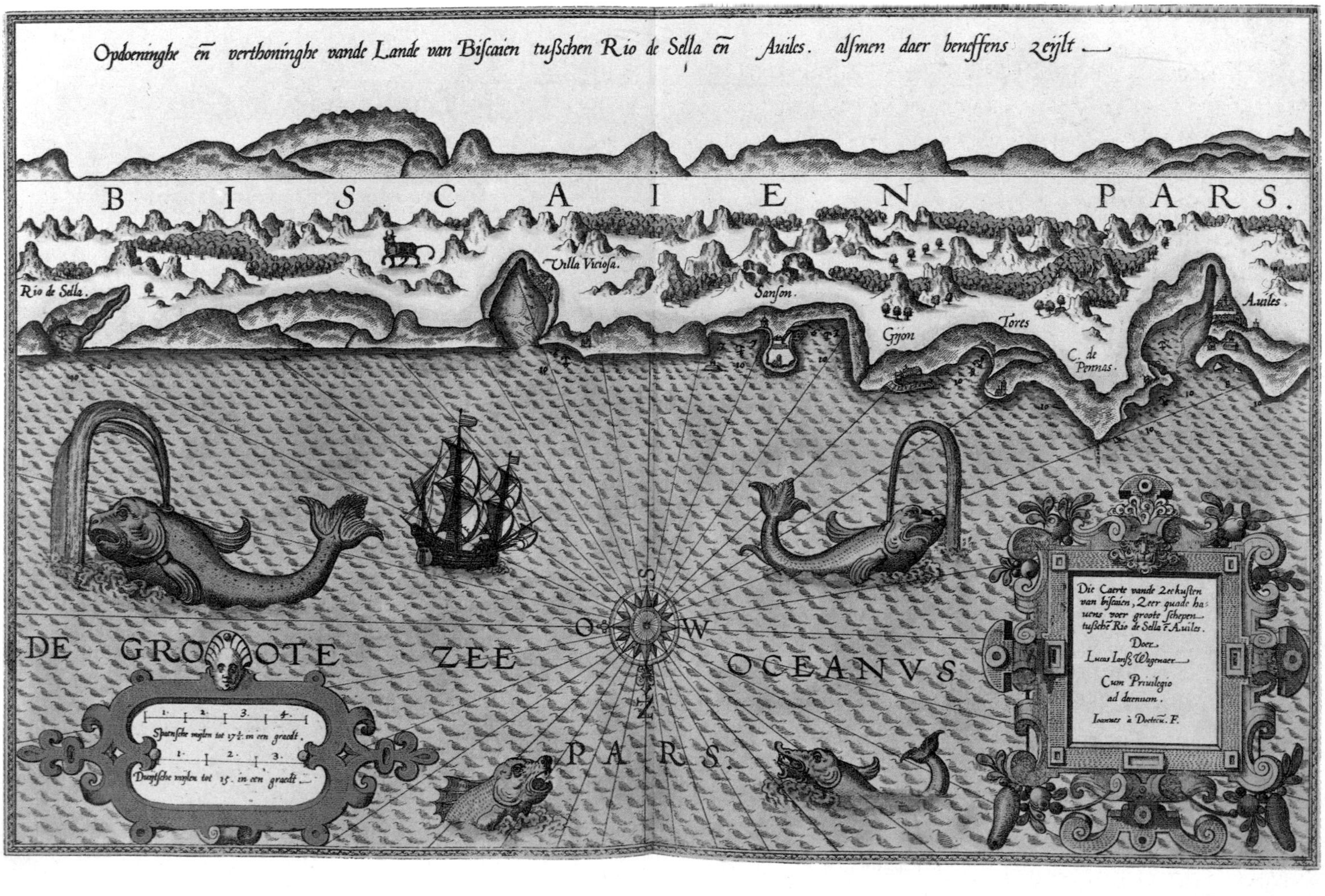

the first harpooned whale of the season *(De Praerogatorium regis)*. In 1573, Ambroise Paré described a whaling expedition that took place in 1565 off the Atlantic Coast of France. Two bundles of whale tongues were presented to Charles IX and his mother, Catherine de' Medici, who had witnessed the operation. "The tongue, being tender, is delicious," the eminent surgeon adds.

The Basques soon ventured beyond their home waters in the Bay of Biscay in search of right whales. By the twelfth century they had reached Iceland; by the thirteenth, Greenland; and by 1372, Newfoundland. Thus, although the Vikings preceded them, the Basques set foot on American soil more than a century before Columbus did. We now know that by the sixteenth century the Basques were dispatching boats by the hundred to Newfoundland and Labrador in time for the "oil season" (June to December). At Red Bay, a team of Canadian archaeologists led by Robert Grenier unearthed the remains of Basque encampments, tryworks, whale bones, and ship wreckage (including the galleon *San Juan*)—along with seventy-five human skeletons (G. Le Blanc, 1984).

So successful were these whaling expeditions that the Biscayan right whale all but vanished from the North Atlantic. It is a migratory species, and when it was no longer seen in European waters during winter, some naturalists believed that its range had shifted. The truth was that the species had been hunted to near-extinction.

*The Basques are credited with having invented most whaling techniques. In 1614, François Sopite, a captain from Saint-Jean-de-Luz, is believed to have perfected tryworks that could be loaded onto whaling ships. Below: An eighteenth-century engraving of a "trying village," one of many the Basques established on the coasts of Iceland, Newfoundland, and Labrador.*

*The Chinese, Koreans, and Japanese started hunting whales in Far Eastern waters many centuries ago, taking mainly Pacific right whales and minke whales. As seen in the Chinese print opposite, whalers first incapacitated their quarry with nets then approached in small boats, armed with harpoons and spears.*

*The following excerpts are from* Traité sur la pêche que font les Basques, *an anonymous eighteenth-century French treatise that explains in considerable detail how the Basques went about the business of catching and butchering whales.*

*"An alert sailor keeps watch high up on the topmast. As soon as he spots a whale, he cries out* 'Balia! Balia!' *which means 'whale' in the Basque language. At once the crew scramble to the whaleboats. Pulling away at the oars, they pursue the sighted quarry. . . .*

*"After the whale has been harpooned, flensers climb onto it; the soles of their boots have iron cleats to keep them from slipping. As a further precaution they are secured to the ship by a rope slung about the body. They pull out specially made knives with wooden handles. As they cut away the blubber from the suspended whale, it is brought on board and chopped into smaller chunks for quicker melting in the try-pots. To speed up the process, two men stir it constantly with long iron implements. First they stoke the fire with wood; then they switch to unrendered blubber, which burns very hot. After the whale has been turned completely around and stripped of all its blubber, the baleen or spikes—they are not outside the mouth, contrary to what several naturalists maintain—are sliced out of its maw. The crew of each ship receives half the proceeds from the oil; the captain, pilot, and flensers receive the proceeds from the baleen as a bonus."*

## AGARI KUJIRA, SAGARI KUJIRA

The oldest Japanese book, the *Kojiki (Record of Ancient Matters)*, dates from the year 712; the fact that it mentions whales comes as no surprise. For centuries the Japanese (and, to a lesser extent, the Koreans and the Chinese) had been taking whales near their coastline. Like their Basque counterparts, the Japanese whaled on a limited scale at first, but before long they were hunting at a furious pace. Japan boasted a sizeable whaling fleet by the seventeenth century, when the Wada family of Daichi, on Kyushu, reaped handsome profits from the whale fishery.

Humpbacks, grays, and rorquals all fell victim to Japanese harpooners; but no species was hunted more relentlessly than the Pacific right whale, first cousin of the Biscayan (Atlantic) right whale. Depending on the season, the men of the Rising Sun referred to it as *agari kujira* (whale traveling northward) or *sagari kujira* (whale traveling southward)—proof that they were familiar with its migration pattern. An illustrated account of the Japanese fishery at the time, *Isanatoru Ekotaba (Pictures of Whale-Fishing)*, was published in 1829.

The author, Yosei Oyamada, tells us that every spring and fall lookout stations *(yamamiba)* were established on hills overlooking the sea. The lookouts kept to a strict diet that was thought to sharpen their vision and powers of concentration. When they spotted a "blow" on the horizon, they gave the alarm with flags or rockets, and the whaling fleet weighed anchor. Swift catcher boats, propelled by sail and oar, maneuvered the panic-stricken whale into nets cast by special net-carrying vessels. Once their quarry was entangled, the fleet encircled it and the crew stabbed away with spears. One of the seamen, a veritable Tarzan, would dive into the water, swim toward the crippled whale, climb onto its head, and make a hole in its snout for the towing line.

After the whale stopped moving, a rope was passed through the hole and the dying animal was hauled back to shore and finished off with a long lance. Then the flensing began. Although the Japanese were interested primarily in the meat, they

鯨切解圖
肉納屋
腸納屋
骨納屋
アリ

did not let the blubber go to waste. Indeed, they found a use for nearly everything, including the bones (but not the liver). A cookbook from 1829 entitled *Kujira Chomi Ho*, or *How to Prepare Whale*, is filled with recipes; it notes that the choicest morsels are the eyes and the mammary glands.

Religion accounts in part for the Japanese taste for whale meat: both Buddhism and Shintoism frown on the eating of meat, but whales were considered fish. Out of dietary convenience, they continued to be regarded as such long after Japanese naturalists had assigned them their correct zoological niche. (As early as 1758, a treatise on natural history published in Kyoto explicitly classified whales as mammals.)

## INTO THE ARCTIC

The story of man's discovery of the seas is always recounted with epic hyperbole: Hail the dauntless navigators who braved ice, storm, and scurvy for the good of science and the well-being of mankind! To be sure. But many an explorer endured blizzard and suffering for the good of his own pocketbook! If the right whale could chronicle man's incursions into subarctic waters, it would be sure to point to itself as the main attraction for quite some time.

Bowheads rarely venture south of 60° N in any season. (This latitude also marks the approximate northernmost boundary of the northern right whale's summer migration.) Without the peaceable and good-natured—some would say "slow and stupid"—bowhead, explorers like Davis, Willoughby, Barents, and Hudson might not have proved their mettle as they searched for the Northeast and Northwest Passages. It would probably not strain the truth to speculate that there were several right whale carcasses for every mile these explorers gained through the icy seas.

Generally speaking, bowheads fell victim to four successive waves of harpooners: the Basques, the Dutch, the British, and—deadliest of all—the Americans.

Having all but extirpated the whale that bears their name by the seventeenth century, the Basques pressed northward and became the first to track down a species of whale peculiar to the Arctic. And although their whaling industry was nearing its end, the Basques' accumulated experience lived on; they served as teachers and guides for whalemen from Norway, Denmark, Hamburg, England, and, above all, the Netherlands. At one point, it looked as if competition might degenerate into an all-out "whale war," and catch sectors had to be allocated through negotiation—a step that spelled disaster for the whales. "Rivalries subsided," writes Lacépède (1804). "They parceled out the coastal areas most likely to further their interests. . . . Everything conspired to destroy the whale."

For a while, the Dutch set the pace, thanks to the famous Captain Willem Barents and his discovery of Bear Island and the Spitsbergen archipelago (1596). Bases for hunting whales and processing oil sprang up there and on Jan Mayen, Iceland, Greenland, and the Canadian side of the Davis Strait. In 1630, the Dutch sent some 400 ships and 20,000 men to Amsterdam Island, a forbidding, windswept rock 500 miles north of the Arctic Circle, to establish the boomtown of Smeerenberg (literally, "Blubbertown"). There was nothing the whaling crews could not find in the village, including brothels and taverns. According to P.-J. van Beneden (1867–92), "[the Dutch] made themselves so completely at home that bakers would signal [their ships] when fresh bread was coming out of their ovens." Onshore, the smell of blubber was everywhere; offshore, the sea was red with blood.

*The Japanese turned whaling into an art. Their whaling fleets consisted of a command vessel, twenty beater boats (each with a crew of fifteen), six net boats, and four tow boats. Crewmen beat the sides of the boats with sticks to drive the whales forward and into the nets. When the spout turned red, the fishermen chanted three times, "May its soul rest in peace!" and sang hymns of thanks to Buddha. Flensing (as seen in this anonymous print, c. 1800) was cause for great celebration. "The catchers do the 'Catcher Dance' and mime the catching of the whale" (Oyamada, 1829).*

*The Japanese boiled down whale blubber for lighting oil, but it was the meat that interested them most. Every part of these sea mammals was considered suitable for cooking, except the liver. Whaling in Japan began to hit its stride in the seventeenth century and, as this print (c. 1850) attests, developed into a full-fledged industry.*

## RULE, BRITANNIA

Between 1669 and 1778, the Dutch harvested no fewer than 57,560 whales. But whale stocks were not inexhaustible, and every year Dutch whalemen had to venture farther out into northern waters. The British soon joined in the great Arctic whale rush and before long they dominated it. Like the Dutch, they had hired Basque whalemen, and early on had proved themselves able harpooners. In 1598, Elizabeth I dispatched a whaling fleet to Greenland. The year before, Henry Hudson had spotted vast stocks of whales in the waters off Bear Island, and by 1611 the Muscovy Company of London was busy slaughtering them.

The British government began to throw its full weight behind the whaling industry in the mid-seventeenth century. In 1672, London started offering handsome bounties as an added incentive. In 1695, it encouraged the formation of a powerful whaling company by sponsoring a public subscription that raised £82,000. In the eighteenth century, the government compensated unsuccessful shipowners or outfitters for losses and allowed them to lay in supplies duty free. Small wonder, then, that the British whaling industry outstripped the competition so quickly.

Many other countries tried to catch up, but failed: In 1768, Frederick II of Prussia decreed the town of Embden to be a trading center for oil and baleen. Four years later, Sweden subsidized the creation of a large-scale whaling station at Göteborg, and in 1755, the king of Denmark provided his harpooners with ships free of charge to give them "a competitive edge." In an attempt to recapture the glory of the Basque fishery, the French government fitted out six whalers in 1784 and manned them with dozens of harpooners from Nantucket, who settled in Dunkirk.

Nor did Russia stand idly by. "She hit upon the idea of creating permanent settlements on the desolate, inhospitable coasts of northern lands," wrote Louis Thiercelin (1866). "She rounded up some prisoners that had been sentenced to death, deposited them on Spitsbergen, gave them some money, and promised them par-

*Having all but wiped out northern right whales in the North Atlantic, harpooners doggedly ventured into the Arctic in search of the equally massive and unaggressive bowhead. Above: This eighteenth-century engraving gives a fairly accurate idea of the perils that awaited whalers during these expeditions. More lives were lost to the sea and the ice than to the whale's thrashing tail.*

*The prospect of finding bowhead whales was a major incentive for voyages of discovery into the Arctic. Opposite: As we see in this German watercolor from 1778, European and North American seamen boldly ventured into ice-clogged waters in search of whales.*

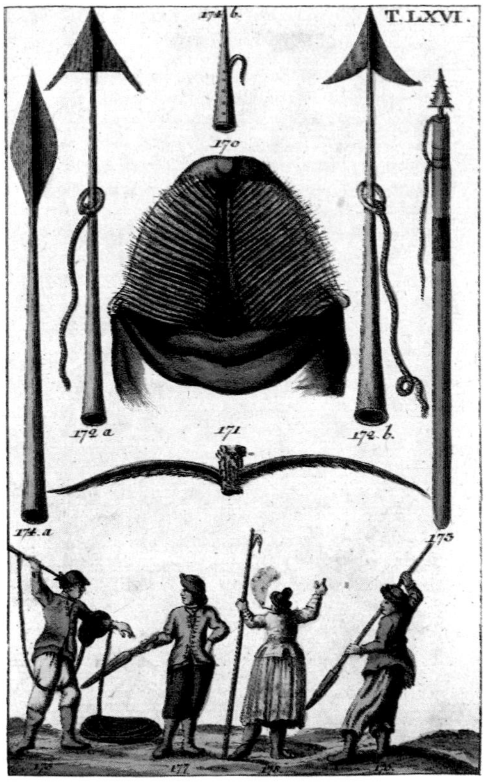


*Above: This engraving from 1805 shows the baleen of a right whale surrounded by hunting and flensing equipment and by the harpooner, flenser, and mate that wielded them.*

dons if they could bear up under the severe climate. . . . This gang of wretched convicts perished to the last man."

## THE GOLDEN AGE OF THE HARPOON

In the eighteenth century, the technique of whaling with hand-held harpoon—essentially unchanged since the days of Basque whaling—proved its mettle. It remained the technique of choice until the advent of the revolutionary harpoon gun. In late spring, whalemen headed for Arctic waters in 100-foot three-masters with oak-lined hulls designed to withstand dagger-sharp drift ice. They hoisted sails, rode out storms, and beseeched God to have pity on them as they maneuvered between icebergs in dense fog.

All of a sudden, the cry would go up from the crow's nest: "Thar she blows!" Commotion on deck as the whaleboats—four to six of them, each 30 feet long and 6 feet wide, were lowered into the water. Pull away, mates! On and on they rowed until the swarthy hulk of the gigantic creature came within range. The harpooner took aim and pitched. The whale shuddered with pain and sounded to escape; too late. Mortally wounded, the animal sought refuge beneath the ice. When it surfaced to breathe, the hunters finished it off.

The right whale stays afloat after it dies—one reason that it was known as the "right" whale to catch. (Another was that it did not put up much of a struggle.) Now the whaleboat would haul its quarry to the mother ship, where the whale was secured to heavy tackle so that it could be slowly rotated, like a chicken on a spit. Seamen with special flensing knives—and an uncanny sense of balance—perched themselves atop the whale and peeled away strips of blubber two feet wide and as long as the animal itself. While the butchering was under way, a complement of assistants known as "cormorants" stood in whaleboats fore and aft of the carcass and did their best to shoo away any birds hoping to partake of the banquet. Occasionally, sharks would be drawn by the scent of blood, and woe betide the sailor who lost his footing!

VIS. VINCIT

R·ARTE·

The tongue was removed with care, since "that of the average right whale generally yields six barrels of oil" (Lacépède, 1804). The valuable baleen plates were sliced off at the base. After the carcass was unlashed and consigned to the scavengers of the sea, the blubber was tried out, or rendered into oil, and collected and stowed in barrels. Illumination for the homes of Europe: let us not forget that the Enlightenment was the age of the whale-oil lamp. We have these northerly cetaceans to thank, in part, for the irony of Swift and Voltaire, the science of Newton and Buffon, the philosophy of Kant, and the musings of Jean-Jacques Rousseau.

*Yankee whalemen turned the sperm whale fishery into big business. "Launching a navy of great ships on the sea [these Nantucketers] explored this watery world; put an incessant belt of circumnavigations round it; peeped in at Bhering's Straits; and in all seasons and all oceans declared everlasting war with the mightiest animated mass that has survived the flood; most monstrous and most mountainous!" (Melville,* Moby-Dick*). A watercolor (above) by Louis Garneray, painted in 1835, and an illustration from an American edition of* Moby-Dick *(right) suggest the gruesome grandeur of this epic adventure.*

## EXPANSION TO THE SOUTH SEAS

At the beginning of the nineteenth century, Europeans and Americans discovered that there was a wealth of whales on the other side of Cape Horn, just waiting to be taken. Whalemen were active in the South Atlantic, the Indian Ocean (off southern Africa, in particular), and even the Pacific, off New Zealand and Chile. Once again, the right whale bore the brunt of the slaughter: Europeans and Americans began to go after the same North Pacific subspecies that the Japanese had been hunting for centuries. The southern right whale was besieged on all sides, and in thirteen years—between 1804 and 1817—as many as 190,000 of them were flensed.

In the "Extracts" section of *Moby-Dick*, Melville quotes from Captain Cowley's *Voyage Round the Globe* (1729): "We also saw abundance of large whales, there being more in these southern seas, as I may say, by a hundred to one, than we have to the northward of us." In 1792, Captain Colnett came across quite a few of them at roughly 40° S in waters off Chile. At the same latitude, but off the coast of Argentina, he had already sighted "herds of whales so vast that the oil they would yield could, it seemed to him, fill half the whaleships in London" (Lacépède, 1804). Today, preservationists shudder when they read descriptions like this. Paradise lost!

In the early nineteenth century, a new generation of whaling fleets put out to sea. The Russians whaled zealously in the Arctic and the North Pacific; by 1821 they had gone so far as to bar foreign whaling vessels from the Bering Sea by force of arms. The Japanese stepped up the hunt on their end, as did the Koreans. Whaling stations mushroomed the world over, from Norway to Canada, the Azores, Argentina, Chile, and New Zealand. Great Britain still held the lead, but not for long: her former colony in North America threw down the gauntlet. We will not go so far as to suggest that there was a harpooner aboard the *Mayflower*, but in the shiploads of immigrants that followed, most assuredly. Within a few short years, the Americans would become the kings of blubber and baleen.

## YANKEE WHALING COMES OF AGE

In the late eighteenth and early nineteenth centuries, the whaling industry along the eastern seaboard of the United States expanded at a staggering pace. From New France to New England, from the Gulf of St. Lawrence to the waters off Massachusetts, harpooners plied their trade as never before. In *Moby-Dick* (1851), Melville quotes from Obed Macy's *History of Nantucket*: "In the year 1690 some persons were on a high hill observing the whales spouting and sporting with each

*This whaling scene in the Arctic (pages 22–23) was painted by an unknown German artist in 1776. As Jules Verne correctly noted in* Twenty Thousand Leagues Under the Sea *(1869), "The role played by whales in the marine world and their influence on geographical discoveries have been considerable."*

other, when one observed: there—pointing to the sea—is a green pasture where our children's grandchildren will go for bread." New Haven, New London, and Mystic in Connecticut; Newport and Providence in Rhode Island; Cape Cod, New Bedford, Martha's Vineyard, and Nantucket in Massachusetts—these and other whaling centers came into their own.

Yankee whalemen circled the globe in search of right whales and humpbacks, and they stalked the last of the bowheads where no whaler had ever dared to go: the open waters of the Arctic Ocean. One New England whaler had passed through the Bering Strait as early as 1819, but the *Superior*, under the command of Captain Roys, was the first vessel to spend an entire whaling season in Arctic waters (1848). Many a crew followed suit, and the floes turned red with blood.

The American whaling fleet, however, built its reputation on the carcasses of a swifter, cleverer, and more belligerent giant than the right whale: the sperm whale.

The leviathan known as *Physeter macrocephalus* had long tempted man, but it also struck fear in his heart. As Richard Stafford noted in *Letter from the Bermudas* (1668), "I could never hear of any of that sort that was killed by any man, such is his fierceness and swiftness." But before long, the lure of profit won out over apprehension.

The sperm-whale fishery got off to a modest start when colonial America was still in its infancy. In 1712, rough weather drove a whaleship under the command of Captain Christopher Hussey into the midst of a herd of sperm whales. A member of the crew harpooned one of them, almost by accident, and the blubber was boiled down for oil. Word got around that it had yielded a respectable return, and the race was on for the mighty toothed cetacean.

Soon the sperm whale was hunted for its spermaceti (the finest of all oils), its ambergris (worth a fortune to perfumers and pharmacists), its ivory teeth, and its blubber, which was tried out for lamp oil. Candles made of spermaceti burned with a smokeless, odorless flame. Herman Melville summed it up in *Moby-Dick* (1851). "But though the world scouts at us whale hunters, yet does it unwittingly pay us the profoundest homage; yea, an all-abounding admiration! for almost all the tapers, lamps, and candles that burn round the globe, burn, as before so many shrines, to our glory!"

The sperm-whale fishery began in the Atlantic, spread to the Pacific, and on to the Indian Ocean. One Nantucket whaler made a modest sally into the Pacific as early as 1789, but it was not until 1791 that two whaleship captains, Joseph Russel and Cornelius Howard, rounded Cape Horn and roamed the South Seas for sperm whales. They returned to port with their holds crammed with barrels of blubber oil and spermaceti oil, and the pace picked up considerably after that.

In the early nineteenth century, little sloops were still setting out with just one or two catcher boats and returning to home port after taking five or six whales. But by the middle of the century, everything changed. Mighty 300-ton three-masters, among the sturdiest craft that have ever sailed the seas, boasted a crew of forty and were fitted out with as many as eight whaleboats. On-board tryworks made the job of rendering that much more efficient.

Of course, this was the heroic age of harpooners like Queequeg, poised at the bows of their spray-drenched whaleboats; of skippers like Ahab, scouring the seas for monstrous whales; and of wide-eyed seamen like Ishmael. There was nothing to match the Yankee fleet out of Mystic, New Bedford, Providence, and Nantucket. By 1850, New Bedford had emerged as the foremost whaling port in the world and the fourth-busiest harbor in the United States. At its zenith in 1876, the American whaling industry boasted 735 whalers and employed some 70,000 people.

As these ships went farther and farther afield, the expeditions became increasingly risky. Whalers remained at sea for up to five years at a time, returning home only when their holds were full. That is, when they did come back.

Aboard ship, the standards of sanitation and other amenities were dreadful. The crew consisted of unemployed workers or penniless hayseeds recruited in taverns by fair means or foul. Wages were notoriously low. "In 1860," Paul Budker points out, "a sailor on an American whaler earned twenty cents a day . . . . Now, an unskilled laborer on land was paid ninety cents a day."

Owners and outfitters took on tremendous quantities of supplies in anticipation of a virtually nonstop voyage. When provisions went bad, the men made do. Among the hands, only the harpooners received decent treatment; they ate properly and bunked aft, where the officers slept.

The abysmal pay and the hardships of life at sea made recruitment difficult, but

*"She blows!" That magical cry from the crow's nest sent everyone on deck scurrying. Below: An engraving of a lookout perched high atop a mast. The barrels of oil that the Yankee whalers brought back turned New Bedford, Nantucket, and Mystic into thriving ports. In the nineteenth century, lamp oil and sperm whale oil were so closely associated in people's minds that when petroleum was discovered in Pennsylvania in 1858, many believed it came from decayed prehistoric whale carcasses. Left: The docks of New Bedford, c. 1860.*

not impossible: crewmen could always be shanghaied. Perfected on the trans-Pacific line between the United States and China (whence its name), this technique was straightforward, if nothing else. The "crimp" might accost some poor down-and-out in a tavern, buy him a drink, and then drug it; or he might start a brawl, with an accomplice on hand to knock a "recruit" senseless with a sandbag. The luckless fellow woke up on board after the whaler had weighed anchor.

Not surprisingly, this convict's life encouraged desertion. Whaling skippers were reluctant to put in at ports of call, so seamen often had to make an escape on remote islands, while the ship took on drinking water and other supplies. One of the most famous runaways of all was Herman Melville, who had signed on as a

*The ghastly demise of a whale, as pictured in an engraving from a book by Thomas Beale (1821). Louis Thiercelin was but one of many who tried to convey the moving grandeur of dramatic scenes such as this one. "The animal thrashes about furiously," he wrote in 1866, "lets out rumbling sounds that sound like thunder, spews forth clouds of mist that blot out the sun—to no avail. Soon the spout takes on a reddish hue; the column of water spray turns crimson. He proffers his blood to the winds, and with it his life."*

hand aboard the *Acushnet* and escaped during just such a stopover at the Marquesas Islands. In *Typee* (1846), he recounts his getaway from the ship (rechristened the *Dolly* in his novel) and his life among the savages of a "paradise of cannibals."

## THE FATAL FLURRY

"Thar! Thar! She blows!" the lookout yelled from the crow's nest. The whaleboats were lowered. Each of these 30-foot craft—how flimsy they looked alongside a 60-foot, 40-ton sperm whale!—was manned by an officer (who acted as temporary helmsman astern), a harpooner aft, and a complement of four oarsmen.

The little whaleboats had to reach striking distance of the whale. "It is at this point that the crew must obey without question," notes Thiercelin (1866). "At this solemn moment some sailors are numbed with fear; their minds wander; they see nothing, hear nothing . . . . The surprising thing is that old sailors are more susceptible to this uncontrollable terror than are young ones."

The harpooner, standing in the bow, braced his knee in a notched thwart (known as the "clumsy-cleat") to take aim at the whale's flank behind the eye. As soon as the quarry was struck, the boat-steerer went aft to take the helm, while the superior officer rushed to the bow. This maneuver was probably intended to maintain the prestige of the officer in charge, who was given the honor of finishing off the whale. Melville noted in *Moby-Dick* that to scurry about in a catcher while being towed by a raging whale was the height of folly.

A dramatic tug-of-war ensued. Frantic with pain, the whale would sound savagely in an attempt to escape. The harpoon line, coiled down in a tub and wound

*When a harpoon pierces a whale's lungs, the stricken animal inevitably lets out a last bloody gasp that whalemen referred to as the "flurry." "In a final desperate outcry, the giant's spout rains blood on the crew, at long last relieved and completely satisfied by this hideous baptism" (Georges Blond, 1953). Left: Whaling scenes like this were still common in the Azores just a few years ago.*

*In its heyday in 1876, the American whaling fleet boasted more than seven hundred vessels, but by 1890 only two hundred were still in operation. The depletion of sperm whale stocks and increased use of petroleum for lamp oil spelled ruin for a once-flourishing industry. Below: Scores of icebound Yankee whalers abandoned in the Arctic, c. 1871.*

about a loggerhead, spun out at a dizzying speed, and it had to be constantly sprinkled with water to keep it from charring the wood. Bridled by the whaleboat and weakened by loss of blood, the whale could not dive very deep. It would come back up for air, skim the surface with the whaleboat in tow, and dive again; in this fashion the chase could last an entire day. Inevitably, however, the whale could flee no more. The crew manned their oars and again brought the boat to within striking range of the exhausted creature. The boat-header lifted his spear and drove it into the whale's lungs, twisting the blade in the wound. This was a moment of great risk: in a final involuntary display of rage, a sperm whale might smash the sturdy whaleboat to pieces with its tail or head, or crush his tormentors in his vise-like jaws.

More often than not, however, the final thrust proved fatal to the whale. "Flurry! Flurry!" they cried, as the spout of the whale turned red and the animal went into violent spasms. Yankee whalers referred to these death throes as the flurry; their French counterparts shouted "*Il fleurit!*" ("He's blossoming!")—a gruesomely ironic phonetic equivalent.

The death of a whale was an awful thing to behold; eyewitnesses were invariably struck by the tragic grandeur of the event. But after the last scarlet sigh, it was back to work. The mother ship arrived at the scene. The carcass was lashed to the starboard side, with its tail facing the bow; then men wearing cleated boots clambered onto the body and began the gruelling task of carving out long strips of gory blubber, which their shipmates hoisted aboard with special hooks. It took about five hours to flense a single whale. The strips of blubber were chopped into chunks, then sliced into "bibles"or leaves to be boiled down. The try-pots gave off a nauseating stench as acrid smoke filled the air.

*Right: As this old lithograph shows, the California gray whale summers in icy waters. When winter approaches, the whales migrate from Alaska, the Bering Strait, and the Chukchi Sea to their only breeding grounds—the warm, shallow lagoons of Baja California where they mate and calve. Charles Scammon (pictured above), one of the greatest Yankee whaling skippers of his day, discovered these refuges in 1852. The appalling massacre that ensued nearly wiped out the entire species. Gray whales have made a miraculous comeback since then.*

A sperm whale's head was hauled on deck and butchered separately. Flensers made a hole in the bulbous forehead, and removed the valuable spermaceti with a special dipper that was hoisted up with a rope and pulley. The teeth were yanked out for sailors to carve into scrimshaw and sell when they went ashore. Sometimes the whale's intestines contained a waxy, shimmering lump that hardened when exposed to air. This lump would be greeted with shouts of joy, for ambergris was worth its weight in gold.

Hunted the world over, sperm whales were growing harder and harder to come by on the vast, featureless seas. The scarcer they got, the less profitable it became for shipowners to go looking for them. As synthetic substances were perfected, moreover, not even ambergris could bring in enough to cover the costs of whaling expeditions. And before long, the development of electricity, gas, and other sources of illumination brought to an end the golden age of Yankee sperm-whale fishery. The focus shifted to the gray whale.

## LAGUNA OJO DE LIEBRE

The California gray whale's troubles began the day man discovered its breeding grounds. This cetacean winters in the lagoons of Baja California, where it mates, calves, and nurses its young. In the summer, it heads back to the Bering Strait to feed on bottom-dwelling invertebrates.

In 1852 the *Boston*, under the command of Captain Charles Melville Scammon, followed its reconnaissance schooner to the entrance of a lagoon in Baja California. There, in the warm shallows of the place Spaniards called Laguna Ojo de Liebre, he beheld a concentration of gray whales such as no whaleman before him had ever dreamed of, much less seen.

A massacre ensued. As a rule, gray whales—nicknamed "devilfish" by Yankee whalemen—are more combative than right whales. But these mating couples and pregnant females were trapped, unable to flee the lagoon and their executioners.

The following year, Scammon returned to the lagoon, trailing more whalers eager to fill their ships with barrels of oil. For approximately a decade, the carnage continued. The gray whale was an easy victim; its consistent migratory path and its pattern of swimming in shallow water made quick work of the "hunt." Scammon himself returned only once more to the lagoon that now bears his name.

*Before whaling came into its own, whales used to congregate by the hundreds in certain lagoons. Judging by the accounts of seamen at the time, these crowds made for a spectacular sight. Above: This watercolor (c. 1880) shows whalemen attacking a large herd of sperm whales in a fjord in Iceland. With the advent of the harpoon gun, whaling became a far more efficient and far more cold-blooded industry than the dangerous business pictured here.*

The original stock of California gray whales must have numbered between 10,000 and 20,000—a population of some considerable size. More than 8,000 disappeared between 1846 and 1874, at a rate of over 500 a year. The effect of this hunting zeal soon became all too clear: the gray whale disappeared from view. In 1866, a scant 41 grays were taken and only 160 spotted migrating off San Simeon.

In the 1880s, the gray whale was thought to be extinct, and thus enjoyed a respite, until its numbers recovered somewhat and factory ships were introduced. In 1925—the peak year for this century—133 mature grays of both sexes fell victim to harpoons; on average, 52 gray whales vanished every year between 1933 and 1946, and once again, the species was feared to be at the brink of extinction. *Perseverare diabolicum.*

## THE ROAR OF THE GUN

For centuries, the hunt was limited to bowheads, right whales, sperm whales, and gray whales; except for humpbacks and small species, the balaenopterids, or rorquals, fared much better than their fellow cetaceans. For one thing, their baleen plates are too short to be of much use; for another, these whales yield less oil. A rorqual is leaner, lighter, and sleeker than a right whale of equal length; furthermore, rorquals have no spermaceti or ambergris.

The main reason that rorquals escaped the harpoon, however, was that they are astonishingly swift and powerful; hunting them with hand-held harpoons was an exercise in futility. Even in the event that a lucky shot found its mark, there was nothing to gain by it, for rorquals are denser than seawater and sink as soon as they stop breathing.

When it comes to killing, however, human ingenuity knows no bounds. Other nations had pioneered other styles of slaughter; now it was Norway—whose waters fairly teemed with rorquals—that ushered in the age of industrial whaling.

*Harpooners were always trying to increase the effectiveness of their weapons. Poison was one alternative: Scottish whalemen tried using harpoon tips dipped in prussic acid in 1831, and in 1866 Louis Thiercelin suggested using either prussic acid or a mixture of curare and strychnine; his experiment claimed the lives of ten whales. The most "sensible" improvement, however, was the harpoon gun (above and right), perfected in 1868 by Svend Foyn.*

As P.-J. van Beneden noted, "The first years they took to hunting these animals in Varanger Fjord, they were so plentiful in the summer months that at times the sea seemed to seethe with them. Ships were reluctant to venture into the midst of this living surface that stretched as far as the eye could see."

This bounty of rorquals was too much of a challenge for hand-held harpoons, and the Norwegians had to improve the efficiency of their equipment. Some attempted to augment the destructive power of the harpoon by replacing the harpooner's arm with a mechanical or chemical device that would do the job more effectively, always fire true, and never tire. According to Thiercelin (1866), Norwegians had been hunting whales with catapults and ballistae since the twelfth century. In the eighteenth century, English and Dutch whalemen had tried inserting the shafts of their harpoons into muskets in order to reach whales "at a distance well in excess of ten meters" (Lacépède, 1804). Between 1850 and 1860, Yankee whalemen perfected a contraption known as the "bomb-gun," and its use became widespread.

These persistent efforts occasionally proved successful. The dubious honor of perfecting a bona fide grenade-harpoon gun, however, fell to a Norwegian by the name of Svend Foyn. A native of Tönsberg, he studied every manual or explosive harpoon-throwing device then in use and probably knew about the work of Cordes, a gunsmith from Bremen who later laid claim to the invention.

In 1864, Foyn mounted a battery of seven prototype harpoon cannons onto his steam-powered catcher, the *Spes et Fides*, and tested them during an experimental cruise off the county of Finnmark. By 1868, he managed to kill thirty whales in rapid succession, and the weapon was considered ready for general use.

A harpoon fired from a gun is a lethal weapon, but adding a grenade makes it deadlier still. The Americans were the first to hit upon the idea of an exploding harpoon; the Norwegians perfected it. Within a few short years, the device had taken on the general characteristics of grenade-harpoons in use to this day. The gun, perched on a raised platform at the bow of a catcher boat, swivels on its base so that the gunner can aim at his target unimpeded. The front part of the harpoon is equipped with movable flanges and a grenade, containing gunpowder, that is set to go off three seconds after the head is embedded in the whale's body.

Here is how W. Besnard (1948) describes the technique. "The harpoon penetrates deep into the body, and the grenade explodes. Before that, as the harpoon pierces the skin, the lashing comes undone, releasing the movable flanges; . . . The barbed tips spread outward in different directions, ripping into the flesh and lodging the grenade in the whale."

The explosion causes massive internal injury, and the whale may die within seconds. But not necessarily: on the high seas, hitting a vital spot is easier said than done, and the whale's agonized death throes can last for hours.

The development of the whaling arsenal did not stop with the use of gunpowder. Whalemen had to devise ways to keep rorquals afloat until the flensers arrived. The only way to manage this on the high seas was to inflate the body with air; again we quote from W. Besnard (1948). "A long tube that looks like some monstrous hypodermic needle is hooked up to an air compressor, and the other end is inserted into the belly of the whale. The compressed air blows the whale up like a balloon. They take out the tube and plug up the hole. Now buoyant, the carcass is left floating in the sea with the company flag pinned on top."

One last problem remained: Rorquals are extraordinarily fast swimmers, moving at speeds in excess of 15 knots when frightened. Obviously, sailing ships that

*The deadly combination of harpoon guns and fast steam-powered boats allowed whalemen to track down surviving specimens of already depleted species: right whales, humpbacks, and sperm whales. Now more than ever, whalers had the tools to catch swift, powerful rorquals—notably the fin whale and the biggest quarry of them all, the blue whale. This activity was largely confined to Antarctica, where in 1931 no fewer than 31,000 whales were killed. The shores of some subantarctic islands are still strewn with the bones of whales. Above: The Cousteau team reassembled this skeleton on Deception Island, in the South Shetlands.*

*For many years, whaling was primarily a coastal activity, dictated by the places and times of year whales ventured near shore. A sperm whale fishery of this kind has existed in the Azores for centuries and survives to this day. Opposite: The flensing of a sperm whale is about to begin.*

had to strain to reach 12 knots could not keep pace. For the whaling industry, the technological revolution that ushered in the age of steam and diesel power came in the nick of time. A few decades saw the emergence of 300-ton steam-powered catchers, then 600-ton diesel supercatchers. Propelled by 2,500-horsepower engines, these 200-foot vessels can reach speeds of 15 knots and remain at sea for more than a month, regardless of the weather.

Bigger, faster, more powerful ships meant that pelagic whaling—far more lucrative than the near-shore fishery—could now be carried out on a truly massive scale. Minke, sei, and Bryde's whales were not the only species to succumb to the harpoon gunner; now humpbacks, fin whales, and the colossal blue whales started to vanish by the thousands. Although activity in the Atlantic, Pacific, and Indian oceans continued unabated, the whaling drama soon shifted to a different stage: the waters of the Antarctic, home to more whales than all other regions combined. Row upon row of misty spouts against a fantastic backdrop of ice.

No one knew more about the staggering concentrations of rorquals in southern seas than those enthusiastic polar explorers, the Norwegians. In 1904, Carl Anton Larsen, a sea captain, established the first onshore whaling station in the Antarctic, on the island of South Georgia. In the years that followed, land-based stations sprang up on subantarctic archipelagos and the Antarctic Peninsula proper. Whale blood frothed on the seas, while tryworks spewed clouds of reeking smoke into the air. The desolate shores at the ends of the earth are still strewn with heaps of bones that bear mute witness to the deplorable fate of these giants.

## RADAR, HELICOPTER, AND SATELLITE

Onward and upward: there was no end to "progress" in catching and processing whales. For a while, the promise of a quick, clean kill by means of electric harpoons generated considerable excitement. As Besnard candidly noted (1948), "An animal immersed in a conductor like seawater can be electrocuted quite easily." (This was not an entirely new idea: in 1868, two Englishmen, Frederick Bennet and Richard Ward, had a patent for "an electric method of capturing whales.")

*Once a spectacular, thrilling, dangerous adventure, whaling had degenerated into mere butchery by the twentieth century. Above: A whaling scene in Norway.*

From the whaleman's point of view, the chief advantage of the electric harpoon was not that it spared animals needless suffering, but that whales would no longer be able to drag catcher boats behind them for hours on end. That was such a waste of everyone's time! And what is more, the splinters that grenade harpoons leave in a whale's body often damage flensing equipment.

Its technical advantages notwithstanding, the electric harpoon had one major drawback: the slightest defect in insulation might send the deadly current through the harpooner instead of the whale. The spray-drenched firing platform of a whaleship is hardly the ideal location for an electrical device of this sort.

As whales became scarcer and harder to find on the open seas, the need for sophisticated spotting techniques grew more urgent. As early as 1929, Kosmos, a Norwegian firm, used a Gypsy Moth reconnaissance plane to help locate whales. After a few lucrative sorties, it disappeared into the fog over the North Atlantic, never to return. In 1946, the United Whalers Co. put two amphibious Walrus aircraft on board the factory ship *Balena* to improve the performance of its fleet. During the 1950s, helicopters were pressed into service for the first time. There was even talk of shelling whales from the air, but nothing ever came of this because no one could figure out how to inflate bombed whales.

Although airplanes and helicopters are still part of the standard whaling arsenal, they have not proven as effective as originally hoped. Weather is a persistent problem, and the cost of purchasing and maintaining aircraft is prohibitive for smaller operations. Of course, whalemen have been using radar to spot flagged whales for retrieval since World War II. Sonar is used to monitor echolocation clicks to spot whales and track them after they dive.

In recent years, whaling fleets have enhanced their spotting capability with extremely sophisticated teledetection devices; satellite pictures, for example, can help to locate the shoals of krill that whales feed on in winter. Whalers have also learned to make use of information—such as the locations of migration routes and breeding grounds—that scientists gather.

## FLOATING FACTORIES

The modern-day whaling industry hit its stride when it devised working platforms commensurate with the marine giants it butchered. Twentieth-century factory ships are huge 20,000- to 30,000-ton vessels. They serve as supply ships for catcher fleets as well as floating stations, where whales are flensed and processed.

In 1925, a Norwegian factory ship called the *Lancing* was the first to make use of a stern slipway. A dead whale could be hauled up to the stern and hoisted onto the cutting deck. The idea quickly caught on.

Now companies could process the animal quickly and completely. The tongue, subcutaneous blubber, oil-rich organs, and internal tissue were rendered. The choicest meat could be salted or frozen for human consumption, animal feed, and pet food. The muscles, intestines, residues, and bones could be ground into fertilizer. No waste — of time or whale.

In 1910, for the first time in the history of whaling, the annual catch worldwide exceeded 10,000. By 1911, the figure had more than doubled, and after only a brief slowdown during World War I, the harvest figures skyrocketed. It was a systematic, mindless, shameless slaughter. For a while, it looked as though the catch was growing exponentially: 27,000 whales were taken in 1926, and nearly 44,000 in 1931. Between 1930 and 1940, an average of 2.5 to 3 million tons of whale were "harvested" every year—12 to 15 percent of the total biomass that man removed from the seas. Blue whales, fin whales, and humpbacks bore the brunt.

In 1931, the enthusiasm of the whaling companies backfired. Overproduction triggered a precipitous slump in world whale-oil prices, which plummeted from £27 per ton in 1929 to less than £10 in 1934.

The lull was short-lived. Governments stepped in to safeguard whaling indus-

*This rorqual, towed to a whaling station for flensing, makes for a forbidding picture. All that bloodletting, all that suffering, for some oil, meat, and baleen. All that slaughter to guarantee a profit for an operation that can flourish only briefly. To quote Australian poet John Blight (b. 1913), "How must a whale die to wring a tear?"*

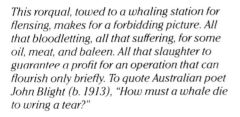

tries; new markets for whale products were sought and found, and the slaughter resumed with a vengeance. In 1935, the worldwide catch bounced back to nearly 40,000. All previous records were shattered in 1938, when whaling companies butchered nearly 55,000 whales. More individuals were taken during certain seasons after 1945, but in terms of tonnage, the catch of the 1938 season has never been surpassed.

During World War II, while countries turned their instruments of destruction on one another, the nation of the whales enjoyed a reprieve (though they still had to run a gauntlet of depth charges and unexploded bombs). From 1941 to 1943, all pelagic whaling in the Antarctic came to a halt. Factory ships were converted into tankers, but these slow vessels proved easy prey for enemy submarines; by the end of the war, two-thirds of them lay at the bottom of the sea. Beginning with the 1943–44 season, however, the Norwegians resumed the hunt in the Antarctic.

At the war's end, even though whaling had nearly ceased for five seasons, whale stocks had not yet recovered. Experts published the facts, but whalemen refused to acknowledge the significance of them: still dreaming of immense herds of fin and blue whales, they greedily hunted the survivors of those species. When that fishery did not suffice, they turned their attention once again to sperm whales (which, by and large, had been left in peace since the end of the nineteenth century) and to sei, minke, and Bryde's whales. Mankind kills first and counts later.

### *THE GRISLY STATISTICS*

*The following table lists worldwide whale catches since 1868, as reported to and published by the Committee for Whaling Statistics in Oslo. The figures represent the number of whales harpooned, not tonnage; a thousand Bryde's whales killed today yield far less oil and meat than a thousand blue whales would have back in the 1920s and 1930s. Note that catches are for every fifth year until 1960, and then every whaling season thereafter until 1986.*

| | | | |
|---|---|---|---|
| 1868* | 30 | 1963-64 | 63,001 |
| 1873 | 36 | 1964-65 | 64,680 |
| 1878 | 116 | 1965-66 | 57,891 |
| 1883 | 569 | 1966-67 | 52,238 |
| 1888 | 709 | 1967-68 | 46,645 |
| 1893 | 1,607 | 1968-69 | 42,126 |
| 1898 | 1,993 | 1969-70 | 42,480 |
| 1903 | 3,867 | 1970-71 | 38,771 |
| 1908 | 5,509 | 1971-72 | 32,133 |
| 1913 | 25,673 | 1972-73 | 32,605 |
| 1918 | 9,468 | 1973-74 | 31,629 |
| 1923 | 18,120 | 1974-75 | 29,961 |
| 1928 | 23,593 | 1975-76 | 22,049 |
| 1933 | 28,907 | 1976-77 | 16,309 |
| 1938** | 54,835 | 1977-78 | 13,638 |
| 1943 | 8,372 | 1978-79 | 10,668 |
| 1948 | 44,002 | 1979-80 | 3,542 |
| 1953 | 53,642 | 1980-81 | 2,928 |
| 1958 | 64,075 | 1981-82 | 2,050 |
| 1960-61 | 65,641 | 1982-83 | 1,683 |
| 1961-62*** | 66,090 | 1983-84 | 1,683 |
| 1962-63 | 63,579 | 1984-85 | — |
| | | 1985-86 | — |

**The year the harpoon gun was invented*
***World catch record, in tonnage*
****Season catch record in individuals taken*

## MORATORIUM! MORATORIUM!

Government measures to protect whales have been a long, long time in coming. Even today, when all but a handful of nations have agreed to put an end to the carnage, poachers are handled with astonishing leniency. Harpooning a protected whale is less risky than shoplifting cosmetics made with whale oil.

Attempts to regulate the exploitation of whales date from the early part of this century; for example, in 1904, Norway banned coastal whaling (but declared war on rorquals in the Antarctic). The need for regulation was perhaps made more urgent by the hard facts of economics: too many whalers were trying to sell too much oil in a finite market. Norway's whaling legislation of 1929, which became the model for subsequent international efforts, established standards for open-sea whaling and, importantly, provided for the creation of the Committee for Whaling Statistics and the publication of ***International Whaling Statistics***. The League of Nations, in recognition of the need for international rule, assembled a committee to draw up an agreement along the lines of the Norwegian legislation; in 1931, the Geneva Convention was signed and adopted by twenty-six countries. This convention led to the first use of limited hunting seasons and quotas for whaling. In 1937, the London Agreement to protect whaling stocks was signed by major whaling nations, excluding Germany and Japan. Despite failed attempts to reduce numbers and sizes of species taken, the agreement did establish shorter seasons and exclude whaling from certain sectors of the world's oceans.

The war years of 1939–45 saw a tremendous decrease in whaling activity, as three-quarters of all factory ships, having been requisitioned to carry supplies, were sunk. Before the war had ended, a preliminary meeting that was held in Lon-

"Y sobre el mar lo sangre se extendia
Como un manto de púrpura flotante . . ."
*Chilean poet Samuel A. Lillo was referring to the whale massacre when he wrote about a "crimson mantle floating on the sea" in 1940. And a systematic, unrelenting, ruthless slaughter it was, whether perpetrated with relatively primitive equipment (as in the Azores, above, where a local sperm whale fishery survives) or on an industrial scale. Opposite: A factory ship, where whales taken by catcher fleets are towed for processing.*

*Think nothing of the whale; you may be sure*
*He thinks nothing of you . . .*
*Except for an expletive when you come near him.*
*(C. H. Sisson, British, b. 1914)*

*May the spirit that once moved upon the waters*
*speak to these men, and give them consciousness*
*of shame, for all the murderous deeds they do!*
*(James Kirkup, British, b. 1918)*

*The murder of whales*
*is only one example*
*to show that man no longer*
*wishes to live in this world.*
*(Wieland Schmied, West German, b. 1929)*

don (February 7, 1944) laid the groundwork for the establishment of the International Whaling Commission (I.W.C.) and postwar regulation of the industry. Two years later, the I.W.C. was formally brought into being, and it now has some forty member nations, both whaling and nonwhaling.

The provisions adopted by the I.W.C., based on the protective measures from 1937, have four key objectives: to safeguard future breeders; to establish scientific

### *THE INCONSISTENCY OF THE INTERNATIONAL WHALING COMMISSION*

*The International Whaling Commission is empowered to make recommendations and suggestions, but has no means at its disposal to enforce them: the decision to comply or not to comply rests solely with member governments. Article Five of the Charter provides the "ninety-day rule"; this stipulates that a signatory who disagrees with a catch quota or a motion to protect a species may simply object to the measure within ninety days and the adopted measure will not apply to that signatory.*

*What is more, no whaling nation is obliged to belong to the I.W.C. If the rules promulgated by the organization do not please a member, the member can simply withdraw.*

*There have been a great many objections and defections since 1946. Whaling nations that still belong to the I.W.C. have formed effective minority blocs to vote down proposals, which must be passed by a three-quarter majority. More often than not, the representatives of whaling nations to the I.W.C. are also principal shareholders in whaling companies—a situation that leaves ecologists feeling that the goats are tending the lettuce patch.*

*The I.W.C. has provided a forum on whaling—but the depletion of whale stocks continues. Credit for most progress the Commission has made belongs, in fact, to a few scientists within the I.W.C. and to outside pressure groups, which have proven a stronger and more effective voice.*

*For years, the Cousteau Foundation has advocated the creation of an internationally recognized Marine High Commission, made up of experts that are not beholden to any private concern or government agency. One of the most urgent pieces of business on its agenda would be to make sure that the whales of the world are protected for the sake of generations to come.*

*Long before international bodies were formed to monitor whaling activity, the slaughter of whales outraged the friends of nature. "I do not approve of these murderous pastimes," says Captain Nemo in Verne's classic* Twenty Thousand Leagues Under the Sea *(1869). "The destruction of these harmless and inoffensive creatures by whalers like you, Ned, is a crime." In* La Mer *(1886), poet Jean Richepin lamented, "A little while longer, and those sovereigns of the sea, the sperm whale and the right whale, shall be seen no more." Above: A Spanish poster denounces whaling in Galicia.*

limits for the number of whales taken; to set up sanctuaries, particularly in breeding areas; and to prohibit completely the capture of individuals belonging to any endangered species.

To protect immature whales, the I.W.C. included the earlier ban on the taking of any female accompanied by her calf and recognized minimum catch lengths (measured from the tip of the snout to the notch separating the flukes): 70 feet for blue whales, 35 feet for humpbacks, and so on.

The "science" used to establish quotas for individual species was economics. Under pressure from whaling interests, the Commission adopted an idiosyncratic (some think absurd) system of measuring whale catches—the "blue whale unit." According to this system, nonspecific quotas were expressed in terms of the oil yield of the blue whale; one blue is "worth" two fin whales, two and a half humpback whales, or six sei whales. The postwar catch quota was set at half the pre-war yield, or 16,000 B.W.U.—whaling interests were in no hurry to change the status quo, only the level of prices. In 1956, the quota still hovered around 14,000 B.W.U. It was not until the annual meeting of 1971 that the I.W.C. finally did away with quotas measured in B.W.U. and considered individual stocks. Meanwhile, limits were observed mainly in the breach, and poaching was rife.

Protecting whale populations also meant establishing strict opening and closing dates for the whaling season; this the I.W.C. did. In addition, sanctuaries in the Antarctic, proposed in 1938, were officially approved.

By 1955, a ban on the taking of blue whales in the North Atlantic was considered; a decade later, the I.W.C. gave them full protection.

In the meantime, humpback and fin whales were declared endangered species in 1957; in 1963, Great Britain suspended all whaling operations, and a year later humpback whales were given full protection in the southern hemisphere; in the same year, The Netherlands ceased all whaling.

The bans on humpback and blue whales were extended to the North Pacific in 1966; full protection for the pygmy blue whale in the Antarctic was given the same year. In 1971, the United States added eight whales to its list of endangered species. The government banned all whaling by American vessels and the importing of whale products into American territory. Unfortunately, however, the import ban strategy often adds up to nothing more than wishful thinking. There are complex issues to resolve: Is a Japanese car to be refused entry because its automatic transmission fluid contains sperm oil? Or a French perfume because it is made with ambergris?

1972 was a year of expanding pressure toward whale protection on the international front. The United States instituted its Marine Mammal Protection Act, a commitment to "long-term management and research programs to conserve and protect these animals." The United Nations Conference on the Human Environment, held in Stockholm, called for a ten-year moratorium on commercial whaling. The I.W.C., at its annual meeting, also in Stockholm, considered a ten-year moratorium, as proposed by the United States; the ban was rejected, scuttled by opposition led by Japan and the U.S.S.R.

The following year, a call for a moratorium was once again on the agenda of the I.W.C.; again the Russians and the Japanese objected, but they did accept quotas by species, a notion they had contested for years.

In 1981, the U.S.S.R. announced that it was retiring its whaling fleet. The hopes of preservationists, however, were dashed when the Soviets explained that the cessation of activity would be confined to a particular sector of the North Pacific. In

*PIRATE WHALERS*

*The recommendations of the International Whaling Commission are one thing; the interests of self-serving shipowners are another. Pirate whalers sail the seven seas with impunity, harpooning any whales they please, including species that are endangered or nearly extinct (right whales, humpbacks, blue whales). A number of these pirates have been named in* Outlaw Whalers, *a pamphlet put out by the I.W.C. The Greenpeace organization has caught some of them red-handed.*

*In* Greenpeace *(nos. 11 and 12), René Parmentier tells the story of the* Sierra, *one of the most notorious illegal whalers in history. Originally a Dutch ship known as the* A.M.4, *it was sold to a firm based in the Bahamas and rechristened the* Run. *Then it found its way into the hands of some Norwegian businessmen, who in turn sold it to some South Africans; these owners registered it in Liechtenstein, then Liberia, as the* Sierra. *It also sailed under the flag of Somalia. Every season between 1968 and 1978 the* Sierra *took between four hundred and five hundred whales, primarily off the west coast of Africa. Its skipper never bothered to ascertain whether he was killing protected species, or mothers with calves. "Why should we deprive ourselves?" asked Andrew Behr, a South African and principal owner of the* Sierra, *in 1975. "The whales are doomed to die out anyway!" The whale meat flensed and butchered aboard the* Sierra *was delivered to Taiyo Canada Limited, the Canadian subsidiary of Japan's Taiyo Fisheries, the biggest privately owned whaling and fishing company in the world.*

*An accident brought the inglorious career of the* Sierra *to an unsensational close. It was rammed by an American ship as it sailed out of Oporto, Portugal. But other pirate whalers carry on its dirty work, for the most part under flags of convenience. Although registered in a number of different countries, they actually belong to the Japanese or resell what they catch to Japanese firms.*

the fall, the I.W.C. set zero quotas for commercial sperm whaling and forbade the use of "cold" (nonexplosive) harpoons, needlessly cruel weapons that prolong the death of the whale for up to twenty-four hours.

1982 marked the great turning point for the protection of whales. At its annual meeting in Brighton, England, the I.W.C. adopted a resolution banning all commercial whaling, effective 1986. The organization's membership has doubled, and includes large nations such as China, India, and Egypt as well as tiny island states (the Seychelles, St. Lucia, St. Vincent, Antigua), for whom the protection of marine life is a highly important issue.

The moratorium was approved despite pressure and lobbying by the Soviets and the Japanese, and despite long, drawn-out bargaining sessions involving Brazilian coffee sales, the shaky economic relationship between the Seychelles and Japan, and the Falkland Islands war. For preservationists, the pleasantest surprise came from Spain, which reversed its longstanding position and voted in favor of the moratorium. Observing the moratorium, or any other I.W.C. regulation, is a matter of choice for members. Any member has ninety days in which to register an objection or set its own quotas. The U.S.S.R. and Japan, backed by Norway and Peru, availed themselves of this rule and objected to the measure.

The next few years saw the same kind of slow progress. In 1983, Peru, Brazil, South Korea, and Iceland agreed to the moratorium; but the Philippines, pressured by Japan, announced that it would begin to take 200 Bryde's whales a year.

At the next annual meeting of the I.W.C., Argentina approved the erection, on an island off Peninsula Valdés, of a monument to the right whale. Along with this symbolic gesture came strict interim quotas. Exceptions were allowed for aboriginal subsistence and scientific research.

Diehard whaling nations continue to maneuver to keep their operations afloat, in particular by stretching the "scientific research" loophole. Counter-pressure is applied by the United States and the Common Market countries through economic sanctions. On April 5, 1985, Japan's Minister of Agriculture and Fishing announced that his country would suspend all whaling in 1988. Will the Japanese keep their promise, or is this just another ploy to circumvent the moratorium?

In 1986, the I.W.C. adopted the "zero quota"—in effect, a moratorium on whaling. But Japan, the U.S.S.R., and other whaling nations have declined to abide by the quota, invoking the ninety-day rule again.

*RECENT CATCH QUOTAS AUTHORIZED BY THE INTERNATIONAL WHALING COMMISSION*

| | 1981–1982 | 1982–1983 | 1983–1984 | 1984–1985 | 1985–1986 |
|---|---|---|---|---|---|
| North Atlantic | | | | | |
| *sperm whales* | 130 | 0 | 0 | 0 | 0 |
| *fin whales* | 701 | 293 | 257 | 281 | 0 |
| *sei whales* | 100 | 100 | 100 | 100 | 0 |
| *minke whales* | 2,554 | 2,434 | 1,226 | 1,177 | 0 |
| North Pacific | | | | | |
| *sperm whales* | 890 | 400 | 0 | 0 | 0 |
| *minke whales* | 1,361 | 1,361 | 721 | 320 | 0 |
| *Bryde's whales* | 529 | 546 | 536 | 357 | 0 |
| Southern Hemisphere | | | | | |
| *sperm whales* | 300 | 0 | 0 | 0 | 0 |
| *minke whales* | 6,718 | 7,072 | 6,655 | 4,224 | 0 |
| *Bryde's whales* | 264 | 165 | 165 | 164 | 0 |
| Aboriginal hunters | | | | | |
| *bowheads* | 17 | 17 | 27 | 27 | 26 |
| *humpbacks* | 10 | 10 | 9 | 8 | 0 |
| *gray whales* | 179 | 179 | 179 | 179 | 179 |
| Totals | 13,753 | 12,577 | 9,875 | 6,837 | 205 |

*Man's mistreatment of whales galvanized wildlife organizations into action. Thanks in part to their protests (above, in Paris; at right, in Sacramento, California), the International Whaling Commission adopted partial protection for whales, followed by an across-the-board moratorium on commercial whaling.*

# 鯨はこんなに役にたつ

㊝大洋漁業

鯨は地球上でいちばん大きな動物です。その体からは、たくさんの油や肉がとれるのをはじめ、すみずみまで役にたって、私たちの生活をゆたかにしてくれます。

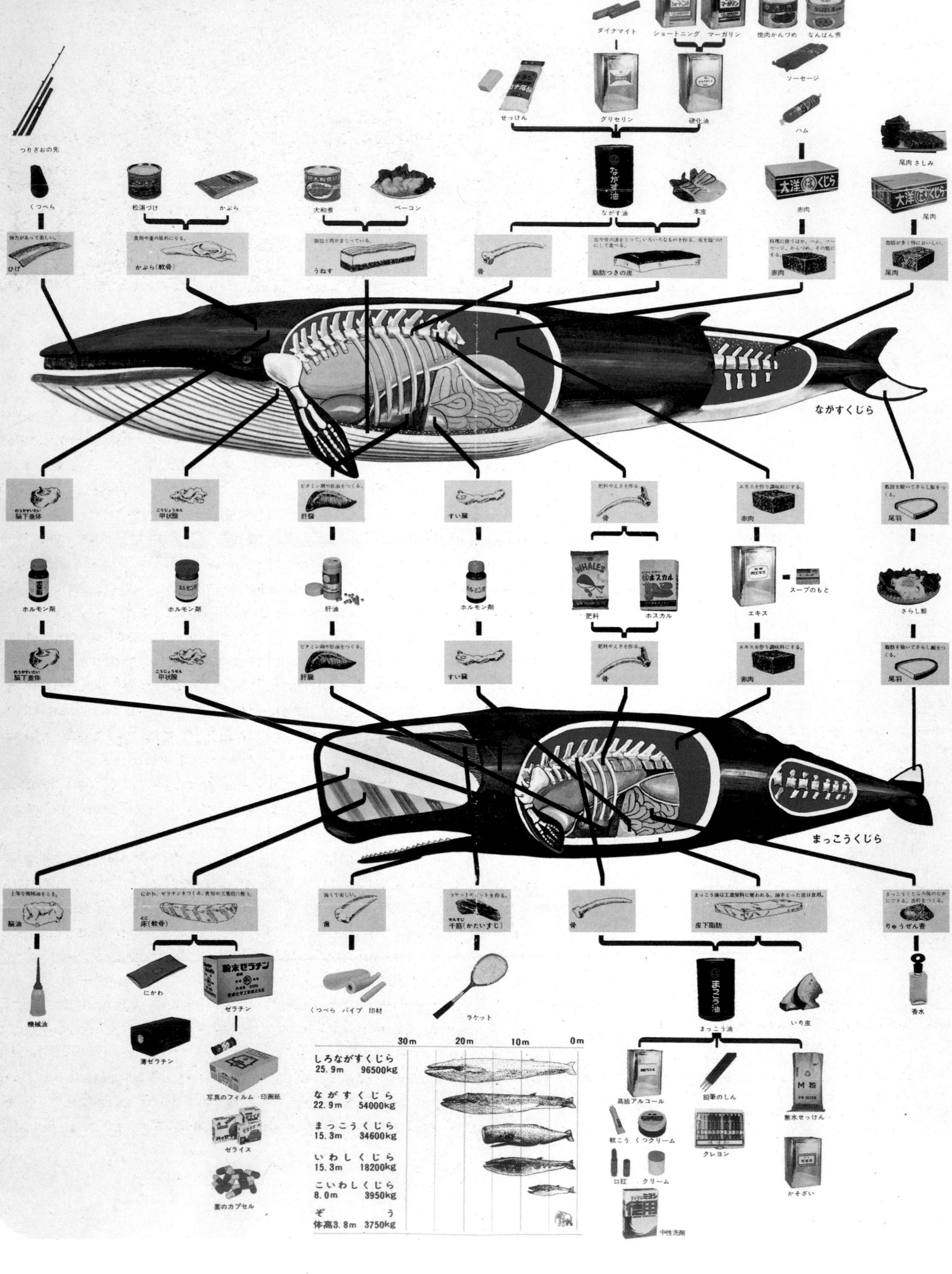


| | 30m | 20m | 10m | 0m |
|---|---|---|---|---|
| しろながすくじら 25.9m 96500kg | | | | |
| ながすくじら 22.9m 54000kg | | | | |
| まっこうくじら 15.3m 34600kg | | | | |
| いわしくじら 15.3m 18200kg | | | | |
| こいわしくじら 8.0m 3950kg | | | | |
| ぞう 体高3.8m 3750kg | | | | |

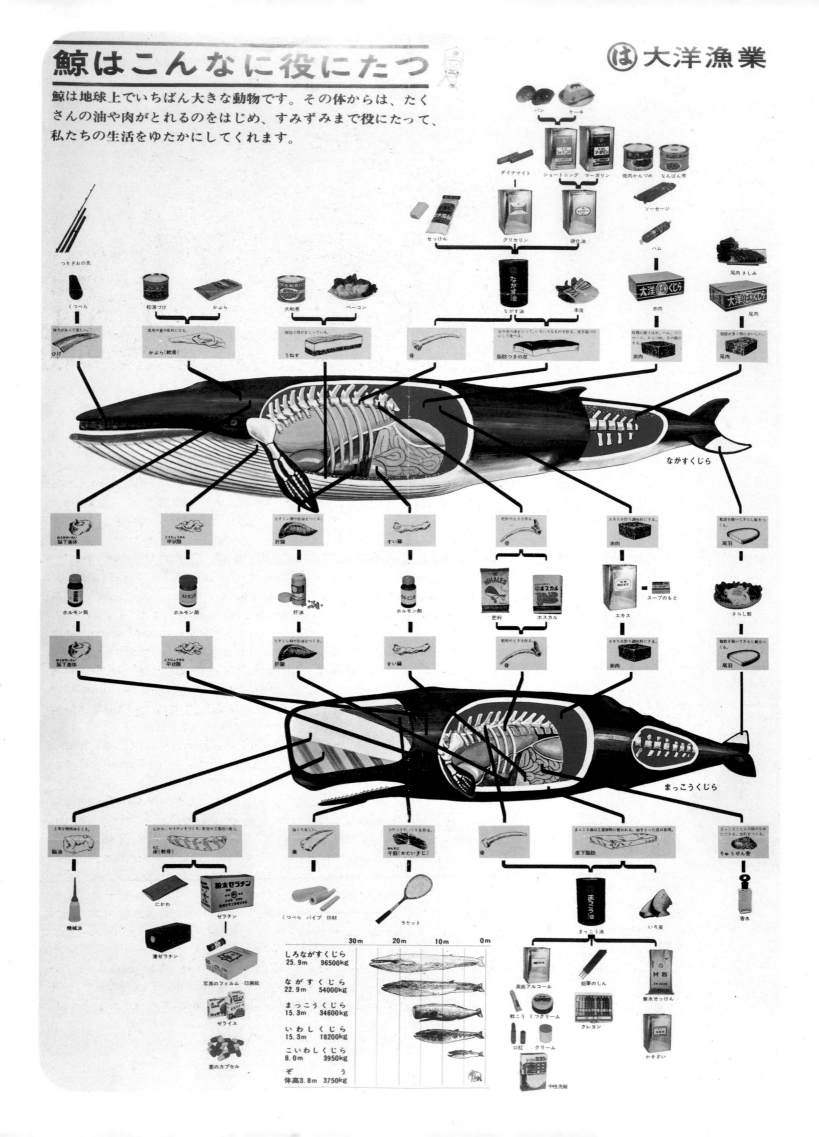

Above: One of the biggest lumps of ambergris ever found was recovered in the Antarctic on December 21, 1953. Ambergris was already a well-known substance when Lacépède wrote about it in 1804. "Once it was highly recommended in medicine. It was administered in a raw state or as a tincture. It was considered an effective stomachic, a stimulant, and an antispasmodic. . . . Now, however, it is primarily sought after for perfumes." This organic conglomerate, which contains ambrein and various other substances, builds up in the intestines of whales.

Left: This poster, published by a Japanese whaling and processing firm, illustrates in chart form some of the many by-products yielded by the body of a baleen whale (above) and a sperm whale (below). No one disputes the profitability of these substances, but continued demand will cost the world its whales. Japan wins no respect by using the tremendous technological resources at its command to pick the seas clean of cetaceans.

## WHALE PRODUCTS

What is it that makes whales such valuable prey for mankind? The most familiar whale products are probably ambergris, baleen, oil, ivory, and meat. But human ingenuity has found a use for nearly every part of a whale, from its teeth to its viscera. Pound for pound, ambergris is the most valuable whale product, but others, such as oil and ivory, are big money-makers. Valued for centuries, they have become important in the manufacture of hundreds of products most of us use daily, from industrial solvents and lubricants to pet food, clothing, and cosmetics.

References to ambergris go back many centuries; an early Arab chronicler, Al-Mas'udi (died 945), mentions it in a text entitled *The Ivory Trade*. Curiously, he believed that this substance was produced in the sea and washed ashore, where sperm whales then ate it. "When the sea is very rough it vomits up pieces of amber as large as rocks, and this fish swallows them. It is asphyxiated by them and then swims up to the surface. Then the Zanj, or men from other lands, who have been biding their time in their boats, seize the fish with harpoons and tackle, cut its stomach open, and take the amber out."

Marco Polo, Albertus Magnus, and medieval alchemists were also familiar with ambergris. Since the Renaissance, it has been used in perfumes and pharmaceuticals.

Considerable ink has been spilled in speculating about the source of ambergris. Some thought it was a waste product of seals, crocodiles, or birds. Others held that it came from underwater bituminous springs. In the seventeenth century, ambergris was classified as a plant substance (R. Boyle, 1673), then correctly reclassified as an animal product (R. Tredway, 1697). In 1866, Thiercelin came to the (incorrect) conclusion that these lumps were gallstones.

In point of fact, ambergris is a concretion that forms in the lower end of a sperm whale's large intestine. Its status as a normal or pathological occurrence remains a subject of controversy to this day. Found in the digestive tract of a tiny percentage of all sperm whales, ambergris is a dark, waxy substance that often contains pieces of squid beaks. The bolus builds up as new layers of detritus accumulate on its surface. A lump of ambergris vomited by a whale remains afloat and occasionally

washes up onto beaches. "In drying," Budker (1957) points out, "it gradually loses its smell and acquires an odor recalling that of a very dry cigar."

Ambergris is primarily made up of ambrein, a fatty substance similar to cholesterol. It is still used as a fixative in perfumes and in the making of cosmetics and high-quality soaps. Ambergris was once valued as an antispasmodic, but its pharmaceutical applications are now limited.

One of the largest lumps of ambergris ever found weighed nearly a thousand pounds; sold in London in 1912, it fetched £23,000, and is credited with saving a small Norwegian whaling company from bankruptcy.

Baleen, or "whalebone," was once one of the most widely used of whale products. For many years, whalemen reaped handsome profits from the baleen plates of the bowhead, which may grow to be several yards long. Until the 1930s, baleen was used in the making of ladies' wear (corsets, brassieres, bustles, hoops), whip handles, riding crops, watch springs, stays for peaked caps, and, of course, umbrella ribs. Demand also came from manufacturers of chairs, mattresses, store shutters, brushes, wigs (to keep the shape of the curls), and plumes on soldiers' helmets. In the Far East, baleen was commonly used for tea trays and shoehorns. Baleen has also been used in orthopedic medicine and ". . . in the making of cylindrical brushes for motorized street sweepers" (W. Besnard, 1948). You name it. The introduction of plastics—not to mention the depletion of suitable whale stocks—brought about the demise of the baleen industry.

Until the nineteenth century, whales and seals provided the manufacturers of lamps and lamp oil with most of the oil they needed. The discovery of petroleum and the advent of electricity sounded the death knell of this industry, which was forced to reorganize in the twentieth century. After new refining processes made it possible to standardize and classify whale oils ("pure Arctic," "pale," "dark," "black," and so forth), they were used in the making of stearin for candles as well as products for dressing leather. The chief market for whale oil, however, was in the manufacture of margarine and cooking-fat compounds.

Today, whale oil is processed into a wide range of products, from glycerine (for dynamite and medicines), preservatives, and stearates for soaps, detergents, and shampoos; to varnishes, paints, printing inks, oilcloth, linoleum, and polishing waxes; margarine and cooking fats; and candles and crayons.

Sperm oil, or spermaceti, is the finest oil of all. "The only thing to be considered here is this," Melville wrote in *Moby-Dick* (1851). "What kind of oil is used at coronations? . . . What then can it possibly be, but sperm oil in its unmanufactured, unpolluted state, the sweetest of all oils?" Lacépède (1804), who swore by its medicinal properties, proclaimed it effective for catarrh, pulmonary ulcers, and renal colic. It was also recommended to soothe, cleanse, and promote the closing of open wounds.

*Yankee whalers used to carve or engrave ivory from the teeth of harpooned sperm whales and sold these pieces of scrimshaw at ports of call to supplement their meager wages.*

*The baleen plates of right whales measure up to 16 feet long, and in the nineteenth century they spawned a brisk trade in "whalebone." Around 1880, Parisians had four grades to choose from: "Polar Whales (deluxe)," "Okhotsk," "Southern Whales," and "Northwest Whales." Only three grades were available in London: "Greenland Whales," "South Sea," and "North West Coast."*

Sperm oil fills the huge spermaceti organ occupying much of the enormous, square forehead of the sperm whale. Composed of 76 percent unbranched fatty-acid esters and 23 percent triglycerides, it is incomparably pure, emulsifies very easily, and is unsurpassed among natural oils as a lubricant. Here is a quick rundown of its uses.

Unrefined sperm oil is mixed with mineral oils and used in leather processing and finishing. Refined and filtered sperm oil (spermaceti) goes into some cosmetics, cold cream, lipstick, shaving cream, and ointments. Filtered sperm oil is an ingredient in motor oil, in cutting and quenching oils for metalworking, and in lubricants for precision instruments. Sulfurized sperm oil is used to dress hides and process textiles. A whole range of products depends on saponified sperm oil and sperm-oil alcohols: cosmetics, dye solvents, blending agents in printing inks, carbon stencils, germicides, plastics, detergents, and paste!

Used in the pharmaceutical industry, the oil in a whale's liver is richer in vitamins (especially A) than cod-liver oil. A fin whale's liver may weigh up to 900 pounds and yield more than 6 pounds of vitamin A. The endocrine glands (pituitary, pancreas, and adrenal glands) are a source of various hormones and medicines.

The ivory from the teeth of sperm whales and other odontocetes is used in the small-scale or semi-industrial production of carved objects (scrimshaw). Whalers once fashioned the ivory into buttons and dice; in Japan, it is still used for seals and piano keys.

The bones of whales also found their uses. The Vikings sat on chairs made of whale vertebrae; so did Martin Luther, as the interior of his house in Wartburg attests. Many primitive cultures used whale bones as building material for structural framework and doorways; the bones could also be carved into kitchen utensils, knitting needles, and chess pieces. Today, whale bones are ground into meal and blended with fertilizers or animal feeds.

*The bones of stranded whales provided primitive societies with beams and other building materials as early as prehistoric times. Above: The jawbones of a right whale make for an unusual "porch" (gate arch) for a house in Iceland.*

*The fishermen-peasants of the Faeroe Islands came up with original uses for the by-products of their whaling activity. Here we see an entire wall made of pilot whale skulls and vertebrae! Today, modern industrial processing plants grind the bones into meal for blending into fertilizers and animal feed.*

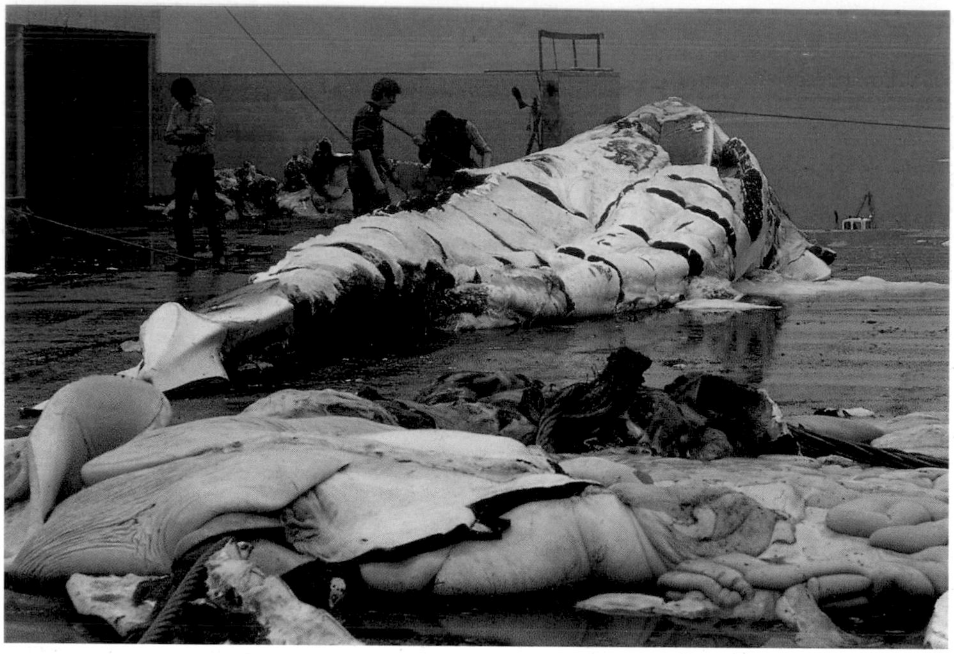

Even such products as skin, blood, and tendons have been found to have commercial application. Tanned sperm-whale skin is turned into bicycle saddles, handbags, and shoes. In the nineteenth century, a factory on the North Cape of Norway used whale blood as an ingredient in sausage. Nowadays, the blood that factory ships salvage is processed into fertilizers or plywood adhesives. Whale tendons are used as strings for tennis racquets and surgical thread. The connective proteins in the tendons, skin, and bones of larger cetaceans yield a gelatin that is used in candy, delicatessen products, and photographic film.

In Scandinavian countries, whale intestines were once used as a substitute for window glass. Nowadays, the gut (and any matter therein) is, like the bones, cooked, dried, and processed into fertilizer.

The consumption of whale meat has long been a subject of controversy and justification. In the thirteenth century, Albertus Magnus referred to whale meat as "*graspois*" or "*craspois*," noting that it could be eaten during Lent "since the whale is a fish." Rondelet (1568) wrote that "except for the tongue, its flesh is not considered good to eat." Ambroise Paré (1573), however, pointed out that in the provinces blubber "is eaten with peas during Lent." In 1804, Lacépède wrote that "Greenlanders and other inhabitants of northern lands consider the skin and flippers pleasant to the taste." Except in a few villages in the Far East, the nearly black, foul-smelling meat of the sperm whale is not considered suitable for cooking. But we read in *Moby-Dick* that "in the case of a small Sperm Whale, the brains are accounted a fine dish."

People in Iceland and Norway still eat whale meat; Icelanders consider *rengi*, a piece of blubber from the belly that is cooked and pickled in vinegar, especially toothsome fare. The biggest market for whale meat is Japan; the Japanese are especially partial to the right whale and smaller rorquals.

Whale meat deemed unfit for human consumption does not go to waste. It is used in canned dog and cat food; in feed for mink, sable, and other animals raised on fur farms; as food for carnivorous animals in zoos; in the production of culture media for bacteria and insect larvae; and as powdered feed for poultry and livestock. Occasionally, by a circuitous route, whale meat ends up on our dinner table, for the extract is used in the making of packaged soups, freeze-dried bouillons, and ready-cooked gravies and concentrates. *Bon appétit.*

*The biggest markets for whale meat have always been Korea and Japan. "One whale taken, seven villages prosperous," an old Japanese saying goes. For one thing, whale meat—unlike pork or beef—cannot transmit parasites to people. In Japan and Korea, the favorite cuts are* akaniku, *the red meat of the subaxial muscle;* onomi, *a piece of tail meat eaten raw as* sashimi; *and* sunoko, *meat from the throat pleats of rorquals used in the making of whale "ham" and "bacon."*

*The Inuit (Eskimo) are one of the cultures for whom the Exemption Clause was intended. People included within the meaning of the clause may continue to take a certain number of individuals of protected species every year. Right: A bowhead whale, chopped up in an Inuit village near Barrow, Alaska. Of the Eskimos Charles Scammon wrote in 1874, "The choice pieces for a dainty repast, for them, are the flukes, lips, and fins."*

### THE ABORIGINE EXEMPTION CLAUSE

*Many cultures—Eskimos, the Indonesians of Timor, the Polynesians of Tonga, the Indians of Vancouver Island or the Magellanic Islands, among others—have for centuries owed their survival to the meat, blubber, and bones of whales. Some still depend on cetaceans, at least in part, for subsistence and raw materials.*

*The so-called civilized nations of the world were to blame for the wholesale slaughter of whales, so it would not have been fair to use depleted whale stocks as a pretext for depriving more traditional societies of their ancestral resources. That is why an aborigine exemption clause has been included in protection agreements from the very start.*

*Article Three of the International Convention for the Regulation of Whaling (September 24, 1931) stipulates as follows:*

*"The present convention does not apply to aborigines dwelling on the coasts of the territories of the High Contracting Parties provided that —*

1. *They only use canoes, pirogues, or other exclusively native craft propelled by oars or sails.*
2. *They do not carry firearms.*
3. *They are not in the employment of persons other than aborigines.*
4. *They are not under contract to deliver the products of their whaling to any third person."*

*This proviso was irreproachable just as it stood. In 1946, however, when the I.W.C. came into being, it was replaced by a differently worded exemption clause in a new Convention. The new language was much less restrictive and omitted all reference to boats or weaponry.*

*The problem is that there is no way to enforce these regulations. Most people covered by the clause have added motors to their traditional craft. They also have guns, and many wounded animals drift out to sea and die, which benefits no one. Lastly, like it or not, aboriginal peoples are becoming fully integrated into the world economy. Nearly all of them market at least some of what they catch.*

*There would be no need to debate the validity of an aborigine exemption clause if native whaling really existed. At present, however, a deplorable perversion of the system is taking place. The Japanese are buying back most of what is taken in the vicinity of the Azores (sperm whales, scarce humpbacks). They oversee what has turned into a phony aborigine whaling operation that extends from Tonga to the Philippines. A Greenpeace inquiry revealed that the Soviets have commissioned a modern whaler, complete with harpoon gun, to take 100 to 200 grays and a few bowheads every year, ostensibly to provide food for the Chukchi and other native peoples of eastern Siberia. Experts agree that the only appropriate catch quota for the region is zero.*

## THE JOJOBA AND THE SPERM WHALE

*One can find just about anything in nature, including a shrub whose seeds yield an oil as fine and as valuable as spermaceti oil. Botanists named it* Simmondsia chinensis, *but the plant is indigenous to Mexico and the southwestern United States and does not grow anywhere in China. The Aztecs called this cousin of the box tree (family Buxaceae)* johowi; *nowadays it is commonly referred to by its Spanish name, jojoba.*

*The jojoba grows plentifully in the Sonoran Desert, from Mexico to Arizona. Averaging 6 to 13 feet high, it has thick, waxy leaves and every year produces 13 to 14 pounds of small brown beans with white centers. These seeds contain (40-60 percent) a very fine multipurpose oil that Indians once used as an ointment for wounds, a pomade for hair, lighting oil, and a dressing to soften leather.*

*Scientists discovered that this pale yellow oil with the aroma of hazelnuts consists of unsaturated fatty-acid esters and alcohols. It is easily extracted from the seeds. It can be stored for twenty-five* years *without turning rancid. It remains viscous at very high temperatures. It is an incomparable lubricant and outperforms spermaceti oil itself in that respect. If we used it in our car engines, we would only need an oil change every 20,000 miles!*

*With the jojoba, nothing goes to waste. The oil is used in the manufacture of countless chemical products (varnishes, inks, glues, plastics, resins), cosmetics (soaps, sun lotions,) and pharmaceuticals (antibiotics, products to prevent hair loss, ointments, excipients). The residue from the pressing process yields a protein-rich flour that is fed to livestock.*

*This miraculous plant tolerates the poorest soils, even salty ones, withstands temperatures of 120° F (but freezes at 18° F), thrives in arid conditions (less than 10 inches of rainfall a year), can live through eighteen-month dry spells, and is virtually parasite-free.*

*The Mexicans, who pioneered jojoba cultivation, have planted 5,000 acres of the shrub in the desert regions of Sonora and Baja California. Its virtues have not gone unnoticed north of the border; jojoba farms are being planned for Arizona and California. This substitute for spermaceti oil has also generated interest in South Africa, India, Israel, Australia, and the Sudan. A laboratory affiliated with the Institut National de la Recherche Agronomique in Angers, France, is looking into the feasibility of* in vitro *propagation of the species.*

*A truly desert form of vegetation that will sink its roots up to 90 feet deep to find water, the jojoba is a plant whose time has come. For one thing, it would save the sperm whales of the world, once and for all. Two hectares yield between 3.3 and 4.4 tons of oil a year; the biggest sperm whale, which takes thirty years to "grow," yields only 3.85 tons. Jojoba also holds great promise for the impoverished countries of the Third World. The introduction of a new agro-industry would generate desperately needed cash for governments in places like Central America or the Sahel.*

*Other plants may prove as valuable as the jojoba. For example, the seeds of two herbs native to Oregon and California, both commonly known as meadow foam* (Limnanthes alba, L. douglasii), *are 25-30 percent high-quality oil (W. Calhoun, 1976).*

*The jojoba, a hedgelike shrub indigenous to the deserts of southwestern North America, may not be much to look at, but what riches lie within!*

*Opposite: The leap of a breaching humpback is a work of art.*

CHAPTER 2

# A Hundred and Fifty Tons of Beauty

4. 1/75
5. 1/40
6. 1/40
2. 1/75
3. 1/75
1. 1/40
9. 1/160
7. 1/75
8. 1/160

*For all these reasons, then, any way you may look at it, you must needs conclude that the great Leviathan is that one creature in the world which must remain unpainted to the last. True, one portrait may hit the mark much nearer than another, but none can hit it with any very considerable degree of exactness. So there is no earthly way of finding out precisely what the whale really looks like. And the only mode in which you can derive even a tolerable idea of his living contour is by going a-whaling yourself; but by doing so, you run no small risk of being eternally stove and sunk by him. Wherefore, it seems to me you had best not be too fastidious in your curiosity touching this Leviathan.*

Herman Melville (1851)

Very, very few human beings have had the good fortune to watch as whales describe flawless arabesques beneath the ocean surface. The combination of gigantic size and effortless grace is a wonderful thing to behold. The animals' movements are as fluid as their environment, and their adaptation to it is most clearly seen underwater.

Everything about the whale is designed for swimming. Its limbs are pared to essentials: completely atrophied hindlimbs (except for a few small bones embedded in the side muscle) and a pair of paddle-like appendages in front for steering and stability. Its body—a smooth, bulky head fitted seamlessly onto a neckless torso—is shaped like a torpedo. Its tail ends in a pair of highly efficient flukes that, unlike the caudal fins of fish and marine reptiles, are flattened horizontally.

No protrusions. Nothing to slow it down. Nothing to impede the flow of water over its streamlined bulk. It is nearly devoid of hair; a thick layer of blubber serves as insulation instead. The whale's nostrils—turned into blowholes—have migrated to the top of its rostrum, enabling it to breathe without interruption while cruising at the surface. The cow's inconspicuous nipples lie within two clefts on each side of the vulva. In males, the testicles are internal, and the penis retracts into a slit within the abdominal wall.

## THE BEACONS OF CETOLOGY

Cetology is the science of cetaceans (from *cetaceus*, a Latin derivative of the Greek word *ketos*, "big fish"). Cetologists are not given to boasting about their accomplishments, for few branches of knowledge have made smaller strides since ancient times.

Why this sluggish pace? For one thing, most whales are huge; there is no aquarium big enough to hold them for close study. For another, they can surface with a couple of strokes of their tail and dive out of view just as quickly. The main reason, however, is that man has harpooned first and asked questions later.

We are not the first to make this observation. Aristotle deplored our ignorance of whales, and his comments were echoed by Rondelet (1568) and Lacépède (1804). "No branch of Zoology is so much involved as that which is entitled Cetology," William Scoresby noted in 1823. Three years later, Frédéric Cuvier wrote that

*Whales dumbfounded navigators, naturalists, and philosophers alike. The strange creatures artists referred to in their illustrations as whales indicate how very little they knew about them. Above: Engravings of a "boar whale" and a "bearded whale" from* Historia de Gentibus Septentrionalibus *(1555) by Norwegian archbishop Olaus Magnus.*

*Opposite: This engraving from T. Bromme's* Systematischer Atlas der Naturgeschichte *(1861) is far more accurate. Top to bottom and left to right: A manatee, a sea cow (dugong), a dolphin, a walrus, a sea lion, a seal, a right whale, a narwhal, and a sperm whale.*

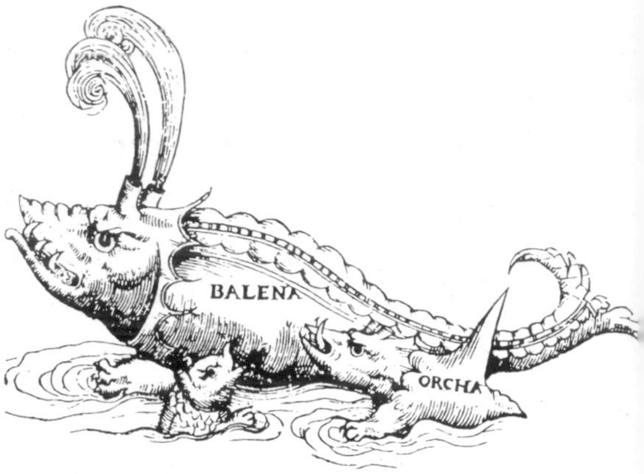


"Many have observed these animals, but by and large their findings are haphazard." According to Thomas Beale (1839), "Utter confusion exists among the historians of that animal." In 1862, Alphonse Toussenel made the following observation: "Painful though it may be, we must acknowledge that, of all the animals on earth, the gigantic, consummate organism known as the whale is the one scientists know least about."

Here we are, just a step from the twenty-first century. New techniques and heightened interest have drawn platoons of scientists and laymen to the study of whales, yet we still debate and wonder. Time and again, the stacks of current publications on the subject sound a familiar refrain: "Insufficient data available."

Discounting the accumulated empirical knowledge of Eskimos, Indians, and other "primitive" peoples, the first cetologist in history was Aristotle (384–322 B.C.). In *Historia animalium*, the master of the Lyceum describes dolphins, orcas (killer whales), sperm whales, and right whales, all of which he correctly classifies as mammals. "Thus, the dolphin is viviparous, and accordingly we find it furnished with two breasts, not situated high up, but in the vicinity of the genitals . . . and its young have to follow after it to suckle." Aristotle knew that cetaceans, unlike fish, breathe with lungs. He differentiated between odontocetes (toothed whales) and mysticetes (baleen whales): "The [latter] has no teeth, but does have hairs that resemble hog bristles." These species, he adds, have a language. "The dolphin, too, utters a murmuring sound that is the equivalent of a voice."

*. . .This great and wide sea, wherein all things are creeping innumerably, both small and great beasts,*
*There go the ships; there is that Leviathan whom Thou hast made to play therein.*
*—(Psalm 104, verses 25 and 26)*

*From time immemorial, whales have inspired all sorts of legends and stories as well as fantastic illustrations. Opposite, top: A whale spouting a double jet, from the treatise by Olaus Magnus. Left: Arrival on the coast of America, from* Americae Tertia Pars *(1662) by Théodore de Bry. Above: An engraving from* Traité des Prodiges, *a sixteenth-century work by Conrad Lycosthène.*

The other great authority on whales in ancient times was Pliny the Elder (A.D. 23–79). In his *Natural History* he fleshes out Aristotle's findings with a mixture of original firsthand observations and fanciful comments. Pliny was familiar with several whale species and knew, for example, that right whales in the "ocean of Cadiz" set out on migrations, that in winter the females gave birth just offshore, and that they were subject to devastating sporadic attacks by killer whales.

Whales are mentioned by a number of ancient authors, from Virgil (*Aeneid*) and Strabo (*Geography*) in the first century B.C. to Arrien and Aulus Gellius in the second century A.D. Then cetology, like so many other sciences, foundered in the neglect of the Dark Ages. For hundreds of years, knowledge about whales was pretty much confined to Aristotle's observations and the Book of Jonah. However, Toussenel (1862) tells us that the Norwegians "prided themselves on knowing twenty-three species of whales" as far back as the ninth century. In the thirteenth century, Albertus Magnus described whaling in *De Animalibus*. About that time, whales were discussed at length in the *Kongespiel* (better known by its Latin title, *Speculum Regale*, or *The Mirror of Royalty*), an anonymous account of Iceland that considered whales the only truly interesting sight the island nation had to offer. Its author correctly distinguished between northern right whales and bowhead whales. Five centuries later, eminent naturalists with goatees and pince-nez were still confusing the two species.

Came the Renaissance, and cetology burst forth like the mighty blow of a rorqual coming up for air. Conrad Gesner (*Historiae animalium*, Zurich, 1551–87) and Ambroise Paré (*Des Monstres tant terrestres que marins*, Paris, 1573) waxed rhapsodic about the size of whales, described them, enumerated distinguishing

*For many years, the only way naturalists could satisfy their curiosity about whales was to examine individuals that had been randomly washed ashore. Reports and illustrations were inevitably inaccurate, since carcasses found on the beach were in various stages of decomposition. Left: An English engraving "after nature" of a sperm whale stranded in 1764 at Egmond-aan-Zee, Holland. Below: Another version of the same stranding, by a Dutch engraver.*

CAGELOT of POTWALVIS lang omtrent 60 Voeten,
den J Maart aldaar in Veiling Verkogt voor 810 Guldens

features, and passed on information about whaling techniques. But the real pioneers of cetology (not to mention biological oceanography) were two medical men, Pierre Belon and Guillaume Rondelet. In 1551, Belon published *Histoire naturelle des estranges Poissons marins* in Paris and two years later followed up with a Latin version, *De Aquatilibus*. Rondelet, a friend of Ambroise Paré and François Rabelais, had his *De Piscibus* printed in Lyons in 1554; a translated revised version entitled *L'Histoire entière des Poissons* came out in 1568.

The seventeenth century witnessed a number of noteworthy contributions, including books by Ulisse Aldrovandi (*Historiae naturalis*, Bologna, 1599); Clusius (*Exoticorum libri decem*, Antwerp, 1605); Athanasius Kircher (*Ars magnifica*, Rome, 1641); Jonston (*Historiae naturalis*, London, 1649–53); and Olaus Wormius (*Museum Wormianum*, Leyden, 1655). However, no three works did more to lay the groundwork of cetology in the 1600s than Friderich Martens' *Spitzbergische oder Groenlandische Reise-Beschreibung* (Hamburg, 1675), *Historia piscium* (Oxford, 1686) by the great British explorer Sir Hugh Willoughby, and the *Phalainologia nova* (Edinburgh, 1692), by Sir Robert Sibbald, the Scottish naturalist.

In 1713, John Ray published *Synopsis methodica avium et piscium* in London. Seven years later, in Amsterdam, Cornelius G. Zorgdrager published his account of the northern whale fishery, *Bloeyende Opkomst der Aloude en Hedendaagsche Groenlandische Visschery*. Hasaeus' *De Leviathan Jobi et Ceto Jonae* appeared in Bremen in 1723. The Hon. Paul Dudley, FRS, communicated *An Essay on the Natural History of Whales* to the Royal Society in 1725. Shortly thereafter, Hans Egede recapitulated current knowledge about right whales in his superb *History of Greenland* (Copenhagen, 1741; London, 1745). Georges Buffon devoted an entire volume of his monumental *Histoire naturelle, générale et particulière* (the first part of which appeared in 1749) to whales. In *Systema naturae* (1758), Linnaeus ranked cetaceans in his classification of organisms, not without considerable uncertainty. From then on, treatises dealing either primarily or incidentally with whales appeared in rapid succession: Othon Fabricius' *Fauna Groenlandica* (Leipzig, 1780); Duhamel's *Traité générale des pêches* (Paris, 1782); John Hunter's *Observations on the Structure and Economy of Whales*, a paper he communicated to the Royal Society in 1787; and Capt. Colnett's exciting *Voyage to the South Atlantic* (London, 1792).

In the first half of the nineteenth century, seminal additions to cetological literature included: Peter Camper's *Observations anatomiques sur plusieurs espèces de cétacés* (Paris, 1820); Harlan's *Fauna Americana* (Philadelphia, 1825); René Lesson's *Histoire naturelle des cétacés* (Paris, 1828); Henry W. Dewhurst's *The Natural History of the Order Cetacea* (London, 1834); and Georges Cuvier's *Leçons d'anatomie comparée* (Paris, 1835), in which the father of paleontology discussed the first whale fossils ever discovered.

However, three other contributions were to prove far more important. In 1820, William Scoresby, the greatest captain in the history of English whaling, published *A Journal of a Voyage to the Northern Whale Fishery*, still considered one of the finest accounts of right whales. In *Histoire naturelle des mammifères* (Paris, 1826), Frédéric Cuvier (brother of Georges) devoted many an impassioned page to cetaceans. Last but not least, there is Lacépède's *Histoire naturelle des cétacés* (Paris, 1804). In this highly romanticized interpretation of natural history, the writer indulges in excesses befitting the monstrous proportions of the animals he describes. This book is liberally sprinkled with quotes from Lacépède, and our hope is that they will help to instill in some of our contemporaries a renewed passion for science.

With naturalists like Lacépède and Cuvier generating an impetus, French cetology made considerable headway and expanded its sphere of influence. The new science drew on the discoveries of explorer-naturalists such as Dumont d'Urville in Antarctica, as well as on research by armchair zoologists like M. de Blainville, Etienne Geoffroy Saint-Hilaire, Alcide d'Orbigny, and, most of all, Paul Gervais, who published *Histoire naturelle des mammifères* in 1843.

Meanwhile, British cetologists were also gaining ground. The pioneering work begun by John Hunter was carried on by his secretary, William Clift. In 1866, Sir Richard Owen published *The Comparative Anatomy and Physiology of the Verte-*

en Egmond op Zee Levend Gestrand op den 15 February 1764.
Getekend en in't Koper gebragt te Haarlem door Cornelis van Noorde


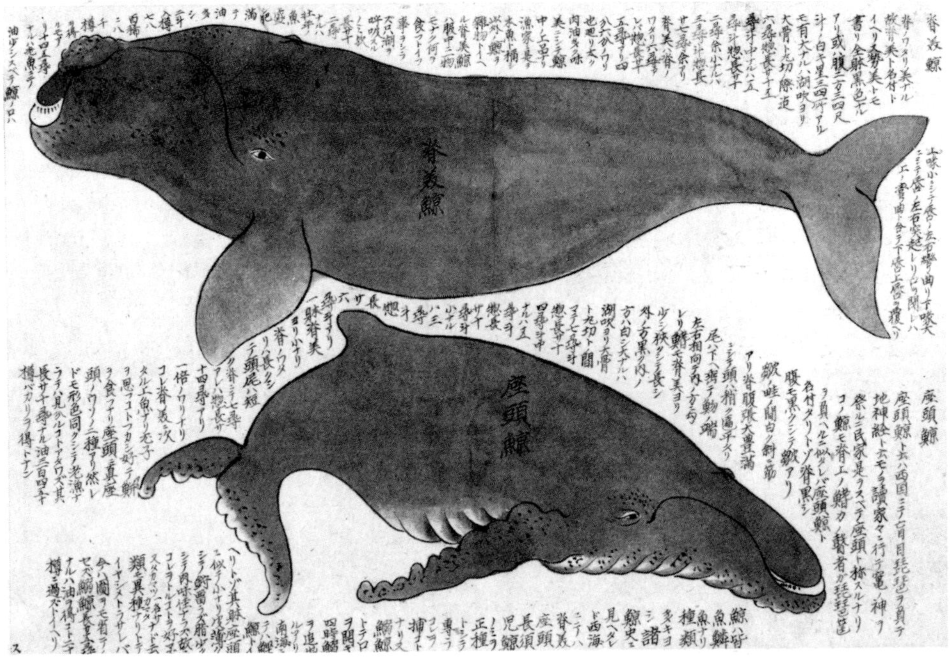

*The Japanese long classified whales as fish so that they could eat whale meat without compromising their religious beliefs. But Japanese naturalists were not swayed by these purely culinary considerations and classified whales as mammals. Their illustrations from the sixteenth to the nineteenth centuries were more accurate than the drawings made by their Western contemporaries. One nineteenth-century manuscript on whaling includes an illustration of a Pacific right whale (above) and a humpback whale (below).*

*brates*. John Edward Gray, who started out as an assistant at the British Museum and went on to become the Keeper of the Zoology Department, published his *Catalogue of Seals and Whales in the British Museum* in 1866. In addition, he established a worldwide network of contacts with field naturalists, including John Anderson in India. The indefatigable Sir William Flower followed in his footsteps.

Indeed, Europeans everywhere were busy observing and classifying cetaceans. In Germany, Prof. Karl Asmund Rudolphi, founder of the Berlin Zoological Museum, first described the sei whale, which was known for a time as "Rudolphi's rorqual." Several studies by Karl Siebold and Hermann Burmeister appeared around this time. Daniel Eschricht, who taught cetology at the University of Copenhagen, was accorded the posthumous honor of having the gray whale (genus *Eschrichtius*) named after him. From the Netherlands came the writings of Hermann Schlegel, director of the Rijksmuseum in Amsterdam. Sweden's representative was Wilhelm Lilljeborg, a specialist in whale fossils who shed considerable light on their genealogy. However, the foremost European cetologist of the second half of the nineteenth century was P.-J. van Beneden, a Belgian zoologist whose many monographs on whales (including *Histoire naturelle des cétacés des mers d'Europe*, 1889) were published in Brussels between 1867 and 1892.

In the United States, where the sperm whale fishery reigned supreme, cetology made strides thanks to gifted immigrants such as Swiss-born Louis Agassiz and Leonhard Stejneger of Norway. Herman Melville's *Moby-Dick* (1851) has no equal in whaling literature; but Charles Scammon, one of the most formidable whalemen of his day, penned a lesser-known masterpiece, *The Marine Mammals of the North-western Coast of North America* (1874). To this day it is an unsurpassed account of the California gray whale, the species Scammon himself brought to the unsympathetic attention of profit-minded Yankee whalemen.

With the turn of the century, our concise who's who of cetological luminaries draws to a close. The age of pioneers was history, description and conjecture gave way to statistics. In but one example of the new trend, N. A. Mackintosh and J. F. G. Wheeler, two British scientists, examined no fewer than 1,500 blue whale and fin whale carcasses at Antarctic stations during one of the *Discovery* expeditions.

*The cetacean family tree is riddled with gaps. Presumably the land-dwelling forebears of the whales returned to the sea some 65 million years ago, but the evolutionary stages leading to the development of modern cetaceans are still largely unknown. Even the greatly simplified diagram below is open to question, and paleontologists remain divided on a number of issues. What confluence of random genetic events could have produced the humpback whale (opposite), that thirty-ton acrobat and expert lobtailer?*

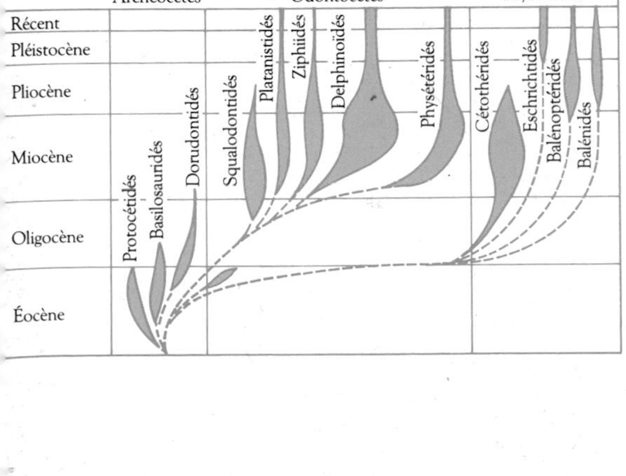


## ARCHAEOCETES, OR THE CASE OF THE IMPROBABLE ADAPTATION

Cetaceans are flawlessly adapted to a marine existence, and one cannot help wondering how these descendants of land animals managed such a successful return to the sea. The issue is highly problematic. According to paleontology and Neo-Darwinism, species evolve through the combined effects of chance mutation and natural selection, the process by which those organisms best adapted to their environment survive. To the lover of whales, however, even the process of evolution seems insufficient to account for this animal. It was a miraculous confluence of random characteristics that allowed a terrestrial creature to acquire, over millions of years, the streamlined shape, innovative skeleton, specialized physiology, and echolocation systems cetaceans now possess.

We know very little about the distant forebears of cetaceans, and our ignorance makes the mystery even more unfathomable. There are missing links between the earliest land-dwelling mammals that waded back into the water and the Archaeoceti (after Flower, 1883), the order of "ancient whales" that were thoroughly adapted to an aquatic habitat.

Aquatic mammals, they share a number of anatomical adaptations with the whale of today: an elongated body, reduced hindlimbs, paddle-shaped front limbs, a tail that can move up and down; the head shows dense ear bones with space around them for insulating fat and air, a long snout and nostrils on top of it.

Archeocete fossils have been found throughout the world. Beginning in the United States in 1834, *Basilosaurus* (temporarily misidentified as "king of reptiles") was found and dated to the middle of the late Eocene era, from 38 million to 45 million years ago. For the next century and a half after this discovery, fossils appeared to confirm this dating for archeocetes; attempts to clarify linkages and distinctions were based on the assumption that proto-whales arose in the mid-Eocene. The most recently discovered archeocete, however, is also the oldest to be identified. Between 1980 and 1983, paleontologists described representatives of the genus *Pakicetus* from a skull and other bones found in the Himalayan region, in sediment dating to 50 million years ago. The discovery pushes the documentation of cetacean development back to the early Eocene period and opens a new chapter in whale evolution.

Any outline of the development of cetaceans is subject to challenge and reinterpretation, particularly in light of fast-paced advances in paleontological applications of modern technology—amino-acid sequencing, chromosome analysis, and other procedures—as well as in discoveries and syntheses of fragments. The following discussion relies heavily on the current work of paleontologist Lawrence G. Barnes.

The *Pakicetus* archeocete lived in an era when the tectonic plate that is now India was shifting up to collide with Asia and formed the Himalayas, and shallow continental seas spread eastward from today's Mediterranean. Dental remains, skull characteristics and biochemical evidence indicate that the archeocete derived from a Paleocene family of large-bodied terrestrial animals called mesonychids; the mesonychids colonized the fringes of the shallow seas and evolved to an aquatic existence through the adaptations common to all cetaceans.

Some experts hold that archeocetes lived at the same time with divergent cetacean branches of primitive odontocetes (the suborder of the sperm whale) and primitive mysticetes (baleen whales). Other authorities, however, believe that the odontocetes and mysticetes derived from archeocetes. In either case, the Oligocene era (25 million to 38 million years ago) saw an intermediate stage of animals sharing characteristics with modern cetacea and with archeocetes. The nostrils shifted backwards; the body streamlined; heterodont teeth were replaced by a uniform shape or by baleen plates; the skull began telescoping; and acoustic scanning organs arose.

Deposits from the Miocene era (5 million to 25 million years ago) have yielded fossils of the sperm whale, the oldest of living whale families. The right whales and bowheads have been documented in deposits from the late Miocene and early Pliocene (2 million to 5 million years ago). The rorquals (humpback, minke, Bryde's, sei, fin, and blue whales) are relative newcomers. The only fossil gray whale that has been described dates to the late Pleistocene and is virtually the same animal that exists today; the anatomical features that separate the gray whale from other baleen whales are so distinctive as to suggest that much earlier ancestors existed as far back as the Miocene. Their remains just came to rest in a spot that has proven less accessible for paleontologists and cetologists.

*For paleontologists, cetaceans are a baffling and provocative riddle. Archaeocetes evolved so swiftly and adapted body shape and physiology to environment so flawlessly that some experts have seized on the cetacean issue to challenge the neo-Darwinian theory of species evolution (that is, random mutation and survival of the fittest). As P.-P. Grassé noted in 1973, "Who would be so bold as to maintain that a creature so wonderfully adapted to life in the water and to deep diving evolved through a chance confluence of random characteristics that just happened to dovetail with a habitat and modus vivendi the animal had not yet even adopted?"*

*Below and opposite, top: These balaenopterid fossils are between 5 and 10 million years old. They were discovered at Sacato, on the southern coast of Peru, by a Franco-Peruvian team led by Professor C. de Muizon. Opposite, bottom: Artist's conception of a primordial underwater scene with a basilosaurus and large sharks.*

*Overleaf: Power and grace. A breaching humpback is one of the most spectacular sights nature has to offer.*

*The whales turn and glisten, plunge*
*and sound and rise again,*
*Hanging over subtly darkening deeps*
*Flowing like breathing planets*
*in the sparkling whorls of*
*living light—*

*(Gary Snyder, American, b. 1930)*

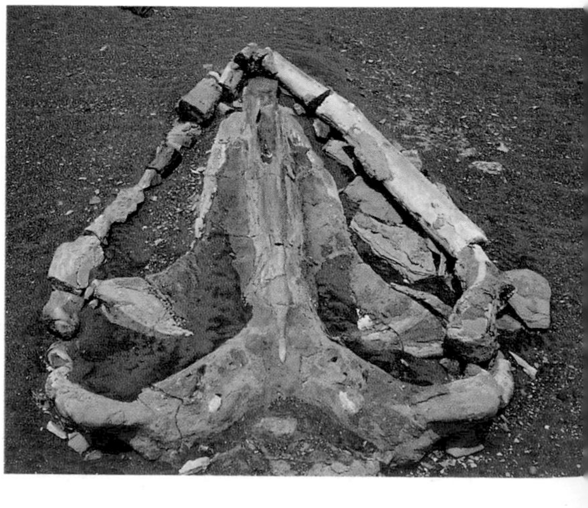

*BASILOSAURUS: "KING LIZARD"*

*"In 1832," writes Lyall Watson (1981), "a column of 28 giant vertebrae was unearthed in Louisiana. It was identified as the remains of a dinosaur by the American geologist Harlan and named* Basilosaurus, *or 'King Lizard'. . . . By 1839 a skull had been discovered and Sir Richard Owen at the Royal College of Surgeons realized that it was not a reptile at all but a mammal. He described the complex, multi-cusped grinding teeth in detail and decided to change the alleged dinosaur's name to* Zeuglodon, *from the Greek* zugotos, *yoked or joined, and* odous, *a tooth. During the next few years, many similar fossils were discovered in the Eocene beds of Alabama and South Carolina. An American fossil-hunter, Albert Koch, . . . strung the vertebrae from several individuals together to produce a monster 35 meters (114 feet) long, which he identified as a 'Sea Serpent' and exhibited in New York in 1845."*

*Actually,* Zeuglodon *was "only" 50 to 65 feet long and weighed between 5 and 6 tons. Its skull accounted for only 7 per cent of its total length. Its neck was short, with seven vertebrae, while the rest of the spinal column was "extraordinarily long and sinuous" (Watson, 1981). The tail was flattened horizontally; the forelimbs had already developed into paddle-like appendages. Its nostrils (blowholes) had migrated to the top of its snout, but not yet to the top of the skull. Diving must not have been one of its strong points, because it kept to coastal shallows and sought its prey (fish, squid) in shallow water.*

## RIGHT WHALE *Eubalaena glacialis*; Family Balaenidae

Right whales are rotund, stocky, and unaggressive. Their skin is as black as night, but their hundreds of baleen plates form a milky smile when they swim near the surface. The mouth of the right whale looks like a gaping buskin, its body like a keg of cider. When it glides through the water, however, this grotesque assemblage takes on the weird beauty of a phantom ship.

There are three geographic ranges of right whales; this fact has led some naturalists to posit three distinct species. They differ only in minor respects, notably in skull structure (W. E. Schevill, 1972) and skin pigmentation. Substantiation of this theory is so incomplete that the current preference is to treat the whales of the northern hemisphere as *Eubalaena glacialis* and those of the southern hemisphere as *E. australis.* Both have coal-black skin that occasionally shades off to slate gray, irregular white splotches on the throat and belly, and callosities on the head and jaw.

It is easy to tell the right whale from its cousin, the bowhead, by the striking callosities that right whales display. These jagged, scablike encrustations, more than 4 inches thick in spots, teem with barnacles, cyamid crustaceans ("whale lice"), and other parasites.

Yankee whalemen referred to the massive horny prominence on the right whale's rostrum as the "Japanese garden" or "rock garden" (Melville, 1851). The French dubbed it *le bonnet*, and the term "bonnet" prevails in English to this day. According to P.-J. van Beneden (1867–92), harpooners used to "scalp the rostrum and keep this part of the chamfron as a trophy or good-luck charm."

An adult right whale measures 46 to 60 feet long (average: 50 feet) and weighs 55 tons (maximum: 96 tons). The female of the species is more powerful than the male. The huge oval head with its scooplike mouth accounts for nearly a third of its total length; unlike the bowhead, the right whale has only a slight depression between the head and back. Herman Melville (1851) was quick to bring out the more humorous aspects of the right whale's appearance: "The Right Whale's head bears a rather inelegant resemblance to a gigantic galliot-toed shoe. Two hundred years ago an old Dutch voyager likened its shape to that of a shoemaker's last. And in this same last or shoe, that old woman of the nursery tale, with her swarming brood, might very comfortably be lodged, she and all her progeny. . . . A great pity, now, that this unfortunate whale should be hare-lipped. The fissure is about a foot across."

The pair of blowholes on its back look a bit like the sound holes of a violin. The capacious mouth of the right whale contains some 260 pairs of light gray baleen plates; these are occasionally milky white but darken with age. They are lined with dark bristles that take on an olive iridescence in sunlight. The longest plates measure nearly 9 feet long and a foot across at the base. The tongue, with its sheath of tender, sensitive skin, can weigh as much as 1.5 tons. Its lower jaw is arched to accommodate the baleen, but less so than that of the bowhead, which has longer baleen. The right whale also lacks the snowy white patch, or "vest," that its cousin sports on its chin.

From the eyes to the beginning of the tail, the right whale's body looks like a barrel. This bulky, slow-swimming species has broad, tapered trapezoidal flippers, expressive, nimble appendages that offset the initial impression of laboring corpulence. The uniformly black, tapered tail stock ends in flukes separated by a deep notch. The concave trailing edge has a somewhat frayed appearance. The

*In the sixteenth century, right whales still ventured into the shallows of the Bay of Biscay to bellow and deliver their young. At the other end of the world, the Japanese wrote wonderful poems in their honor. This is a huge, slow-moving, gentle species. Each individual sports large, distinctive, parasite-ridden callosities over its head and body. According to Dr. Payne (1976), who has spent years studying the southern right whales of Peninsula Valdés, Argentina (where this photograph was taken), "an adult's callosity patterns are constant over long periods" and are a reliable means of identifying individuals.*

breadth of the flukes when fully spread is equal to nearly one-half of total body length (almost 20 feet in the biggest specimens). Right whales have no dorsal fin or throat grooves.

The right whale is the hairiest of all cetaceans; at least it retains more of its hair after birth than any other whale. In 1820, Petrus Camper noted that in right whales "there are towards the tip of the snout a few scattered bristles similar to a moustache." Melville (1851) characteristically brought out the lighter side of this phenomenon. "This reminds us that the Right Whale really has a sort of whisker, or rather a moustache, consisting of a few scattered white hairs on the upper part of the outer end of the lower jar. Sometimes these tufts impart a rather brigandish expression to his otherwise solemn countenance." For once, anthropomorphic imagery such as this does not rub scientists the wrong way: The right whale does indeed grow facial hair in places where humans do, and it sports the rough equivalents of eyebrows, moustache, and scraggly beard.

### *RIGHT WHALE*

*In 1776 a German naturalist, O. S. Müller, gave this species its scientific name,* Balaena glacialis. *Another German, Georg Borowski, described it in 1781. In 1864, J. E. Gray of the British Museum decided to create a new genus* (Eubalaena) *for the right whale to distinguish it from the bowhead* (Balaena). *The idea was resurrected in 1908 by an American taxonomist, J. A. Allen. Nowadays, some advocate separate genera for the right and bowhead whales. In the early nineteenth century, Lacépède saw a Japanese print of a right whale from the North Pacific and proposed the existence of* Balaena japonica. *In 1822 Antoine Delalande sent Antoine Desmoulins a right whale skeleton from the southern hemisphere. (It is still in the Musée d'Histoire Naturelle, Paris.)*

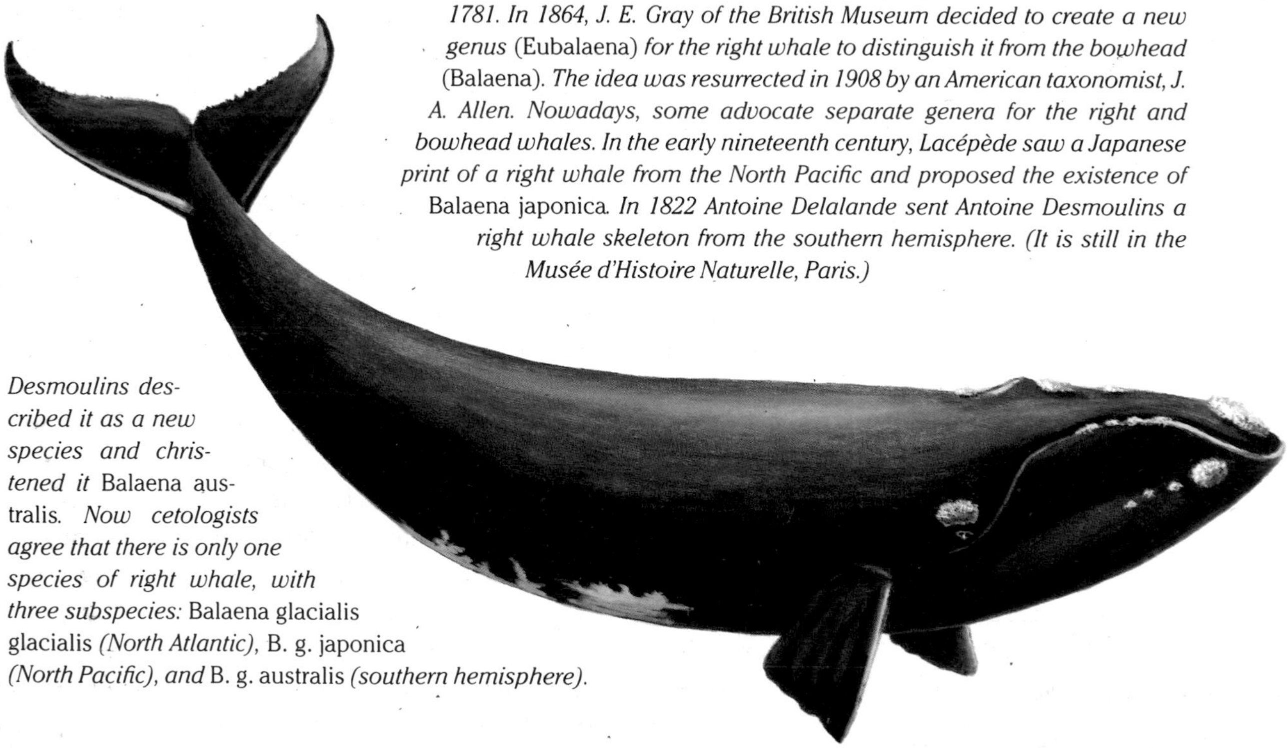

*Desmoulins described it as a new species and christened it* Balaena australis. *Now cetologists agree that there is only one species of right whale, with three subspecies:* Balaena glacialis glacialis *(North Atlantic),* B. g. japonica *(North Pacific), and* B. g. australis *(southern hemisphere).*

*English:* black right whale, great right whale, southern right whale
*French:* baleine franche noire, baleine des Basques, sarde, baleine des Sardes
*Russian:* nastoiaschchii kit, youjnyi kit *Japanese:* sebi kujira, akari kujira
*Spanish:* ballena franca *German:* Nordkaper *Italian:* balena nera
*Norwegian:* nordkapper *Dutch:* noordkaper *Icelandic:* sletbag, sletback, hauswhal
*Danish:* svarthval *Aleutian:* cullamach

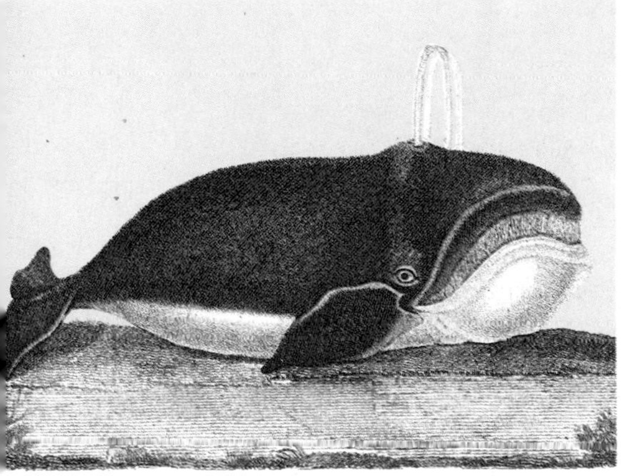

Famous for its long baleen plates and phenomenally thick jacket of blubber, the bowhead whale has been ruthlessly hunted in the Arctic Sea for centuries. The Inuit are still entitled to take a certain number of them every year. Top: The head of a bowhead carcass, lying on its back. Above: An engraving from the 1839 edition of Lacépède's Histoire Naturelle des Cétacés (1804). About the same time, English poet and essayist Charles Lamb (1775–1834) wrote "Triumph of the Whale," later quoted by Melville in Moby-Dick (1851):

*Not a mightier whale than this*
*In the vast Atlantic is;*
*Not a fatter fish than he,*
*Flounders round the Polar Sea.*

## BOWHEAD WHALE *Balaena mysticetus*; Family Balaenidae

Picture a veritable mountain of muscle and blubber with an unaggressive yet obstinate demeanor—a gleaming, compact, stocky hulk 50 to 60 feet long (average: 52.5 feet) and weighing up to 110 tons—and still you will have only a vague idea of this superb, peaceable colossus that plies dark leads in the glistening pack ice. The sheer bulk of the species so captivated some observers (including leading cetologists) that they credited it with being as big as an island. Lacépède, for example, believed that 325-foot specimens may have existed in ancient times. According to P.-J. van Beneden, Captain Alex Deuchars took an individual from the Davis Strait that measured 78 feet long and weighed 120 tons. William Scoresby, however, who personally inspected hundreds of bowheads, reported that he never came across any longer than 64 feet.

The head, which accounts for about 40 percent of the whale's total length, is a tremendous, conelike affair whose bowed appearance inspired the nickname Yankee whalemen gave the species. Below the parabolic rostrum is a mouth up to 20 feet deep and 10 feet across with thick lips turned down at the corners.

The surprisingly small, almost invisible eyes are located just above the corners of the bowhead's huge lips. Each of the blowholes—"two f-shaped spout-holes," to quote Melville (1851)—extend some 5 to 7 inches across the top of the head. Between 300 and 360 baleen plates hang from each side of the upper jaw; old whalemen used to say that a bowhead has as many plates as there are days in a year. Occasionally mottled but usually black, the smooth baleen are fringed with dark bristles that take on a silvery sheen in sunlight. All told, these horny plates, which measure 15 inches across at the base and up to 15 feet (once in a great while, over 16 feet) in length, can together weigh as much as 2.5 tons. "Seeing all these colonnades of bone so methodically ranged about," wrote Melville in *Moby-Dick*, "would you not think you were inside of the great Haarlem organ, and gazing upon its thousand pipes? For a carpet to the organ we have a rug of the softest Turkey—the tongue."

## BOWHEAD WHALE

*Icelanders knew a surprising amount about whales even centuries ago. They must have been aware of migratory patterns, because an account of Ohthere's voyage to the North Cape mentions that "sailors sailed for three days beyond the point where the whales go back." As long ago as the thirteenth century, the* Kongespiel *or* Speculum Regale, *an anonymous account of Iceland, describes two different types of baleen whales whose northern and southern migration ranges meet but do not overlap. One they called* sletbag, sletback, *or* hauswhal *(the right whale); it came from the south in the spring. The other came from the north in the fall, so they called it* nordwhal *(our bowhead). Icelanders also noticed that the southern species was infested with parasites, whereas the cold-water northern species was virtually parasite-free. Centuries later, scientists from "advanced" countries were still confusing them. In* Géographie universelle *(1875–94), Elisée Reclus maintained that the Biscayan right whale had been wiped out in the North Atlantic but had found refuge in the Arctic Ocean.*

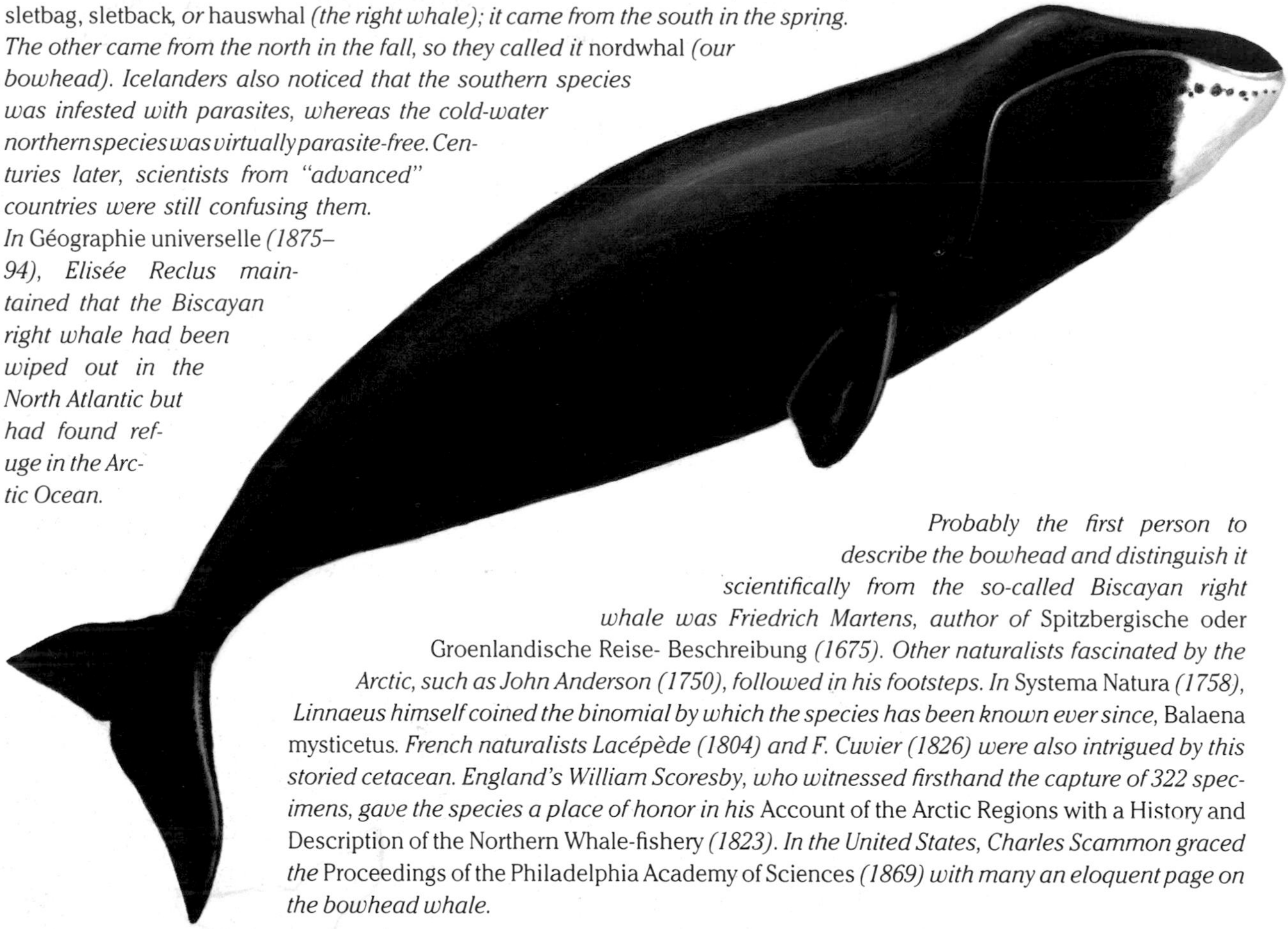

*Probably the first person to describe the bowhead and distinguish it scientifically from the so-called Biscayan right whale was Friedrich Martens, author of* Spitzbergische oder Groenlandische Reise- Beschreibung *(1675). Other naturalists fascinated by the Arctic, such as John Anderson (1750), followed in his footsteps. In* Systema Natura *(1758), Linnaeus himself coined the binomial by which the species has been known ever since,* Balaena mysticetus. *French naturalists Lacépède (1804) and F. Cuvier (1826) were also intrigued by this storied cetacean. England's William Scoresby, who witnessed firsthand the capture of 322 specimens, gave the species a place of honor in his* Account of the Arctic Regions with a History and Description of the Northern Whale-fishery *(1823). In the United States, Charles Scammon graced the* Proceedings of the Philadelphia Academy of Sciences *(1869) with many an eloquent page on the bowhead whale.*

*English:* bowhead, northern right whale, Greenland right whale, common right whale
*French:* baleine franche de Groenland, baleine franche arctique
*Russian:* grenlandskyi kit, polyarnyi kit *Japanese:* ko-kujira, hokkyoku kujira
*German:* Walfish, Bogenkop *Spanish:* ballena franca *Italian:* balena de Groenlandia
*Norwegian:* nordwhal *Dutch:* groenlandse walvisch *Swedish:* grönlandsval
*Greenland Eskimo:* akbek *Alaskan Eskimo:* kairalik (adult), ingotok (juvenile)
*Icelandic:* Greenlandsvalur *Aleutian:* ugamachcach *Yakut:* kakhlim

The bowhead's flippers are shorter and narrower than those of the right whale. Its body, which lacks both dorsal fin and throat grooves, is encased in a substantial protective layer of subcutaneous blubber more than 20 inches thick in spots. The tail stretches as much as 27 feet across and has a less concave rear margin than that of its southern cousin.

The skin, locally bluish or grayish in juveniles, normally turns an inky black in adulthood. In most specimens, light gray to snowy white patches can be seen on the upper lip, chin, periphery of the eyes, and tail. The underside of the lower jaw is usually unpigmented, or at the very least flecked with yellowish-white spots. Frédéric Cuvier (1826) commented on the color range of the species. "Not all common right whales have been found to have the same pigmentation. Some were completely black; others had irregular gray areas against a black ground; still others turned out to be blackish above and white underneath. Sightings of completely white specimens have even been reported. . . . According to Mr. Scoresby, very old individuals usually have more white or gray areas than do adults."

## PYGMY RIGHT WHALE *Caperea marginata*; Family Balaenidae

Little is known about this scaled-down right whale, which measures "only" 16 feet long and weighs a paltry 3.5 tons. Sightings of free-swimming individuals are extremely rare (Ivashin, 1972). The most reliable data we have on pygmy right whales is a 1967 film taken by T. Dicks at Plettenberg Bay, South Africa. The balance of our scant knowledge has come from examining fewer than a hundred or so individuals washed ashore in New Zealand, Australia, Tasmania, South Africa, Crozet Island, the Falkland Islands, Argentina (one specimen, confirmed) and Chile (one specimen, unconfirmed). More pygmy right whales beach themselves along the coast of South Africa and in the Great Australian Bight than anywhere else.

It has a tapered snout, a well-defined nape, and a strongly bowed lower jaw. Its head accounts for about one-fourth of total body length. A lateral compression just

*The little-known pygmy right whale does not stray outside of the temperate and cold waters of the South Atlantic, the South Pacific, and the Indian Ocean. The species is naturally scarce and undemonstrative. Our primary sources of information are the specimens that have beached themselves over the years. Below: The only free-swimming pygmy right whale ever filmed underwater (T. Dicks, Plettenberg Bay, South Africa; December 1967).*

behind the eye marks the dividing line between the head and trunk. Its mouth is not as turned down at the corners as that of other right whales, but is more bowed than that of the gray whale. Deep furrows run along the roof of the mouth. The pygmy right whale's 230 pairs of ivory-colored baleen plates (4 inches across at the base and up to 27 inches long) are darker on the outer edge and are fringed with fine, soft, silvery bristles.

The pygmy right whale is comparatively long and sleek. It differs from its two larger cousins in that it has a triangular, falcate dorsal fin, placed well back, and two throat grooves (although these longitudinal furrows are indistinct and, in some individuals, absent). Its cheeks, snout, and sides are free of callosities. The narrow flippers are rounded at the tips. Its thick tail ends in flukes whose breadth is one-fifth the animal's total length. Another distinguishing trait is a larger number of ribs—17, compared with 13 in the bowhead and 14 in the right whale—and the fact that there are only 4 "finger" bones in its forelimbs.

Since our knowledge of the pygmy right whale is limited to stranded specimens, and cetacean carcasses tend to darken, the color range of the species is still in doubt. Hence, the assertion that it is "black above and gray below, or else black all over" (Davies and Guiler, 1957) should be taken with a grain of salt. The one C. K. Tayler sighted (1963) was gray above and a delicate silvery color underneath. In some individuals a blurred grayish-white line arches across the back from and between the flippers.

*PYGMY RIGHT WHALE*

*During the famous expedition led by Sir John Ross from 1839 to 1843, naturalists discovered some bones and baleen plates similar to, but smaller than, those of right whales. In his* Zoology of the Voyage of HMS Erebus and Terror *(1846), J. E. Gray described the diminutive, virtually unknown species and named it* Balaena marginata. *In 1864 Gray established a new genus* (Caperea) *for some bones and a skull that had been submitted to him for inspection. He received yet another find in 1870; a third name,* Neobalaena, *was added to the list. Shortly thereafter, Gray himself realized that the three species he had described were, in fact, one and the same:* Caperea marginata, *the pygmy right whale.*

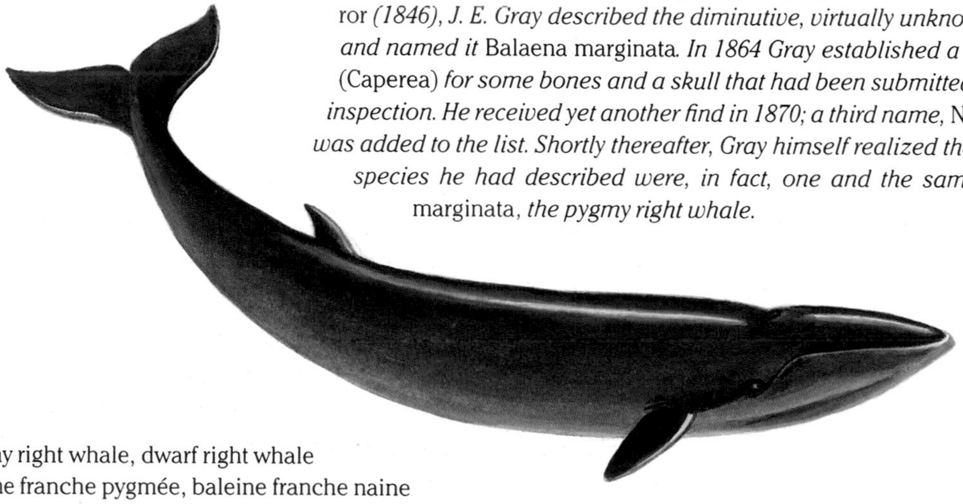

*English:* pygmy right whale, dwarf right whale
*French:* baleine franche pygmée, baleine franche naine
*Russian:* gladkii kit *Japanese:* kosemi kujira
*German:* Zwergglattwal *Italian:* balena pigmea
*Spanish:* ballena franca pigmea *Dutch:* dwerg walvis
*Norwegian:* dvergretthval

*The California gray whale—Yankee whalers nicknamed them "devilfish" because of their fierce resistance under attack—has made a miraculous comeback since the species was severely depleted in the nineteenth century. Today we have the good fortune to see grays wintering in the lagoons of Baja California, where females deliver their young. Above: This spyhopping gray has poked its arched, parasite-studded snout above the water to have a look around.*

## GRAY WHALE *Eschrichtius robustus*; Family Eschrichtiidae

The pale, sandy lagoons along the barren Baja California coastline are the winter retreat of gigantic gray whales. Their silvery plumelike blows glisten against the deep blue water. Grays are more belligerent than right whales and defend their calves more aggressively when threatened; for this reason, Yankee whalemen nicknamed the species "devilfish."

The gray whale is the only species in its family, and only the California population promises to survive exploitation. The Korean stock is so reduced that it may no longer be viable. The Atlantic stock may have disappeared as recently as the seventeenth century, not because of commercial whaling in the region but perhaps because of early near-shore hunting.

The gray whale is rarely longer than 45 feet and weighs in at 30 tons. The biggest individual ever taken, a female, measured 50 feet from snout to tail notch and tipped the scales at 36 tons.

This species always has a clumsy, ungainly look about it despite the fact that it is not as rotund as right whales. (Its subcutaneous blubber is about 10 inches thick at the most, half that of the bowhead.) Appearances to the contrary notwithstanding, grays are limber, agile creatures and excel in water acrobatics. They breach with tremendous gusto and can maneuver in water just a few yards deep without running aground—a feat no other whale dares even to attempt.

A slight dip at the nape separates its massive arched head from the trunk. Bristles are scattered about the front part of the head, the tip of the snout, and the lower jaw. The mouth of the gray whale contains approximately 160 pairs of broad, sturdy, smooth, short baleen plates, the largest of which are 20 inches long. The light-colored bristles are thicker and coarser than those of other mysticetes.

*GRAY WHALE*

*The first naturalist to describe this species was the Hon. Paul Dudley (1725), who dubbed it the "scrag" whale because of its parasite-flecked skin. In 1777 a German veterinarian, Johann Polycarp Erxleben, called it* Balaena gibbosa *("humped whale"), a name that stuck for about a century. In 1868 Edward D. Cope, an American palaeontologist, created the binomial* Rhachianectes glaucus. *Four years earlier, in 1864, J. E. Gray of the British Museum had created the genus* Eschrichtius *(in honor of Daniel Eschricht, a zoology professor in Copenhagen); he based the new genus on a gray whale skeleton that Swedish professor Wilhelm Lilljeborg had excavated in Sweden in 1861 and named* Balaenoptera robusta. *So, Gray added* robustus *to his new genus, resulting in what turned out to be the definitive binomial,* Eschrichtius robustus. *Such are the tortuous byways of taxonomy.*

*English:* gray whale, California whale, devilfish, hard-head, mussel-digger, grayback, ripsack
*French:* baleine grise, baleine grise de Californie, baleine à six bosses, baleine de Californie
*Russian:* seryi kit *Japanese:* koku kujira *Spanish:* ballena gris *Italian:* balena grigia del Pacifico
*German:* Knotenfisch *Norwegian:* grähval *Swedish:* gräso val *Dutch:* grijze walvisch
*Aleutian:* chickakhluk *Chukchi:* kentaen uiiut *Alaskan Eskimo:* antokhak

The right baleen plates are more worn than those on the left; as the bottom-feeding whale plows up sediments from which to filter organisms, it probably feeds mostly on its right side—occasioning greater wear and tear. The narrow, salmon-pink tongue has a gray tip and weighs from 1 to 1.5 tons.

The gray whale has two (occasionally four) throat grooves, each about 5 feet long. The broad, sinewy flippers often have tears in them and, now and again, ragged or frayed edges reminiscent of a scarecrow's sleeves. It has no dorsal fin proper, but there is a string of a half-dozen to fifteen irregular bumps along the spine from the midback to the flukes. These "knuckles" extend all the way to the base of the tail and are scarred in older individuals. The average-sized tail flukes sometimes trail shreds of skin and are studded with patches of parasites that give it the appearance of a tattered piece of clothing.

As for its pigmentation, the gray whale, true to its name, is a mellow, glistening slate-gray, with lighter areas scattered here and there on the belly and flippers. In addition, the thousands of external parasites that infest its skin create an elaborate patchwork of spots, blotches, and markings that range from off-white to pale yellow.

## BLUE WHALE *Balaenoptera musculus*; Family Balaenopteridae

Behold the largest animal that ever roamed our planet! Observe as it makes its way along the ocean's surface, its blowhole spewing like a chimney. When it dives, its rolling back looks like an island in motion.

The blue whale's realm is the seven seas. In winter, these whales mate in the warmth of tropical waters, where mothers suckle their seven-ton newborns. In the spring, they repair to the hushed splendor of the poles to build up their reserves of blubber—with icebergs for palace walls and the northern lights for tapestries.

The blue whale's relatives include several other graceful divers—members of the family Balaenopteridae. In 1804, Lacépède grafted the Greek suffix *pteron* ("wing") onto the French word for whale, *baleine*, and thus coined the term *balénoptère*, or "winged whales." English-speaking whalemen referred to balaenopterids by the all-purpose name "finbacks" or "fin whales" because one of their hallmarks is an arched, pointed dorsal fin in the hindmost quarter of the back. However, this sail-like protuberance is not the only feature that distinguishes these mysticetes from right whales and grays. Balaenopterids are noted for their sleeker, slenderer, more elongated proportions; they have, you might say, a more elegant look about them.

*What words can do justice to the colossal blue whale, the biggest creature ever to roam land or sea, the giant among giants? Below: This blue whale, identifiable by its long tail stock and tiny, nubbin-like dorsal fin, belongs to the small but faithful group still seen at the entrance to the Sea of Cortez.*

*the diving eye sometimes collides with*
*great blue whales of innocence.*
*(Gwen MacEwen, Canadian, b. 1941)*

In most species, a balaenopterid's head accounts for only one-fourth of its total length. The flat rostrum and pointed snout inspired Frédéric Cuvier (1826) to nickname them "pikehead" (*tête de brochet*). The long, narrow flippers are located close to the corner of the lips. The tail is proportionately smaller than those of the Balaenidae and Eschrichtiidae. The numerous grooves running lengthwise along the throat and belly prompted the Norwegians to call them

*rörhval* (rör = "tube" or "furrow"), whence *rorqual* in French and English. These deep, functional pleats fan out like an accordion, enabling rorquals to take in a greater amount of food. Rarely visible in living cetaceans when not feeding, these ventral grooves, or throat pleats, show up in slain or stranded individuals, especially after compressed air has been pumped into them. Naturalists often exaggerated this characteristic in illustrations.

The blue whale is distributed in temperate and cold waters worldwide, although populations in certain areas have been drastically reduced. This whale's average length is 82 feet, its weight range between 80 and 120 tons. (In the early 1900s, some whalemen reportedly took a blue whale measuring nearly 110 feet long and weighing more than 200 tons, but this has never been confirmed.) Females are 3 to 7 feet longer than males and a good 10 tons or so heavier. According to C. Lockyer (1975), the record individuals taken in the postwar years were a female nearly 91 feet long and weighing 171 tons, and another female more than 94 feet long, weighing 174 tons.

The head of the blue whale is less pointed than that of other rorquals, and the animal has an almost straight mouth and a curved rostrum that, from above, looks like a Gothic arch. Its tongue alone weighs 4 tons. From its bluish gums hang smooth, jet-black baleen that take on a magnificent blue sheen in sunlight. There are between 270 and 395 pairs of baleen plates (average, 320) that weigh more than 200 pounds. Broad at the base (2 feet) and relatively short (3 feet), the baleen plates are fringed with thick bristles that range from purplish-violet to charcoal-gray.

The evenly spaced throat grooves—of which there are from 55 to 118—extend from the chin to the navel. In front of and to the sides of the two blowholes are fleshy ridges that some whalemen refer to as "mudguards." The falcate or scimitar-shaped flippers are rarely longer than 8 feet, small compared to total body length. At scarcely more than 12 to 14 inches high, the triangular or falcate dorsal fin is ludicrously tiny; it is located well back on the tail stock, more or less across from the anus. When a blue whale surfaces to breathe, it rolls a seemingly endless expanse of back, only to bring the magnificent spectacle to an incongruous conclusion with this insignificant nubbin. The markedly concave flukes are no more than 23 feet across and seem quite small for the animal's size. Blue whales lift the flukes just above the surface before diving.

Blue whales are mainly a soft blue-gray, as mellow as an Oriental carpet, with

*For many years, the wondrous blue whale was considered so much harpoon fodder, 150 tons of life measured solely in terms of the number of dollars its blubber, bones, and baleen could fetch on the market. Until the nineteenth century (below) and even later, illustrations invariably showed blue whales as fat because the only "models" artists ever saw were stranded individuals, bloated from decomposition or from the compressed air whalers pumped into them to keep them afloat. Actually, blue whales are long, slender, almost serpentine (right). Compared with right whales, all rorquals look "lean and emaciated" (Van Beneden).*

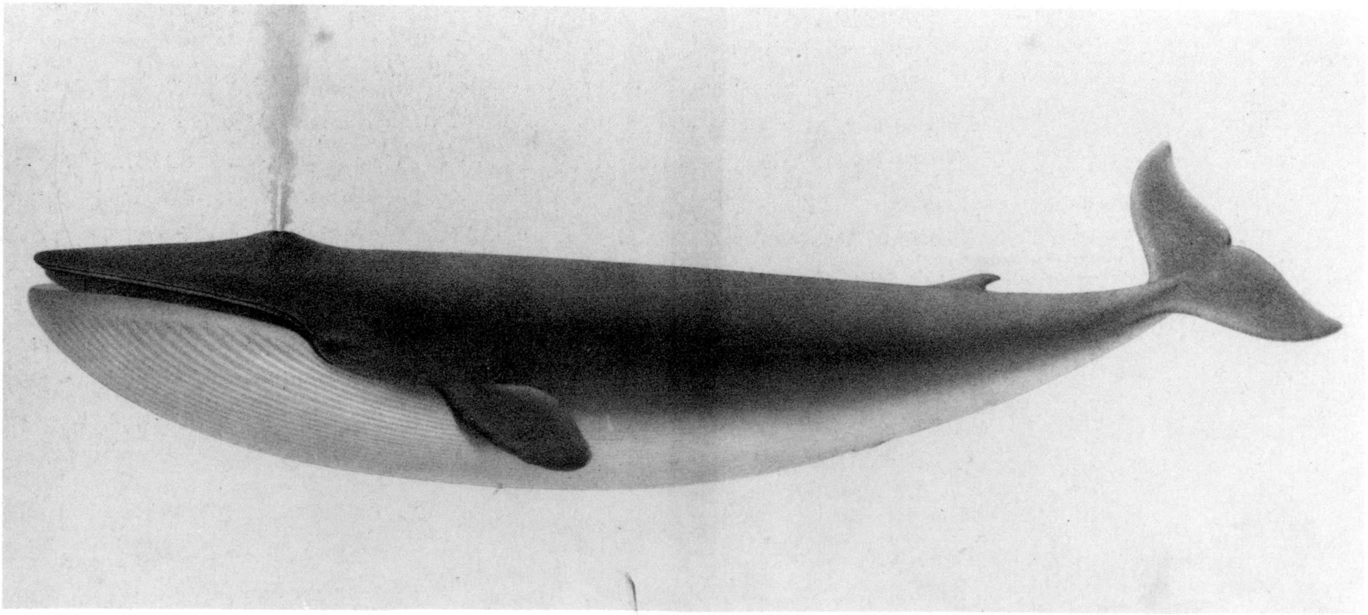

## BLUE WHALE

*The giant of them all was long known as* Balaena *(or* Balaenoptera*)* sibbaldi, *in honor of Sir Robert Sibbald, the Scots naturalist who had described two specimens that stranded on the coast of Scotland in 1692. Thereafter treatises referred to the species by many other names—*Balaena maximus, Rorqualis borealis, Sibbaldus musculus, Sibbaldus sulphureus*—each with its advocates and detractors. In 1903, E. G. Racovitza classified the blue whale in the genus* Balaenoptera *once and for all.*

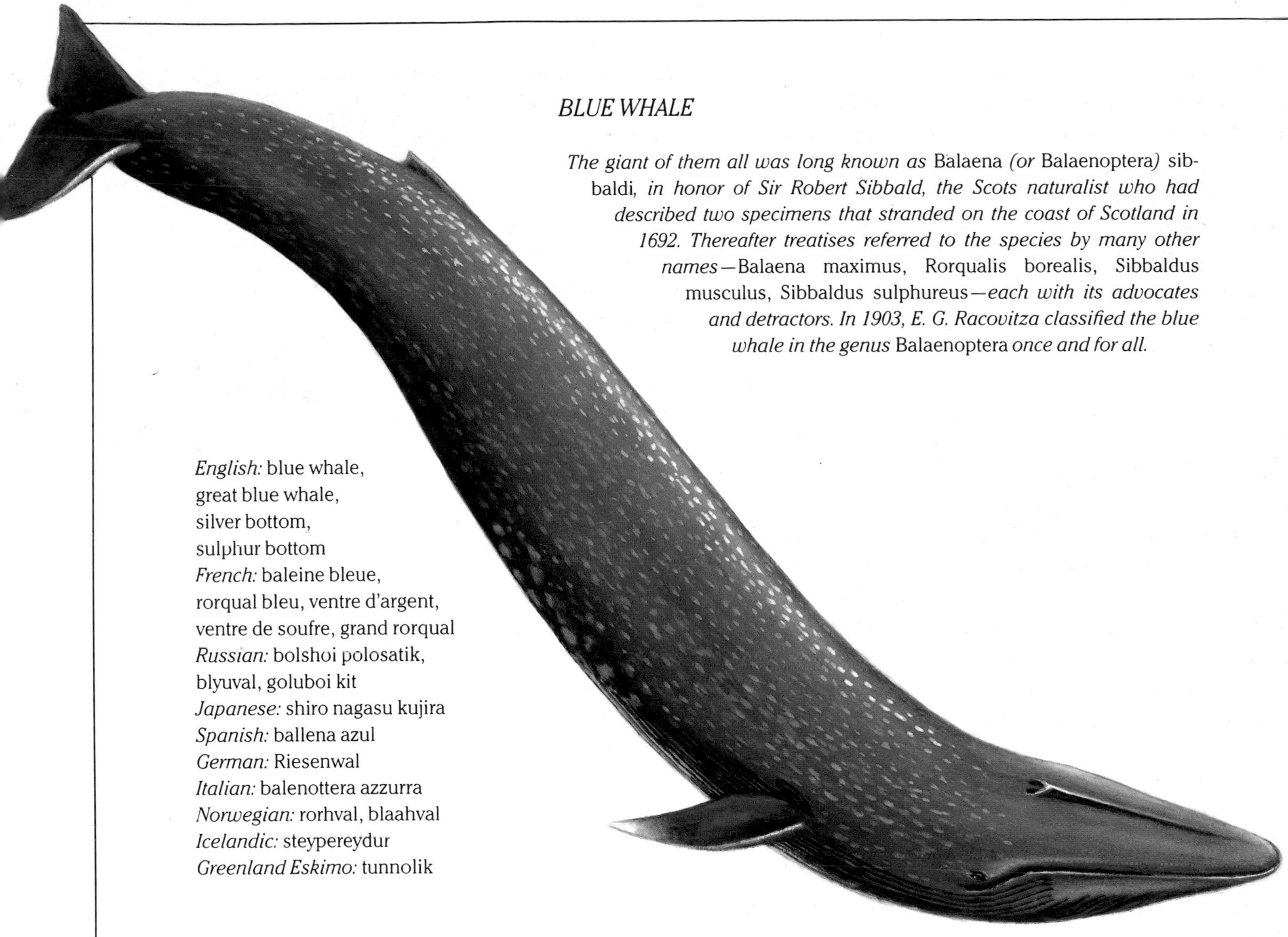

*English:* blue whale, great blue whale, silver bottom, sulphur bottom
*French:* baleine bleue, rorqual bleu, ventre d'argent, ventre de soufre, grand rorqual
*Russian:* bolshoi polosatik, blyuval, goluboi kit
*Japanese:* shiro nagasu kujira
*Spanish:* ballena azul
*German:* Riesenwal
*Italian:* balenottera azzurra
*Norwegian:* rorhval, blaahval
*Icelandic:* steypereydur
*Greenland Eskimo:* tunnolik

light gray to snow-white areas on the tips and undersides of the flippers. The belly and sides are often flecked with pearl-gray, yellowish, or brownish markings. During the summer feeding season in polar waters, the underside of the whale may take on a thick, sticky coating of silvery or yellowish diatoms—whence the popular names "sulphur bottom" and "silver bottom." Herman Melville (1851) could not help marveling at its "brimstone belly, doubtless got by scraping along the Tartarian tiles in some of his profounder divings."

Whalemen active south of the equator between 0° and 80° E (eastern Atlantic and western Indian oceans), particularly in the area around Kerguelen and Crozet islands, were astonished to find that some of the blue whales they harpooned had shorter tails. Cetologists did not start to take a closer look at these strange animals until 1961. They had the head and body of *Balaenoptera musculus*, but much shorter baleen plates, a grayer pigmentation overall, and a caudal appendage of bafflingly small proportions. T. Ichihara (1975), a Japanese cetologist, suggested that these pygmy blue whales be considered a subspecies of the blue whale instead of a separate species. As one might expect, he gave it the scientific name of *Balaenoptera musculus brevicauda*. The I.W.C. has acknowledged the subspecies while awaiting further clarification.

FIN WHALE *Balaenoptera physalus*; Family Balaenopteridae

More than any other whale, this swift, gigantic cetacean creates an immediate impression of power. Though almost as big as the blue, the fin whale is a magnificently efficient swimmer. It seems to revel in rough weather and ocean swells; as it cavorts in the unbridled fury of the storm, it seems to be taking the measure of its own energy.

The animal Lacépède (1804) referred to as *Balaenoptera gibbar* "can match the right whale in terms of length, but not bulk." Indeed, the fin whale easily outstrips the right whale in size; individuals 80 feet long have been reported and the biggest one on record was a female that measured 89 feet. The average length is about 65 feet. As with most mysticetes, the female is larger than the male and may weigh up to 70 tons—still less than a right whale.

The fin whale is slimmer, more sinewy, and more lithe than the blue whale. Its body consists of 24 percent blubber (compared with 27 percent in the blue whale), and its muscles account for 45 percent of total body weight (compared with 39 percent in the blue whale). It therefore yields about half the oil of a blue whale and must be killed in twice the numbers to maintain harvest levels.

Its bulk notwithstanding, the fin whale is sleekness incarnate. "With its flat head, it looks as though it is always smiling," notes Philippe Diolé (1972). "If you see a finback directly from the front, it looks like one big smile, as though there were something friendly about it, or as though it has a sense of humor." Its tapered head would seem better suited to a bird than a whale. Its rostrum sports a sprinkling of hairs, and there is a tuft of bristles at the tip of the lower jaw. The brain of the fin whale weighs around 11 pounds. Its mouth contains 270 to 470 pairs of baleen plates; the average is 360. These plates have a bluish cast in juveniles, but in time

*Its size notwithstanding—an individual can weigh more than 60 tons—the fin whale is the very picture of sleekness. It is a swift, powerful, brawny species. "Of a retiring nature, he eludes both hunters and philosophers. Though no coward, he has never yet shown any part of him but his back, which rises in a long, sharp ridge. Let him go. I know little more of him, nor does anyone else" (Melville, 1851).*

*Wearing what looks like a perpetual smile, the fin whale is as long as a bus; but its eyes have a knowing, mischievous twinkle in them. As a rule, the species does not pay much attention to people, but now and again an individual will swim right up to a boat. Opposite, below: A fin whale spyhopping to get a better look at the strangest species of them all.*

they turn smoke-gray or, less frequently, greenish-gray streaked with white; some plates on the right front are white. The largest plates do not exceed 3 feet in length. The thick, fairly coarse bristles range in color from brownish-gray to yellowish-white.

The fin whale's flippers are short and lanceolate; the falcate dorsal fin, though longer than that of the blue whale, does not stand more than 27 inches high. There are between 50 and 114 ventral grooves (average, 64) that start at the underside of the lower lip and run along the throat and belly to the navel or slightly beyond. Between the dorsal fin and the broad tail flukes that curve only slightly along the rear margin, the body narrows and is strongly compressed laterally, resulting in a prominently ridged tail stock that earned the species its nickname, "razorback."

The dorsal surface of the fin whale is gray, occasionally shading into black, and its throat and belly are snow-white. The dividing line between these contrasting areas runs obliquely along the sides from the flippers down to the tail. The under-

## *FIN WHALE*

*Since fin whales readily venture into the Mediterranean Sea, they were the first baleen whales to be described, classified, and admired. Aristotle referred to it as* mysticetus, *noting that "in its mouth are spikes that look like hog bristles." Pliny the Elder wrote of its awesome size and named it* musculus. *"In [the province of] Saintonge," noted Guillaume Rondelet in 1568, "it is known as* gibbar *because of its arched, humped back. It is as big as the common right whale, but not as thick-set or rotund." In* Spitzbergische oder Groenlandische Reise-Beschreibung *(Hamburg, 1675), Friedrich Martens described what he called a* Finfisch *in minute detail.*

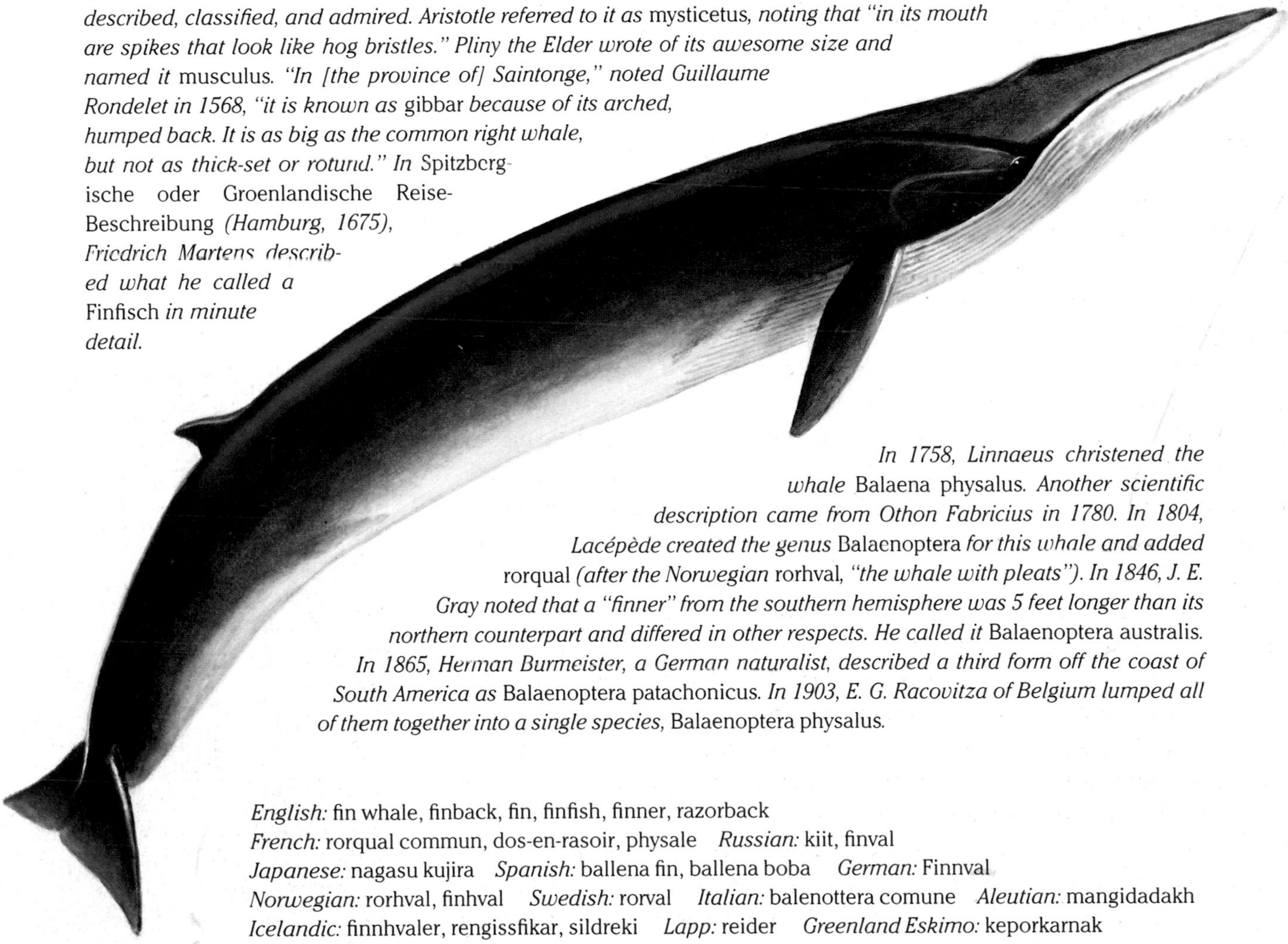

*In 1758, Linnaeus christened the whale* Balaena physalus. *Another scientific description came from Othon Fabricius in 1780. In 1804, Lacépède created the genus* Balaenoptera *for this whale and added* rorqual *(after the Norwegian* rorhval, *"the whale with pleats"). In 1846, J. E. Gray noted that a "finner" from the southern hemisphere was 5 feet longer than its northern counterpart and differed in other respects. He called it* Balaenoptera australis. *In 1865, Herman Burmeister, a German naturalist, described a third form off the coast of South America as* Balaenoptera patachonicus. *In 1903, E. G. Racovitza of Belgium lumped all of them together into a single species,* Balaenoptera physalus.

*English:* fin whale, finback, fin, finfish, finner, razorback
*French:* rorqual commun, dos-en-rasoir, physale *Russian:* kiit, finval
*Japanese:* nagasu kujira *Spanish:* ballena fin, ballena boba *German:* Finnval
*Norwegian:* rorhval, finhval *Swedish:* rorval *Italian:* balenottera comune *Aleutian:* mangidadakh
*Icelandic:* finnhvaler, rengissfikar, sildreki *Lapp:* reider *Greenland Eskimo:* keporkarnak

sides of the flippers and flukes, like the belly, are white. In many individuals, a grayish-white chevron runs across the back, just behind the head and between the flippers. The asymmetrical coloring on the fin whale's head is as beautiful as it is peculiar. The lower jaw is light on the right side, dark on the left, echoing the color of the baleen plates. The color pattern may be related to right-side feeding. Since some of the right baleen plates are also white and the rest on that side are gray, one would think (to paraphrase Melville) that the fin whale's mother ran afoul of a chessboard when she was pregnant.

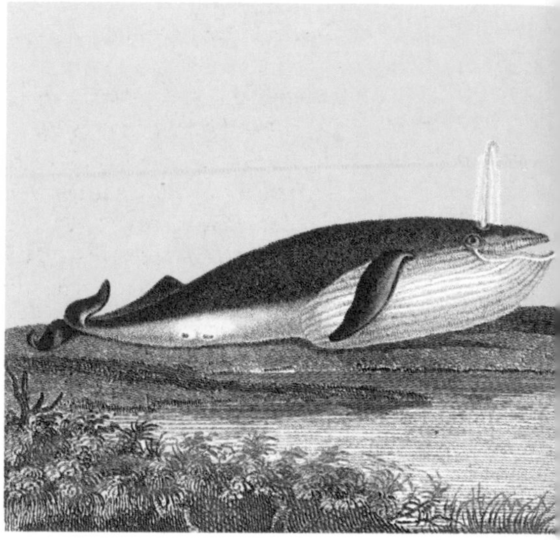

## SEI WHALE *Balaenoptera borealis*; Family Balaenopteridae

In migration, this swarthy, graceful swimmer with the broad, inscrutable smile comes close to the coast of Finnmark at the same time of year as the coalfish or pollack. Norwegians call this fish the *seje*, and the whale the sei. This popular name is the one commonly used today.

Adult sei whales range in length between 40 and 50 feet (average: 15 meters), but the largest females can measure up to nearly 70 feet. Although one specimen reportedly weighed in at 29 tons and 20-ton individuals are occasionally taken, they typically weigh between 15 and 18 tons. Like all rorquals, seis are sleek and "flatheaded"; but they are not as streamlined as fin whales. The sei's head is slender, and its upper jaw has a noticeably higher arch. A single median ridge runs along the rostrum from the forehead to the snout. (Minke whales also have a single rostral ridge; Bryde's whales have three.) Its 219 to 402 slender baleen plates are short, reaching a maximum length of 29 inches; the plates are gray-black, with fine, silky, soft bristles, very long and snow-white. This two-toned smile is one of the sei whale's more beguiling characteristics. A few bristles are also scattered about the blowhole and the periphery of the lower lip.

*Albeit about half as long and one-fifth as heavy as a blue whale, the average sei whale still weighs as much as three or four elephants. Like its cousin the fin whale, the sei was long thought to be fat and bloated (as in this engraving). In fact, sei whales are lean, streamlined creatures with wonderfully hydrodynamic bodies. Below: The sei is a good diver and can keep pace with a dolphin.*

## *SEI WHALE*

*When a specimen of this species stranded on the coast of Holstein in 1819, a German, Carl Rudolphi, described it as* Balaena rostrata *because he believed it to be a new form of right whale. Seven years later, F. Cuvier reexamined the skeleton in the Berlin Museum (where it may still be seen) and corrected the mistake by naming it* rorqual du nord. *In 1828, René Lesson took the genus* Balaenoptera, *which Lacépède had established in 1804, and latinized the name Cuvier had given it, yielding the binomial by which the species has been known ever since;* Balaenoptera borealis. *For nearly a century, however, it was also known as Rudolphi's rorqual* (Rudolphius borealis) *in honor of the man who first described it. The name currently in favor among cetologists is* Balaenoptera borealis.

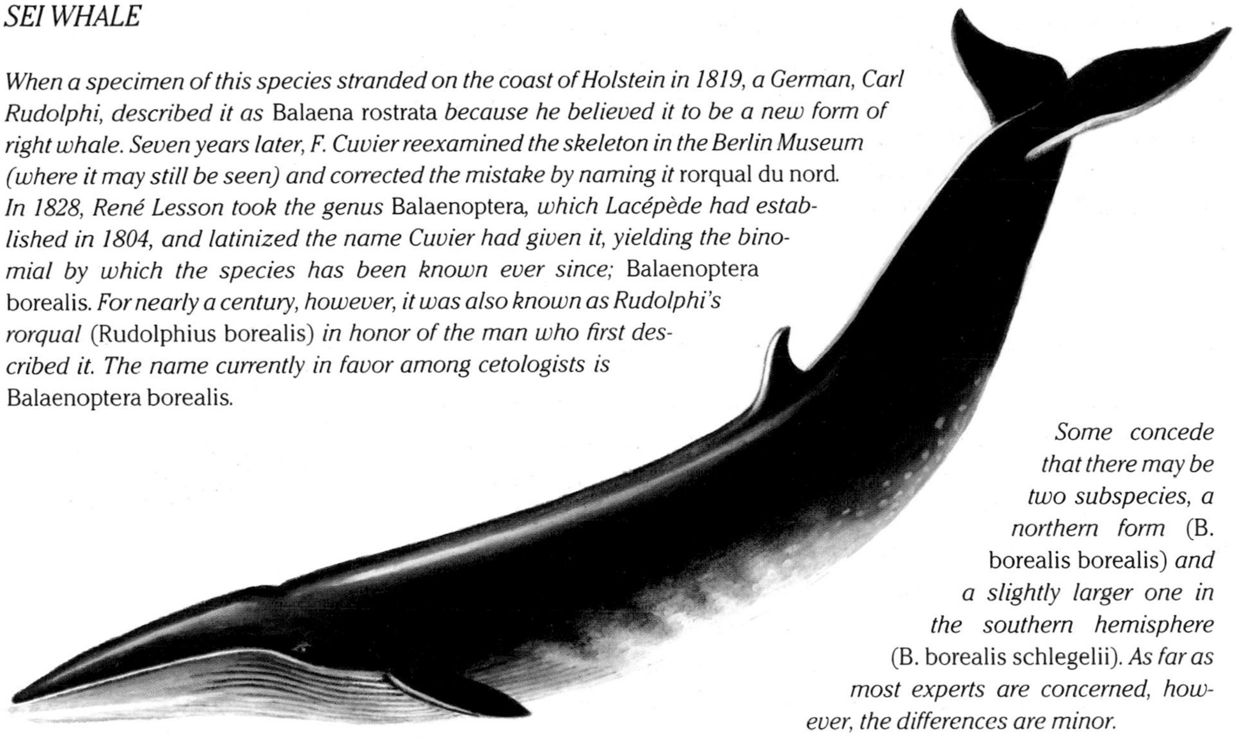

*Some concede that there may be two subspecies, a northern form* (B. borealis borealis) *and a slightly larger one in the southern hemisphere* (B. borealis schlegelii). *As far as most experts are concerned, however, the differences are minor.*

*English:* sei whale, sei, Rudolphi's rorqual, sardine whale
*French:* rorqual boréal, rorqual du Nord, sei, rorqual de Rudolphi
*Russian:* saidiaoni kit, ivasevyi polosatik *Japanese:* iwashi kujira
*Norwegian:* sei, sejval *Spanish:* rorcual negro, balleno sei
*Italian:* balenottera boreale *Dutch:* sei, noordische vinvisch
*Aleutian:* agalagitag

The sei whale's flippers are only one-tenth the animal's total length. The falcate dorsal fin, located farther forward than those of other large balaenopterids, is proportionately larger—approximately 2 feet high. The hind part of the body is compressed laterally (as in all balaenopterids), and its broad flukes seem never to be properly hitched on to the sharp upper and lower ridge. The 32 to 60 ventral grooves extend from the chin to only midway between the flippers and the umbilicus. (In comparison, Bryde's whales have roughly the same number of grooves, but they run all the way to the navel.)

Overall, sei whales are steely gray, but the species' back often appears to be nearly black—and that is why some whalemen refer to the species as the "black rorqual." Small, light scars speckle the flanks. On the undersurface, a broad, irregularly shaped area of grayish-white to white extends back from the chin. The undersides of the flippers and tail flukes are also light gray. All in all, a free-swimming sei whale brings to mind some strange extraterrestrial creature made of an unknown metal. Before a long dive, sei whales never "throw the flukes"—that is, raise their flukes out of the water; this behavior is diagnostic. Old whalemen used to say that a sei does not show the light underside of its tail so long as there is still life in it.

## BRYDE'S WHALE *Balaenoptera edeni*; Family Balaenopteridae

The spring migration of this species takes it to waters that are warmer than the summering grounds of other rorquals. As a result, Bryde's whales seldom crossed paths with whalemen—they lived in peace for many years. But the suffering of the Bryde's whales was simply postponed; recently they, too, have come under the eye of harpoon gunners. The I.W.C. moratorium will be their salvation.

Bryde's whales, also known as tropical whales, are between 36 and 46 feet long and weigh up to 23 tons. The biggest individual ever taken measured almost 47 feet from snout to flukes and weighed 20 tons. According to Peter B. Best (1975), the waters off the west coast of South Africa are home to two slightly different forms of the species: a smaller, sedentary, coastal variety that almost never strays beyond the continental shelf, and a larger, migratory, pelagic variety. Another difference: the baleen of the coastal stock are very narrow, similar to those of the sei whale, although the former's are shorter and thicker, and the fringe is different.

Like the sei, Bryde's whale has an arched upper jaw that occasionally gives it a haughty appearance. Three converging ridges—a distinctive mark, as other rorquals have only one—run along the broad rostrum from the blowholes to the tip of the snout. These prominences, at times studded with parasite-infested growths, look like ritual scarifications. The 250 to 370 pairs of light gray baleen plates are fairly wide at the base but relatively short—with a maximum length of

*BRYDE'S WHALE*

*In 1878, John Anderson of Scotland, then Superintendent of the Indian Museum in Calcutta, described this species for the first time and called it* Balaenoptera edeni *in honor of Sir Ashley Eden, Chief Commissioner of Burma. In 1912–13, the Norwegian zoologist O. Olsen, just back from South Africa, published several papers on a rorqual from the southern hemisphere he called* Balaenoptera brydei. *(J. Bryde, the Norwegian consul to South Africa, built the first whaling factory in Durban.)*

*Soon it became clear that the two species were, in fact, the same. Whalers still refer to it as Bryde's whale, but some scientists give priority to Anderson's 1878 description. The current trend is to call it the "tropical whale"; if the name catches on, it may ultimately satisfy all concerned.*

*English:* Bryde's whale, tropical whale
*French:* rorqual (balénoptère) tropical, rorqual de Bryde, baleine de Bryde, rorqual d'Eden
*Russian:* brayda kit *Japanese:* nitari kujira
*Spanish:* ballena de Bryde *Italian:* balenottera tropicale

*A free-swimming Bryde's whale looks even duskier than its fellow rorqual, the sei whale. Its distinguishing field mark is three parallel longitudinal ridges on the snout; other rorquals have only one. Above: This superb individual was photographed in the Sea of Cortez.*

*. . . Read the whale in all the ways clouds*
*are read . . .*
*the whale seems simpler than it is:*
*an easy water-to-land knot.*
*(Roy Fisher, British, b. 1930)*

about 17 inches; the plates are fringed with stiff gray bristles. The pelagic variety off South Africa has two-toned baleen, very light gray to white at the front of the mouth and dark gray to black toward the rear.

Bryde's whales and sei whales have a number of characteristics in common—diminutive flippers (one-tenth body length), an extremely falcate dorsal fin, and a powerful tail. Other features, however, make it possible to tell the species apart: Bryde's whale is sleeker and more streamlined than its comparatively brawny cousin. Its 30 to 65 throat grooves extend from the chin to or beyond the umbilicus, making them 3 to 5 feet longer than those of the sei. Both sei whales and Bryde's whales have dark gray backs, but the chin, throat, and belly of the former are white, while the underside of the latter is indistinctly delineated lighter gray. In addition, Bryde's whales sport a wide, dark gray band that relieves the lightly pigmented belly. Generally speaking, a free-swimming Bryde's whale looks even darker than the dusky sei.

## MINKE WHALE · *Balaenoptera acutorostrata*; Family Balaenopteridae

The minke whale is the runt of the family—even though it still measures a respectable 25 to 30 feet long! Minke whales are friendly creatures, apparently not skittish around boats. The sturdy species' firmly packed physique, insulated by several inches of blubber, makes it the roly-poly of the rorqual clan; it is a spirited, robust swimmer known for its whimsical acrobatic stunts.

The average male minke whale is about 25 feet long, the average female about 2 feet longer. (The maximum length is about 35 feet.) Minkes weigh between 6 and 7.5 tons (the record weight is 9.5 tons). The most distinctive trait of the species is a narrow, acutely pointed, nearly triangular snout that earned it both its scientific name and nicknames, "little piked whale" and "sharp-headed finner." The minke has a single prominent head ridge, typical of the rorquals. Its lower jaw protrudes well beyond the upper one on all sides. The mouth contains about 300 pairs of baleen plates. Fringed with very fine, snow-white bristles, these small, horny plates of less than a foot in length range in color from yellowish-white to white.

The minke's trunk is bulkier than that of its fellow rorquals. Its flippers are well developed and comparatively long (one-eighth of total length); the dorsal fin and deeply notched tail flukes are also relatively large. The 50 to 70 throat grooves extend from the chin to near the umbilicus.

The back and sides are slate-gray (occasionally charcoal-gray) from the tip of the snout to the tail. But in yet another example of nature's penchant for contrast, the minke whale's underside is considerably lighter. The undersides of the flippers are white, and the top sides are often marked with a broad white trapezoidal band.

The minke actually shows considerable variation in shading and markings. Some stocks sport a pair of large, light gray chevrons that arch across the back just above the flippers. In some individuals, a triangular patch of light gray extends along each side between the belly and the dorsal fin. Dr. W. L. van Utrecht of the Amsterdam Zoological Laboratory (1961) argued long and hard in favor of a subspecies peculiar to the southern hemisphere, known as *Balaenoptera acutorostrata huttoni* or *B. a. bonaerensis*—a subdivision not all cetologists accept. The southern minke has even larger flippers than its northern counterpart. The southern minke's flippers lack the distinctive white patch, a field mark for positive identification in other waters. The baleen is white in front to grayish-brown at the rear.

*Opposite, top: Swift, alert, and playful, the fish-eating minke whale joins the large rorquals (blue and fin whales) on krill-rich feeding grounds in the summer. During the first half of the twentieth century, minkes indirectly benefited from the blue whale fishery, which resulted in less competition for food. In the last thirty years, however, this species has become a prime target of harpoon gunners.*

*MINKE WHALE*

*The first naturalist to describe this species as such was Othon Fabricius (1780), but Icelanders and Norwegians had known about its existence for centuries. Lacépède (1804) examined the remains of a juvenile stranded near Cherbourg in 1781, created a new genus* Balaenoptera, *and added* acutorostrata *because of its pointed snout. Whalers commonly refer to it as the minke whale, after the Norwegian* minkehval.

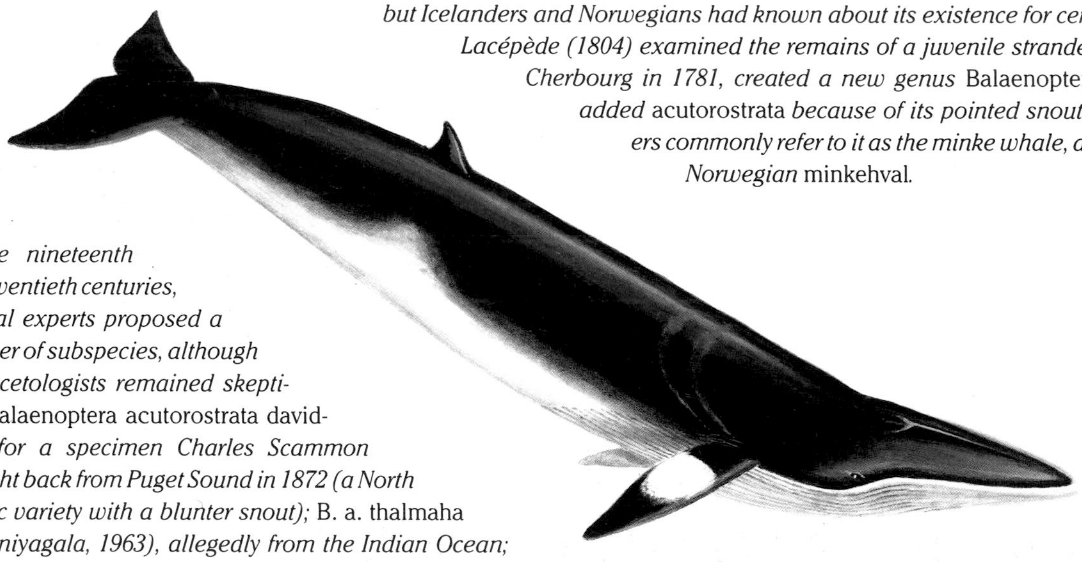

*In the nineteenth and twentieth centuries, several experts proposed a number of subspecies, although most cetologists remained skeptical:* Balaenoptera acutorostrata davidsoni *for a specimen Charles Scammon brought back from Puget Sound in 1872 (a North Pacific variety with a blunter snout);* B. a. thalmaha *(Deraniyagala, 1963), allegedly from the Indian Ocean; and* B. a. huttoni *(Gray, 1874) or* B. a. bonaerensis *(Burmeister, 1867), a southern subspecies whose unusually large flippers lack the characteristic band of white on the upper surface.*

*English:* minke, Minke's whale, piked whale, lesser rorqual, sharp-headed finner, little finner, pikehead, summer whale, baywhale *French:* rorqual (balénoptère) museau-pointu, baleine (rorqual) de Minke, petit rorqual, rorqual nain *Russian:* malyi polosatik, zalivov *Japanese:* koiwashi kujira, minku *German:* Zwergwal *Italian:* balenottera minore *Spanish:* ballena enana, rorcual pequeño, ballena minke *Dutch:* dwerg vinvisch *Icelandic:* andarna fin *Norwegian:* minkehval, rebbehval, vaageval *Greenland Eskimo:* tikagulik *Aleutian:* agamakhchik

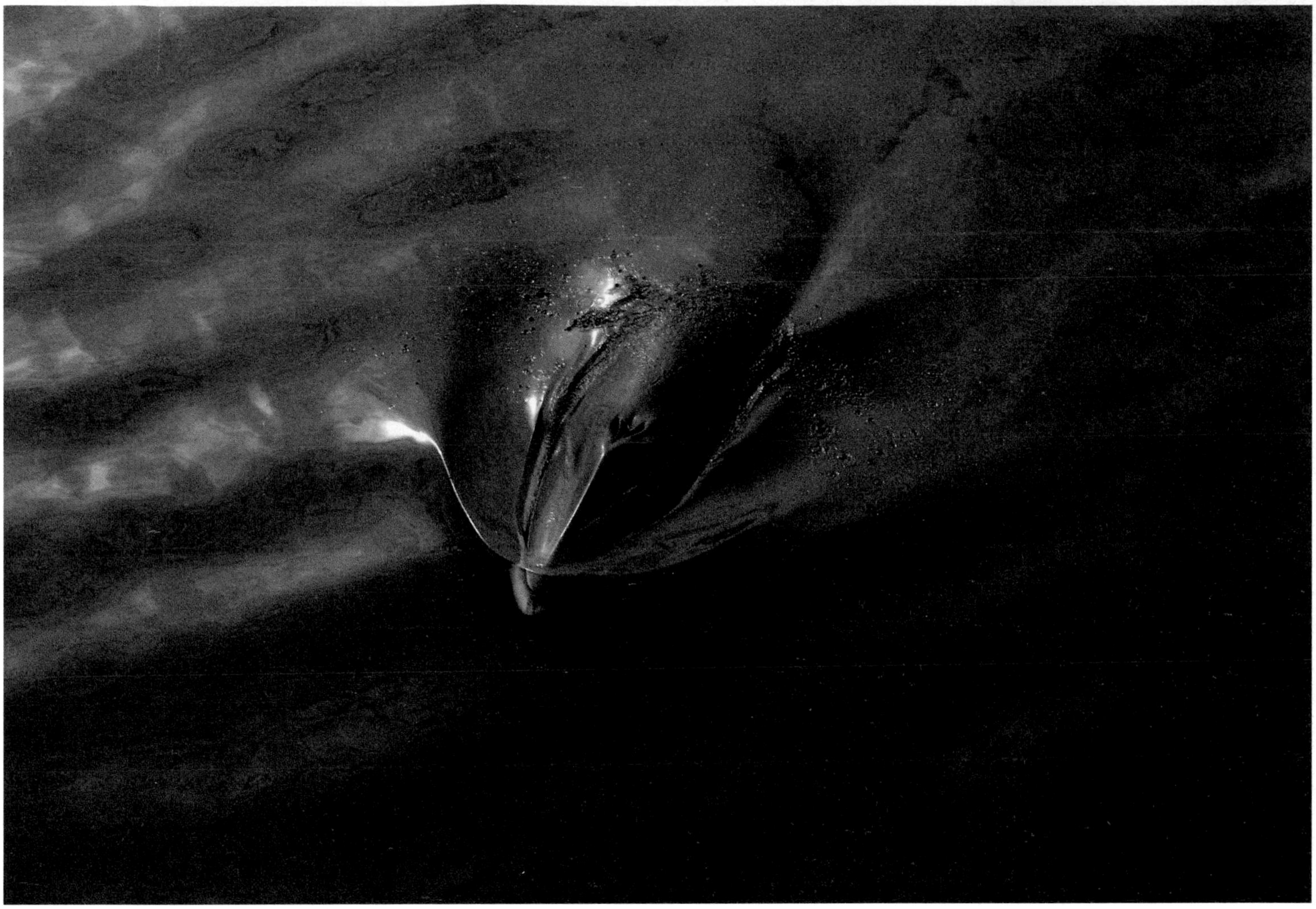

*Below: In this lithograph from Scammon's* The Marine Mammals of the North-western Coast of North America *(1874), the light-colored band on the flipper positively identifies this individual as a minke whale. Until recently, artists made minkes (and other whales) too big, too rotund, too pot-bellied.*

*HUMPBACK WHALE*

*The humpback whale was described quite a few times before the eighteenth century. The "hump" that so often makes up part of its name refers not to the nodules on its head, but to the exaggerated roll of the back when the whale sounds. One of the French names of the species,* gibbar, *has the same Latin root as the French word for "hump." Another French name,* jubarte *(possibly a variant of* gibbar*) may be derived from Jupiter; in England the species was once known as jupiterfish (Anderson, 1746). Yet another French term,* mégaptère, *refers to the humpback's inordinately long flippers. The first cetologist to enter the taxonomic fray was Klein, who in his* Historiae naturalis piscium *(Leipzig, 1740–49) named the species* Balaena gibbo unico, *"the one-humped whale." In* Regnum animale *(1756), Brisson, who created the order Cetacea, came up with* baleine de la Nouvelle Angleterre. *Fabricius, in 1780, named it* Balaena boops, *which gained currency for quite some time. In 1781, the German naturalist Georg Borowski latinized the name Brisson had given it, coming up with* Balaena novaeangliae. *The discerning Lacépède (1804) removed it from the family Balaenidae, reclassified it as a balaenopterid, and dubbed it* Balaenoptera jubartes.

*F. Cuvier (1826) took his cue from Linnaeus and created the name* rorqual boops. *In 1846, J. E. Gray established the genus* Megaptera *(Greek for "big wing") and added* longipinna, *which means precisely the same thing in Latin!*

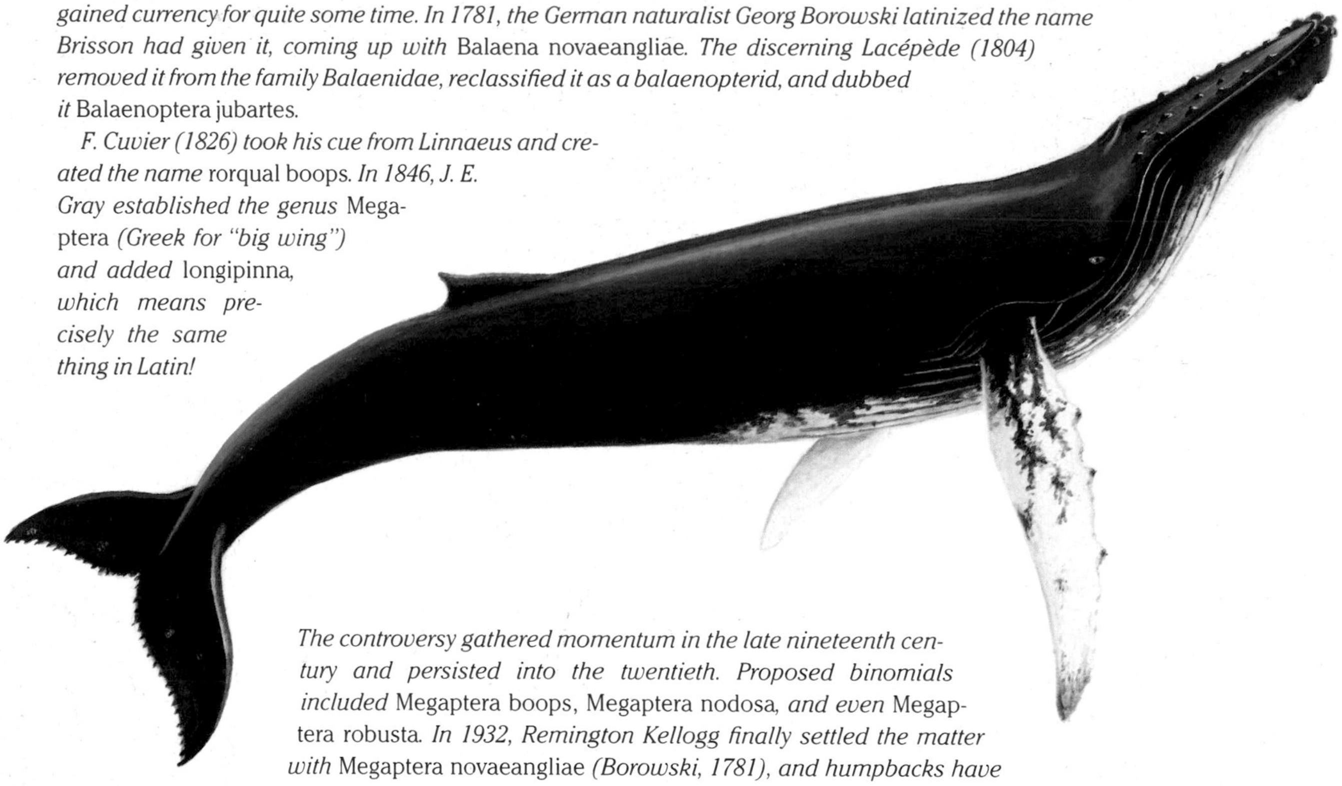

*The controversy gathered momentum in the late nineteenth century and persisted into the twentieth. Proposed binomials included* Megaptera boops, Megaptera nodosa, *and even* Megaptera robusta. *In 1932, Remington Kellogg finally settled the matter with* Megaptera novaeangliae *(Borowski, 1781), and humpbacks have been known by that scientific name ever since.*

*English:* humpback, hunchback, bunch whale, knucklehead
*French:* baleine à bosse, mégaptère, jubarte, gibbar, baleine bossue
*Russian:* gorbach *Japanese:* zato kujira *Spanish:* yubarta, gubarta, ballena jorobada
*Norwegian:* knølhval *German:* Knurrval, Buckelwal *Swedish:* hnufubakur *Italian:* megattera
*Icelandic:* hrafnreydar *Polish:* pletwal *Greenland Eskimo:* keporkak *Aleutian:* aliama, kaipekak

## HUMPBACK WHALE *Megaptera novaeangliae*; Family Balaenopteridae

The playful, affectionate humpback seems made for entertainment; watch as it frolics, breaches, sings amid ocean swells, or waves at passing ocean liners with its flippers. Stocky and ill-proportioned, this brawny entertainer is the clown, acrobat, and crooner of the seas.

*Wonderful humpback! Splendor of the seas!*
*Oceangoing vessel! It swims, breaches, sings,*
*and lulls its young in its big white "arms."*

*I am the whale,*
*last of our kind*
*in this polluted sea,*
*Merlin master of old mysteries.*
*(Desmond O'Grady, Irish, b. 1935)*

The average length of the male humpback is about 47 feet, and of the female, about 50 feet; the longest female on record was 62.5 feet. Males and females alike weigh between 30 and 50 tons, depending on seasonal variations in blubber.

The humpback's head is proportionately bulkier than that of other rorquals, and the line of its mouth is more contorted. The lips, chin, and entire snout are studded with fleshy protuberances, or tubercules. A single, coarse bristle grows out of the center of each of these strange, wartlike bumps or knobs.

The humpback's lower jaw is more bowed than that of its fellow rorquals, and there is no rostral ridge. Its thick, spongy tongue is sometimes coated with asperities. There are 250 to 400 pairs of dark gray baleen plates; they are narrow and short, with a maximum length of just over 2 feet. The short, coarse bristles are dark gray as a rule, but occasionally shade off to a lighter color. Humpbacks have only 14 to 35 throat grooves, set widely apart and extending all the way to the navel.

It is impossible to look at a humpback's body and not find its power deeply impressive. More thickset than other rorquals, it narrows abruptly forward of the tail. The variously shaped dorsal fin often looks like a blunted triangle, but is sometimes falcate, or, as in dogfish, pointed; the fin is "mounted" on a thick, fleshy step, not present in any other balaenopterid.

The humpback's tail is, in a word, glorious. Its broad, deeply notched flukes, with their serrated or frayed rear margins and sharp white markings on the undersides, have always inspired awe among whalemen. Humpbacks throw the flukes high into the air when starting a long dive—and who can blame them for proudly displaying this twelve-foot-wide propeller?

The fact that attempts have been made to classify humpbacks into four color categories, from practically white to completely black, suggests just how wide the pigmentation range of the species really is. For the "average" individual, Lacépède's description of 1804 is as good as any: "The upper part of this cetacean is black or darkish; the underside of the head and arms, quite white; the underside of the belly and tail, mixed black and white."

It is difficult to do justice to the humpback's enormous flippers. Picture impossibly long forelimbs, ranging in color from light gray to white and black to snow-white: aquatic angel's wings with edges scalloped like cumulus clouds, powerful yet tender appendages that are constantly in motion, constantly communicating, protecting young, or locked in passionate embraces during the mating season. These flippers can measure up to one-third body length. Seldom has a species been given so appropriate a scientific name; *megapteron* is new Latin for "big wing."

*Once nothing more than cannon fodder, the humpback whale now inspires poetry and captivates people the world over. But the concern of its newfound human friends is not uppermost in its mind. It has other things with which to concern itself—like the many varieties of parasites that infest its body. This dorsal view (above) and lateral view of an individual infested with* Penella *(below) are from Scammon's* Marine Mammals of the North-western Coast of North America *(1874).*

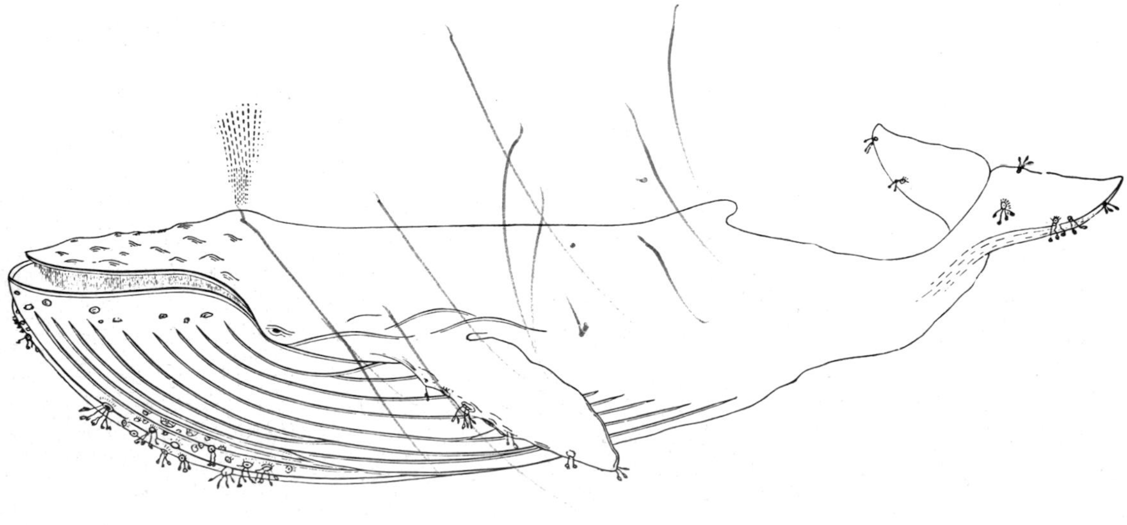

*There is no mistaking a sperm whale; nothing else in the world is shaped like it. It is said to have the biggest nose on earth; but it also has the biggest brain and puts it to good use. Deep inside the whale's rough-hewn exterior lie the melon (spermaceti organ) and other sophisticated adaptations that enable the species to echolocate, dive to tremendous depths, and communicate.*

## SPERM WHALE *Physeter macrocephalus* ( = *Catodon*); Family Physeteridae

The sperm whale is a colossus—a panting forge, a stupendous assemblage of muscles, a formidable predator that rules the seas from the surface to the ocean floor. The first thing one notices about this odontocete is its tremendous, boxlike head—which is the inspiration for the species name *macrocephalus.* "Its head," notes Lacépède (1804), "is one of the biggest, if not the biggest of any known. It almost always accounts for more than a third of its total length. This huge, cubical mass looks as though it has been lopped off in front, resulting in a broad, squarish, nearly vertical snout."

The adult male of the species is between 50 and 52 feet long, once in a great while reaching 65 feet. In 1826, Frédéric Cuvier wrote that "sightings of 80 to 100-foot [specimens] have been reported," but these reports must have been exaggerated. The sperm whale weighs about 40 tons on average, occasionally as much as 50 tons; lone bulls of 60 to 65 tons have been sighted, but they must form a tiny minority. Unlike female baleen whales, female sperm whales are considerably smaller than males, averaging 33 to 36 feet long (maximum: 40 feet) and between 14 and 18 tons.

Its monstrous head—20 feet long, 10 feet high, and 7 feet across—rough-hewn like some unfinished piece of sculpture, creates an overwhelming impression of wild, rugged beauty. It is no wonder *Physeter macrocephalus* managed to send many a whaler to the bottom with a single butt of its noggin!

The dentition of the sperm whale is homodont, or uniform, and monophydont—that is, there are no milk teeth. The teeth in the upper jaw atrophy before birth and usually remain unerupted. The almost needlelike lower jaw, a sharply pointed triangle 16 feet long, comes equipped with a spectacular set of huge, conical teeth. They are oval in cross section, 7 inches long, and weigh more than 2 pounds apiece. The 24 to 30 teeth on each side fit into sockets in the upper jaw when the whale closes its mouth.

The eyes are placed well back, just above the convergence of the upper and

## *SPERM WHALE*

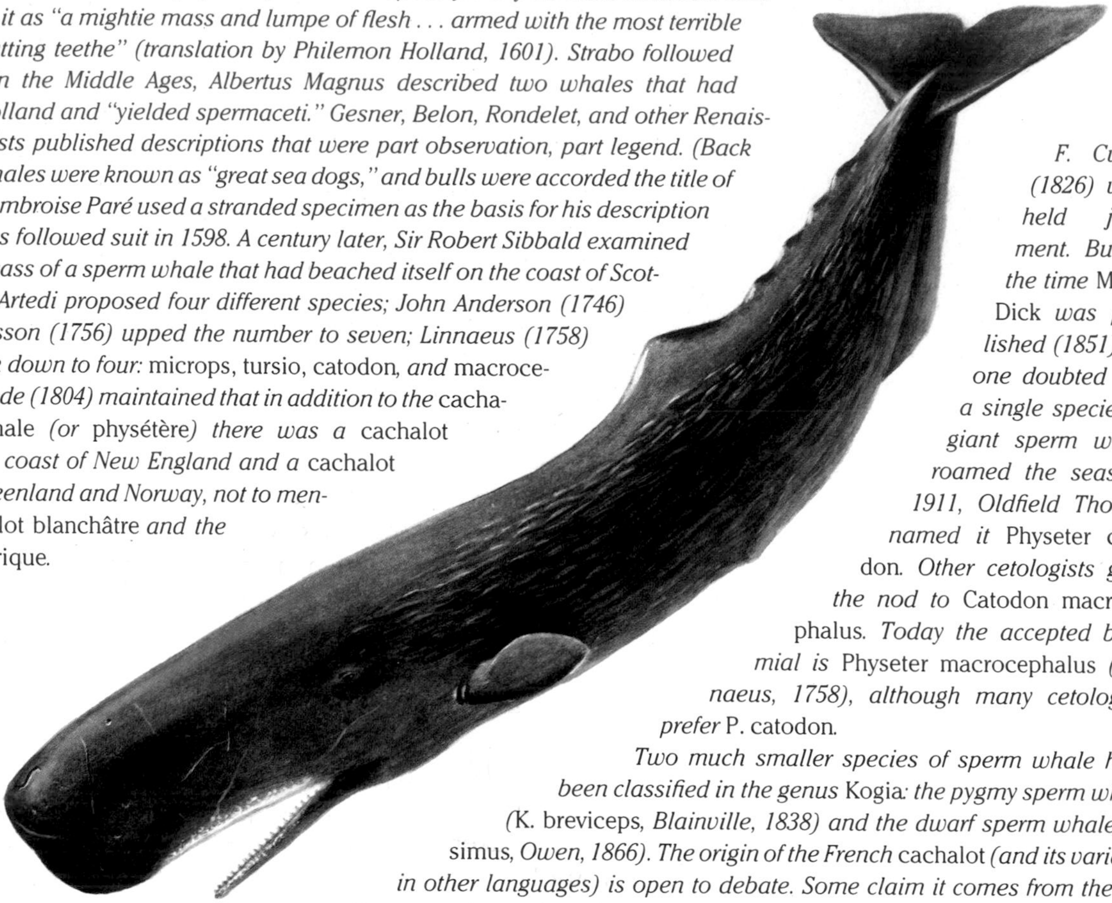

*The sperm whale has long been an inexhaustible source of inspiration for poets, painters, and philosophers. Aristotle named it* physeter *("blow" or "spout"). Pliny the Elder dubbed it* orca *and described it as "a mightie mass and lumpe of flesh . . . armed with the most terrible sharpe and cutting teethe" (translation by Philemon Holland, 1601). Strabo followed Pliny's lead. In the Middle Ages, Albertus Magnus described two whales that had stranded in Holland and "yielded spermaceti." Gesner, Belon, Rondelet, and other Renaissance naturalists published descriptions that were part observation, part legend. (Back then, sperm whales were known as "great sea dogs," and bulls were accorded the title of "emperors.") Ambroise Paré used a stranded specimen as the basis for his description in 1577. Clusius followed suit in 1598. A century later, Sir Robert Sibbald examined (1692) the carcass of a sperm whale that had beached itself on the coast of Scotland. In 1738, Artedi proposed four different species; John Anderson (1746) concurred; Brisson (1756) upped the number to seven; Linnaeus (1758) brought it back down to four:* microps, tursio, catodon, *and* macrocephalus. *Lacépède (1804) maintained that in addition to the* cachalot macrocéphale *(or* physétère*) there was a* cachalot trumpo *off the coast of New England and a* cachalot svineval *off Greenland and Norway, not to mention the* cachalot blanchâtre *and the* physale cylindrique.

*F. Cuvier (1826) withheld judgment. But by the time* Moby-Dick *was published (1851), no one doubted that a single species of giant sperm whale roamed the seas. In 1911, Oldfield Thomas named it* Physeter catodon. *Other cetologists gave the nod to* Catodon macrocephalus. *Today the accepted binomial is* Physeter macrocephalus *(Linnaeus, 1758), although many cetologists prefer* P. catodon.

*Two much smaller species of sperm whale have been classified in the genus* Kogia*: the pygmy sperm whale (*K. breviceps*, Blainville, 1838) and the dwarf sperm whale (*K. simus*, Owen, 1866). The origin of the French* cachalot *(and its variants in other languages) is open to debate. Some claim it comes from the old Gascon* cachau*, others from the Catalan* quachal *("big teeth"), still others from the old Spanish* quixal*, meaning "jaw" or "set of teeth." It was once believed that the oil inside the whale's melon or bulbous forehead was a reservoir of semen; hence it was called spermaceti and the species came to be known in English as the sperm whale.*

*English:* sperm whale, great sperm whale, trumpet whale, cachalot
*French:* cachalot, macrocéphale, grand souffleur, trumpo, baleine-trompette, physétère
*Russian:* bolshoi plevum ("great spouter"), kashalot *Japanese:* makko kujira *Italian:* capidoglio
*Spanish:* cachalote, ballena esperma *German:* Pottfisch, Pottwall, Caschelott *Norwegian:* potfisk, suehval, hunshval, bardvalir
*Swedish:* kaskelot *Dutch:* potvisch, kaisilot *Icelandic:* buthvalue, rod kammen
*Provençal:* peis mular *Polish:* olbrotowick *Greenland Eskimo:* kigutilik

lower jaws. Gleaming with intelligence and a seeming craftiness that have always fascinated whalemen, the eyes of the sperm whale inspired a number of haunting passages in *Moby-Dick* (1851). At 20 pounds, the spherical brain is not only proportionately much larger than that of baleen whales, but the largest of any creature that has ever lived. The single, S-shaped blowhole, about 20 inches long, is located on the left side of the front end of the head, when the sperm whale blows, the spout travels to the left and forward at a 45° angle.

*"Look at the colossus before us!" exclaimed Lacépède in 1804. "Behold a giant of the sea, a sovereign of the deep! . . . It wields daunting weapons. . . . It does not rule its watery realm the way peaceable right whales do; it holds dreaded dominion over the seas. It does not stop at driving back aggressors, smashing obstacles in its path, destroying anything that has the audacity to do it harm. It seeks out its prey." The sperm whale has fascinated generations of whalers, and curiosity-seekers still come in droves to gawk at stranded individuals. Below: An attempt at reproducing a sperm whale; an engraving from the 1839 edition of Lacépède's* Histoire naturelle des Cétacés *(1804).*

The thick, rounded, stubby flippers, 5 feet long, 2 to 3 feet across, are used primarily for braking and steering. Instead of a dorsal fin there is a hump, two-thirds of the way along the body, followed by a string of small, uneven knobs or "knuckles" that run down the lower back to the tail. The number of these projections varies from one individual to another. Females have a characteristic callus on the forward part of the largest knuckle.

The sperm whale's tail is an extraordinarily mobile appendage. "The largest sized Sperm Whale's tail," we read in one descriptive passage in *Moby-Dick*, "comprises upon its upper surface alone, an area of at least fifty square feet. The compact round body of its root expands into two broad, firm, flat palms or flukes, gradually shoaling away to less than an inch in thickness. At the crotch or junction, these flukes slightly overlap, then sideways recede from each other like wings, leaving a wide vacancy between. In no living thing are the lines of beauty more exquisitely defined than in the crescentic borders of these flukes." An uneven ridge runs along the underside from the anus to the tail.

Sperm whales are almost entirely black or dark gray on the back, head, and dorsal surface of the tail. (However, light gray specimens have been reported.) In some individuals, very pale spots and patches with blurred edges appear on the sides and belly, which are not as dark as the rest of the body. In old bulls, the head is studded with grayish spots and numerous scars, earned during contests with other bulls or giant squid. Even among juveniles, the skin has a shriveled, corrugated texture worthy of the most weather-beaten of old salts.

Since the publication of *Moby-Dick*, it has been common knowledge that white whales exist, and actual sightings at sea have indeed been reported. On August 21, 1951, the French whaler *Anglo-Norse* took an albino individual in the Pacific. According to the captain's report, "its hide was white as snow, with only a slight grayish-blue patch at the rear of the back" (G. Blond, 1953). Another unpigmented sperm whale was taken and flensed off Hokkaido by the Japanese whaler *Seki Maru III* on April 19, 1957; this individual did not have the red pupils or pink irises typical of albinos of other mammalian species. Of course, none of them could match Melville's white whale for awesome, brute force and fiendish malice, especially " . . . when seen gliding at high noon through a dark blue sea, leaving a milky-way wake of creamy foam, all spangled with golden gleamings."

CHAPTER 3

# Nomads in Jeopardy

*The spouts of whales have become scarce, all too scarce; and no one is to blame but man. The wholesale slaughter of whales has been relentless and unbridled. Only recently have we learned to appreciate the unutterable beauty of a trio of diving humpbacks (pp. 90–91), or of a rainbow glistening in a humpback's spout (below).*

*In the smell of death*
*In the* luxe of *plants,*
*In the blood of the whale . . .*
*Is the knowledge of the end of time.*
*(David Mamet, American, b. 1947)*

*There will be nothing left of this gigantic species but a few vestiges. Its remains shall turn to dust and shall be scattered to the winds. It will live on only in human memory and in paintings. Everything on our planet wastes away and dies out. What drastic change shall give it a new lease on life? Nature is deathless, but only in the aggregate. Man artfully contrives to beautify and revive some of her works; but there are so many others he damages, disfigures, and destroys.*

Lacépède (1804)

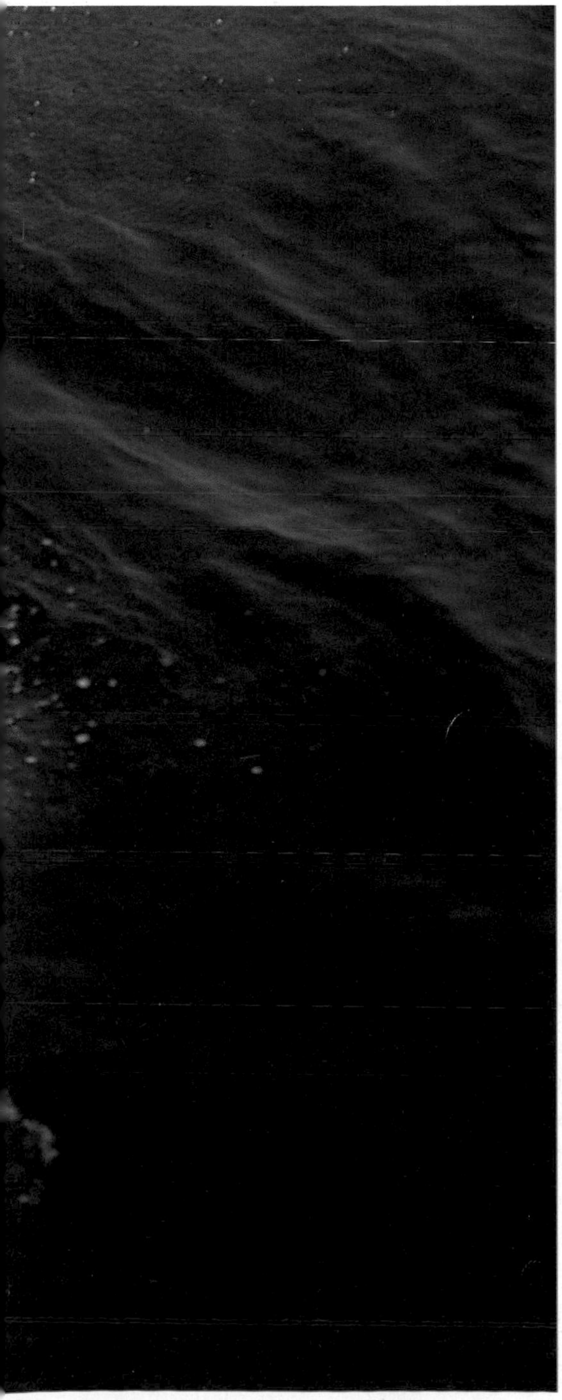

Five centuries ago, the oceans teemed with magnificent monsters, mischievous leviathans, frolicsome hundred-ton tots—all tirelessly plying the waters of our planet. Some headed poleward to slumber beneath the tapestry of the northern lights, others toward the tropics to court splashingly in the glistening foam. Today, the seas are nearly empty of such gamboling.

Have we taken leave of our senses? Even if it took fifty or a hundred years of hard work and self-restraint, should we not at least try and restore to nature—and to future generations—the staggering sight of massed whales breaching, mating, or gorging themselves on wriggling shoals of pink plankton?

## SOUND RECKONINGS

There are two ways of going about the business of estimating whale populations. One relies on direct observation, using appropriate marking and tallying procedures, or inspection of specific biological parameters in stranded carcasses or specimens supplied by whaling ships. The direct-count method inevitably yields incomplete data. The other technique involves constant extrapolation (individual to group, group to population, current conditions to previous conditions, and so forth). Any logician will tell you that inferences like these are a tricky business, the more so when the party doing the inferring has a vested interest in the results.

Some of the statistics presented in this chapter must be greeted with skepticism. Stocks have often been assessed for the express purpose of maximizing exploitation, and therefore the assessment is often open to optimistic interpretation. We are dealing with an area in which sound reckonings are hard to come by. Whale population estimates have often been modeled on the ones commercial interests use when calculating potential resources for pelagic fisheries. Is there any reason to assume that procedures for counting fish stocks can be applied to whales? There is an enormous biological, ethological, and ecological gap between herrings and sperm whales, for example, but they share biological parameters of mortality, reproduction, and maturation.

Any population of living things may be reckoned by an in-the-field "head count." But whales are distributed over vast reaches of water; taking a direct census is easier said than done. Very few stocks stay in one place long enough for each individual to be spotted and photographed. Species with clearly defined migration routes and timetables, such as the right whale, the gray whale, and the humpback, may be counted with relative ease from land, sea, or air. (Teams of vehicles—two aircraft, two ships, or a plane and a ship—yield the best results.) Direct observation was the technique Dr. Payne used for his extraordinary census of the right whales that mate and calve off Peninsula Valdés, in Argentina. The method also proved fruitful in estimating the population of certain humpback stocks that winter off the Bahamas or Hawaii, then head toward Cape Cod, Newfoundland, or Alaska come summer. The most reliable set of figures is for the California gray whale, which passes very close to shore during migration. In all of these species, it is usually possible to identify individuals within a group by means of body markings, location of parasite-infested growths, or morphological details such as the shape of the fluke notch or dorsal fin.

When the census shifts to the high seas, daunting problems arise. Which regions should be monitored? The operation would require hundreds upon hundreds of ships. No results could be obtained at night or in rough weather. A certain number of whales on deep dives would escape detection. And so on. To enhance spotting capability, scientists have turned to sonar and other sophisticated techniques that yield excellent results with fish but prove less effective with cetaceans. Whales often elude sonar and are too widely scattered.

## MATHEMATICS TO THE RESCUE

In what was hoped would be a change for the better, some cetologists (from Japan and the Soviet Union, for the most part) came up with mathematical models for estimating population size based on the number of whales a spotting vehicle (usually a ship) encounters during sample runs over sample lengths of time. The numbers recorded in the sample area are extrapolated to a total area and total population.

Clearly, calculations such as these are not without logical pitfalls. Is the sample spotted typical of the entire region? Is there any guarantee that the same individuals are never counted twice? Weather may obscure sightings, or diving time may be improperly accounted for. An observer's impressions may be colored by training or bias.

This model was applied to minke whale stocks in the Antarctic. In 1970 the population was estimated at 70,000. Then, thanks to miraculous "new parameters," the figures were revised upward to 150,000 just two years later. More than double the original estimate! During the same period Japan substantially increased its annual catch of smaller rorquals, from 289 in 1971 to 3,354 in 1972, and was arguing before the I.W.C. that the species could withstand higher quotas.

Another method for estimating population size involves marking individuals and subsequently analyzing data from recovered tags. The devices themselves have been tested and improved. Most are internal "Discovery" tags—small stainless-steel tubes shot deep enough into the blubber to stay in place, but (theoretically) not so deep as to interfere with the whale's activity; in fact, tissue damage and, rarely, deaths caused by marking have been reported. The most serious drawback with this approach is that the whale has to be killed and flensed in order to retrieve the information.

Marking has never proved an unequivocal success. For one thing, some whale-

men have cheated by failing to return marks to scientists or by providing inaccurate information when they do. (It was later discovered that some whalemen had filed false reports concerning actual provenance of whale carcasses. How shortsighted of them to doctor the results!) Moreover, only a very small percentage of marks has ever been recovered. From 1932 to 1973, scientists marked 1,154 blue whales, 7,080 fin whales, 812 sei whales, and 4,609 humpbacks. The rates of recovery were 11.6 percent, 11.9 percent, 5.6 percent, and 3.2 percent, respectively. Hit-or-miss data such as these cannot be considered a sound basis for conclusions about whale populations.

In the not-too-distant future, scientists may fare better by making use of observation techniques that are not only more accurate, but also more respectful of the physical integrity of the whales themselves. One of their tools will be telemetry—the high-speed transmission of scientific data. And now that high-resolution photography from space, even through cloud cover, is a reality, scientists also may monitor whales by satellite.

Another alternative is "radio-tagging" whales by fitting a backpack onto the animal's body. Whenever the whale surfaces, the transmitter emits a signal that is picked up by an airplane or satellite. Scientists on the receiving end cannot only keep track of an individual's movements, but also monitor the frequency of dives, number of feeding periods per day, and many other aspects of cetacean biology and behavior. Tremendous strides are being made in electronics and miniaturization, so there is every reason to expect that science will perfect increasingly reliable and durable radio transmitters equipped with multiple sensors. These devices will be shot into or implanted in the whale without serious harm; immediately, radio locator beacons will start sending updates on water temperature, depth and duration of dives, cardiac and respiratory rates, blood chemistry, and any other internal or external factors they have been programmed to detect.

*Scientists estimate whale populations a number of ways. Some involve direct observation from shore or from a ship or airplane. Individuals are identified one by one by means of distinguishing characteristics, such as pigmentation, callosity patches, or (as with these humpbacks, above) shape of the dorsal fin. These methods work especially well when the target species readily ventures near the coast (like the whale these divers from the Cousteau team have accosted, right); humpbacks and California grays are excellent candidates for direct counting. In other instances, however, this method has to be supplemented by indirect techniques of varying complexity and reliability.*

Right Whale

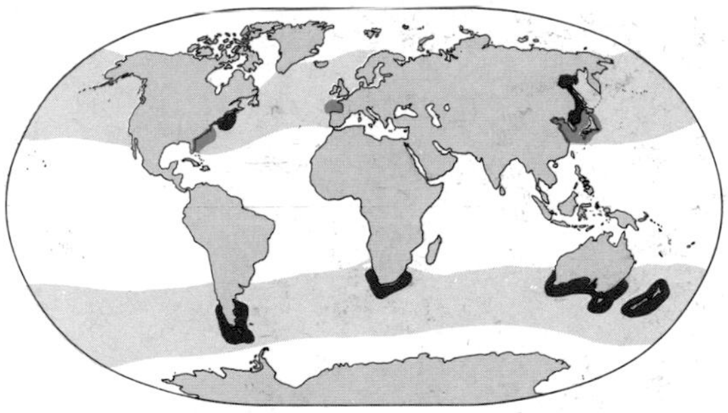

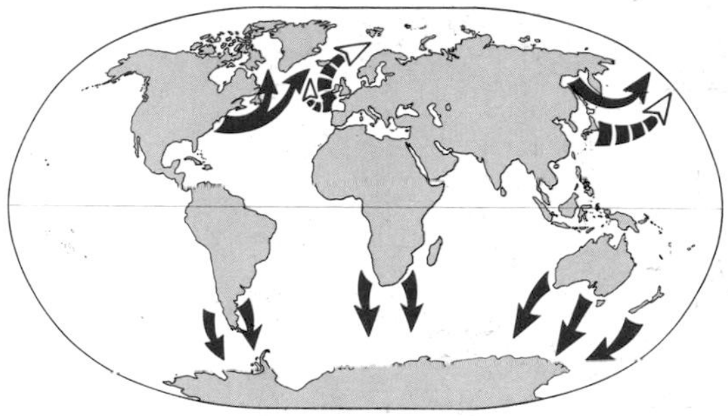

■ Known breeding areas

■ Abandoned or uncertain breeding areas

□ Migration zones

Probable routes

Uncertain routes, diminishing populations

At the beginning of the summer (June–July in the northern hemisphere, December–January in the southern hemisphere), most baleen whales head for their feeding grounds in polar waters. They return to the warm waters of the tropics in autumn.

*Whalers used to refer to the distinctive callosity on northern right whales as the "bonnet" or "rock garden." Actually located on the upper lip, this crusty skin growth is studded with barnacles, worms, and "whale lice" and can grow to an enormous size. Melville (1851) likened it to "the trunk of some huge oak, with a bird's nest in its crotch." Left: These right whales—an individual at the surface (above) and mother and calf underwater (below)—were photographed off Peninsula Valdés, Argentina, a breeding ground that has been declared a wildlife sanctuary.*

## CHECKLIST

Now that we have all of these methods at the ready, the question remains: How many whales are there? How many are left? How many still enrapture the boundless seas on either side of the equator? Can they look forward to recapturing their former grandeur? To be sure, pollution, coastal development, maritime traffic, and other factors take their toll on these fragile giants. Only a long-term, across-the-board moratorium on whaling everywhere, however, will save the whales.

### *RIGHT WHALE*

Populations of right whales have been reduced since the late eighteenth century. Although the remaining populations have been fully protected since the 1930s, they are still taken by whalers operating outside the strictures of the I.W.C.

In the North Atlantic, where the right whale was known as the Biscayan right whale, there may have once been three distinct stocks. The first was centered around Spain and the Bay of Biscay, where the slaughter first got under way; they migrated to Iceland and Norway for the summer. The second cruised the waters off Norway—this was the whale formerly known as the *nordcaper* or *sarde*—and summered around Spitsbergen and Jan Mayen Island. The third shuttled from Georgia to Newfoundland, Labrador, and Greenland, and back again. Each of these stocks once numbered in the thousands. Tragically, the first two have likely been wiped out. An individual taken in the Azores during the 1969–70 season was probably a stray. A handful of survivors are believed to live off Madeira, but cetologists have not verified their provenance. The third group is estimated at 200 to 500 individuals, and although they appear to be recovering there is no assurance of a "comeback." This stock is centered around the Bay of Fundy in Nova Scotia.

The destruction of the right whale in the North Pacific was just as appalling. We do not even know how many groups may have once lived in the region. Probably there was one in the vicinity of Japan and Korea that migrated in the summer toward the Kamchatka peninsula and the Bering Strait, and another near British Columbia that set out for Alaska and the Aleutians come spring. Today, between 200 and 300 at the most are thought to survive in both areas combined. And not the slightest sign of recovery.

In the southern hemisphere, the massacre of the southern right whale (*E. australis*) was just as ruthless, albeit late to transpire. Consider the effects of the kill around New Zealand. In the early nineteenth century, 14,000 right whales were taken every year in that region alone; by 1935, the catch had dwindled to four. Aside from the New Zealand stock—which is actually a hopelessly stagnant relict population centered around Campbell Island—there was a southwestern Atlantic group that shuttled between South Georgia and the waters off Argentina and Brazil as well as a third "south Indian" group that traveled from Crozet and Kerguelen islands to Amsterdam Island and South Africa. Right whales in this hemisphere have fared somewhat better than their northern counterparts. Several hundred individuals congregate every year off Peninsula Valdés (Argentina) to breed. Another stock 200 strong is regularly sighted in the coastal waters of South Africa. The Japanese and South Africans claim that a total of 3,000 right whales survive south of the equator and allege an upward trend on the order of 10 percent a year. This contention has yet to be confirmed; Dr. Payne's 1976 estimate of 1,500 southern right whales is probably closer to the mark.

*BOWHEAD WHALE*

Bowheads have never lived anywhere but in the Arctic Ocean from the Bering Sea to Greenland and Baffin Bay. The species once thrived around Spitsbergen, but few have been seen recently; it rarely ventured into the waters off eastern Siberia. Bowhead whales spend summers at the edge of the pack ice, as far north as 78°–80° N. In September and October, they start out on an annual migration that takes them past the islands of the Canadian north and southward into the Atlantic, but they never venture south of 60° N in the Atlantic. No bowhead has ever been sighted below Cape Farewell, the southernmost tip of Greenland. In the Pacific, Charles Scammon noted in 1874, the species travels a bit farther south to 55° N. In both oceans, the southern boundary of the bowhead's range generally marks the northern limit of the right whale's range. The migration northward gets under way in late April and early May.

At present, the bowhead population appears to be distributed in four remnant stocks. The largest lives in the Arctic waters off extreme northwestern Canada; the population summers from the Beaufort Sea to the Chukchi Sea (especially the area around Banks Island); in winter these whales travel south through the Bering Strait. The second group is confined to the Sea of Okhotsk; its winter migration takes it to relatively low latitudes in the northwestern Pacific. The range of the third—the "Northeast Canada" group—extends from Hudson Bay to Baffin Bay. The fourth moves about in the waters off eastern Greenland and occasionally strays as far east as the Barents Sea. The survival of this group is in jeopardy.

There is no point in recounting the heartrending story of how man decimated bowhead populations. Like its cousin, the right whale, the bowhead has been fully protected since 1937. However, a certain number of them may be taken each year under the "native exemption clause" of the International Whaling Commission. An estimate based on a "census" taken in the Chukchi and Beaufort seas in 1978 put the bowhead population in that area at between 1,783 and 2,865 (H. Braham et

*Behold the rarest of sights: a bowhead whale spouting at the edge of the Arctic pack ice. Fewer than 3,000 of them survive. Toussenel inveighed against the wholesale slaughter of bowheads in* L'Esprit des Bêtes *(1862). "Every year the French government spends vast sums of money, heaven knows why, to promote the extermination of a species that never did it the least bit harm."*

Bowhead

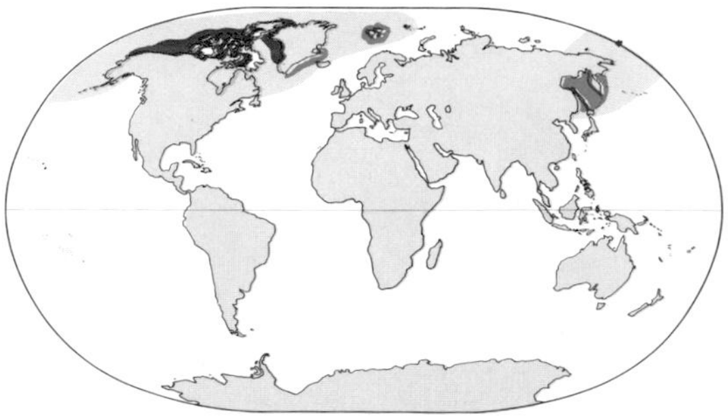

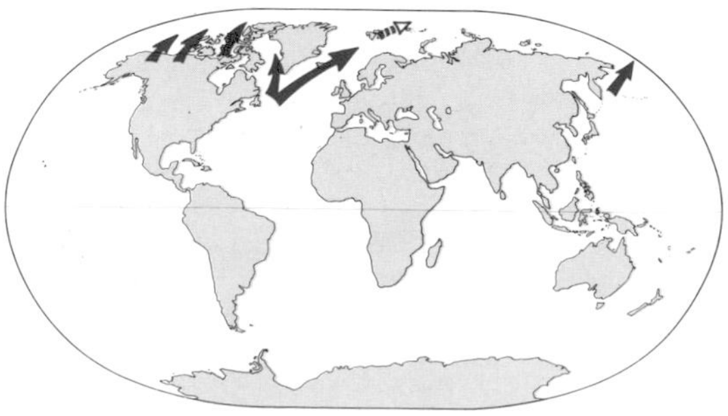

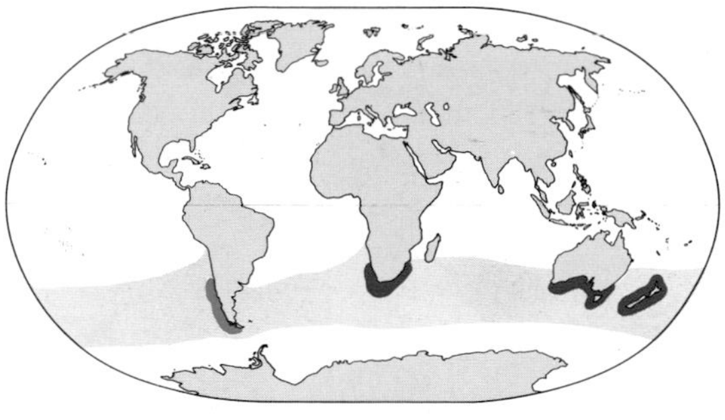

Pygmy Right Whale

al., 1979). The size of other stocks is well below that figure. In 1976, 23 bowheads were sighted in Lancaster Sound, and since then, there have been isolated sightings. At present, there are probably fewer than 4,000 bowhead whales worldwide, and the prognosis for recovery is uncertain.

*PYGMY RIGHT WHALE*

Whalemen have never taken much interest in pygmy right whales, which are diminutive (in comparison to right whales) and naturally scarce. This little-known species is confined to the southern hemisphere. Since 1846, there have been fewer than a hundred strandings, all in Australia, Tasmania, New Zealand, South Africa, Crozet Island, and the Falkland Islands.

Pygmy right whales are circumpolar, distributed between the isotherm of 20° C on the north and the Antarctic convergence (a boundary formed by currents) on the south. In 1907, Wilson claimed to have sighted a few specimens in the Ross Sea, but Lillie (1915) disproved his assertion; the animals were, in fact, minke whales. The cold Benguela current sweeps the rare pygmy right whale as far north as Mozambique, while others ride the cold Humboldt current up to Argentina. The total population of the species is unknown.

*GRAY WHALE*

Gray whales have made a miraculous comeback—provided we limit the discussion to the California stock. Other populations have not been as fortunate. Until not so long ago, a stock of grays made its home in the North Atlantic. Scattered bone finds and historical references suggest that the species lived in Icelandic waters until the seventeenth century. It is thought that the Atlantic stock of gray whales was not completely wiped out until about 1725.

Another, far larger group wintered off Sakhalin, Korea, and Japan, migrating to summering grounds in the Sea of Okhotsk. This population was virtually exterminated by whaling activity; the last of the west Pacific stock were reportedly taken off the east coast of Japan in 1914 and off Korea in 1933. (Two or three individuals were reportedly taken by the Koreans in subsequent years.) Since then, a few sightings—a very few—have been reported: one in 1942 north of the Kuril Islands, another in 1959 near Sakhalin, another in 1968 southeast of Honshu; if a western Pacific population still exists, its ranks must be severely depleted. Nevertheless, the situation is not hopeless. In October 1983, Soviet biologists from the

*A California gray whale vaulting above the ocean surface makes for a majestic sight. By 1874, even Charles Scammon, who figured prominently in its massacre, had to acknowledge the obvious: "None of the species are so constantly and variously pursued as the one we have endeavored to describe, and the large bays and lagoons, where these animals once congregated, brought forth and nurtured their young, are already nearly deserted. The mammoth bones of the California Gray lie bleaching on the shores of those silvery waters . . . and ere long it may be questioned whether this mammal will not be numbered among the extinct species of the Pacific." Today,* mirabile dictu, *gray whales are abundant once more.*

Research Institute of Fishing and Oceanography on Sakhalin spotted about twenty gray whales in the Gulf of Pil'tun Zaliv. This is heartening news.

The eastern Pacific stock was more fortunate. California grays winter and calve in lagoons along the western coast of Mexico: Scammon's and San Ignacio lagoons and the bays of Magdalena, Reforma, Sinaboa, Matancitas, and Ballenas. Some individuals make their way into the Sea of Cortez. In the spring, gray whales cruise along the West Coast of North America toward summering grounds in the Bering Sea, the southern Chukchi Sea, and the southwestern Beaufort Sea (D. W. Rice, 1975). The migration south starts in late September or early October. Grays cross the Gulf of Alaska at a brisk pace, covering between 90 and 160 miles a day; they reach San Diego by Christmas.

The first round of whaling (1846–86) severely depleted the species—which made a resurgence, only to be hunted again in its most secluded breeding grounds. A ban against the taking of California gray whales has been in effect since 1946, and the population of the stock has been slowly rising ever since.

According to Scammon, 8,000 to 10,000 grays were still alive in the second half of the nineteenth century. His estimates are now considered to have been on the high side. Recent research (D. A. Henderson, 1972) suggests that the preexploitation level probably did not exceed between 15,000 and 18,000. Be that as it may, by the 1885–86 season, a scant 160 migrating individuals were sighted south of San Simeon, and the population was estimated at 4,400–5,000. In 1916, zoologist R. C. Andrews sadly noted that the species had been lost to science for twenty years; in 1930, another cetologist feared that there were only a few dozen individuals.

After 1946, the ranks of the California stock swelled at a rate of about 10 percent a year. However, the gray whale "explosion" seems to have slowed considerably since 1959–60, to 2 or 3 percent. A census has been taken every year since 1967 near Monterey, California, where 95 percent of the population passes within a mile and a half of shore. Based on these findings, the California stock has reached 15,000 or more—close to the original optimum population.

Over the last decade, native hunters have taken an average of 165 grays a year, not to mention the 316 kills made from 1959 to 1969 by "special scientific permission." The Soviets have tended to interpret the Native Exemption Clause according to their own lights. Invoking the whaling tradition of eastern Siberia, the U.S.S.R. has started taking gray whales (and right whales) in the Chukchi Sea.

*BLUE WHALE*

How is the giant of giants faring these days? What has become of this wondrous animal, fashioned over millions of years by the forces of nature? Although the blue whale has been fully protected since 1967, the species is not yet out of danger.

G. L. Small (1971) reckoned the world population of blue whales at fewer than 200. Fortunately his estimate was, in all likelihood, unduly pessimistic. However, even cetologists not given to dire predictions believe that it will take blue whales at least 50 years to recover to only half of the preexploitation population—and that is assuming a total suspension of all whaling. A half-century, and provided there are no hitches!

The North Atlantic stocks were depleted between 1883 and 1915 during a frenzy of whaling in the waters off Norway, Scotland, Iceland, Newfoundland, and Greenland. Although it is difficult to estimate the original population, it numbered at least 10,000 and probably included several distinct subgroups. The first cruised the waters off Cape Cod and southern Newfoundland in winter, migrating toward

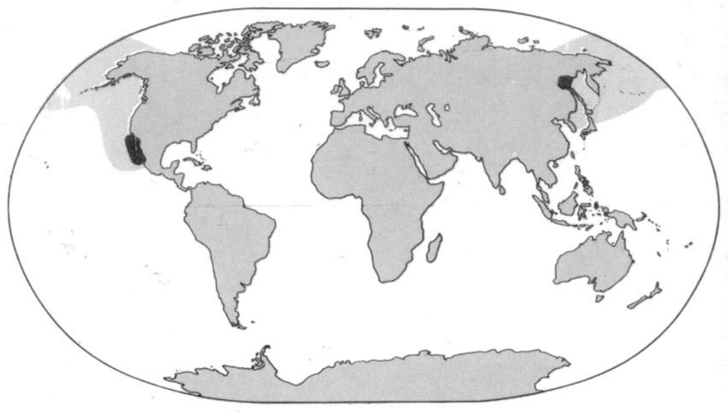

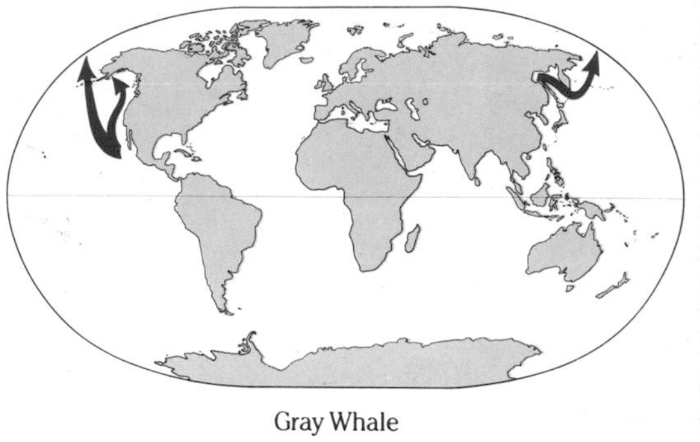

Gray Whale

*Pity the blue whale! More than 20,000 of them perished every year between the wars (some 30,000 in 1931 alone), and in the 1950s every whaling season claimed several thousand more. The species has been protected since 1967.*

*Intestines, hoses sliding about,*
*vats bubbling, crane-chains clattering*
*—all that is stilled: the factory closed,*
*but always, I think, a bad prospect.*
*(Douglas Livingstone, South African, b. 1932)*

*The outlook is bleak indeed. Although blue whale populations are recovering in some areas, the biggest animals on earth are finding it difficult to meet and mate.*

the Gulf of St. Lawrence, the west coast of Greenland, and the Baffin Sea in summer. A second subgroup—the only one whose original size has been reliably estimated (several thousand)—started out from the middle of the North Atlantic, skirted the east coast of Greenland, passed through the Denmark Strait, and ended its summer migration at the edge of the pack ice, above 80° N. A third set out from the Azores in the fall, pressing northward past Ireland, the Hebrides, and the Faroes and into the Arctic Ocean. A fourth migrated from the coast of Spain to Norway and Spitsbergen, reversing the pattern in the fall. There is nothing definitive about this breakdown by stocks: Blue whales are known to have made east-west transatlantic crossings. The one thing about which there is no speculation is that there has been a dramatic decline in the blue whale population worldwide.

The North Pacific population is divided into two main stocks. An eastern subgroup shuttles between the Sea of Cortez and the Bering Sea by way of the waters off Baja California. The western subgroup winters in the vicinity of the Marianas and the Ryukyu Islands, but also heads back to the Bering Sea in the summer. Combined, the two stocks did not number more than 5,000 individuals in 1910. In 1972, an optimistic estimate (Nishiwaki, in K. S. Norris, 1972) put the figure at 1,500, after the population bottomed out at a few hundred in the 1930s.

The most horrifying chapter in the history of the blue whale fishery took place south of the equator. No fewer than 331,142 blue whales were taken in the southern hemisphere between the 1904-05 and 1978 seasons. The preexploitation population must have been at least 200,000, fully three-fourths of which lived in the Antarctic. By 1955 fewer than 5,000 remained; in 1964, perhaps less than a thousand. That was probably on the low side. Today, however, most cetologists feel that there are no more than 7,000 to 12,000 blue whales left in the entire region.

So far as we know, these survivors are distributed in six well-defined stocks (J. A. Gulland, 1976). Like the humpbacks, they summer at the edge of the pack ice and winter in the temperate subequatorial waters of the three great oceans. Blue whales, fin whales, and humpbacks spend an average of 120 days a year in the Antarctic, arriving in a steady flow: pregnant females first and males last. They reverse the order when they head back north: males first, calves and juveniles in the middle, and pregnant females bringing up the rear. One stock of blue whales probably travels between the Weddell Sea and the coast of Brazil; the second, between the Weddell Sea and the coast of South Africa and Namibia; the third, between Antarctica and the Gulf of Oman by way of Mauritius; the fourth, between Australia and Indonesia by way of the waters off the west coast of Australia; the fifth, between the Ross Sea and New Zealand; and the sixth, between the Ross Sea and the offshore waters of Peru and Ecuador, particularly around the Galápagos.

The pygmy blue whale (subspecies *Balaenoptera musculus brevicauda*) is confined, at least in summer, to a fairly restricted range in the Southern Atlantic and Indian oceans—roughly from Tristan da Cunha and Gough Island, off southwestern Africa, to Amsterdam and St. Paul islands, 1,500 miles from Australia. A few individuals stray beyond this area toward Chile or the west coast of Australia, but only once in a great while. Ichihara (1975) estimated that, prior to the 1960–61 season that marked the start of the pygmy blue whale massacre, the population stood at about 10,000. Just before full protection was extended to the subspecies in 1967, there may have been no more than a few hundred left. Lack of sufficient data distinguishing young blue whales from pygmy blue whales makes gauging the recovery rate difficult, but authorities currently estimate that there are just a few hundred pygmy right whales.

Blue Whale

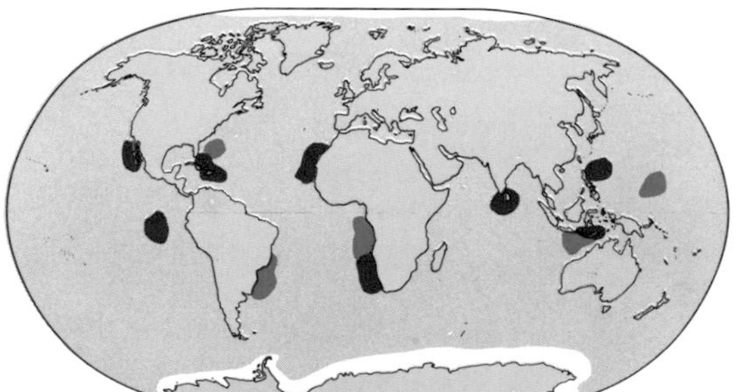

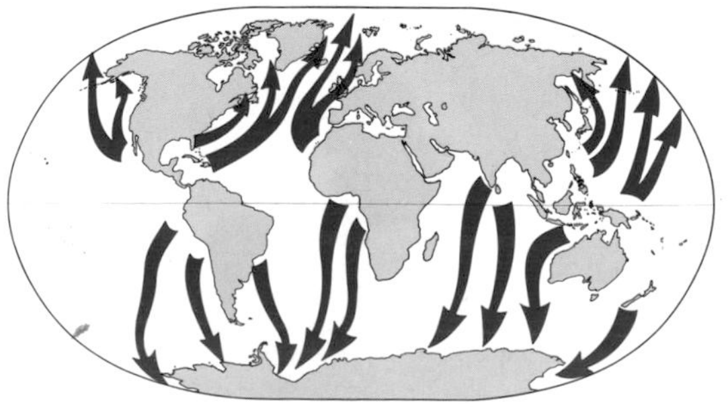

*Like the blue whale, the fin whale is a predominantly pelagic species that prefers swimming in deeper waters. Hence, direct observation from the coast is difficult at best, and direct counting of stocks is largely hit-or-miss. Certainly there are fewer than 100,000 fin whales worldwide. This mother and her calf are a symbol. One day, perhaps, no one will be forced to write: "Dear friend, the sea is red with blood; / The tide a bloody bed for these souls of the sea" (Ron Ridell, New Zealander, b. 1952).*

*FIN WHALE*

Chronologically, fin whales were the first species to fall victim to the harpoon gun: Svend Foyn himself gave the order to fire. Whaling for "razorbacks" in the North Atlantic proved highly productive at first, particularly off Norway, the Scottish islands, and Iceland. One Icelandic shore station has been in continuous operation from 1883 to the present day. In this region alone, between 240 and 250 individuals were regularly taken every year for twenty-six consecutive seasons.

Since fin whale populations overlap considerably and migrate toward the same shoals of plankton, it is difficult to plot the range of individual stocks. Not counting a few clusters of a few dozen specimens each (one in the Mediterranean, another in the Barents Sea, and a third that shuttles between Bermuda and Nova Scotia), the North Atlantic is home to five distinct fin whale groups (D. E. Sergeant, 1976). The first group (probably made up of two groups) migrates from Newfoundland and Nova Scotia to Davis Strait. A western Greenland group summers in the Baffin Sea, while a group off Iceland and the east coast of Greenland passes through the Denmark Strait. The fourth group migrates from the Faroes and the west coast of Norway to summer around Spitsbergen, and the fifth—likely containing several subpopulations—heads for the islands off Scotland in spring.

A reliable count of fin whales remains elusive. For the entire North Atlantic region, estimates range from 3,000–5,000 (L. Watson, 1981) to an overly optimistic figure of 31,230 (D. E. Sergeant, 1976). Moreover, quite a few anomalies have yet to be accounted for. Data concerning the corpus luteum (part of the ovary) and the growth rate of females suggest that fin whales to the west and north of Norway belong to different populations. But if our criterion is the abundance of iodine in blubber, there may be as many as five different stocks in the eastern Atlantic alone (C. J. Rørvik and A. Jonsgård, 1975).

Of the approximately 50,000 fin whales that once lived in the North Pacific, no more than 14,000 or 15,000 survive. The "American" stock off Mexico that migrates to summering grounds off Vancouver Island, Alaska, and the Aleutians held steady until 1954, then took a nosedive. The "Asian" stock consists of a group off Indonesia and the Philippines, which migrates to the Marianas, and two other groups that press northward from the China Sea and eastern Japan to Kamchatka, the Bering Sea, and the Arctic Ocean. The population of this stock plummeted until 1920, then leveled off until 1952, at which time it resumed its downward trend.

South of the equator, the fin whale was the primary target of a relentless pelagic fishery from 1938 to 1964. Until 1953, stock levels managed to keep pace with catches; then whalemen, having hunted the blue whale nearly to extinction, turned their full attention to "razorbacks." Things have calmed down somewhat since 1965, but the damage has already been done: 671,092 fin whales taken between 1904–05 and 1965–66!

The following chart outlines the distribution and approximate range of the eight fin whale populations in the Antarctic (R. Gambell, 1975):

| *Stock* | *Summering Grounds* | *Antarctic Wintering Grounds* |
|---|---|---|
| Chile-Peru | West of Chile and Peru | 110° W–60° W |
| South Georgia | East of Brazil | 60° W–25° W |
| West Africa | West of Africa | 25° W–0° |
| East Africa | East of Africa | 0°–40° E |
| Crozet-Kerguelen | East of Madagascar | 40° E–80° E |
| West Australia | North of Western Australia | 80° E–110° E |
| East Australia | Coral Sea | 140° E–170° E |
| New Zealand | Fiji Sea | 170° E–145° W |

Some experts maintain that a ninth, "mid-Indian" cluster winters in the vicinity of the Maldive Islands and heads toward summering grounds between 110° E and 130° E.

According to R. Gambell (1975, quoting D. B. De Lury), the total fin whale population in the southern hemisphere originally stood at more than 400,000. By 1958 there were 180,000 left; by 1975 the figure had dropped to 80,000. The current estimate is about 100,000.

*SEI WHALE*

Systematic, intensive exploitation of the swift, dusky sei whale did not get under way until 1960, at which time the hunt began on both sides of the equator. From the 1964–65 season on, sei whales became the primary target of pelagic whaling in the Antarctic.

Although sei whales have long been hunted in the vicinity of Iceland, information about the size of the North Atlantic population is sketchy. We do know (according to P. B. Best, 1975) that in winter seis can be found off Venezuela and Senegal; that generally they do not head back to very high latitudes in the summer (although individuals have been sighted west of Spitsbergen, at 79° N); that in the 1930s the species was plentiful from the Faroes to Norway, but shifted more and more to Icelandic waters from 1948 on; and that a spotty count in the Labrador Sea yielded a figure of 800 individuals. The general estimate for the entire sei population in the North Atlantic is about 3,000. Not enough is known about the population to give a breakdown by stocks.

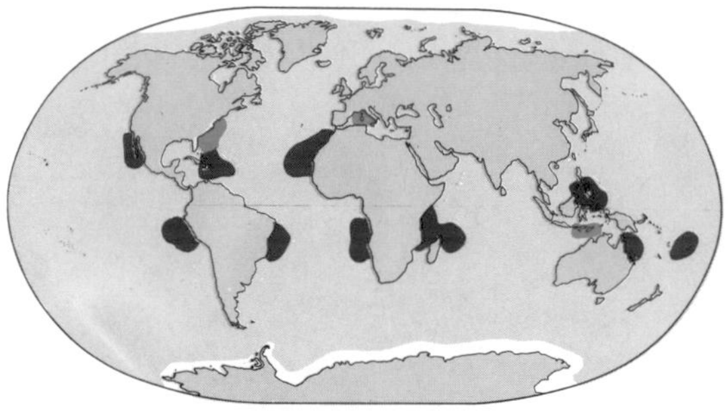

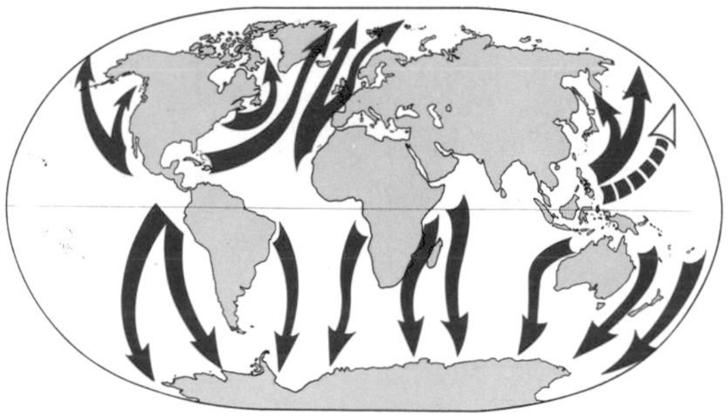

Fin Whale

Reliable data about North Pacific stocks are just as scarce. Sei whales have been seen wintering as far east as Central America and as far west as Indonesia and New Guinea. Sightings in summer have been reported in a huge quadrilateral roughly defined by connecting Taiwan, Kamchatka, Vancouver Island, and northern California. That is all we know. The original population was between 50,000 and 60,000; today there are probably no more than 18,000 left.

In the southern hemisphere—for all intents and purposes, the Antarctic—no fewer than 87,284 sei whales were slaughtered between 1905–06 and 1965–66; an average of 6,000 were taken every season from 1969 to 1979 alone. The pre-exploitation size of this stock has been estimated at between 130,000 and 180,000. According to the F.A.O., 52,500 individuals were still alive in 1969. In June of that year, J. A. Gulland submitted a more optimistic figure of 73,400 at the annual meeting of the I.W.C. in London. The Japanese, to many people's astonishment, claimed that 150,000 to 250,000 sei whales still plied the seas! Nowadays, it is generally acknowledged that 70,000–75,000 sei whales survive south of the equator.

We are as ignorant of the distribution of sei whale stocks in the southern hemisphere as we are of their numbers. It has been suggested that there is a separate group in each of the six rather arbitrary zones into which Antarctica has been carved. This, however, is pure speculation. Apparently some cruise along the coast of Peru and Chile to the Galápagos Islands; others shuttle between the Falkland Islands and Brazil by way of the Argentine coastline; still others follow the coast of Namibia and Angola to the Gulf of Guinea; and a last group heads past southern Africa and either side of Madagascar on its way to the Gulf of Oman. However, that is pretty much the extent of what we know about the range of the species.

Sei Whale

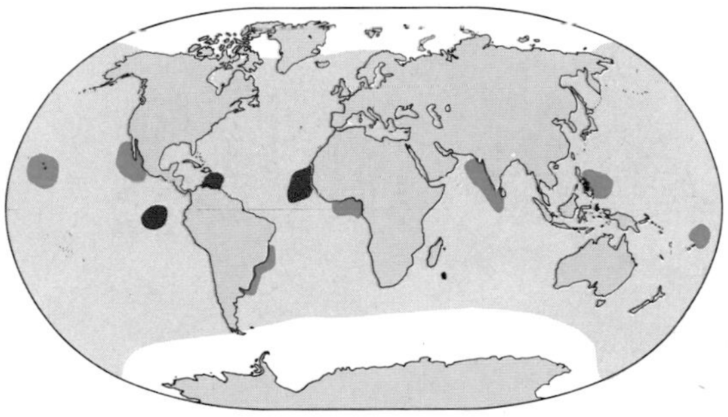

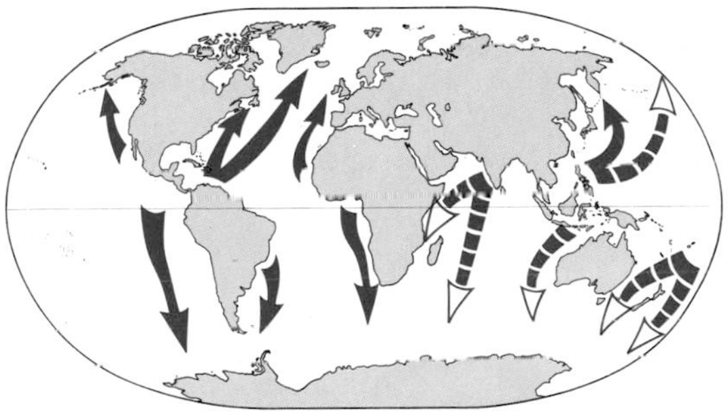

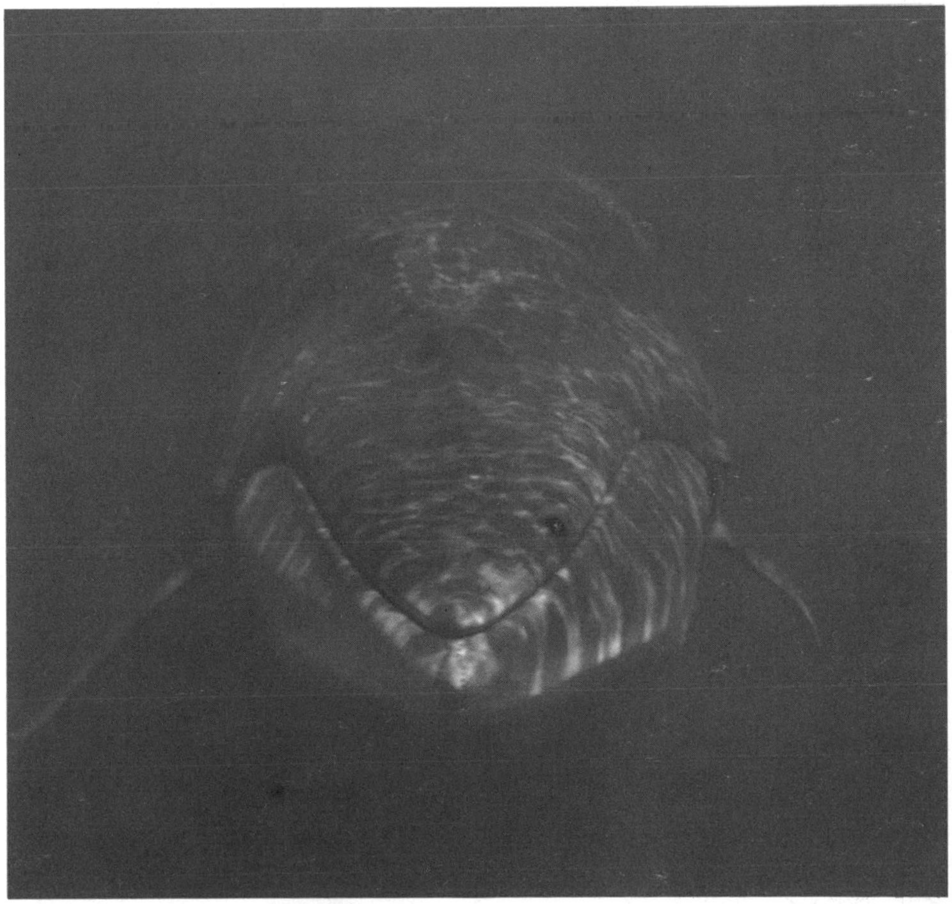

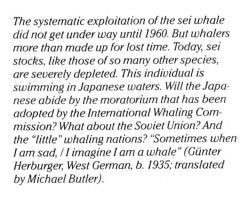

*The systematic exploitation of the sei whale did not get under way until 1960. But whalers more than made up for lost time. Today, sei stocks, like those of so many other species, are severely depleted. This individual is swimming in Japanese waters. Will the Japanese abide by the moratorium that has been adopted by the International Whaling Commission? What about the Soviet Union? And the "little" whaling nations? "Sometimes when I am sad, / I imagine I am a whale" (Günter Herburger, West German, b. 1935; translated by Michael Butler).*

*BRYDE'S WHALE*

Not much is known about this retiring, prepossessing whale, except that it is naturally scarce and that its range is defined primarily by the limits of the 20°C isotherm—that is, the species is intertropical. Yet, from 1965 to 1980, whalemen exploited Bryde's whales in increasing numbers just the same.

According to one questionable estimate, there were approximately 15,000 to 19,000 Bryde's whales in Japanese waters between 1955 and 1962. Today, more than 18,000 survive in the region. Only one other stock—the one off the western coast of South Africa—has been targeted for a census. Originally it may have numbered some 9,000 to 10,000; the current population is believed to be half that. Many cetologists are of the opinion that today there are more than 80,000 Bryde's whales worldwide.

The species is thought to be distributed into a number of distinct geographic areas (P. B. Best, 1975). One near-shore group is centered around the Gulf of Mexico and Florida, ranging from the Chesapeake Bay to the southernmost West Indies to the south. In the North Pacific, there is a near-shore stock off the west coast of Kyushu and in the east China Sea; a central pelagic stock from Japan to the Bonin Islands; and another coastal stock off Mexico and California that cruises as far north as La Jolla. An eastern group in the South Pacific shuttles between Chile and the Galápagos Islands, and a western group travels from Australia to Fiji and Polynesia. In the South Atlantic, there is a near-shore stock off Brazil, a pelagic stock migrating between Brazil and southern Africa, and a coastal stock that shuttles between the Cape of Good Hope and the mouth of Orange River. A "western" group lives in the Indian Ocean off the eastern coast of South Africa; it migrates to the Seychelles by way of Madagascar. A near-shore group ranges from the Bay of Bengal to Sumatra and Java, and another near-shore group makes its way along the west coast of Australia to western New Guinea and Timor.

*Both blowholes wide open, a Bryde's whale surfaces for air in the Sea of Cortez. To what depths will it take that big, sleek body, that knowing look, that flawless mammalian structure that left* terra firma *for the primordial seas? "Under the ever-moving, mighty dreams, / You sound our seas, / Powers, strong angels of the world" (Kathleen Raine, British, b. 1908).*

Bryde's Whale

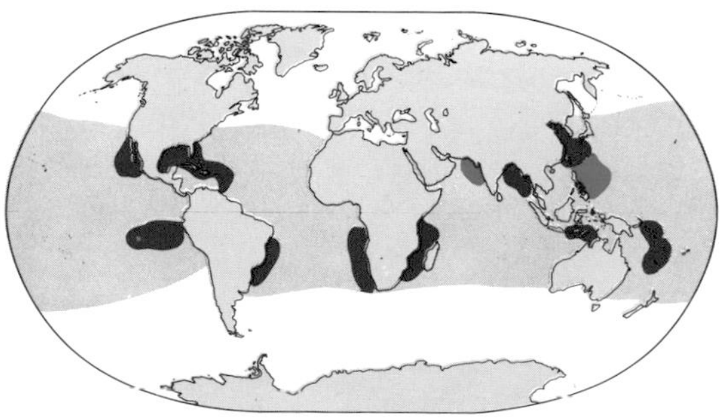

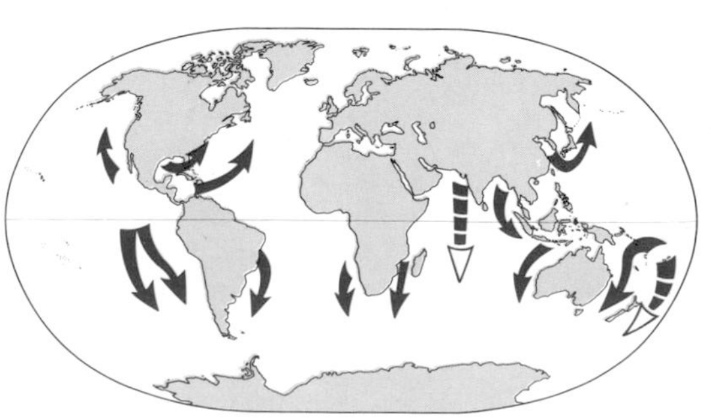

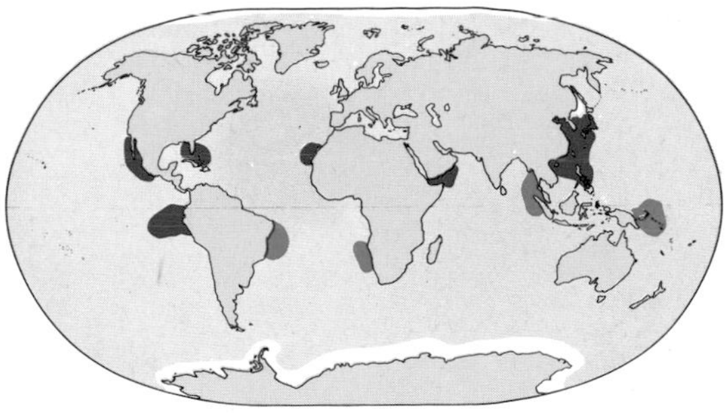

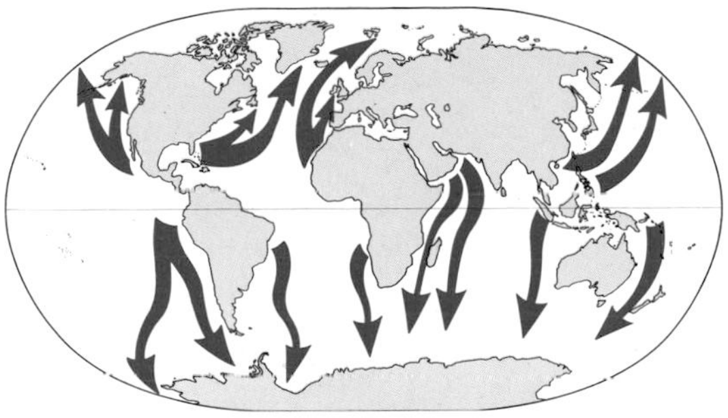

Minke Whale

*MINKE WHALE*

At first, the killing of larger cetaceans worked to the advantage of the diminutive, frisky minke whale. Ultimately, however, it too fell victim to the ruthless grenade harpoon. We have little in the way of solid information about the species. Scarce in the tropics proper, minke whales are distributed in all waters, but securing an accurate census is difficult, as they swim right up to ships, vitiating direct counts tremendously. The minke is a wide-ranging species. In summer, individuals are seen threading their way through leads in the pack ice; in winter, they are seen along continental and island coasts.

Norwegians initiated a systematic, mechanized minke fishery in the Atlantic at the end of World War II. In the North Pacific, the Japanese, Koreans, and Chinese did most of the killing. But whaling nations the world over declared open season on minkes in the Antarctic; between 1970 and 1974, over 18,500 were taken.

The North Atlantic population is thought to be divided into an eastern stock—found from Morocco to Scotland in winter, and Iceland to Norway and the Barents Sea in summer—and a western stock, which lives off Florida in winter, and from Cape Cod to Greenland in summer. The size of these two groups is not known.

A similar east-west division is believed to exist in the North Pacific, where a Mexico-California group summers around Alaska and the Bering Strait, while another group winters around the Philippines, Japan, and Korea, migrating in summer to the Sea of Okhotsk and the east coast of Kamchatka.

South of the equator, the minke's migration corridors roughly coincide with those of the fin whale. All Southern hemisphere minke whales spend the summer in Antarctic waters. In the winter, a number of groups go their separate ways. One group is found off Chile and Peru. The East African stock is subdivided into a local group that cruises west of Madagascar to the Gulf of Aden, and another that veers east of Madagascar on its way to Sri Lanka. There are also Brazilian and New Zealand stocks. As we mentioned earlier in this chapter, Ohsumi, Masaki, and Kawamura estimated the minke whale population in the Antarctic at 70,000 in 1970 and 150,000 in 1972! According to others, there are between 110,000 and 390,000 minke whales south of 20° S. In the opinion of a great many cetologists, however, there are probably 150,000 to 300,000 minke whales worldwide, with 200,000 as the likeliest figure.

*The swift, playful, comical, mischievous minke whale may have countless secrets to share with us, if only we were its friends and understood its language.*

*My whales are not*
*the dream symbols of Jonah or Melville;*
*they are living hyperboles that flow rejoicing*
*in the ineffable submarine sport . . .*
*islands that dance so, changing course*
*responsive one to another,*
*as the petals of time unfold.*
*(Jaime García Terrés, Mexican, b. 1924; translated by Margaret Cullen)*

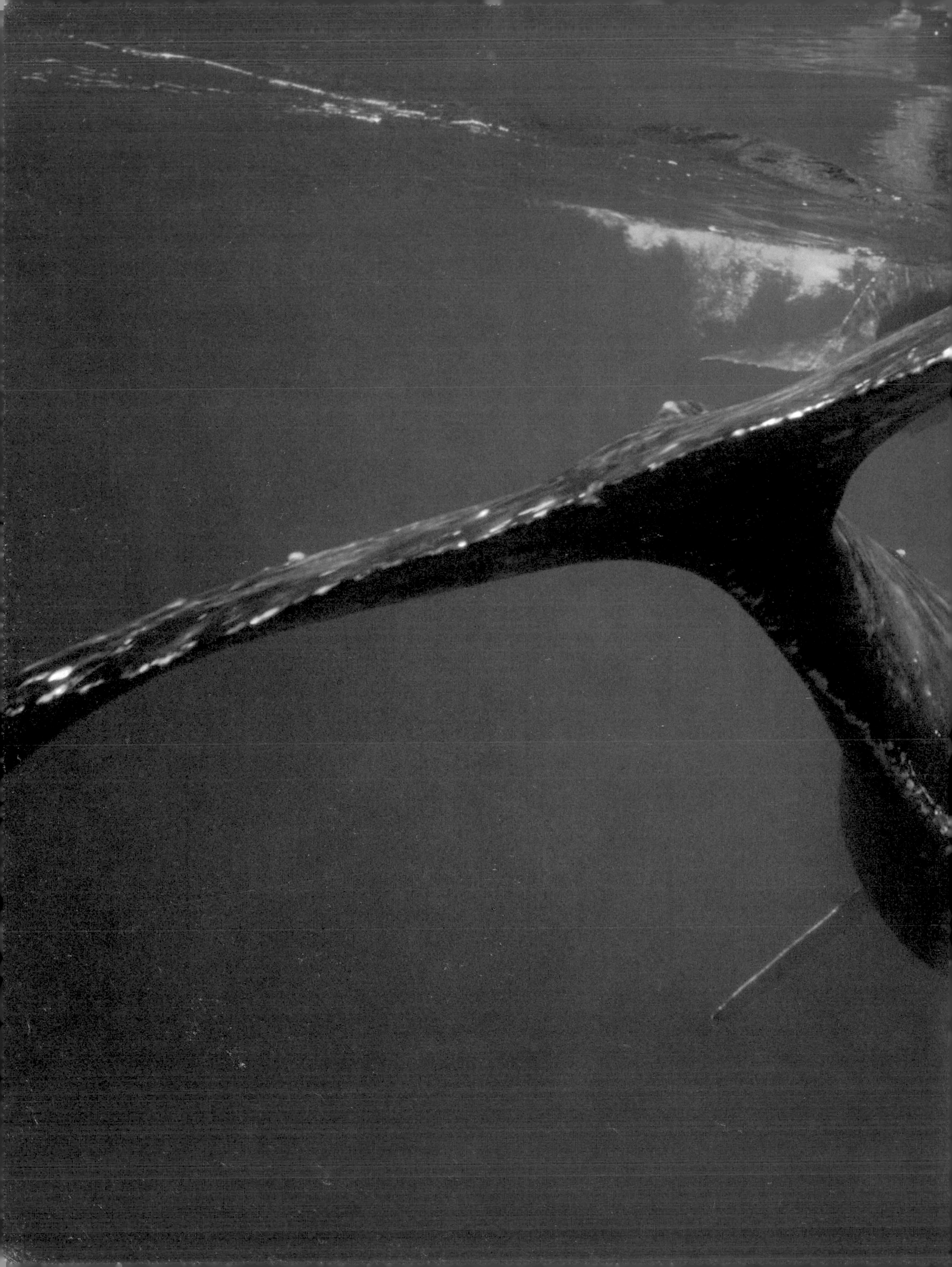

*HUMPBACK WHALE*

Of all the balaenopterids, humpbacks yield the most oil for their size. Consequently, they have suffered more than any other baleen whale. Thanks to Svend Foyn and his specially-mounted harpoon gun, tens of thousands of them ended up in the try-pots. Case in point: from 1904–05 to 1965–66, the total humpback catch in Antarctica was officially put at 145,424, or nearly 2,400 a year. During the 1910–11 season, more than 6,000 of them were taken in the vicinity of South Georgia alone! Though fully protected since 1967, the species is, unfortunately, subject to subsistence hunting and pirate harpooning.

The distribution of the humpback whale is virtually worldwide. The slaughter in the North Atlantic was so swift and so ruthless that it is difficult even to imagine what preexploitation conditions in the region may have been. In all likelihood, there were two fairly small original stocks, each probably subdivided into smaller local stocks. In winter, the eastern Atlantic population is believed to have split up into two groups, one around the Canary and Cape Verde islands, with summering grounds around Scotland and Norway, and an Azores group with a summer migration to Iceland, the tip of Greenland, and as far north as the Arctic Ocean. The western Atlantic subgroup, ranging in winter from Guyana to the West Indies and Bermuda, migrated in the spring to New England, Newfoundland, through the Davis Strait, and into the Arctic Ocean. A single intensive whaling season (1915) practically wiped out these stocks, which originally numbered only 5,000 individuals. Today, the eastern Atlantic group consists of a discouraging 100 specimens, while just a few thousand are thought to ply the waters of the western Atlantic.

The North Pacific stocks, at first even more widely scattered than their counterparts in the Atlantic, had been steadily depleted by American and Japanese whalemen since the nineteenth century, but things took a dramatic turn for the worse in the 1950s. It is thought that humpbacks in the region were once distributed in four groups. The first wintered around the Moluccas, the Philippines, and Japan, traveling in summer toward Kamchatka, the Bering Strait, and into the Arctic Ocean. The Marshall, Mariana, and Caroline islands were the wintering grounds of the second group, which headed for the Aleutians in the spring. The third followed a parallel route, but started out from Hawaii and ended up along the coast of Alaska. The fourth and last group spent the winter near Mexico and the island of Guadalupe,

*The humpback—the singing whale, the Caruso of the deep—is stockier than other rorquals. This made it all the more attractive to whalers, who lost no time bringing the species to the brink of demographic disaster. How splendid a humpback looks as it slowly undulates underwater (preceding pages) or (above) brings its tail crashing down against the ocean surface! "The whale is life incarnate," wrote French poet Jean-Paul de Dadelsen in* Jonah *(1962). "The whale is creation . . . Whales are always bigger, always farther away. Take it from me, there is no getting away from them. They are a necessity."*

migrating in spring to Alaska and the Bering Strait. All of this is conjecture. At present, the vast reaches of the North Pacific are home to a severely depleted population of humpback whales. There may be 1,000 or so in the northeastern Pacific that summer in the Aleutians and Alaska. The northwestern group is estimated at nearly the same figure—not a hopeful level for recovery.

Nowhere were humpbacks more plentiful than in the southern hemisphere; nowhere was the carnage more horrifying. The original population of the group east of South America never exceeded 30,000—fully 27,000 of which perished between 1909 and 1915. By 1934 this population was nearly extinct; it is estimated at perhaps 170. The group in the southeastern Indian Ocean still numbered 12,000–16,000 in 1934; by 1962 it had plummeted to 200 at the most, and it may have risen to 340 today. Likewise, the southeastern Pacific group dropped from 10,000 in 1934 to between 200 and 500 in 1962. Out of a preexploitation population of several tens of thousands in the Antarctic, only 1,500–3,000 survive.

Humpback Whale

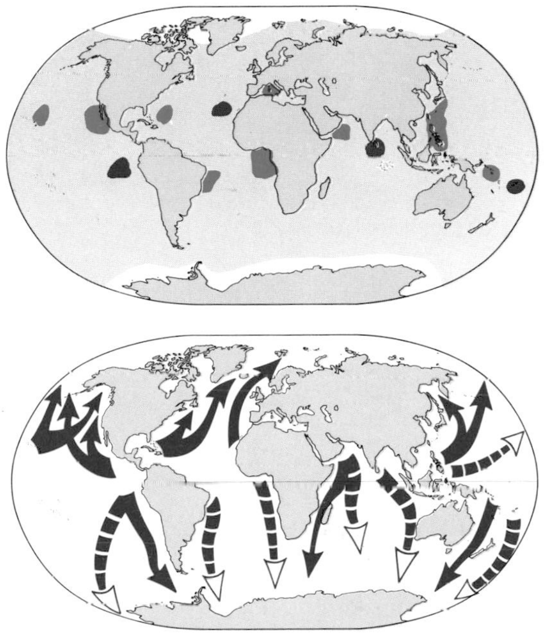

Even this remnant stock may still be subdivided into as many as nine subgroups. The first summers between Tierra del Fuego and the Antarctic peninsula and heads toward the coast of Brazil in the fall. The second starts out from the northern Weddell Sea and also winters off Brazil. The third travels from the Antarctic to the Gulf of Guinea by way of the West African coast. The fourth departs from the same summering grounds as the others, but veers east of Africa, skirts Madagascar, and pauses at the Comoro Islands, after which some individuals press northward to the entrance of the Gulf of Aden and the Persian Gulf. The fifth sets out from Antarctic waters, cruises along the west coast of Australia, and completes its intrepid 3,600-mile migration to the Malabar Coast by way of Indonesia. The sixth group opts for an east Australian route, destination New Guinea. The seventh sets out from the Antarctic and cruises along either side of New Zealand before proceeding to New Caledonia. The more widely scattered eighth group summers in the open waters of the Ross Sea and in the spring follows a number of migration corridors toward Samoa, the Tuamotu Islands, and Easter Island. The ninth, which summers in the same Antarctic waters as the first, rides the Humboldt current, drifting toward the open waters off Ecuador and the Galápagos by way of Chile and Peru.

At any rate, that is the way it must have been. For the time being, the few signs of recovery the southern humpback stocks have shown are more than offset by other, more disconcerting observations.

*SPERM WHALE*

The socially sophisticated sperm whale, with its harem schools and subtle hierarchies, provides an even more compelling example of how whaling, if it had to take place at all, would have been better off sparing breeding groups—that is, using biological parameters instead of geographical ones. The biological unit—the only entity able to breed, migrate, locate food, defend itself, play, and do everything that goes along with living—has taken a back seat to the notion of "exploitable stock," which is subject to miscalculation, hit-or-miss counting techniques, questionable extrapolations from marker data, and biased reporting.

Hundreds of thousands of sperm whales still ply the waters of the globe, perhaps 500,000 to 1 million. This may seem like a great many, but that figure is misleading in two respects. First, a substantial number belong to small groups that may be below the sustainable level; it stands to reason that a hundred stocks of ten individuals each are in a more precarious situation than ten stocks of a hundred individuals each. Biologists are currently studying certain clusters that albeit depleted by only 50 percent over a century ago, show signs of depressed pregnancy rates and still have not managed to regain preexploitation levels. (This may also reflect the sperm whale's pattern of sometimes forming groups by sex or by stage of maturity.) Second, when a cetologist counts sperm whales, there is no guarantee that some other cetologist has not already counted the same individuals. There are documented cases of sperm whales that have been wounded off Peru only to turn up on the East Coast of the United States.

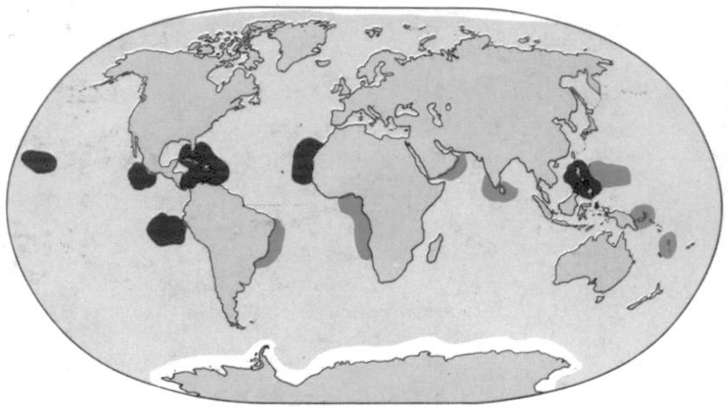

Sperm Whale

The population of sperm whales in the North Atlantic is still trying to make a comeback from the harrowing spate of overfishing in the nineteenth century that nearly extirpated the species (P. B. Best, 1975). We do not know if their numbers are on the rise. Catches have been suspended since 1981, so cetologists rely primarily on extrapolated data from encounters reported by commercial vessels. Very few individuals are ever sighted within the Arctic Circle; those that are invariably are full-grown bulls. However, Slijper et al. (1964) report fairly heavy concentrations off northwestern Africa, around the Azores, in the Caribbean Sea, and within a horizontal swath situated roughly between 30° and 50° N. Mitchell (in P. B. Best, 1975) maintains that another high-density zone lies north of the Sargasso Sea, and that there may be another off the coast of Guinea. One of the most reliable estimates puts the current population density in the North Atlantic at 2.48 individuals per 1,000 square miles, or 21,550 sperm whales over 8,688,895 square miles. A somewhat more optimistic count claims that a total of 27,000 sperm whales may survive in the whole of the North Atlantic.

In the North Pacific, where the battle with Moby-Dick was joined, sperm whales are probably distributed in three stocks (P. B. Best, 1975). The Asiatic (western) stock, confined to a range west of 170° E, is densest in the coastal waters of Japan, the Kuril Islands, Kamchatka, and the Bonin Islands. The "central" stock lives between 170° E and 150° W, and as far north as the Aleutians. The American (eastern) stock does not venture west of 150° W. Of course, cetologists believe that there is considerable overlapping along the borders of these watery territories and that the major stocks are split up into a great many "harems." An occasional lone bull may stray into the vicinity of the Bering Strait, but no seaman has ever reported sighting a sperm whale in the Arctic Ocean.

In the Pacific as in the Atlantic, the demographic data are shrouded in uncertainty at the present time. Some experts maintain that there are 30,000–35,000 males north of 40° N; others, 37,000–38,000 south of 50° N. A few world estimates seem to be on the low side (60,000–90,000 males and females for the whole of the

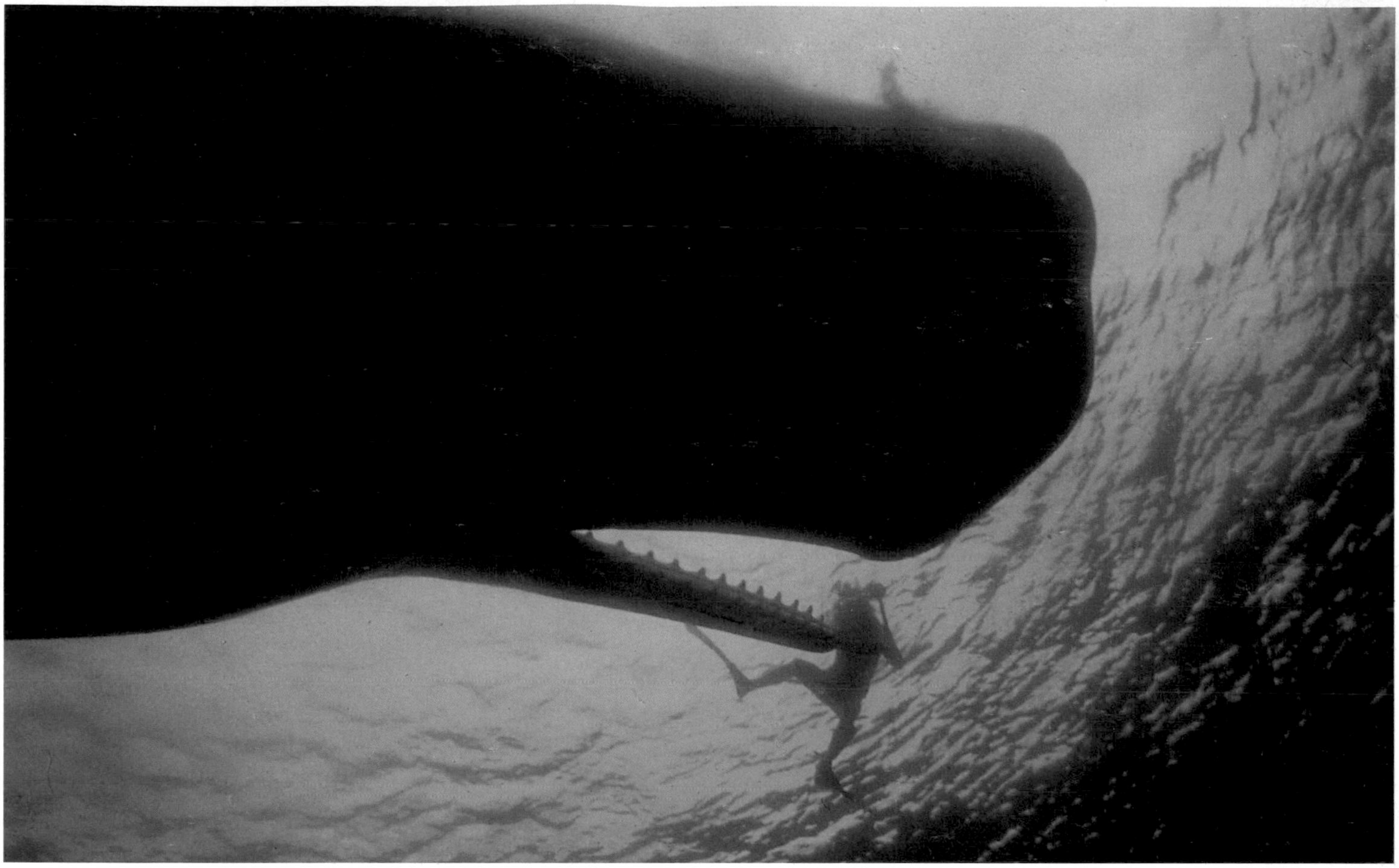

*No seafarers stood more in awe of the sperm whale than whalers themselves. Unlike right whales, they never allow themselves to be taken without a struggle. As Melville (1851) noted, "I am horror-struck at this antemosaic, unsourced existence of the unspeakable terrors of this whale." Actually, the whale has more reason to be "horror-struck" than we, given what we have done to it. Opposite: A pod of sperm whales near the Galápagos Islands. Above: A lesson in the comparative size of man and whale. But this sperm whale is not about to devour a diver, appearances notwithstanding. It has been harpooned by whalers in the Azores and is already dead.*

North Pacific); other estimates are too unrealistically optimistic (250,000 mature females alone!). As an example, one study (Ohsumi and Fukuda, 1974) puts the original number of bulls for the entire region at 167,000 and the current population at 63,000. Chapman (1977) estimates current populations at 118,000 for males and 210,000 for females. According to some estimates, only 37.7 percent of the original male population survives, compared with 83 percent of the female population. It is bad enough that these massacres—English-speaking whalemen prefer to call them "recruitments"—have taken such a heavy toll. But worse is the disparity between male and female catches, which further contributes to population imbalance (and gives the lie to the misguided anthropomorphic belief that it is inherently preferable to spare the women and children).

The benchmark for calculating the original populations of sperm whales south of the equator is 1964, although whalemen were active in the region long before that. Even experts refuse to vouch for the reliability of estimates (P. B. Best, 1975), which range from a low total of 216,000 (both sexes) all the way to 360,000 bulls and 300,000 cows. The first is undoubtedly more accurate than the other two! A realistic estimate might be 330,000 sperm whales in 1964, reduced to 295,000 ten years later in the wake of a resumption of intensive whaling in the southern hemisphere.

Sperm whales south of the equator summer in subpolar waters and migrate north in winter for breeding. (Females and young tend to remain in warmer waters.) They are believed to be distributed in nine groups, reflected in the geographical divisions established by the I.W.C. for population management: two Atlantic groups; an East Australian group; a New Zealand group; groups in the central and eastern Pacific; and—by far the strongest and most important—an Indian Ocean population of eastern, central, and western groups.

## THE STRANGLEHOLD OF POLLUTION AND DEVELOPMENT

Whale populations have fallen sharply the world over. For some local stocks, the outlook is as bleak as ever. One way to increase their chances of survival would be to abide by the moratorium (or zero quota) to bring all forms of whaling to an immediate and unconditional halt. A permanent moratorium would be indispensable—but inadequate.

Whales have always been wonderfully adapted to their environment; they still are. However, the butchery they have had to endure has increased their susceptibility to random or regular fluctuations in their marine habitat (temperature, salinity, etc.). If we are sincere about shifting our priorities from slaughtering cetaceans to saving them, then we must learn more about their ecology. Yet, as if our inexcusable ignorance were not bad enough, we exacerbate the plight of the survivors.

Pollution, of course, is taking up where the harpoon gun left off. Cetaceans constantly ply the ocean surface and are apparently more sensitive to oil slicks than other marine organisms, often avoiding them when possible. They may absorb the residue into their respiratory and digestive tracts. Right whales that skim krill in the Arctic Ocean could be placed in jeopardy by an oil well break in Alaska, which might clog their baleen bristles. The infamous Santa Barbara oil spill did not improve the lot of California gray whales, and they probably do not take kindly to the sheets of hydrocarbons released by the ports of San Diego, Los Angeles, San Francisco, and Seattle. Whales have had to run a gauntlet of oil blobs left over from spills in Brittany (*Torrey Canyon, Amoco Cadiz*), the North Sea (*Ekofisk*), the Gulf of Mexico (*Ixtoc I*), the Persian Gulf, and off the coast of South Africa. Not to mention the fact that hardly a square mile of ocean surface has not already been fouled by tankers, boat engines, and waste runoff from cities and highways.

Unfortunately, petrochemicals are not the only noxious substances we dump into the sea. Industrial waste includes PCBs (polychlorinated biphenyls), the disastrous effects of which on embryos and juveniles of many species have been well documented; PVCs (polyvinyl chlorides); dioxin; acrolein; and other toxic compounds too numerous to mention. Then we have the heavy metals and radioactive isotopes. Abnormal levels of arsenic, lead, cadmium, chromium, and zinc have been detected in some of the lagoons where whales feed or breed. Dutch experiments have demonstrated that sublethal levels of DDT and PCBs affect reproduction in harbor seals. Science must expand its efforts to include monitoring the effects of these toxins on large cetaceans.

Since whales are at the top of their food chain, their tissues accumulate the toxic residue that plants and animals at lower levels pass up through the chain, increasing in concentration at successive levels. Industrial, chemical, and nuclear waste are not the only culprits; municipal effluents also contain compounds that can build up to dangerous levels. Agricultural pesticides are washed into rivers and out to sea, ultimately showing up in the bodies of whales. The blubber of one California gray whale was found to contain 0.50 p.p.m. (parts per million) of DDT, while for some sperm whales the figure was as high as 8.90 p.p.m. For dieldrin, another insecticide, the proportions were 0.075 p.p.m. for grays and 0.019 p.p.m. for sperm whales.

Denise Viale conducted a comprehensive study (1976) of contaminants in the western Mediterranean Sea and their direct impact on whales in the region. The Ligurian and Tyrrhenian seas were found to be cesspools of waste from surface

*Harpooning is not the only crime man has perpetrated on whales. He is forever devising new ways of usurping or polluting the very habitats in which whales congregate to feed, frolic, mate, calve, and raise their young. We realign the coastline, dig harbors, and dump toxic waste from homes, farms, and factories; and all these activities affect the health and demographic stability of the few whale stocks that have managed to elude the harpoon gun. Below: A beached rorqual—a powerful, almost metaphysical commentary on the consequences of the productivity mania on which our civilization prides itself.* "Has the hunt for this mountain / of blubber come to an end?" *(Jean Orizet, French, from* En soi le chaos, *1975)*

mines, toxic refuse from cities and farms, industrial waste, and contaminants dumped into rivers. Autopsies of whale carcasses revealed "hydrocarbon boluses and assorted bits of plastic in the stomach." The most serious threat, however, came from pollution on the high seas. At the time Viale was conducting her research, Montedison, an Italian firm that manufactures titanium dioxide, was dispatching sludge-laden barges to "dumping grounds" sixty kilometers off Cape Corsica. Here, 3,000 tons of sulfuric acid, iron compounds, magnesium, manganese, vanadium, chromium, and other pollutants were being "disposed of" each and every day. "There has been a noticeable increase in the incidence of strandings in the Mediterranean, particularly along the coast of Corsica," she noted. "From May 1972 to May 1974, twenty-four dead or injured whales (including eight rorquals) were reported, whereas the average number of beached rorquals in Corsica since 1670 has been on the order of two every three years. This increase cannot be ascribed to chance."

Although a lack of sufficiently broad data prevents scientists from demonstrating between toxin concentrations and strandings, any such abnormality merits investigation. Among Viale's findings were integuments saturated with "a red substance visible to the naked eye"; iron buildup in the liver, muscles, and lungs; and highly abnormal levels of titanium, chromium, and vanadium in tissues. Worse still, all of these contaminants may have a synergistic effect: they reinforce each other's toxicity, or in combination produce a new effect. For example, mercury in metal form is not overly dangerous, but in the presence of an acid (as in the specimen examined), it produces ethylmercury and methylmercury—organic compounds that can incapacitate or even kill in minute concentrations.

Denials by industrial concerns notwithstanding, Viale correctly concluded that "there could be no escaping the link between the increase in the number of whale strandings and the increase in pollution." And what is true of the Mediterranean is true of other bodies of water. Industrial and agricultural hydrocarbons are found in all the oceans of the world, and—more and more—evidence of trace elements and chlorinated hydrocarbons is being discovered.

Medpoll (1977), the Cousteau team's scientific survey of the Mediterranean Sea, revealed that pollution was not the chief factor in the overall decline in the quality of marine life. An even greater threat comes from the disruption of ecosystems by development.

An unenviable fate awaits the whales we do not harpoon, as well as the fish we fail to trap in our purse seines. We are dredging new marinas and commercial ports in places where whales have always come to feed, frolic, or breed. Every time we encroach on biologically critical areas—mating grounds, breeding grounds for plankton, spawning grounds for fish—we are indirectly mistreating one whale species or another. New steamship lines, stepped-up urbanization of the coastline, breakneck industrial, residential, and recreational development, airports built out over the water, marinas, offshore drilling rigs—these and countless other manifestations of our destructive mania for "growth" are doing irreparable damage to the ocean environment in general and to whale habitats in particular.

Coastal areas, including the highly productive strip of marine life known as wetlands, have borne the brunt of this onslaught. Home to algae as well as flowering plants (such as eelgrass), wetlands are the sea's lungs, pantry, and nursery rolled into one.

The ocean can be compared to a vast desert, dotted here and there with oases bursting with life: areas of upwelling (where nutrient-rich bottom waters are

Whales now have friends the world over. Research teams track them on the open sea, not to increase catch efficiency, but to better understand them in their native habitat. Above: Engine turned off, a motor launch from the Cousteau ship has a close encounter with a right whale off Peninsula Valdés, Argentina. Groups of lay observers—whalewatchers—have formed in the United States, Europe, Australia, and New Zealand.

drawn to the surface), salt marshes, coral reefs, and coastal wetlands. The latter oxygenate the water, provide food for larvae, juveniles, and adults, and serve as sanctuaries for a wide variety of species. In their remarkable study of the coastal wetlands of the Mediterranean, A. Meinesz and C. Boudouresque (1983) noted that plant fragments swept down by currents toward the ocean floor constitute the "primary source" of food for benthic (botton-dwelling) organisms. Without this vegetation, there would be no giant squid in the ocean depths. Since sperm whales feed on giant squid, it may be said that colossal odontocetes also depend on healthy wetlands.

## WITH FRIENDS LIKE THAT . . .

The more man scours the oceans for sources of protein and profit, the more he enters into direct competition with whales. In winter, when nutrition is scarce, several species (especially rorquals) feed on herring, sardines, anchovies, and other varieties of fish that commercial trawlers have targeted for both the human and livestock markets. It has been noted that the taking of capelin in the North Atlantic interferes with relict populations of humpbacks, minke whales, and fin whales. The Cousteau team studied this phenomenon in the Gulf of St. Lawrence and off the coast of Newfoundland. Humpbacks deprived of their customary prey are venturing closer to shore, where they become fouled in fishermen's nets and drown.

To quote from the Preliminary Report on Large Cetaceans issued by the F.A.O. (1976): "Other commercially exploited fish that figure prominently in the diet of whales include: cod and herring for minke whales (North Atlantic); herring for fin whales (North Atlantic); chinchard, anchovy, and pilchard for Bryde's whales (southern Africa); mackerel, which supplements the sei's staple diet of copepods (North Pacific, southern band); anchovy and mackerel for Bryde's whales (North Pacific), . . ." And so on.

An even greater danger looms on the horizon. It is no secret that several countries are looking into the feasibility of harvesting krill in polar and subpolar waters. When this harvest develops into a full-blown industry, as sooner or later it must, it will hinder the recovery of a number of already severely depleted whale stocks and may have an adverse effect on even the hardiest species.

We are poisoning the sea, sterilizing its nurseries, rearranging its coastline, and plundering its schools of fish. Now we are eager to add its shoals of planktonic crustaceans to the booty. Isn't all of this enough to finish what the harpooners have left undone? Apparently not. Even military activity at sea is responsible for the death of whales. Despite protests, the navies of several nations actually use whales for target practice. Every year, dozens of cetacean carcasses are found riddled with shot and shrapnel, victims of a butchery that reaches new heights of folly. Moreover, the shooting is indiscriminate: protected species, unprotected species—anything will do.

But armed forces do not stop at taking potshots at whales. They dump toxic waste and "expired" (but still hazardous) chemical warfare agents, generate radioactive emissions from nuclear-powered submarines, and set off underwater explosions with catastrophic effects. Polaris rockets and other ICBMs fired from beneath the ocean's surface are capable of annihilating all marine life for miles around. Even the ceaseless noise generated by military fleets must be torture for whales and other creatures that are very sensitive to sound.

Lastly, we must come to grips with the fact that whales may well end up victimized by the very people who would befriend them. Off Nantucket, Cape Cod, Newfoundland, and in the Gulf of St. Lawrence, the "in" thing nowadays is to hop on a boat and marvel at humpbacks, fin whales, or blue whales. In these areas, whales are just "passing through," and human curiosity causes little disturbance. This is especially true for near-shore species, such as right whales, grays, and humpbacks. When certain species migrate, the tourist industry ferries sightseers out in chartered boats to gawk—for a fee, of course. Business is booming in San Diego, California, where every fall and spring some 300,000 people stationed on land or at sea turn out to watch migrating gray whales. More problematical, "nature safaris" to the breeding lagoons themselves are becoming popular. A similar fashion has cropped up along Peninsula Valdés in Argentina, where already 36,000 visitors flock each year to watch the arrival of right whales. Fortunately for the gray whales, the Mexican government seems to have sensed how dangerous these "friendly little outings" really are. Not only has sanctuary status been given to Ojo de Liebre (Scammon's Lagoon) and a number of other gray whale haunts, but all maritime traffic during the calving and nursing season has been banned. The general public has become increasingly attuned to nature, and that is a positive trend. But our interest in animals should always be tempered with respect; if not, even the best of intentions can backfire.

*People who have befriended the whales are speaking out against anyone still bent on doing them harm. The whales seem to be active participants in this detente; in these lagoons, some whales approach small boats and appear to solicit touching. The "friendlies" are often accompanied by their calves. One researcher (M. Dahlheim, 1984) has suggested that the noise of the outboard engines attracts the whales. If untempered, however, whalewatching zeal can also interfere with the animals' lives.*

## HARVESTING KRILL: AN INDUSTRY OF THE FUTURE?

*There is growing interest in the small, cold-water crustaceans collectively known as krill. Pound for pound, their highly nutritious flesh contains as much protein as red meat as well as a higher proportion of minerals and trace elements (calcium, iron, phosphorus, magnesium, zinc, and others). Krill is rich in vitamins A, B, and D; a carotenoid pigment that is a precursor of Vitamin A gives euphausiids their pinkish color. Krill consists of about 78 percent water, 5 percent ash and chitin, 4 percent fat, and 13 percent protein, although composition varies with the season and the proportion of* Euphausia superba *in the planktonic "soup." Its average caloric value is 500 kilocalories per pound.*

*For whales, krill is a staple food; for man, it is a potential source of wealth. The shrimp-like euphausiids are processed into a thick paste known as "krill cake" (100 pounds of krill are needed to make 60 pounds of "cake"). In some countries, krill is eaten whole, and krill tails are considered a delicacy. Japan and the Soviet Union were the first to promote krill as the "food of the year 2000." The by-products of a krill fishery (including carapaces, fats, pigments, and enzymes) could be used, among other things, in the manufacture of dyes, glues, cardboard, cosmetics, and pharmaceuticals. This promising industry has generated considerable interest in Poland, West Germany, Chile, and Norway.*

*Harvesting has already begun. A specially equipped West German vessel can remove krill from the sea at a rate of about 9 to 13 tons an hour, with an occasional 60-ton "spurt." During the 1980–81 summer season, a hundred Russian trawlers operating in the Antarctic harvested an estimated 1.1 million tons; the Japanese took another 15.4 tons. According to Chile's Secretary of Fisheries, 20 million tons of krill could be harvested annually in Antarctic waters without adversely affecting whales. That is a moot statement: some experts are already forecasting an annual crop of 100 to 150 million tons! All told, traditional fisheries worldwide take in only 70 million tons a year.*

*In 1991, the signatory nations of the Antarctic Treaty may take advantage of a scheduled revision to join forces and turn the industrial exploitation of krill into a reality. As usual, the advocates of plunder spout lofty ideals; they maintain that harvesting this "steak from the sea" will help feed the starving nations of the Third World. Don't be taken in: the cream of the catch will end up on the plates of the wealthy. The rest (that is, most of it) will be fed to livestock.*

*Most recently, the good news is that krill fishery is on the decline—for the simple reason that, to most of us, krill is unpalatable.* De gustibus non est disputandum.

## A DIFFICULT CHOICE

*Nothing is simple. Ecologists love whales. Ecologists also love alternative energy sources, such as tide-driven electricity. But whales and hydroelectric power do not necessarily mix.*

*Peninsula Valdés in Argentina separates the Gulf of San José from the Golfo Nuevo. Since the range between low and high tides there is on the order of 25 feet, the Gulf of San José would be an ideal location for a generating station (R. Gibrat, 1966).*

*However, the Gulf also happens to be one of the principal breeding and calving grounds of the southern right whale. If a dam were built, the whales would no longer venture into the bay.*

*Canadian authorities are faced with much the same dilemma. The powerful tides in the Bay of Fundy are a potential source of cheap energy. Unfortunately, it is also the home of the sole surviving stock of right whales in the North Atlantic.*

## TRAPPED AT SEA!

Whales feed on schools of sardines, capelin, herring, and other small fish. Occasionally, however, they follow their prey right into gigantic nets put out by trawlers to catch the very same fish. Consequently, increasing numbers of humpbacks, right whales, gray whales, rorquals, sperm whales, and dolphins are falling prey to these fatal traps.

Once entangled, the whales thrash about and occasionally work their way free —destroying the mesh in the process. More often than not, however, there is no escape and eventually they drown. Either way, the net is ruined. For fishermen, the losses are catastrophic. Villagers along the coast of Newfoundland and elsewhere near migration routes have few kind things to say about the hapless leviathans.

During the migration season, a few concerned individuals descend on the coasts most "at risk" and work with the fishermen. When a whale gets fouled in a net, they attempt to release it by cutting the mesh. At least the animal escapes unharmed, and the net can be salvaged. Scores of whales are freed this way every year.

It would be better, of course, if the whales did not get caught in nets in the first place. Research is now under way to see if the problem might be alleviated by enlisting the intelligence of the whales themselves, for they have complex brains and are more than capable of learning. Tests are being conducted to see if they can be trained to understand warning signals that convey the message "danger." It does not take long for whales to recognize beeps or ultrasonic signals from radio beacons attached to the nets. Many of them stop as soon as they hear the warning.

## DANGER: BOAT PROPELLERS

Fortunately, whaling is on the wane. But the decline in catch figures is offset by the rising incidence of individuals that are being wounded or maimed by boat propellers. They suffer deep gashes in the back or sides, torn dorsal fins, and occasionally a severed tail. If the injury is life-threatening, the wounded whales beach themselves and die.

Collisions with large ships pose the greatest threat. Huge 250,000-ton supertankers racing along at 20 knots create currents that literally suck in even the strongest of sea creatures. The captain may notice nothing more than a momentary loss of speed.

D. R. Patton (1980) counted fourteen such collisions between 1975 and 1980 off California alone. Five of the whales were never seen again; nine perished. The ships came out of it unscathed.

Nowadays it is not unusual to come across a whale with a severed tail. In California, Dr. Ray Gilmore (1961) alone found six "amputees": a humpback and five grays. Loss of the lower tail stock and the flukes need not prove fatal for a whale, which swims by moving its entire body up and down. According to Dr. Gilmore, a tailless gray whale that set out from San Diego on February 14, 1958, was sighted near Kodiak Island, Alaska, on May 3. It had traveled 3,000 to 3,500 miles, averaging 40 to 50 miles every twenty-four hours. Uninjured grays making the same migration cover 80 miles a day.

CHAPTER 4

# Adapting to a Watery Realm

*The whale, "this mountain in movement, this dance" (Walter Helmut Fritz, West German, b. 1929). The whale, "moving like clouds at the edge of the world" (Jenny Joseph, British, b. 1932). The entire ocean is their realm. They swim from continent to continent. As the order evolved, it acquired wonderful anatomical and physiological mechanisms that allow modern whales effortlessly to cope with the rigors of life in the water. Few areas of natural history are as exciting as that of cetacean adaptation. Below: Two fin whales about to sound, off the coast of Iceland.*

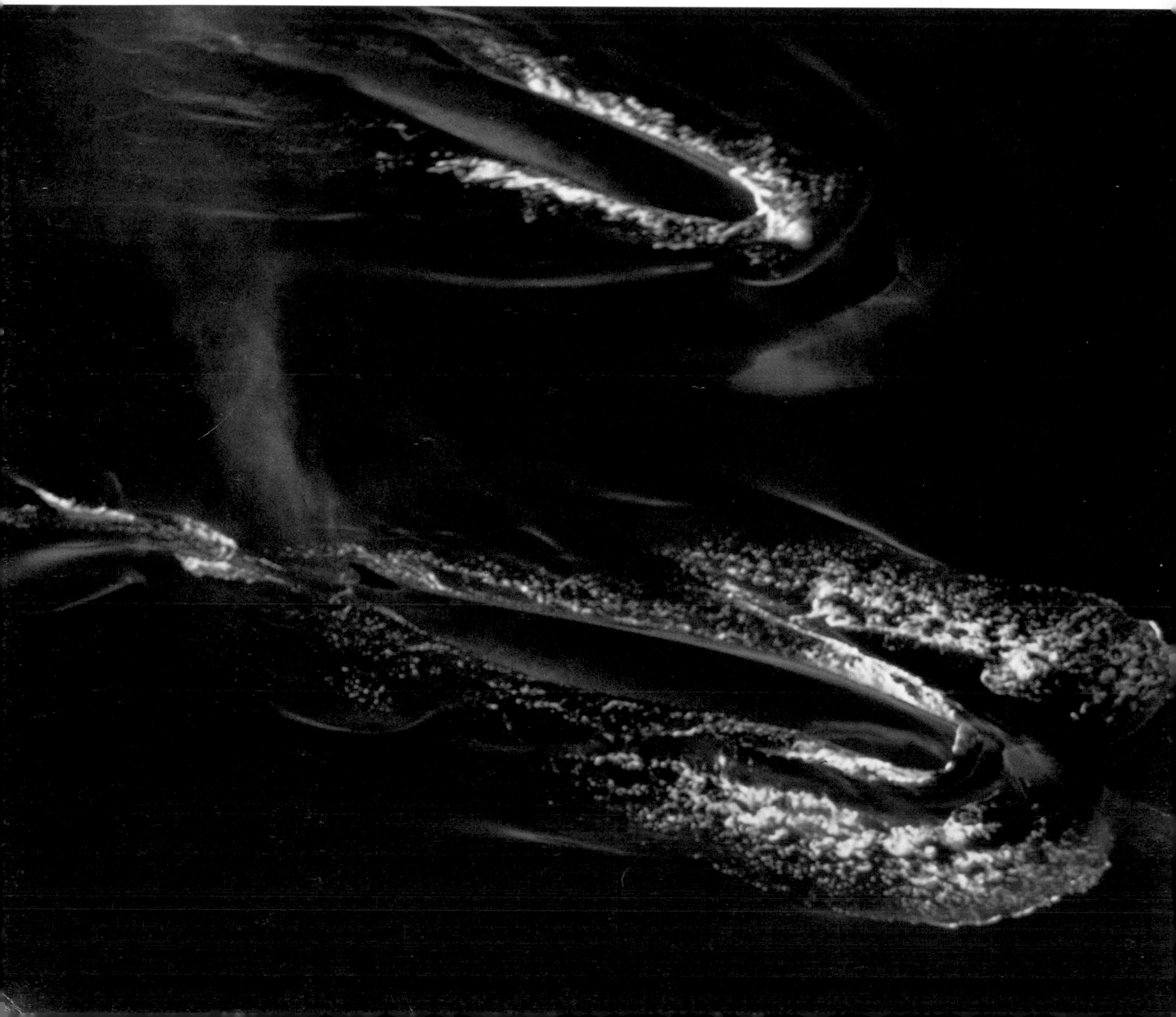

*Curiosity gets the better of us; we draw near to learn what we can. They live in the midst of the sea, like fish; yet they breathe like land species. They dwell in cold-water regions; yet they are warm-blooded and quick to react to the world around them. . . . They are huge; yet they can move about at great speed, even though they have only forelimbs and no feet as such. . . . Of all animals, none holds sway over so vast a dominion; their watery realm extends from the surface to the bottommost depths of the sea.* Lacépède (1804)

No treatise, poem, or painting can convey the overwhelming massiveness of a free-swimming whale. A 150-ton blue whale *is* a monster, but not because there is anything deformed, ungainly, or ferocious about it. One hundred fifty tons of fluidity—one of the most stupendous achievements ever shaped by the forces of nature. The blue whale's tail is broader than the average living room; its tongue alone would fill a bathroom. More than 100 tons of blood (about 2,500 gallons) course through its body. Its heart, encased in a ventricular wall nearly 2 feet thick, measures almost 4 feet across and weighs half a ton. Picture a pipe 18 inches across, and you have an idea of the size of its aorta. Its liver weighs more than a ton; so do the freshly ingested contents of its stomach.

Bulk and capaciousness on this scale give rise to formidable biological problems. How does this floating island propel and steer itself? How does it dive and effortlessly maneuver in crosscurrents? How does it obtain oxygen and nutrition? How does it maintain a steady body temperature? How does it defend itself from attack by parasites and predators?

The story of how whales have adapted to and interact with their environment—that is, their ecology—is just now starting to be told. Despite our centuries-old fascination with these creatures, our knowledge of their way of life is comparatively slim, and many ideas are just now being confirmed.

The first peculiarity is the fact that, like other mammals, these mammoth creatures start out as microscopic eggs comparable in size to that of a human being or a shrew. All the instructions needed to "program" a whale are encoded in twenty-one or twenty-two pairs of chromosomes, the threadlike strands of DNA (deoxyribonucleic acid) that carry and transmit hereditary characteristics. Contrary to what one would expect, there is no easy way to obtain fresh blood from large whales; but the procedure has been successfully carried out, and DNA analysis performed, with two species. Sei whales—and it seems, all baleen whales and most toothed whales—have twenty-two pairs of chromosomes: twenty-one pairs of autosomes and two sex chromosomes (XX for females, XY for males). Gibbons have the same number; *Homo sapiens*, one pair more. Sperm whales have only twenty-one pairs, as do baboons and rats.

## THE PARADOX OF SPEED

The so-called cetacean paradox—later named Gray's paradox after the biologist who first formulated it in 1936—states that cetaceans are theoretically not capable of generating the energy output that enables them to reach the speeds they actually do. Since physics alone cannot account for their prowess, cetaceans do indeed seem to defy the laws of hydrodynamics. However, before we attempt to reconcile the seemingly irreconcilable, let us review the facts.

There was a time when bowhead whales were thought capable of swimming as fast as 24 miles per hour. "So fleet is this cetacean," wrote Lacépède (1804), "that it leaves behind it a wake as wide and deep as that of a ship scudding in full sail. It can travel 11 meters a second. It is swifter than the trade winds." According to the more objective P.-J. van Beneden, "The consensus among whalemen is that it can cover a distance of 3 to 4 [English] miles (that is, 5 to 7 kilometers) in a hour." But he was quick to stress that they were capable of a sustained "escape speed" when persued, citing as proof the fact that "whales harpooned off Spitsbergen have turned up in the North Pacific" after crossing the Arctic Ocean. (In fact, just one such whale was recovered many years later.) Van Beneden was so convinced of the bowhead's swiftness under duress that it led him to incorrect conclusions about polar geography. "The whale can accelerate to high speeds, especially when wounded. Captain Graville tells of an individual wounded off the *east* coast of Greenland and reportedly sighted at the mouth of Omenak Fjord, on the *west* coast of Greenland, the very next day. Hence, a sound must divide Greenland across the middle."

Actually, bowheads cruise or migrate between 3 and 6.5 mph; they slow down to between 1 and 2. 5 mph when feeding. Although they can quicken the pace to 9 to 12 mph when threatened, they cannot keep it up for very long.

When it comes to speed, right whales are pretty much on par with bowheads. The gray whale, however, seems to be a somewhat more lethargic species. According to the crew of the *Calypso*, which clocked some grays under various conditions, their cruising speed is 4 or 5 knots (roughly 4.3 to 5.5 mph). When alarmed, they can double their speed.

Current estimates for blue whales suggest a sustained cruising speed of 3–10 mph and sprints of over 25 mph. The crew of the *Calypso* followed an 88-foot, 100-ton blue whale at 14 or 15 knots for two hours and found it could sustain a 20-knot sprint for ten minutes. The equally swift fin whale probably has even greater stamina; it can accelerate to 12 knots (over 13 mph) and hold that speed for forty minutes to an hour. It is believed that during the spring migration toward the poles, this species covers 2,400 miles in a month; that would bring its average speed (not allowing for rest periods) to over 4 mph. R. M. Laws (1961) estimated that migrating fin whales travel some 2,700 miles at an average (nonstop) speed of 4.5 mph.

For sheer speed sei whales seem able to outperform fin whales and even dolphins. By all accounts, sei whales can dart away in a flash and are capable of sprinting at 30 knots (33 mph). Brown (1971) notes that the species has phenomenal staying power. An individual marked one summer in the Antarctic reportedly was taken ten days later some 2,200 miles away; this would put its average speed, if it made the trip nonstop, at 10.2 mph.

*When a cetacean swims, it unwittingly scoffs at the laws of hydrodynamics. Assuming we confine ourselves to the accepted laws of objects moving through water, the speed whales achieve in water appears to be greater than the power output their muscles can produce. This phenomenon is known as Gray's paradox, after the British biologist who first advanced it. Above: Two gray whales set out on their 3,000-mile spring migration to the poles, where shoals of plankton await. Opposite: A minke whale spouting in waters off Hokkaido, Japan.*

Confirmed data about the speed of Bryde's whale is as scarce as information concerning all other aspects of the species. It can probably swim as fast as the blue or fin whale. The more frequently observed minke whale is comparatively slow when migrating but can move smartly when hunting fish.

As the crew of the *Calypso* has seen a number of times, the humpback is no match for other rorquals when it comes to speed. Although they can sustain a "burst" in excess of 10 knots if disturbed, humpbacks usually poke along at about 4 knots (4 mph). A female with a calf swims much more slowly; the pod, unwilling to leave her behind, lets her set the pace. Yet the slow-moving humpback is also one of the acrobats of the sea. And it could only leap above the surface if it were able to accelerate to a minimum of 18 mph for several dozen meters.

No one, however, disputes the humpback's endurance. Chittleborough's report (1956) of one humpback that covered 500 miles in six days is by no means unusual. Most humpbacks south of the equator travel more than 3,100 miles during every spring and fall migration, taking little time out to rest along the way. According to W. H. Dawbin (in K. S. Norris, 1966), migrating humpbacks cover almost 1,030 miles a month at an average nonstop speed of 1.4 mph.

Whether traveling alone or in a pod, sperm whales cruising at the surface move along at a leisurely 3 or 4 knots. (In 1874, Scammon clocked them at "three miles per hour.") As soon as they sense danger, however, they quicken their pace to an initial escape speed of 10 to 15 knots (11 to 16 mph), which can be sustained for more than an hour. If harpooned, an individual can spin out the line at 20 to 25 mph. Sperm whales harpooned in the vicinity of the Azores have been known to

SWIMMING SPEEDS OF WHALES (in mph)

| Species | Feeding | Cruising/Migrating | Fleeing |
|---|---|---|---|
| Bowhead | 1.2–2.5 | 3–6.5 | 10–12 |
| Right whale | 1.2–2.5 | 3–6.5 | 7–11 |
| Pygmy right whale | 1.2–2.5(?) | 3–6(?) | ? |
| Gray whale | 1.2–2.5 | 2.5–6 | 10–11 |
| Blue whale | 1.2–4 | 3–20 | 24–30 |
| Fin whale | 1.2–4 | 3–22 | 25–33 |
| Sei whale | 1.2–4 | 3–22 | 36–40 |
| Bryde's whale | 1.2–4 | 3–18 | 25.5 |
| Minke whale | 1.2–6 | 3–15.5 | 18–21 |
| Humpback | 1.2–2.5 | 3–9 | 15–16.5 |
| Sperm whale | 1.2–3.5 | 3–9 | 21–27 |

## HITCHING A RIDE ON A WAVE: BERNOULLI'S PRINCIPLE

*Whale calves learn to swim in no time. But how do they survive their first poleward migration of several thousand miles when they are only a few months old? How do they keep up with a mother trying to escape a pursuing whaler or some other danger? The answer may be that they use the backwash created by the moving adult to propel themselves. This is known as Bernoulli's Principle, named for Daniel Bernoulli (1700–82), the Swiss physicist who pioneered the science of hydrodynamics.*

*When the need for sustained or high-speed swimming arises, "calves place themselves slightly behind the point of maximum diameter of their parents, just below and beside the dorsal fin," notes Lyall Watson (1981). "The speed of water flow in the narrow channel between their bodies is increased, and the pressure in that area is correspondingly decreased, . . . increasing thrust (or decreasing drag) on the smaller body. The result could be more than a 25 percent increase in efficiency (Lang, 1966)."*

*Shortly before his death, painter Henri Matisse visited the Oceanographic Museum in Monaco. "Just look at those bones!" he cried out when he saw a whale skeleton. "Impossible to conceive of contours better suited to their purpose. And to think that these creatures make them and aren't even aware of how astonishingly beautiful they are." Above: The reconstructed skeleton of a rorqual. Below: The skull of a sperm whale (dorsal view).*

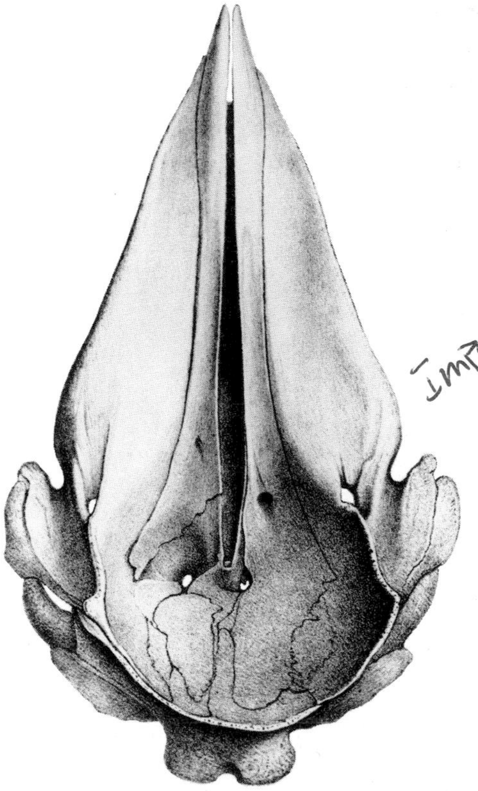

tow catcher boats at 20 knots. Whaling literature is filled with countless tales of terrified oarsmen holding on for dear life while a sperm whale dragged their craft along at breakneck speeds.

## THE SKELETON OF A BIRD

As one might expect, cetaceans owe their swimming prowess to a great many factors that bear investigation if ever we are to account for Gray's baffling paradox. The first of these is skeletal configuration.

The bones of whales are designed not so much to support the weight of organs (which are nearly weightless in water) as to serve as anchorages for muscles. Sturdiness is essential, but the bones must also be light; that way, they do not increase the average density of the tissues they structure. Birds, which move about in an ocean of air, have light, hollow bones penetrated by air sacs. The bones of whales, which ply the liquid counterpart of the atmosphere, are lightened in much the same way. The hard, dense shell covers a spongy, weblike inner structure irrigated by blood vessels. The interstices are filled with a marrow that has a very high oil content. Fully one-third of all the oil whalemen extract from their quarry comes from the bones, and those bones that are richest in marrow actually float on the surface.

Thus a whale's relatively light skeleton accounts for only 17 percent of total body weight; for a 130-ton blue whale, that comes to about 22 tons. In addition, whale skeletons differ structurally from those of other mammals: 45 percent of a whale's bones are located in the spinal column and related components—the core of the cetacean "swimming machine"; the skull, jawbones, and ribs account for another 45 percent. That leaves a scant 10 percent for the forelimbs (flippers) and vestigial hind limbs.

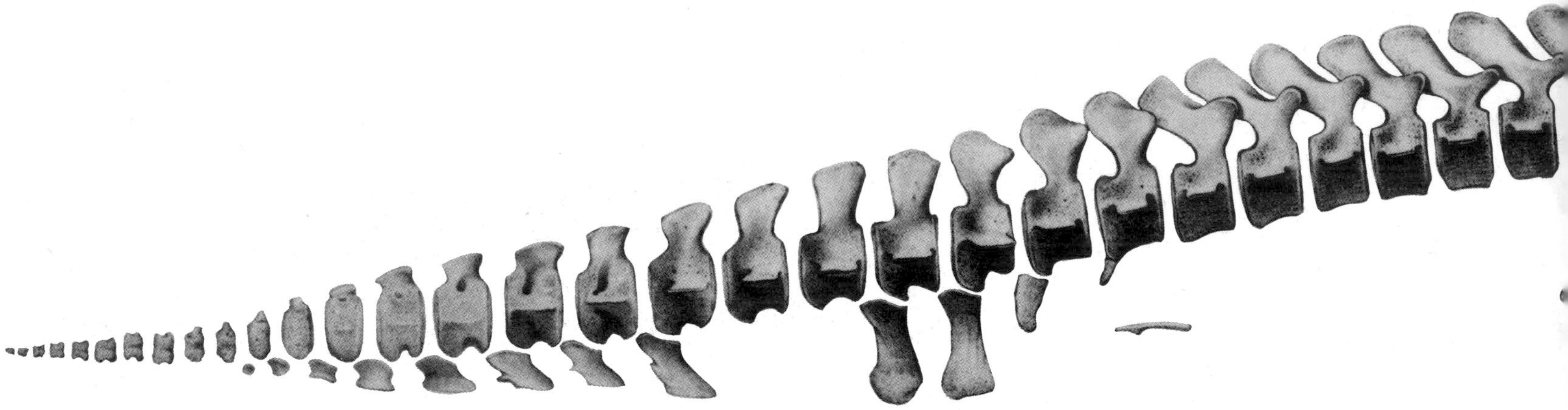

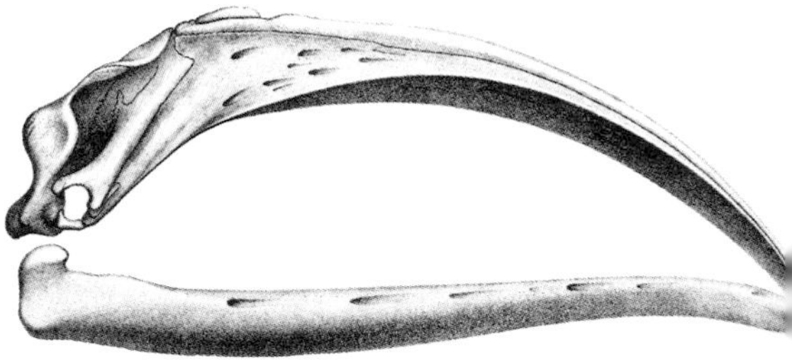

The cetacean cranium differs from the "standard" mammalian skull configuration in a number of ways. Whales lack certain bones, while others have undergone changes in position and relative size. "These changes," note Bourdelle and Grassé (1955), "resulted in telescoping, that is, the part of the skull behind the snout became shorter, but not so much through anteroposterior reduction as by overriding or sandwiching of certain bones." In embryos, cranial structure resembles that of typical mammals throughout most of the gestation period. The massive, yet tapered, skull makes it possible for whales to slice through the water.

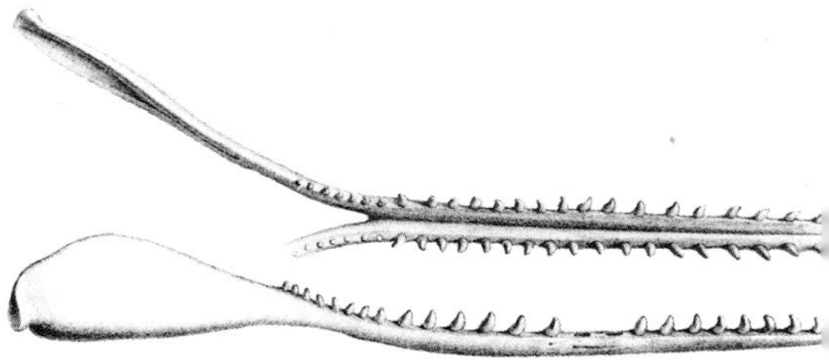

Whales have seven cervical vertebrae, as do all mammals. In cetaceans, however, these vertebrae are unusually short, and they may be partly fused, as in the right whale, or unattached, as in the fin whale. A short, rigid neck virtually eliminates "head wobble" when the tail is propelling the body at full tilt. This arrangement improves swimming efficiency and enhances hydrodynamic flow.

The whale's trunk and tail vertebrae are distinctive in a number of ways. For one thing, the thoracic, lumbar (waist), and caudal (tail) vertebrae all describe a single, uninterrupted arch from the neck to the tip of the tail. The propelling muscles are attached directly to this powerful yet supple framework to improve energy output. In archaeocetes, as in all four-legged mammals with a pelvic girdle, the sacral vertebrae still formed a distinctive bone cluster; in modern-day cetaceans, they have assumed the shape of lumbar vertebrae. The undersides of the caudal vertebrae extend downward at the extremities. Although these chevron bones do provide additional sites for muscle attachment, their primary function is to protect the tail blood vessels.

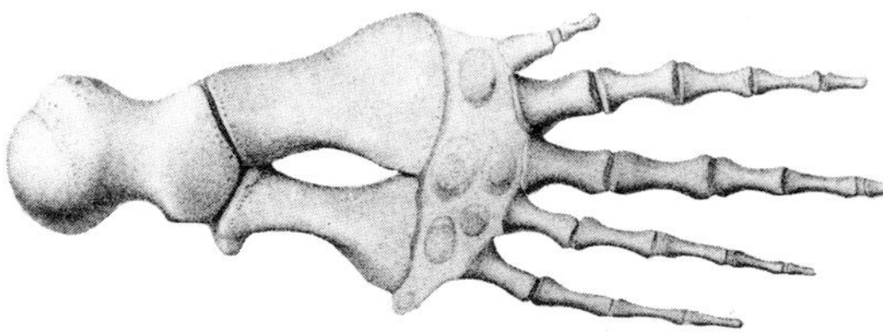

Most whales have twelve or fourteen pairs of ribs. In mysticetes, only the first two pairs are joined to a shortened sternum. In odontocetes, the breastbone is longer and consists of several bony elements.

The forelimbs are attached to a shoulder girdle that consists of a very broad, fan-shaped shoulder blade (scapular); there is no collarbone (clavicle). The humerus, radius, and ulna are stubby, thick, and less elaborate than those of land mammals. The flattened, paddlelike "hands" consist of a wrist and four or five short, thick metacarpals.

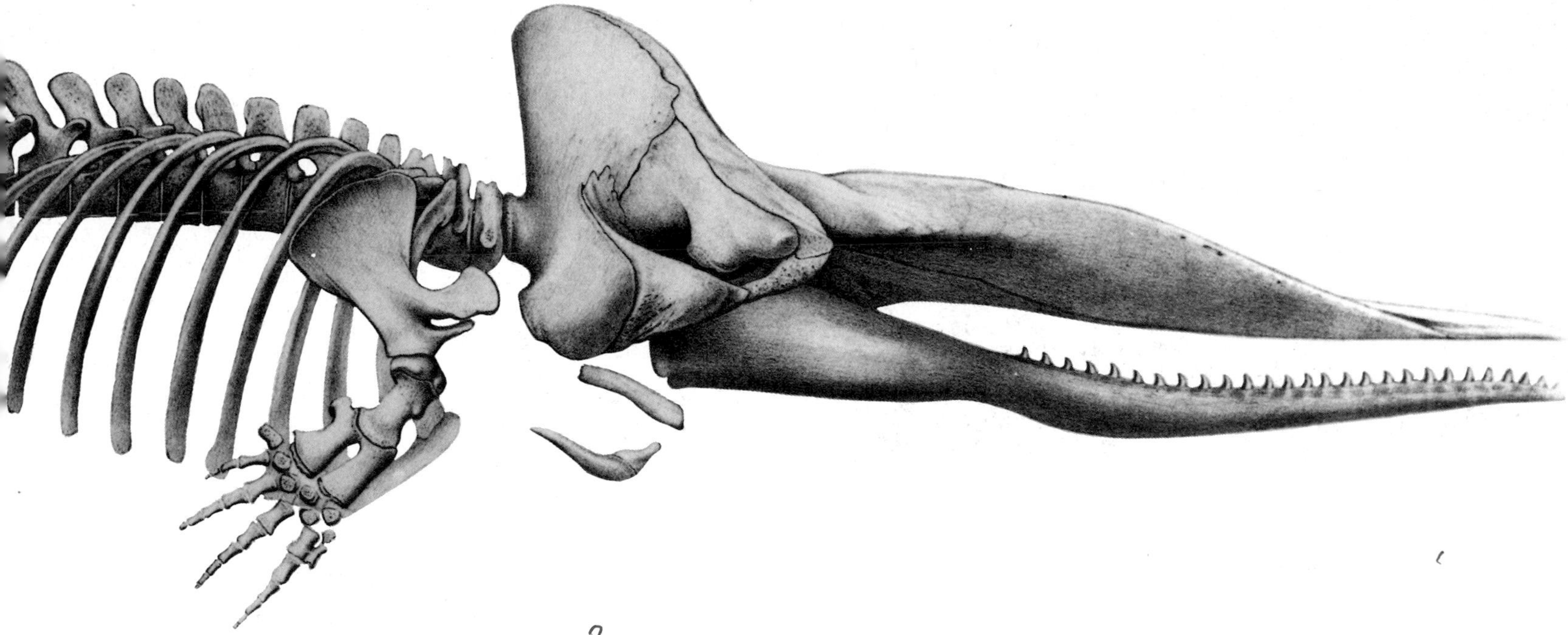

The archaeocetes had five digits. Although right whales still have a vestigial thumb, most present-day baleen whales (especially rorquals) have lost this. The most obvious characteristic of whale forelimbs is hyperphalangism. The second and third "fingers" are disproportionately long and can include as many as fourteen phalanges. Paradoxically the humpback whale, whose gigantic white flippers

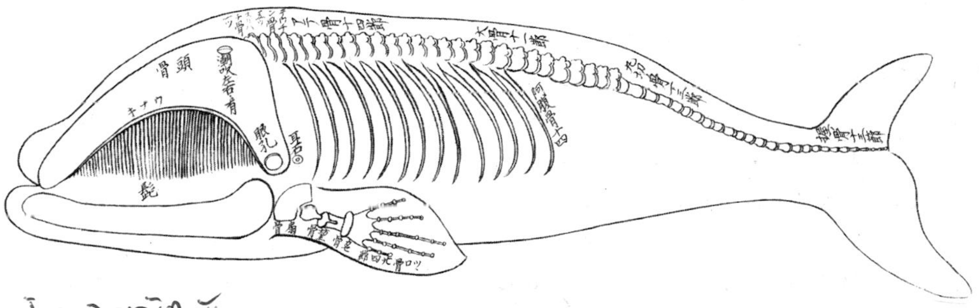

*The skeleton of a whale is light relative to its total body weight; it also differs considerably from that of most other mammals. The bones of a whale's skull and trunk account for 90 percent of total skeleton weight, the limbs only 10 percent. The hind limbs are vestigial. Above and opposite: Drawings from* Ostéographie des cétacés vivants et fossiles *(1868–79) by P.-J. van Beneden and P. Gervais. From top to bottom: The complete skeleton of a sperm whale, the skull of a right whale, the lower jaw of a sperm whale, and the skeleton of a fin whale flipper. Right: Drawing from an early nineteenth-century Chinese treatise on whales.*

IMPORTANT

*WHALE VERTEBRAE*

| *Species* | *Cervical* | *Thoracic* | *Lumbar* | *Caudal* | *Total* |
|---|---|---|---|---|---|
| *Right whale* (Balæna glacialis) | 7 | 14 | 12 | 24 | 57 |
| *Bowhead* (Balæna mysticetus) | 7 | 13 | 12 | 23 | 55 |
| *Pygmy right whale* (Caperea marginata) | 7 | 17 | 2 | 15 | 41 |
| *Gray whale* (Eschrichtius robustus) | 7 | 14 | 12 | 23 | 56 |
| *Blue whale* (Balænoptera musculus) | 7 | 15 | 15 | 27 | 64 |
| *Fin whale* (Balænoptera physalus) | 7 | 15 | 15 | 27 | 64 |
| *Sei whale* (Balænoptera borealis) | 7 | 14 | 13 | 23 | 57 |
| *Bryde's whale* (Balænoptera edeni) | 7 | 13 | 13 | 21 | 54 |
| *Minke whale* (Balænoptera acutorostrata) | 7 | 11 | 12 | 18 | 48 |
| *Humpback* (Megaptera novæangliæ) | 7 | 14 | 10 | 22 | 53 |
| *Sperm whale* (Physeter macrocephalus) | 7 | 11 | 8 | 24 | 50 |

*The whale skeleton:*
*I walk slowly through it, as*
*in a bare forest.*

*The whale skeleton:*
*I lay here my own bones, as*
*in a sea's graveyard.*

*(Sen Akira, Japanese, b. 1926; translated by James Kirkup in collaboration with the poet)*

typically extend more than 10 feet from the body wall, have shorter fingers than do their fellow balaenopterids. It is the radius and ulna that are stretched far out, not the phalanges.

Whales no longer have hind limbs; at least, what is left of them is not deserving of the name. The pelvic girdle, reduced to two small, rodlike bones embedded in the side muscle, is detached from the spinal column (but used in males to anchor muscles attached to the penis). Except for an occasional tiny vestigial femur in the sperm whale, odontocetes show no evidence of leg bones. Some mysticetes do have the rudiments of a femur and tibia just across from the anus, but they are embedded in the muscle and are completely detached from the rest of the skeleton. The buds of hind limbs are visible in the embryos of baleen whales, but these recede before birth.

## POWER AND GRACE

Physiologists, who are sticklers for accuracy, have calculated that mammalian muscle has an average energy output of 7.4 watts per pound. Therefore, a 130-ton whale, with 50 tons of first-rate muscle at its command, corresponds to an "installed capacity" of 820,000 watts, or just over 1,100 horsepower. Granted, some of these muscles are antagonists. But even if only half of them worked in the same direction, the whale's output would still be equivalent to that of a 550-horsepower locomotive.

Power and speed go hand in hand, but in this case the weight that has to be moved is colossal and the resistance of the water is tremendous. If we are to shed any light on Gray's paradox, we shall have to probe more deeply.

A 550-horsepower machine could not possibly propel 130 tons through water at 25 mph unless it came equipped with a number of elaborate adaptations. In the case of the whales, these adaptations involve morphology, physiology, and tissue structure.

The muscle system of the whale is an impressive assemblage of dark, coarse-grained flesh that accounts for more than a third of the animal's total weight. Well-developed pectorals enable its forelimbs to move as broadly or as precisely as needed. The masseters (jaw muscles) are well developed, too. But for sheer bulk, nothing can match the groups of trunk muscles that lie along the spinal column. Powerful aponeuroses make it possible for these muscles to pull efficiently on their insertions. The obliquely aligned diaphragm has highly developed muscles responsible for the mighty exhalations whales are known for when they come up for air after a long dive.

Not all whales have a dorsal fin, and those that do are unable to move it. It has no internal bone structure, no rays (unlike those of fish), not even any muscle; it is simply a mass of soft connective tissue strengthened by tougher fibers. This passive appendage helps maintain stability, much like the centerboard of a sailboat.

Whales have what appears to be a disproportionately large tail. In the largest species, the horizontally aligned, falcate flukes, which flare out like the wings of a butterfly, may have a surface area of up to 80 square feet. No bones connect the

*No whale species developed flippers as long as those of the humpback (scientific name* megaptera, *Greek for "big wing"). Humpbacks use these flattened, paddlelike forelimbs not as propellers, but as horizontal and vertical stabilizers and to help them brake and steer. The two main purposes of the flippers have nothing to do with locomotion. Rich in superficial blood vessels, they abet heat exchange between the organism and its environment. Secondly, these highly mobile, expressive appendages are vitally important in sexual display, mating behavior, contact between mother and young, and other manifestations of "body language."*

flukes to the spinal column; nor are they modified hind limbs, like the tails of seals and walruses. A whale's tail is a new structure shaped by evolution. It is mostly connective tissue. In cross section, three distinct strata may be seen beneath the epidermis: a thin layer of blubber crisscrossed with connective fibers, a layer of transverse fibers attached to the ten hindmost vertebrae, and a layer of longitudinal fibers set at right angles to those of the layer directly overhead. The spaces between the fibers are honeycombed with oil-filled cells. In the flukes, the tendons of the muscles that drive the caudal peduncle (tail stock) diverge into countless bundles of tendons. To quote Grassé (1955), "The tail forms an extremely tough assemblage of bone and fiber. The tendons are so highly developed that there is no chance of muscular activity, however violent, breaking the spinal column."

The tail stock is a powerful propeller, but it is also instrumental in stabilization and steering. Lacépède noted this back in 1804. "The ease with which the right whale moves not only its two arms but the flukes of its tail independently of each other provides it with an effective means by which to vary its movement, to change direction or position, in particular, to lie on its side, turn over onto its back, or spin about whenever it likes."

*Whales are phenomenal swimming machines. Every spring and fall, rorquals and humpbacks shuttle between winter breeding/calving grounds and summer cold-water feeding grounds that may be as much as 3,500 miles apart. Below: Blue whales, like the ones in this photograph, generate a tremendous amount of energy. The tail of a fin whale (opposite) is equivalent to a 500-horsepower propeller. A highly effective weapon against aggressors, the tail, like the flippers, is involved in body language.*

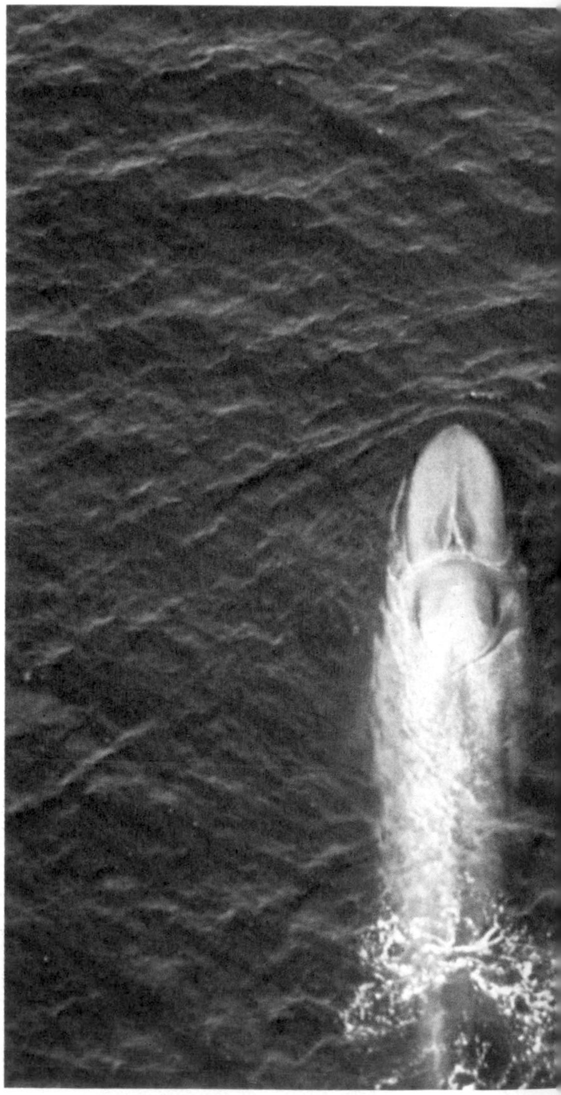

## SWIMMING MACHINES

The cetacean body has been characterized as a virtually flawless "biological seaplane" (K. S. Norris, 1966), and the secret of the whale's swimming prowess indeed lies partly in overall morphology. Typically, these mammals swim with a smooth, measured, up-and-down motion, unlike fish, which move their bodies from side to side. To propel itself through the water, a whale flexes locomotor muscles attached to the spinal column. Most of its swimming muscles are in the second half of its body. The broad tail flukes sweep up and down against the water, alternating upstrokes and downstrokes. But the fact that a whale has a powerful "engine" propelling it through the water does not resolve Gray's paradox. Experts have had to examine still photographs and motion pictures of free-swimming whales to help them discover what other means of propulsion cetaceans may have at their disposal.

P. E. Purves (1963) started with the assumption that whales swim as well as they do because their bodies generate almost complete laminar flow. In other words, water streams over their bodies in a smooth flow, creating little turbulence or drag.

If the bow wave generated at the front end of a whale were to break up in a turbulent flow of eddies along the animal's hindquarters, the drag produced by the collision of water particles with the body surface would be significant. Instead, this wave is effortlessly parted, extended, and dissipated by the whale's own fins and flippers. The dorsal fin, when present, cleaves the flow vertically, splitting it into two perfectly symmetrical sheets of water and drawing out the path of the wave so that it breaks up into impeding vortices well behind the animal's body. (The longer the whale, the farther back the dorsal fin.) The flippers serve the same purpose, only horizontally. However, most of the credit for "damping out" turbu-

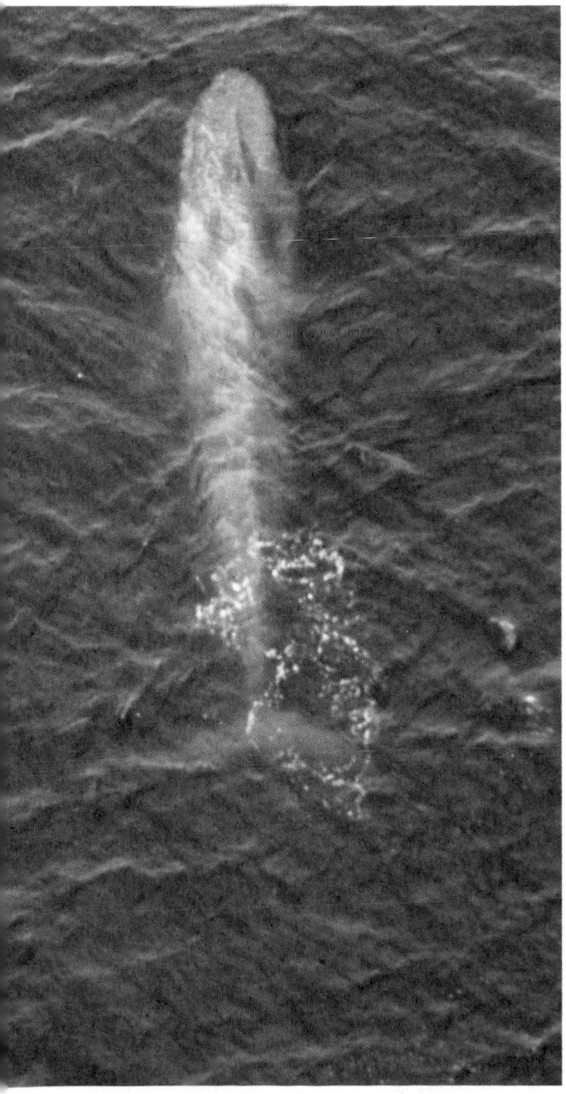

lence goes to the tail stock. Its up-and-down movement speeds up the water particles in direct contact with the rear part of the body and prevents them from forming eddies until they have been driven well back in the animal's wake.

This "antiturbulence" capability is made possible by a number of startling anatomical features. The primary antiturbulence mechanism in whales and dolphins is their outer layer of skin—a pliable, loosely attached, fluid-packed casing a scant half-millimeter thick that sheathes the tougher dermis underneath. This lower layer comes equipped with a complement of tiny ridges running parallel to the long axis of the animal. In cross section, the skin consists of an elastic outer layer over countless tiny, spongy channels that are vertically aligned and gorged with fluid. The slightest external pressure triggers an instantaneous reaction: minute adjustments in the "magic jacket" prevent eddies from forming and enable the animal to move through the water more efficiently. Another example of nature's wondrous resourcefulness.

There are other conjectures of hydrodynamic adaptation. The ridges of the dermis contain tiny capillary loops that, by releasing heat, may help create a microlayer of water next to the skin that is slightly warmer, less dense, and less viscous to improve the animal's "glide."

Since lubricants lower the viscosity of the liquid with which they are mixed, another way of improving water flow over a body surface is to lubricate the surface. Fish secrete a slimy mucus that coats the skin and enables them to glide effortlessly through the water. The more copious the mucus, the better the swimmer; the heaviest secretion occurs in large pelagic predators like tuna, bonito, and marlin. Whales do not have mucus-secreting cells similar to those of fish, but the thin outer layer of a whale's skin secretes a high polymer of ethylene oxide that may act as a lubricant or may slough off skin cells into the water and thereby reduce turbulence.

## THAR SHE BLOWS!

The primary nutrient of animal organisms, whatever they may be, is that incomparable source of energy known as oxygen. Whales and other mammals that made the transition from land to sea had to adapt to breathing while swimming. The nostrils-turned-blowholes had to migrate backward to the top of the head, and the diaphragm had to thicken and tilt to position the lungs dorsally—for the center of gravity. Moreover, any connection between the respiratory and digestive tracts had to be reduced at the rear of the mouth or else the way cetaceans ingest food would have conflicted with the way they take in oxygen.

Now simply a field mark for identifying whale species from a distance, spouts long inspired many a yarn and implausible engraving. The facts are fascinating enough; there is no need to embroider them.

In all species except the sperm whale, the blowholes are located medially and near the top of the head. In odontocetes, a single opening is shared by two breathing passages; in mysticetes, there are two separate orifices with a narrow band of tissue in between. The thick, elastic lips or ridges around the periphery of the blowholes (popularly known as the "cutwater") are controlled by powerful muscles that make a watertight seal when the whale is below the surface. They reopen with a contraction of these muscles. Although this is usually a reflex reaction, whales can open their blowholes whenever they wish.

The nasal passages of baleen whales are uncomplicated tubes with no secondary sacs or cavities. In most toothed whales, however, the blowhole opens a series of paired diverticula, or sacs, that merge before hooking up to the larynx. The nasal system of sperm whales is more elaborate than that of other odontocetes because it must accommodate the huge spermaceti organ. From a single blowhole, located on the left front of the snout, one nasal passage runs back on the left

*Thar she blows! The call that used to go up from the crow's nest when the lookout sighted a spout at the surface has become the rallying cry of those determined to protect endangered whale species. Below: The blowholes of a California gray whale look like the sound holes of a violin. Baleen whales breathe through both nostrils at the top of the head, resulting in a characteristic double column of spray. Above: The spout of a California gray whale.*

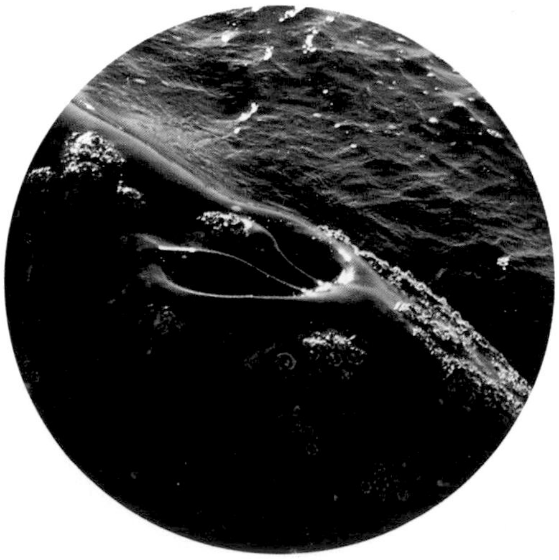

*Baleen whales (like the humpback, above) spout a double blow, but toothed whales have only one functional blowhole that produces a single column of spray when they exhale. Whale spouts have been a source of fascination since man first beheld the sea, inspiring stories about capsized boats and passengers hurled overboard, or about their stench or noxious effects. Even Melville (1851) put some store by these accounts. "You cannot go with your pitcher to this fountain and fill it, and bring it away. . . . I have heard it said, and I do not much doubt it, that if the jet is fairly spouted into your eyes, it will blind you."*

*Overleaf: There is no truth to the stories about whale spouts being poisonous or foul-smelling, except when a whale is feeding. When several of these marine giants (like these humpbacks) congregate in a remote lagoon and spew forth gossamer plumes of mist, the sight is almost too majestic to be real.*

side, curving around the organ as a simple tube. The right passage, however, first runs forward to form a sac in front of the organ and forms another sac at the rear, before branching off to join the left passage.

The structure of the larynx depends on the type of whale. In mysticetes, it is a tubelike affair embedded in the anterior nasal passages; in odontocetes, it looks like a goose's bill. Although all whales lack vocal chords, the larynx does have vibrating parts capable of producing sounds. These "utterances" play a crucial role in social interaction.

The digestive and respiratory systems are kept separate by an elongated pharynx and an enlarged epiglottis that blocks the pathway between the esophagus and the trachea.

The trachea, bronchi, and bronchioles of whales come equipped with rings of cartilage that are amazingly tough. Their lungs, unlike those of many mammals, are not lobed. Typically they have an abundance of elastic tissue, thick pleurae, and alveoli like those of land mammals. Relative to total size, the lungs of whales are no more developed than those of other mammals; in fact, they are somewhat smaller.

## A SUBTLE MIST

We shall return to the physiology of cetacean respiration later on; but let us first take a moment out to consider the spout itself. Despite the scientific advances of our modern age, the sight of a whale spouting still inspires wonder and reverie, quickens the heartbeat of whalemen, and touches a wistful chord in many a poet:

Dawn
Spouting whales
Icy sea

*Gyodai (1732–1792)*

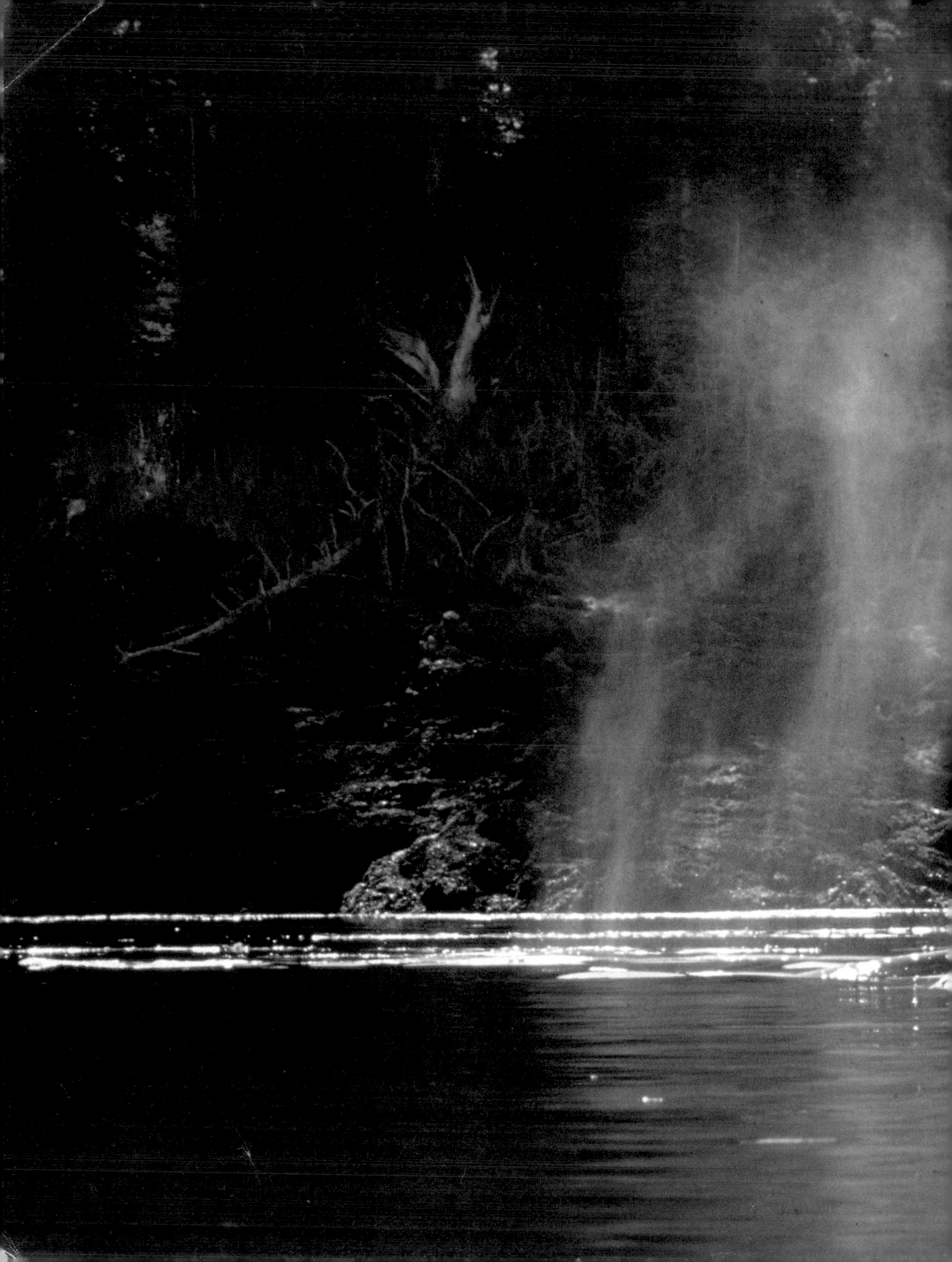

Right whales shoot two powerful, bushy jets 13 to 16 feet into the air; they merge into a V-shaped spout. The bowhead's double blast is similar, but taller (19 to 22 feet). The blow of the pygmy right whale is not prominent (about 3 feet), but hardly anyone has seen it firsthand on the open sea.

The thunderous burst of the gray whale is a single, broad, bushy plume, 10 to 13 feet high. Sometimes it is clearly divided at the top. In calm conditions, it can be heard half a mile away.

Blue whales send up a single, slender jet that soars 40 to 50 feet above the ocean surface. The fin whale's blow is not as tall (16 to 22 feet) and broadens into an ellipse of spray at the top. Sei whales and Bryde's whales both spout an elongated, inverted cone or "pear" 10 to 13 feet high.

The low, inconspicuous spout of the minke whale (6.5 feet or less) can only be seen against a dark background. It is less slender than those of other rorquals, possibly because minkes start to exhale before their blowholes have surfaced.

*Humpback whales (below, a group of three near the western coast of Greenland) spout a fuller, bushier double column than do other members of the rorqual family. Their 10- to 13-foot spout ends in a gossamer balloon of spray whose fleeting beauty defies description. When a whale spouts, it exhales a pressurized mist of pulmonary gases (oxygen, nitrogen, carbon dioxide, water vapor) combined with tiny particles of an oily mucus or "foam" that lines the animal's breathing passages.*

The tall spout of the humpback is bushier than of other rorquals—a 10- foot to 13-foot column crowned with a gossamer balloon of spray whose fleeting, ethereal beauty defies description.

The sperm whale produces the oddest-looking spout of all. The first exhalation after a deep dive is a thunderous blast that can be heard half a mile away. The column is powerful but only moderately tall, although some observers caught up in the excitement of the moment have reported blows up to 50 feet high. Due to the peculiar location of its single blowhole, the sperm whale spouts forward and to the left at about a 45-degree angle.

It is widely believed that the spout of whales is offensive, revolting, caustic, or even poisonous. Van Beneden, for example, maintained that "the exhaled air of the sperm whale is extraordinarily fetid." According to Portier (1938), "Prof. [Emile] Racovitza, a naturalist with the *Belgica* expedition, happened to be on the bridge of the ship just when a whale broke surface alongside the hull. He was drenched by the spout and noted that it was a warm and decidedly foul-smelling mist." "Nor is it prudent for the hunter to be over-curious touching the precise nature of the whale spout," admonishes Melville (1851). "Your skin will feverishly smart from the acridness of the thing so touching it."

The crew of the *Calypso* have been drenched by whale spouts on a number of occasions. It did not cost them their eyesight nor, as Melville feared, the skin of their arms or legs. There was not even anything particularly repulsive about the smell. Here is what happened to Philippe Cousteau when he found himself surrounded by some right whales:

"I inhaled the very breath of the whales. The spout landed right on us, soaking my face and hands and drenching the boat in a fine spray. The mist did not smell bad; it was delicate, with a faint odor of musk." When a whale is feeding, however, its spout has a decidedly stronger smell, like acetone.

All the stories that have perpetuated the myth of the stinking whale spout can be traced to whalemen. It is not inconceivable that the blood rushing into the lungs of a wounded right whale, rorqual, or sperm whale could impart a strong organic smell to its final breaths. But it is more likely that the hunters were simply wrong, or that they succumbed to the impulse of the killer to disparage his victim.

The nature of the spout itself is a more intriguing question. At first it was thought that whales use their tongues to force water from the mouth through the blowholes. This misconception—perpetuated by the otherwise discerning Lacépède—inspired all kinds of farfetched accounts, such as the one about how a sperm whale can fill a boat with water from its spout until it capsizes. (That one dates back to Pliny the Elder.) The composition of whale spouts piqued the curiosity of Daniel Eschricht, a Danish naturalist, and Holböll, the governor of Greenland, who suggested that a blow consists of moist air that condenses as it comes into contact with cool air. However, it soon became apparent that the cloudlets whales shoot into the sky are visible in warm tropical air, too.

By the end of the nineteenth century, the most widely held view was the one expressed by Van Beneden: "Probably we shall be nearer the truth if we say that it is both air and water—but water broken up into extremely fine particles, like the mist expelled by an atomizer." The visible spout is primarily water collected in the blowhole depression and atomized when it is forced out. Other experts soon

added to the "residual water vapor" theory, maintaining that during a dive gases under pressure in the lungs undergo a process known as adiabatic cooling. Here is how Poetier (1938) explains it: "Violently compressed air in the whale's thorax seems to 'expand' the moment it is forcefully expelled through the opened blowhole. Now, physicists tell us that this expansion is accompanied by a significant drop in temperature, meaning that the water vapor in the air a whale exhales undergoes condensation. . . . A quantity of air at 20° C compressed to two atmospheres falls to –33° C at the moment of release."

One more component of the visible blow was suggested by F. C. Fraser and P. E. Purves (1955), who studied the foam that lines the breathing passages, air sinuses, and middle ear of whales. This mixture is composed primarily of oil droplets in a very fine emulsion. When the whale exhales, particles of foam mingle with gases in the air stream (oxygen, nitrogen, carbon dioxide, and water vapor), as if in a giant cough—giving the spout its characteristic appearance. In addition, this "phlegm" is thought to dissolve nitrogen when the whale inhales, enabling the animal to retain a small amount of this gas in its respiratory system. This ability, in turn, could help prevent dissolved nitrogen from entering the bloodstream in significant amounts during deep dives. For this reason, whales coming up from a deep dive can dispense with stage decompression.

*Blue whales send a tremendous, fairly slender single column of mist soaring as much as 40 to 50 feet above the surface. It is one of the most prodigious sights the sea has to offer. Above: The biggest whale of them all spouting in the Sea of Cortez, just off the coast of Baja California.*

## THE BREATH-HOLDING CHAMPIONS OF THE WORLD

The hypothesis that respiratory mucus may help eliminate excess nitrogen in the airways brings us to the extraordinary mechanisms that make it possible for whales to make such deep dives.

Before whales embark on prolonged stints underwater, they prepare themselves by doing their version of breathing exercises. Every species has its own way

Right Whale

of "sounding," or slipping beneath the ocean surface. The right whale, for example, takes about one breath a minute while cruising at the surface. But when it is about to sound, the pace quickens to five or six breaths a minute for five or six minutes, after which it dives almost straight down, raising its flukes high into the air before disappearing. It usually stays under for four to six minutes but can prolong the dive to ten or twenty minutes if alarmed, even up to forty minutes in life-threatening situations. Right whales probably dive no deeper than about 490 feet.

Bowhead

Bowheads take one or two breaths a minute while cruising, four to six a minute for three or four minutes when preparing for a dive. They descend at a steep angle as they begin to sound and raise their splendid flukes high above the surface. They remain underwater between five and fifteen minutes, swim at the surface for two to four minutes, dive again, and repeat the pattern. The more dives it makes, the longer a bowhead takes to recover at the surface. It is conjectured that bowheads will go down to 500 feet; but all that is certain is that, under duress, bowheads are ready to make prolonged dives. According to Scoresby (1823), bowheads stay under for fifteen to twenty minutes but have been known to remain underwater "for up to 56 minutes when harpooned." Scoresby also noted that wounded whales occasionally dived at such high speed that they sometimes crashed into rocks on the ocean floor, more than 100 fathoms (600 feet) down.

A pygmy right whale breathing at the surface will show its snout and blowholes for just a few seconds before slipping out of sight. On one of the rare occasions when it was observed firsthand, this whale spouted about once a minute while cruising. Its dives are brief (four to five minutes, possibly up to fifteen minutes when threatened).

Gray Whale

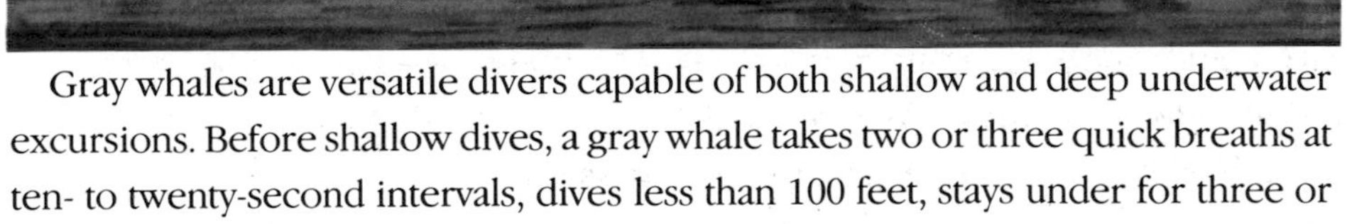

Gray whales are versatile divers capable of both shallow and deep underwater excursions. Before shallow dives, a gray whale takes two or three quick breaths at ten- to twenty-second intervals, dives less than 100 feet, stays under for three or four minutes, and emerges about 1,000 feet from the spot at which it sounded. Before deeper dives, it takes two or three very deep breaths each minute for three to five minutes and stays under for seven to ten minutes, resurfacing some one-third to one-half mile away. If threatened, a gray whale can stay under for as long as thirty minutes and dive to depths of about 500 feet. When sounding, it descends at a very steep angle and lifts its flukes into the air for quite some time.

Blue Whale

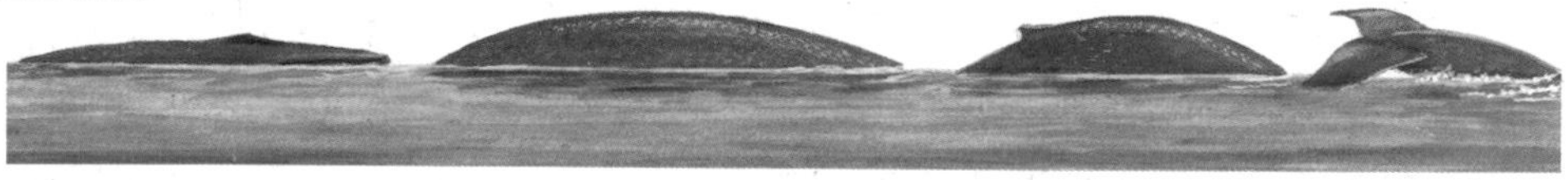

To sound, blue whales raise their flukes ever so slightly above the surface, but before they do they "roll" their gleaming, seemingly endless blue-gray backs. They spout one to four times a minute, depending on circumstances. They make twelve to fifteen quick, shallow dives in a row (100 to 150 feet at thirty-second intervals), followed by a longer, deeper dive to an estimated 350 feet or more. The longer dive can last from ten to thirty minutes to almost an hour if need be. When they surface, blue whales seem hardly "winded" at all. They spout five to twelve times a minute and do not take long to recover.

Fin Whale

The breathing sequence of fin whales is much the same. They spout at a slightly faster rate when at rest (three to six times a minute), but recover more quickly than their mammoth cousins. Then again, their dives do not last as long (five to fifteen minutes, occasionally twenty to thirty minutes). According to an old whaling rule, a sounding fin whale will expose even less of its tail than a blue whale. Howell (in Portier, 1938) tells of a harpooned individual that reportedly dived so precipitously it broke its neck when it hit bottom at 275 fathoms (1,650 feet). Norwegian scientists have confirmed that fin whales reach depths of 1,100 feet.

Sei Whale

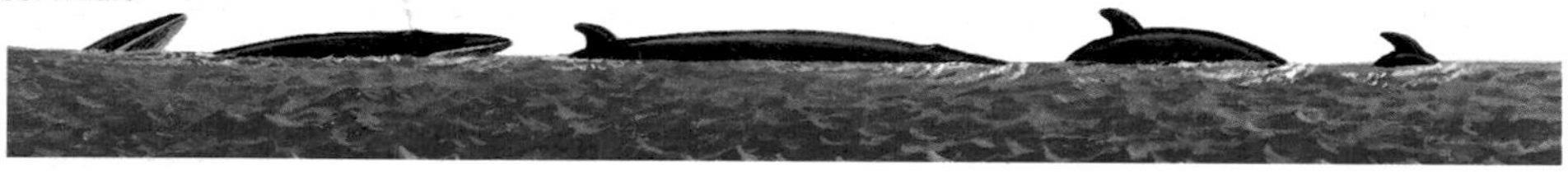

Sei whales breathe and swim at two different paces. They may breathe two or three times in a row at fifteen- to twenty-second intervals, then dive for five to ten minutes; or they may take five or six breaths every thirty to fifty seconds before embarking on dives lasting from fifteen minutes to half an hour. We do not know how deep sei whales dive. Once they surface, they do not arch their backs the way that fin whales do, but sink quietly out of sight without showing one square inch of their flukes.

Bryde's Whale

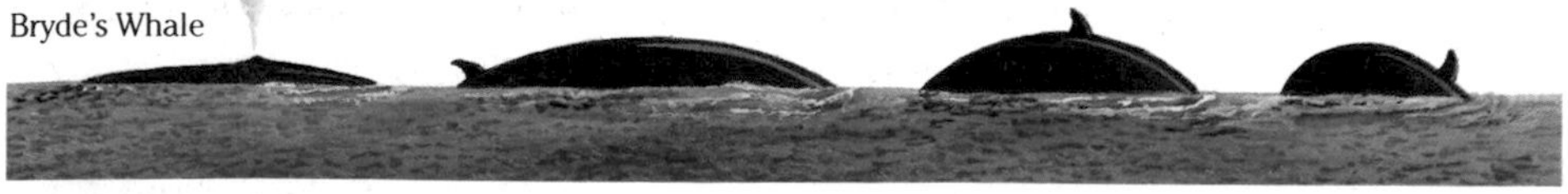

The breathing sequence of Bryde's whales is three or four blows at the surface, followed by dives that can last between five and twenty minutes. Like the sei, it does not raise its flukes when sounding.

*Every whale species has a distinctive breathing pattern at the surface and a particular way of slipping beneath the surface ("sounding"). Some display much of the back and all of the tail; others are far less demonstrative. Whalers were familiar with these diving sequences (pp. 141, 142, 143), which positively identify species on the high seas. The breathing sequence of the minke whale (not included in these illustrations) is much the same as that of Bryde's whale. Minkes spout as soon as they can, sometimes even starting to exhale just before they break the surface. Below: A minke whale in Japanese waters.*

Minke whales breathe five or six times in a row at intervals of less than a minute, make a quick dive, and (like blue and fin whales) repeat the process several times before making a deeper dive of ten or twelve minutes (occasionally twenty or twenty-five minutes). Minkes arch the back high above the surface when sounding but do not expose their flukes.

Humpback Whale

Humpback whales breathe slowly when at rest, especially in warm tropical or subtropical waters. Some experts have reported that humpbacks take one or two breaths a minute at the surface (Lockyer, 1975); others maintain that these whales breathe at a faster rate. A humpback can stay under for three to ten minutes, or up to thirty minutes when threatened. Upon surfacing, it takes four to eight breaths a minute for as long as it takes to recover. Before starting a deep dive to 500 or 700 feet, it arches its back high above the surface of the water, as though deliberately displaying the characteristic that earned the species its popular name. Then the humpback throws its flukes high in the air, as if it were proud to show off its velvety black tail with the variably pigmented undersides.

Sperm Whale

The undisputed deep-diving champion among large whales—indeed, among all cetaceans except for the bottlenose whale—is *Physeter macrocephalus*, the sperm whale. This species' underwater feats have long astounded those fortunate enough to witness them. As far back as 1839, Thomas Beale noted that sperm whales could dive to 800 fathoms (4,800 feet). Van Beneden quoted other first-hand accounts: "Captain Gray claims to have seen sperm whales stay under for two hours at a time and spin out 700 fathoms of line. Captain Scammon saw dives of fifty minutes and even an hour and a quarter." Many scientists, although willing to concede the unsurpassed diving capabilities of the species, took these observations with a grain of salt. At least, they did until 1932 (A. H. Laurie, 1933; R. Kellogg, 1938, in K. S. Norris, 1966; S. R. Riedman and E. T. Gustafson, 1966). That was the year the crew of the *All America*, a cable ship then off the coast of Colombia, hoisted a 46-foot sperm whale entangled in an underwater telegraph cable that had lain on the floor of the Pacific Ocean—3,500 feet below the surface! It had apparently become fouled in the cable and died of asphyxiation.

Several incidents of this kind have been reported since. On six occasions the cable lay more than 450 fathoms (2,700 feet) below the surface (Slijper, 1962). Today most experts agree that sperm whales dive deeper than 4,800 feet, and that large bulls may occasionally touch bottom at depths of 8,000 to 9,500 feet.

Sperm whales spout three to five times a minute when at rest, quickening the pace to six or seven times a minute when they come up from a dive. They are quick to recover, but it takes them longer to "catch their breath" after a series of dives. According to an old whaler's rule of thumb, for every foot of a sperm whale's

*Accomplished divers, sperm whales sound at a very steep angle and descend to tremendous depths. Mature bulls can stay underwater for more than an hour, stalking and feeding on giant squid at depths ranging from 5,000 to 10,000 feet. Clearly, the feeding imperative is one reason for these forays into the deep. But could they also be a source of pleasure? Given the effects extreme pressure is known to have on the nervous system of mammals, is it so farfetched to suggest that sperm whales on deep dives may experience the euphoria that human divers refer to as "rapture of the deep"?*

*Like a whale*
*Let me sleep*
*falling through shoals of silence*
*imponderable, vast*
*displacing darkness upon darkness*
*pricked by oxygen of dreams.*
*(Frances Horovitz, British, b. 1940)*

length, it will spout once at the surface and spend one minute submerged during the subsequent dive. For example, a 60-foot individual would blow sixty times and disappear for about an hour. Juveniles breathe more frequently, and get winded more quickly, than do adults; a calf will not stay under longer than seven minutes. Females do not dive as long (twenty minutes at the most), as deep, or as frequently as males. Only mature bulls over 40 to 45 feet in length manage to suspend respiration for an hour or more.

Even for large bulls, however, a very deep dive is an unusual occurrence warranted only by the prospect of a king-sized helping of giant squid. Lockyer (1976) analyzed some sonar recordings made off Durban, South Africa. A third of the time, the individuals observed dived to depths of less than 325 feet. Sperm whales 23 to 29 feet long did not venture below 2,300 feet (8 percent of all observed dives); individuals 30 to 36 feet long stopped at 3,000 feet (3 percent of all dives); and only specimens 40 to 45 feet long dived more than 3,300 feet below the surface (3 percent of dives).

A sperm whale goes through a magnificent sounding ritual, no matter how deep it dives. It lifts the entire rear part of its body, rounding it into an arch and "rolling" the seemingly endless row of knuckles along its spine. It raises its tail almost vertically and lets it quiver in the air for a moment before diving straight down.

## PHENOMENAL PHYSIOLOGY

How do we account for these *tours de force*? How do whales manage to suspend respiration for so long with so little effort? How can they cruise, look for food, feed, and court underwater—in other words, expend so much energy and oxygen—and not feel an urgent need to come up for air? When we hold our breath, our glottis shuts tight. Pressure builds up inside our chest cavity until it becomes unbearable. Our heart strains to drive venous blood toward the lungs, which have no fresh oxygen to offer. Venous stasis results (slowing of the blood circulating in the veins), leading to fatigue (loss of energy) in our oxygen-starved limbs. Increased pressure and higher levels of carbon dioxide in the blood stimulate the respiratory center in our brain. After one to three minutes (depending on one's stamina), we must either breathe or faint.

How do whales avoid the sequence of unpleasant symptoms most mammals endure when they don't breathe? At first it was thought that these diving champions had extraordinary breathing capacity. The raw statistics are indeed impressive: A 120-ton blue whale has a usable lung capacity of about 100 cubic yards; a 60-ton fin whale, nearly 70 cubic yards; a 40-ton sperm whale, about 35 cubic yards; and man, 200 to 400 cubic *inches*. Relative to body weight, however, large whales actually have rather undersized lungs, accounting for less than 1 percent of total weight in most whales—compared with 1.76 percent for *Homo sapiens* and 2.55 percent for elephants (Lockyer, 1976).

However, cetaceans put their breathing apparatus to much better use than we land mammals do. They have far more alveoli (air cells) than we do. Whale lungs contain two layers of capillaries (the lungs of other mammals have but one), and this arrangement increases the efficiency of gas exchange. The pleurae of whales are thicker and more resilient than ours. The pulmonary tissue proper contains a generous supply of myoelastic fibers for better overall elasticity. The bronchial tubes are lined with muscular tissue. Even tiny bronchioles less than a millimeter across come equipped with sphincters that cut off the alveoli from the rest of the lung. The function of these sphincters is unknown. They may prevent air from entering the alveoli during certain phases—such as when the lungs are compressed—to keep excessive nitrogen from entering the blood and tissues. (This excessive nitrogen is what causes the "bends" in human divers.)

These anatomical mechanisms add up to a higher degree of pulmonary efficiency. Residual air accounts for 28 percent of the total capacity of human lungs; our vital capacity is 72 percent. In whales, residual air never exceeds 15 percent of total capacity, meaning that their vital capacity is over 85 percent and can reach 92 percent. In addition, we renew only 10 to 20 percent of the contents of our lungs in normal breathing (55 percent with forceful exhalations). In whales, the "turnover rate" is 80 to 90 percent. Taking all factors into consideration, S. R. Riedman and E. T. Gustafson (1966) calculated that "a single whale breath is equivalent to eight human breaths."

Efficient replacement and "management" of air, however, are not the main reasons for the whale's diving prowess. The amount of air whales take with them in their lungs as they head underwater is not that great. Even if their lungs were filled to capacity, the contents would not be enough to sustain dives of half an hour or more.

As we noted earlier, whales prepare for dives by taking several deep breaths in rapid succession just before sounding. In so doing, they increase the oxygen content not just of the lungs, but of the entire blood supply—and even in tissues that act as oxygen reservoirs. While underwater, whales do not store oxygen the way people do. As a human diver burns up oxygen, 34 percent of it comes from the lungs, 41 percent from the blood, 13 percent from the muscles, and 12 percent from other tissues. Whales draw only 9 percent of the oxygen they need from the lungs, 41 percent from the blood, an astonishing 41 percent from the muscles, and the remaining 9 percent from other tissues. In sperm whales, as much as 50 percent of the oxygen depleted during deep dives is stored in the muscles (Scholander, 1940).

Whales have a greater number of red blood cells per unit of blood than do humans, and whale blood is therefore richer in hemoglobin than our blood (1.3 to 1.4 times richer, according to Suzuki, 1921). It thus has a greater tendency to combine with oxygen.

Whale muscle is designed for maximum oxygen-storing capacity; experts now feel that this is largely attributable to the unusually high myoglobin content of the tissue. (Myoglobin, or muscle proteins that store $O_2$, is present in most vertebrates. These proteins are oxygen-bonding pigments, and they give the meat of whales its dark color.) Myoglobin stores oxygen, releasing it to cells the instant they send out a signal for it.

*Indirect evidence—stomachs containing deep-sea sharks—suggests that some sperm whales dive as deep as 10,000 feet (nearly two miles) below the surface. Baleen whales cannot match these feats; for them, reaching a depth of 1,200 feet is a major accomplishment. A diving whale is a marvel of adaptation. Whales do not have gigantic lungs relative to body size, but they are able to renew pulmonary contents much more efficiently than we do. They store oxygen in the blood and have developed specialized tangles of blood vessels (*retia mirabilia*) for just that purpose. Their muscles are rich in myoglobin, an oxygen-carrying protein. Opposite: Baleen whales spouting after a dive. Above: A California gray whale; below: fin whales accompanied by a group of white-sided porpoises. Pages 148–49: A humpback whale slips beneath the surface.*

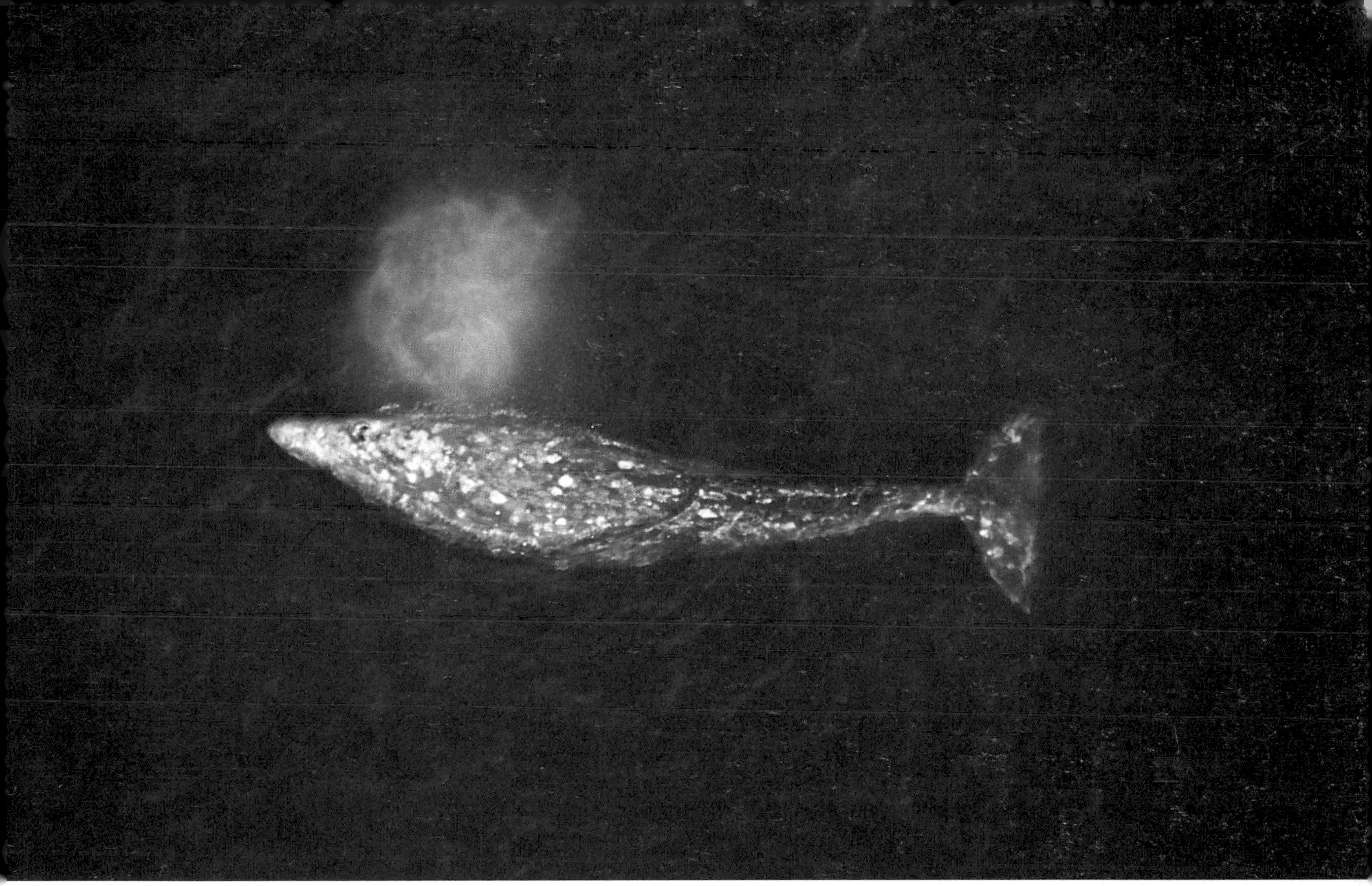

Better pulmonary ventilation and better storage of oxygen in blood and tissues—theoretically, these factors alone would equip whales for self-sufficiency underwater. But in order to travel at great depths for long periods, an organism not only has to store large quantities of oxygen, but also use it sparingly. Everything about a whale's anatomy and physiology is geared to achieving a single objective: husbanding oxygen, its source of energy.

The first secret of successful diving is to provide oxygen only to those organs that most urgently need it: in other words, to reroute almost the entire oxygen supply to the heart and brain. During this reflex reaction, inessential circulation is reduced and ultimately shut down. Peripheral tissues require less oxygen than the heart and brain; when these inessential areas do not get enough oxygen from the blood, they switch over to a "standby" form of metabolism that is not oxygen-dependent—a process called anaerobic metabolism. This now-familiar process, albeit neither as fast nor as efficient as ordinary metabolism, has the advantage of allowing cells to be put "on hold" for a fairly long time without fresh supplies of oxygenated blood.

A whale's motor muscles tap their own myoglobin reserves for oxygen, and when the oxygen stored in the myoglobin has been depleted, the muscle cells switch over to anaerobic metabolism. During a dive, the circulation of the blood is cut off in muscles not essential to swimming. Vasoconstriction slows oxygen use and prevents the release of lactic acid into the blood. (Lactic acid is the primary byproduct of muscular activity during anaerobic metabolism.) Thanks to this mechanism, the fatigue that other mammals experience when they lack oxygen is "masked"; the respiratory center in the whale's brain is not stimulated, and there is no increase in heart rate.

Still other physiological adaptations enable whales to deplete their oxygen supply parsimoniously. For example, mechanisms designed to restrict the return flow of venous blood to the heart prevent the right ventricle from sending oxygen-poor blood to the lungs, preventing unnecessary strain from pressure buildup in the lungs and preserving oxygen supplies in the lungs and blood.

The slowdown in the return blood flow is largely the result of a slowdown in heart rate. This condition, known as bradycardia, is regulated by a reflex response of the pituitary gland and the hypothalamus to the sensation of submersion. A whale's heart rate is not very high under normal conditions: eight to ten beats per minute. During a dive, the reflex reaction cuts this by half, to only four or five beats per minute (Slijper, 1962). All mammals experience some degree of bradycardia when underwater; the human heart rate, for example, drops from seventy to eighty to less than forty. However, whereas our heart starts to race after just a short while, animals adapted to diving can prolong bradycardia for much longer periods of time. Experiments have shown that prolonged bradycardia is indispensable for animals living underwater.

Additional anatomical and physiological mechanisms help slow the return flow of blood to the heart and divert it to the brain. It has been suggested that the two halves of the heart function more independently in whales than in land mammals. After a certain amount of time underwater, the right side may nearly stop beating; by sending almost no venous blood to the lungs for purification, the animal saves

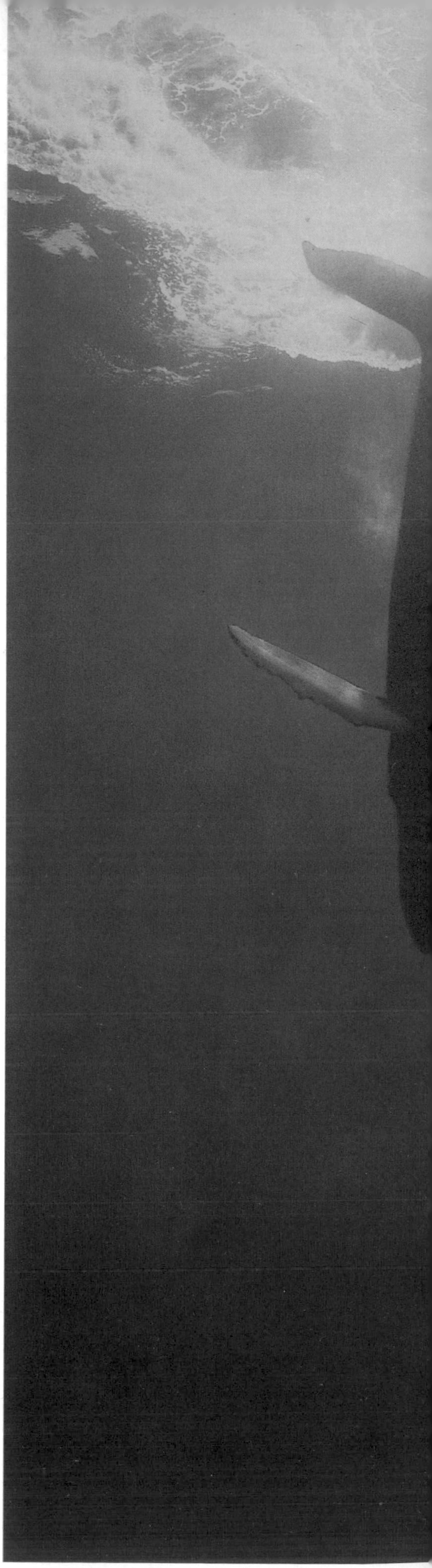

oxygen. Meanwhile, the left side is programmed to dispatch what little reoxygenated blood it does receive directly to the brain. Indeed, the organism seems geared to rerouting its entire reserve of oxygen-rich blood to the brain, which in turn empties its venous blood into specialized "holding chambers" located primarily in the liver and in a huge dilatation of the vena cava, below the diaphragm (Portier, 1938).

Our startling tale does not end there. In whales, selective circulation to the brain is made possible by tangled reservoirs of blood known as the *retia mirabilia*, or "wonderful network." (Pierre Belon observed them in the dolphin as far back as the sixteenth century but did not understand how they worked.) Frédéric Cuvier's description is as serviceable now as it was 150 years ago: "These endlessly convoluted vessels form a massive plexus filled with oxygenated blood, and they are located mostly beneath the pleura, between the ribs, and on either side of the spine. . . . Presumably these intricately interwoven networks exist in cetaceans because of their frequent need to suspend breathing (that is, to interrupt oxygenation of the blood) for substantial periods of time. These tangles act as reservoirs of oxygenated blood which, once it has reentered the circulation, keeps alive those areas that would otherwise deteriorate in the presence of venous blood."

The sturdy yet resilient *retia mirabilia* are not unique to whales. Similar systems in the sole pads of dogs and wolves help prevent frostbite in winter. If sloths and other mammals that live upside down did not have these networks of vessels in their paws, their entire blood supply would rush to the brain.

To recapitulate: efficient lungs, efficient storage of oxygen in the blood and muscles, slowdown of venous flow to the heart, selective circulation to the brain, and *retia mirabilia*. The pieces of the puzzle are starting to fit together, but a few are still missing.

How do whales avoid decompression sickness? Why are they immune to the gas embolisms that have been the undoing of so many human divers? The condition commonly known as the "bends" is caused by the formation of bubbles in the tissues and blood of deep-sea divers who come to the surface too quickly and do not allow nitrogen and other inert gases dissolved under pressure in their bodies to be voided gradually through the lungs. To prevent these deadly bubbles from turning them into a champagne bottle whose cork has just popped, human divers returning from deep, prolonged dives must undergo an extremely gradual, controlled ascent known as stage decompression. Whales dive much deeper and stay down for much longer periods of time; yet they manage quite nicely without stage decompression, ascending rapidly without the slightest ill effect. One reason is that, unlike human divers using scuba gear, whales do not breathe highly compressed air as they descend; hence, they do not dissolve as much gas in their blood. Large whales take along a very small amount of nitrogen with them on their excursions into the ocean depths.

But the explanation works only so long as the animal makes a limited number of consecutive dives. Polynesian fishermen who retrieve pearl oysters and mother-of-pearl dive twenty to forty times a day to depths of 75 to 100 feet. They, too, suffer from decompression sickness, which they call *tarawana*. For humans, repeated diving is as dangerous as prolonged diving. Yet large whales are able to dive over and over again without stopping. A typical sperm whale, for example, dives several times a day, ventures ten to thirty times deeper than Polynesian divers, stays under sixty times longer, and comes up for air only once in a while.

Several physiologists have attempted to shed some light on the mystery of how whales accomplish this. First of all, the scientists have noted that nitrogen is highly soluble in the blood of whales. They also noticed that nitrogen-rich whale blood, when left alone, restores only a small amount of the excess gas dissolved in it. What becomes of the missing nitrogen?

The answer lies not in any one mechanism but in a confluence of adaptations. The all-pervasive blubber of whales reroutes the nitrogen in their blood before it has a chance to reach nerve fibers; it also releases it very gradually as the animal surfaces. In addition, a whale's respiratory system comes equipped with a large number of nasal sacs and sinuses that act as nitrogen traps. As we have already seen, these cavities are lined with an oil-mucus emulsion ("foam") that accumulates dissolved nitrogen and other inert gases. When a surfacing whale takes five or six breaths in a row, it rids itself of far more excess nitrogen than a human diver does as he undergoes stage decompression.

Recently it has even been suggested that the deeper whales dive and the greater the pressure, the more their lungs cave in and that, at depths of more than about 450 feet, their lungs are completely collapsed. Any air still in them would then be forced into nasal passages and adjunct air sacs. Not a single molecule of excess nitrogen could be absorbed into the blood.

*Below: A sperm whale gloriously silhouetted in a nimbus of light. There are fascinating similarities between diving whales and human children at birth. When any mammal is submerged, lack of oxygen (anoxia) triggers the secretion of so-called stress hormones (chiefly epinephrine and norepinephrine, produced by the adrenal glands and sympathetic nerves). The swift, massive influx of these substances into the bloodstream increases arterial pressure and slows the heart rate. Moreover, the circulation of the blood is automatically rerouted, or shunted, from peripheral organs such as skin, muscles, and intestines to the heart and the brain, on which physiological survival depends. This hormonal reflex occurs in all mammals, but none has developed it as highly as the human fetus just before birth and sea mammals. H. Lagercrantz and T. Slotkin (1986) have shown that a baby about to emerge from the womb and a diving whale cope with the lack of oxygen in precisely the same way.*

*THE REMARKABLE HEAD OF THE SPERM WHALE*

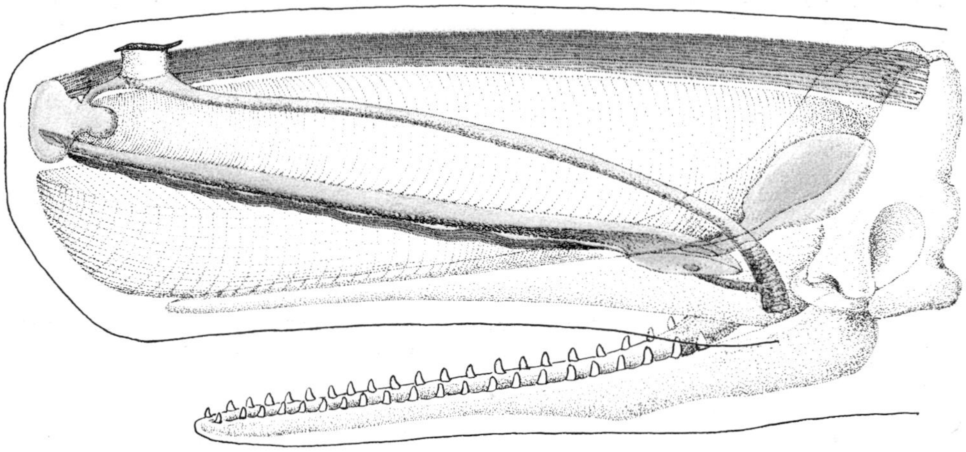

*The scientific name of the sperm whale is* macrocephalus, *and with good reason: It has a truly enormous head. If this rough-hewn, blocklike noggin seems disproportionately large, it is because it houses a peculiar anatomical feature known as the spermaceti organ. "The sperm whale's skull accounts for perhaps 12% of the weight of the head" (M. Clarke, 1979). The remaining 88 percent is taken up by the melon, "a complex mass of muscle and oil-filled connective tissue." Inside this thick-walled, pouchlike container is a substance whalers called spermaceti oil because they thought it was a reservoir of whale semen. "In a large male the organ may hold four tons of spermaceti oil." The organ rests on several layers of fatty and fibrous tissue.*

*This remarkable organ, which weighs as much as a full-grown elephant, is a vitally important adaptation to the whale's environment. A great deal has been written about its possible purposes. For one thing, the melon makes for a bigger head—and more ramming power in scuffles. The spermaceti organ also focuses, amplifies, and directs emitted sounds, especially during echolocation. One researcher has even suggested that "such focusing can concentrate the sound intensely enough to stun the squids that are the sperm whale's main prey."*

*But one aspect of the spermaceti organ—the fact that it contains so much oil—remains unexplained. The properties of the oil itself must be analyzed before its mysteries can be unveiled. Malcolm Clarke undertook just such an analysis. Here is a brief recapitulation of his hypothesis, which was published in* Scientific American *(240[1]: 128–41).*

*To begin with, Clarke reminds us that the sperm whale makes very deep dives (3,200 to 10,000 feet) and can remain underwater for as long as ninety minutes. As whalers often noted, "the animal frequently surfaces within a few hundred yards of the point where it began its dive. The whales are known to descend at a speed of about 4 knots (120 meters/min.) and to ascend at a speed of about 5 knots. Hence, a round trip to a depth of 1000 meters would not take more than 15 minutes. . . . The duration of a dive is sometimes three times longer." What does the whale do the rest of the time?*

*"Both the duration of the dive and the fact that the whale's place of emergence is close to its place of submergence suggest that when the whale comes to the bottom of its dive, it must sometimes lie almost still in the water. Perhaps its hunting strategy relies less on active pursuit and more on silent hovering." But a whale could not do this unless it could be "very nearly neutrally buoyant, that is, by having the same density as the surrounding water." How, then, is it able to vary its density and control its own buoyancy?*

*This is where the spermaceti organ comes in. "Temperature probes of freshly killed sperm whales show that when the whales are resting on the surface, the temperature of the spermaceti oil is 33°C (90°F). The oil begins to crystallize, or congeal into a solid, when its temperature drops below 31°C. Unlike the crystallization of water, which is almost instantaneous at the freezing point, the crystallization of spermaceti oil is a gradual process that is not completed until the temperature drops several degrees. When spermaceti oil freezes, it becomes denser and therefore occupies less volume. And occupying less volume, it displaces less . . . seawater and is less buoyant."*

*How does the whale cool itself down in the first place? It can lose heat either by passive conduction through the blubber and skin, or by "active" heat transport (that is, circulating the blood in a special way that results in heat loss through the nasal passages). The simpler of the passages, the left one, runs from the blowhole to the pharynx; this curving tube is the one through which the animal actually breathes. The more complicated right nasal passage starts out narrow, then "widens and flattens out as it passes downward to form a broad, flat chamber, the vestibular sac. . . . A continuation—a wide, flattened tube that runs back the length of the snout—meets the left nasal passage in a common cavity. Just forward of this narrowing the right nasal passage opens upward to connect with a second sac, the nasofrontal sac. . . . The right nasal passage is thus often more than a meter wide; its roundabout course through the snout is 5 meters or more long." This makes it an ideal cooling mechanism for spermaceti oil.*

*The whale can draw in seawater through its blowhole; the water, in turn, travels into nasal sacs, where it absorbs or "pumps" heat from the melon. The oil congeals as the whale's depth in the water increases. The animal achieves neutral buoyancy almost automatically. "In dives from 200 to 1000 meters deep, exchanging heat via the snout skin alone, the whale would reach neutral buoyancy within five minutes of attaining the desired depth. If both heat-exchange areas come into play, the interval would be shortened to three minutes."*

*When a sperm whale hovers at the bottom, its density equals that of the surrounding seawater, which means that it burns very little oxygen. The oxygen in its blood is shunted to the brain and heart, while the oxygen in its muscles is put on hold so that energy will be readily available to hunt prey that may happen by. "Even if the animal became exhausted during a deep dive"—say, after doing battle with a giant squid—"it could still pop to the surface for air. For example, a sperm whale that has exhausted itself can shunt the heat that is a by-product of its muscular activity into the spermaceti organ and again become positively buoyant. Such an exhausted animal is just as likely to reach the surface again as a fresh whale that can easily swim up."*

At any rate, whales do not suffer from decompression sickness. Moreover, they are not susceptible to nitrogen narcosis ("rapture of the deep")—a condition that comes about when nitrogen in the blood bonds to fatty materials, in particular, the myelin that sheathes nerve fibers. This leads to disorders of varying severity: euphoria, progressive loss of neuromuscular coordination, disorientation, loss of consciousness, and coma.

## MATTERS METABOLIC

An overall assessment of cetacean physiology indicates that whales are much more comfortable underwater than at the surface. We—who are so awkward, so self-conscious in the water—find that difficult to imagine. To be sure, whales must return to the surface to breathe. Aside from that periodic necessity, however, they are naturally inclined to remain submerged. What kinds of adjustments have whales made, through the ages, to be so thoroughly at home underwater?

Whales burn up less oxygen during a dive than at the surface because there is no wave friction underwater to impede their forward motion. It has been calculated that a 75-foot blue whale has to generate 1,175 horsepower and requires 600 cubic yards of oxygen a minute (assuming a conversion efficiency of 20 percent) in order to maintain a speed of 15 knots at the surface. To maintain the same speed underwater, however, only 168 horsepower and less than 70 cubic yards of oxygen per minute are needed. Poking along at the surface calls for 12.2 horsepower and 48 cubic feet of oxygen each minute; underwater, that drops to a remarkably efficient 7.5 horsepower and 30 cubic feet of oxygen per minute. That is why whales make so many long, shallow dives at such slow speeds: they are cutting their physiological expenditures.

Let us delve more deeply into this matter. Wonderful swimmers, unsurpassed divers, nimble acrobats, and indefatigable migrators though they may be, whales use up comparatively little energy, all things considered. Their metabolic rate is low—in fact, it is one of the lowest of any warm-blooded mammal. Metabolic rate—the rate at which heat is produced by the breakdown or building up of organic molecules per unit of weight and time—affects morphology, weight, speed internal structure, behavior, and ecological interaction. Generally speaking, the heavier the organism, the lower the metabolic rate. For example, a guinea pig weighing about 1 pound 4 ounces has a basal metabolic rate of 490 kilocalories per pound of weight per day; a 154-pound man burns 72.6 kilocalories per pound per day; and a four-ton elephant, 28.6 kilocalories per pound per day. Allowing for substantial fluctuation among individuals, the metabolic rate of whales ranges from about 7.9 kilocalories per pound per day for the blue whale and 5.5 kilocalories per pound per day for the fin whale to about 9 kilocalories per pound per day for the sperm whale (Lockyer, 1976). This low metabolism is why the giants of the sea ingest food by the ton, yet in the final analysis require little nutrition relative to body weight. By reducing the body's overall demand for oxygen, a low basal metabolic rate also affects the physiology of diving.

There are a number of other questions one could ask about the inner workings

*Below: Divers from the* Calypso *came across this right whale at the bottom of San José Bay, near Peninsula Valdés, Argentina. It is not unusual for members of this species to lie at the bottom for minutes at a time. According to Dr. Mandojana (1982), right whales do this to elude potential enemies, such as killer whales or people. By keeping perfectly still, the whale conserves precious oxygen, enjoys an excellent view of its surroundings, and avoids creating telltale ripples at the surface.*

*GLANDULAR MATTERS*

*Although whales have a relatively low metabolic rate, they have huge thyroid glands. The thyroid of a 1,100-pound beluga weighs about 3.5 ounces, that of a horse of equal weight only 1.4 (S. R. Riedman and E. T. Gustafson, 1966). Therein lies a contradiction. Metabolic rate is usually determined by the amount of thyroxin the thyroid secretes, and hormone secretion is itself regulated by the pituitary gland and the hypothalamus. This remains a mystery.*

*On the other hand, whales have tiny adrenal glands; comparatively speaking, those of large cetaceans are even smaller than those of diminutive species. The adrenal glands (the medulla, or inner part, to be exact) secrete adrenaline, the celebrated hormone that is pumped into the blood at times of stress or intense emotion (fear, anger, aggression). It mobilizes the body's energy at a moment's notice. Cats, tigers, and racehorses are high-strung "sprinters"; they have huge adrenal glands. Whales, however, are paragons of gentleness, imperturbability, and self-control—just as the size of their adrenal glands would lead one to expect.*

*Above: Occasionally, whales are seen resting motionless at the surface, as this humpback is doing. Sometimes they are sleeping, but not always. A few species, especially right whales, seem to enjoy stretching out like this when the sun is shining, and Dr. Mandojana (1982) has even suggested that they are sunning themselves! This may not be as implausible as it sounds: After a few days of "tanning," their skin turns darker and "peels."*

of a whale. For example, how does a whale manage to withstand the constant cold of polar seas or the extreme low temperatures of depths below 600 feet? The answer is twofold: a low ratio of surface area to body volume, and blubber. Whales are nothing more than two cones—the head and trunk—placed base to base at the back of the head. Therefore, relative to body weight, a proportionally small surface area is available for heat exchange. A 63-foot blue whale weighing 22,000 pounds has a body surface of approximately 630 square feet, or 6.3 square feet per ton. A dolphin weighing 220 pounds has a total body surface of 6.3 square feet. Hence, the dolphin is 100 times more susceptible to fluctuations in temperature than a blue whale (not to mention the fact that dolphins have comparatively longer flippers—which add to heat loss).

Secondly, a layer of blubber (up to 20 inches thick in right whales) acts as an efficient insulator. Lockyer (1976) found that the heat-conducting capacity of whale blubber is very low. In living blubber, capillary networks are arranged to allow only very gradual loss of heat; barely 10 percent of all heat exchange takes place in this layer. Since whales have a relatively low lung capacity and do not "shed" many calories when they exhale, they usually find themselves faced with the unlikely dilemma of overheating while swimming in icy seas!

Dead blubber insulates only half as effectively. Yet blubber insulates so well, in fact, that the internal temperature of a dead whale does not drop below 30°C (85°F) for several days.

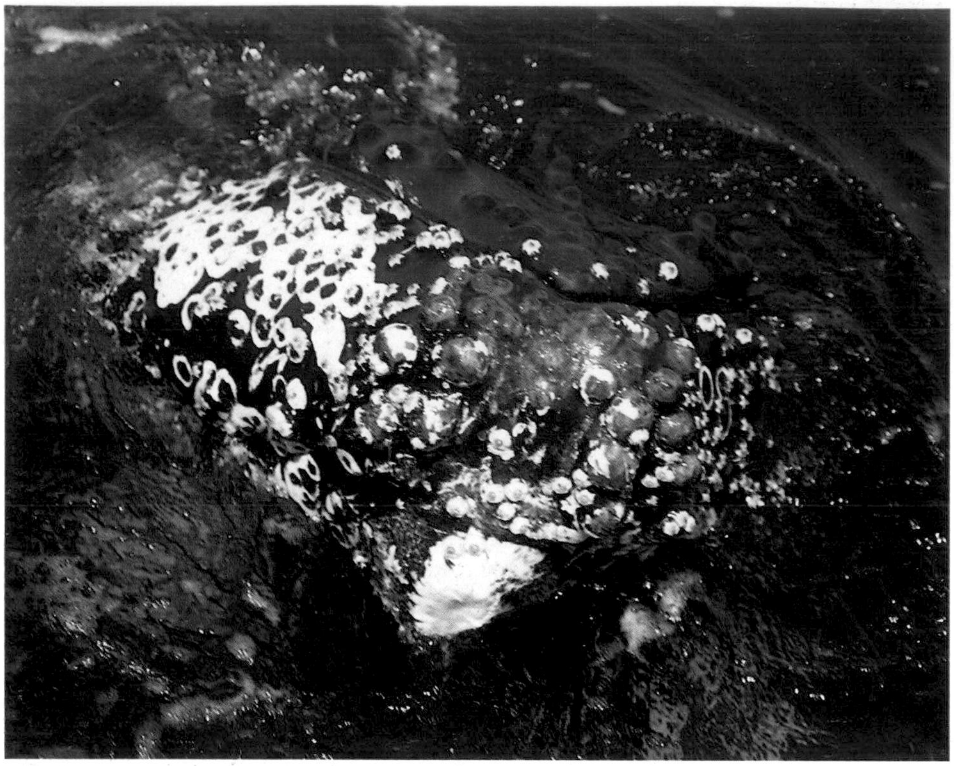

### *A CLOSER LOOK AT WHALE SKIN*

*Whale skin has come under the scrutiny of bionics, the branch of science concerned with the application of biological "performance" to the solution of engineering problems. Few problems bedevil shipbuilders more than turbulence, which creates drag on the hull and slows the vessel down. But water flow over cetacean bodies is virtually laminar—that is, nearly without friction or drag. By learning the secret of drag-free propulsion, we could manufacture a new breed of ultraefficient ships.*

*Most of the laboratory research concerned with this question has been funded by armed forces in the United States, the Soviet Union, and Europe. So far as we know, nothing concrete has come out of these studies, although they have cost many cetaceans their freedom and, in some cases, their lives. To be sure, we have a clearer idea of how sea mammals "damp out" boundary-layer turbulence, particularly by means of minute reflex adjustments in the skin. For the time being, however, the search goes on for inert materials capable of duplicating the sensitive, instantaneous reactions of living tissue.*

Researchers soon realized that, at least in whales, thermoregulation depends almost entirely on the tail, the flippers, and the dorsal fin (if present). Unlike the head and trunk, these appendages have a high surface-to-weight ratio, a generous supply of blood vessels, and very little blubber insulation. As we have seen, whales can shut down most peripheral blood circulation or restore it when needed; and this regulating mechanism seems to work particularly well in the fins and flippers. They take excess heat from within the body and pump it into the surrounding water as soon as the animal's internal temperature starts to rise.

We now know that whales perceive fluctuations in both water and air temperature over their entire body surface. The upper and lower thresholds of sensitivity vary from species to species. Right whales, for example, confine themselves to waters between 5° and 20°C (40° to 70°F), as do gray whales. Blue whales can tolerate 0° to 25°C (32° to 75°F). Minke whales usually limit their range to 5° to 10°C (40 to 50°F), but sightings have been reported in much colder and much warmer seas. The humpback is eurythermal (that is, able to live in a wide range of temperatures) and feels equally at home in below-freezing waters and warm seas of 30°C (85°F).

In sperm whales, temperature tolerance is related to age and sex. Cows and juveniles are hardly seen anywhere except in temperate or warm seas; bulls, however, are given to congregating in large groups "on the line"—that is, along the equator—as well as making lone sojourns toward the poles, where waters dip to freezing. As one might expect, accurate temperature perception may be a factor for all species when it comes time to migrate.

## THE FIVE SENSES

It is something of an oversimplification, but whales are not "tuned in" to their surroundings by means of touch, taste, smell, or even sight—which is not to say that they don't use these senses. Theirs is above all a world of hearing. Through sound, whales take their bearings, detect objects, find food, and evade potential foes. Today we know that the "silent world" of the seas is a vast echo chamber and that its inhabitants are constantly bombarded with noise. In this realm, where a good ear is a key to success, whales reign supreme.

First, a few words about the other senses. Whales have a fairly well-developed sense of touch, which serves important social purposes. Although whales are generally amiable creatures, they do use their bodies for competition, aggression, and defense. In most instances, however, touching relates to play or parental care. Whales love to rub against each other, and not just when they are courting or mating; apparently they indulge in stroking for the sheer pleasure of it. More sensual individuals are given to brushing against the wooden hulls of ships. The flippers (acting as "arms" and "hands") seem to be, as in other mammals, more richly innervated and more generously supplied with tactile cells than the rest of the body. Although "their fingers are fused and wrapped in a glove of tough, thick skin" (Lacépède, 1804) and although the digits cannot be moved individually, the flippers are often used to clasp, coax, and fondle a mate or a newborn calf. Surely no one will accuse us of anthropomorphism if we venture to say that physical contact such as this is a sign of tenderness.

*Opposite: The snout of a humpback whale. Almost all authorities on cetacean physiology maintain that whale skin is not particularly sensitive, especially since it is often studded with parasites. According to divers from the* Calypso, *however, such is not the case; and their findings have been confirmed. However lightly one may touch the skin of a whale, the animal reacts with a shudder. Considering the relative size of a human finger and the body surface of these mammoth creatures, that is an astonishing reflex response. Other evidence suggests that whale skin is rich in nerve endings, and that would help explain the importance of body contact between mother and young (as with these humpbacks, below).*

Whales have no fingernails or other superficial body growth, except for a few hairs. The importance of these few hairs as organs of touch is inversely proportional to their quantity.

Odontocetes are practically hairless after infancy. Mysticetes, however, retain some growth around the mouth and on the snout; its chin hairs are often aligned in two rows. Baleen whales sport a "beard" and "mustache" of between twenty and sixty bristles. The shaggiest species are the bowhead and the right whale.

Richly innervated with up to 400 nerve fibers per hair (Grassé, 1955), these vibrissae are actually highly sensitive organs of touch. They lack the glands and erector pili muscles of other types of mammalian hair, but on closer inspection with a microscope we see that each follicle is honeycombed with blood sinuses. Hence, they are erectile. It is not known what purpose these sensors serve; they remain one of the many cetacean secrets that science has yet to penetrate.

## TASTE AND SMELL

Although we do not know for sure, the organs of taste seem to be rudimentary in cetaceans. This comes as no surprise: since they do not chew their food, they have

### *SKIN AND BLUBBER*

*Whales have very sensitive skin. As P.-P. Grassé notes (1955), "The sheen of its outer surface is unlike that of any other mammal."*

*The epidermis consists of a keratinized outer layer, the* stratum corneum, *and a deeper Malpighian layer (*stratum germinativum*), which contains melanin and other pigments. Sandwiched between them is the* stratum lucidum, *a layer so thin that it is nearly invisible.*

*The dermis, which has few papillae, contains a padding of connective tissue reinforced with stiff fibers. Deeper down is the blubber, or* panniculus adiposus. *Blubber is made up of clusters of tightly packed connective fibers with large oil-filled cells in the interstices. A network of small arteries and veinlets crisscrosses the fatty matter. Whale blubber is not flabby or shapeless; reinforcing fibers keep it firm and compact.*

*Whales have no pores or sweat glands. Excess heat is brought to the surface through the capillaries, not by perspiration. However, droplets of oil ooze through the epidermis, helping to permit drag-free water flow over the body.*

*The average thickness of the blubber layer varies from species to species and fluctuates with the seasons. Whales are fattest in the fall, when they leave the polar feeding grounds, and slimmest at the end of the following spring, after the migration from the tropics.*

*The blubber of a right whale is up to a foot and a half thick; a bowhead's is even thicker. An adult male blue whale is encased in blubber 2 to 14 inches thick; the female's ranges between 6 and 16 inches. The other rorquals are not as plump, except for the fairly rotund humpback. The gray whale has 2 to 8 inches of blubber, the sperm whale 4 to 12. The* panniculus adiposus *is thickest on the upper surface and sides of the rear part of the body, but thins out considerably on the flippers (site of heat exchange), around the blowholes, around the eyes, and on the lower lip.*

*Generally speaking, the combined subcutaneous blubber and internal fats of the gray whale, blue whale, and other rorquals account for an estimated one-fourth of total body weight; for a humpback or sperm whale, one-third; for a right whale, two-fifths.*

*During fetal development, whales grow varying amounts of hair. They are hairless at birth, however, except for some vestigial bristles that form a scraggly "mustache" and "beard" on the snout. In some species, such as right whales and California gray whales, they are clearly visible (like the ones on the snout of this gray whale calf). Whale bristles are, in fact, highly sensitive organs of touch; more accurately known as vibrissae, they heighten the pleasure of physical contact among members of a group.*

little opportunity to taste it. Dolphins that were fed pieces of spoiled whiting and codfish spit out the bad food at once; they apparently could tell that it was putrid. Can sperm whales taste their prey? It is hard to conceive of any higher animal species with so little sense of taste.

Fish have a highly developed sense of smell. Migrating eels and salmon rely on smell, in part, to find their way back to their spawning grounds. When the earliest four-legged land animals (amphibians) appeared, the olfactory cells of these new vertebrates migrated toward the nasal fossae, and came to be used specifically for detecting chemical effluvia in the air. When cetaceans returned to the water, the configuration and physiology of the upper breathing passages underwent tremendous changes that left them with almost no sense of smell.

Fossil skulls indicate that Basilosaurus and other archaeocetes still had fairly well-developed olfactory peduncles. But as they adapted to marine life, the sense of smell was gradually replaced by developing auditory centers and other functions.

In toothed whales, there is no trace of a smell-detection apparatus, not even olfactory nerves or corresponding lobes in the brain (Breathnach, 1960), although vestiges of olfactory organs have been observed in fetuses. But there is evidence that odontocetes may not be completely anosmatic. "Sperm whales, when running, flee to windward. . . . Haley points out that the whales, if the air is calm, usually turn to the direction from which the wind blew last, and never deviate a single compass point from their flight in that direction" (K. S. Norris, 1966). Why would they behave this way if they could not "smell" trouble? Some speculate that this reaction is a holdover from a time when toothed whales still had the sense of smell and that the air acts as a purely tactile stimulus.

Baleen whales have retained olfactory nerves, but these are "quite slender" and "everything suggests that these animals are anosmatic" (P.-P. Grassé, 1955). Other scientists argue that mysticetes are still able to pick up some smells—that of krill, in particular—from quite some distance. Several eyewitness accounts lend weight

to this hypothesis. Vice-Admiral Pleville-le-Peley, onetime minister of the French navy, wrote to Lacépède (1804) about the time he threw overboard some putrid water from the bottom of his cod-fishing boat, whereupon an entire group of right whales was so put off by the stench that it scattered.

## A QUIZZICAL TWINKLE IN THE EYE

A whale's eyes are located directly above the corners of the lips, near the shoulders. They are small: about the size of grapefruit in right whales and sperm whales. The eyelids, though present, are so swollen with fatty matter that they are practically immobile. There are no eyelashes. According to Lacépède (1804), the eye of the whale is "rather oblate," the lens nearly spherical (like that of seals and other marine mammals). The iris, when dilated, reveals a pupil that is "stretched out transversally"; while sacs beneath the upper eyelid discharge a thick, viscous fluid. The substance secreted by these well-developed tear glands (or facsimiles thereof) protects the cornea and conjunctiva from the effects of seawater. This fluid is especially noticeable when a dolphin is moved from one place to another; it seems to be weeping. Theoretically, all of these characteristics should add up to first-rate eyesight.

The eye of the sperm whale caught the attention of Frédéric Cuvier (1835), who

*The sperm whale "blows" forward and to the left through a single blowhole. Melville was captivated by the wild beauty of the sperm whale and its spout: "And how nobly it raises our conceit of the mighty, misty monster . . . his vast, mild head overhung by a canopy of vapor . . . and that vapor—as you will sometimes see it—glorified by a rainbow, as if Heaven itself has put its seal upon his thoughts."*

*The eye of a large whale is about the size of a grapefruit. Relative to body size, however, it seems minuscule. Right: The eye of the California gray whale, as pictured in Scammon's* Marine Mammals of the North-western Coast of North America *(1874). The artist has given it a decidedly human appearance.*

noted that it is 8 to 9 inches across at its widest point and has a strange yellowish tinge to it. He conceded that whales see well "in a calm, transparent sea," but questioned Lacépède's claims about their in-air vision. "Its vision is quite poor once it raises its eyes above the surface."

Cetologists have taken sides with either Lacépède or Cuvier ever since. Many, like Cuvier, still believe that whales have poor eyesight, at least out of the water and at close range. They point out that a whale's eyes are very small indeed (1/350 of total body length in humpbacks, 1/440 in fin whales, 1/600 in blue whales); that the surface of the cornea is uneven; and that an unusually thick sclera (the "white" of the eye in humans) reduces the useful capacity of the posterior and anterior chambers (Grassé, 1955). Experts argue that whales dive so deep or feed in waters so turbid that their eyesight is of little use to them anyway. In a lighter vein, Slijper (1962) mentions that not once in its entire life does a blue whale have the pleasure of contemplating its own tail. Noting that the retina is "almost completely vascularized and rich in rods" (the black-and-white vision cells responsive to faint light), Grassé concludes that a whale's in-water vision is sharp but poor at close range because the lens cannot focus. Above the surface, "the eyes of whales are highly myopic"; the indexes of refraction are such that visual images come to a focus in front of the retina.

Those in the Lacépède camp try to make a case for both first-rate close-up vision in the water and good in-air vision. They note that whales have been known to brush against divers, looking out of the corner of the eye as if to size them up. They remind us that dolphins leap with astonishing precision, and that, unless whales have good in-air vision, it is hard to explain why so many of them "spy hop," or poke their heads straight up out of the water to have a look around. Recent experiments have demonstrated that dolphins, at least, see well both in and out of the water.

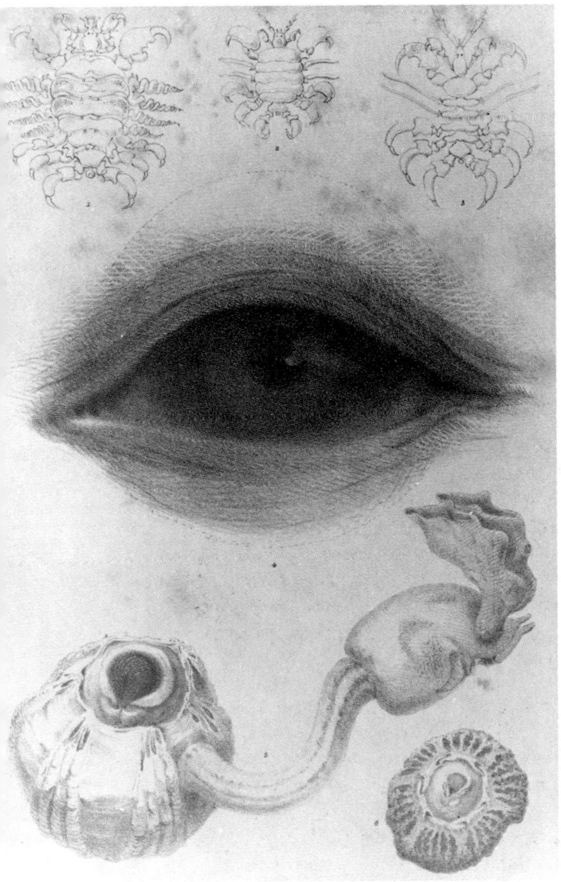

For a whale, light is more than just a visual stimulus. A whale's ability to perceive changes in day length—known as the circadian rhythm—plays a crucial part in triggering the urge to migrate and is at least as important as the animal's sensitivity to fluctuations in air temperature. This set of perception and responses, regulated by the pituitary gland, occurs in all animals that make seasonal migrations. W. H. Dawbin (in K. S. Norris, 1966) noted that nursing female humpbacks leave the Antarctic when there are only eight and a half hours of daylight left, whereas pregnant females of the very same species go on feeding and wait until the days are no more than six and a half hours long.

## EARS: ALL THE BETTER TO SEE YOU WITH

Whalemen knew that their quarry could hear them from a distance. According to Scoresby (1823), whales are very quick to notice and flee the impact of ripples generated by moving ships. Yet whales have no ears—at least none that anyone can see. Ever since Petrus Camper's pioneering treatise on the subject (*Traité de l'ouïe du cachalot*, 1765), people have suspected that the hearing apparatus of the whale is a marvelous example of successful adaptation to an aquatic environment.

We now know that they are wonderful listening machines whose ability to pick up sounds both above and below the surface far surpasses ours. They have been called "acoustic creatures," and deservedly so.

Since the oldest known archaeocetes already had an ear similar to that of modern species, all we know about the evolution of hearing in whales is that it occurred eons ago. Sound waves had to be heard through water, and their auditory tract adapted accordingly.

The absence of an external ear is simply a concession to the laws of hydrodynamics. Mysticetes even retain the vestiges of two muscles that once moved the auricle. Land mammals rely on ear pinnae to collect airborne sounds, but scientists currently suggest that echolocating whales receive underwater sounds through the lower jaw. In this respect, it can be said that toothed whales hear with the mouth.

The opening of the ear, just behind the eye, is so unobtrusive that it long went unnoticed. In the great blue whale, this pinhole of an orifice is no more than 2 millimeters across (0.04 inches). The auditory ear canal is also extremely narrow, and in mysticetes part of it is actually interrupted by a solid band of tissue. At the point where the meatus flares out, it is clogged by an elongated accumulation of wax and shedded skin cells. The ear plug builds up, layer upon layer, rather like a strata of sedimentary rocks; scientists use the "laminations" in the ears of har-

*All the divers from the* Calypso *agree that, up close, the most striking thing about a whale is the expressive, inquisitive, knowing look in its eyes. Here is how Albert Falco describes the experience. "Underwater, the right whale has drawn a bead on me. Its little oval eyeball, with a large, white hemispherical callosity for an eyebrow, seems to have no trouble seeing me. We stare at each other (it with its left eye) for a good thirty seconds. I am struck by the way they twinkle with intelligence, as if to ask: What kind of creature are you? What species do you belong to? Perhaps it thinks I am a dolphin in distress, unable to swim properly, enveloped in a horrible rubbery skin with yellow striping."*

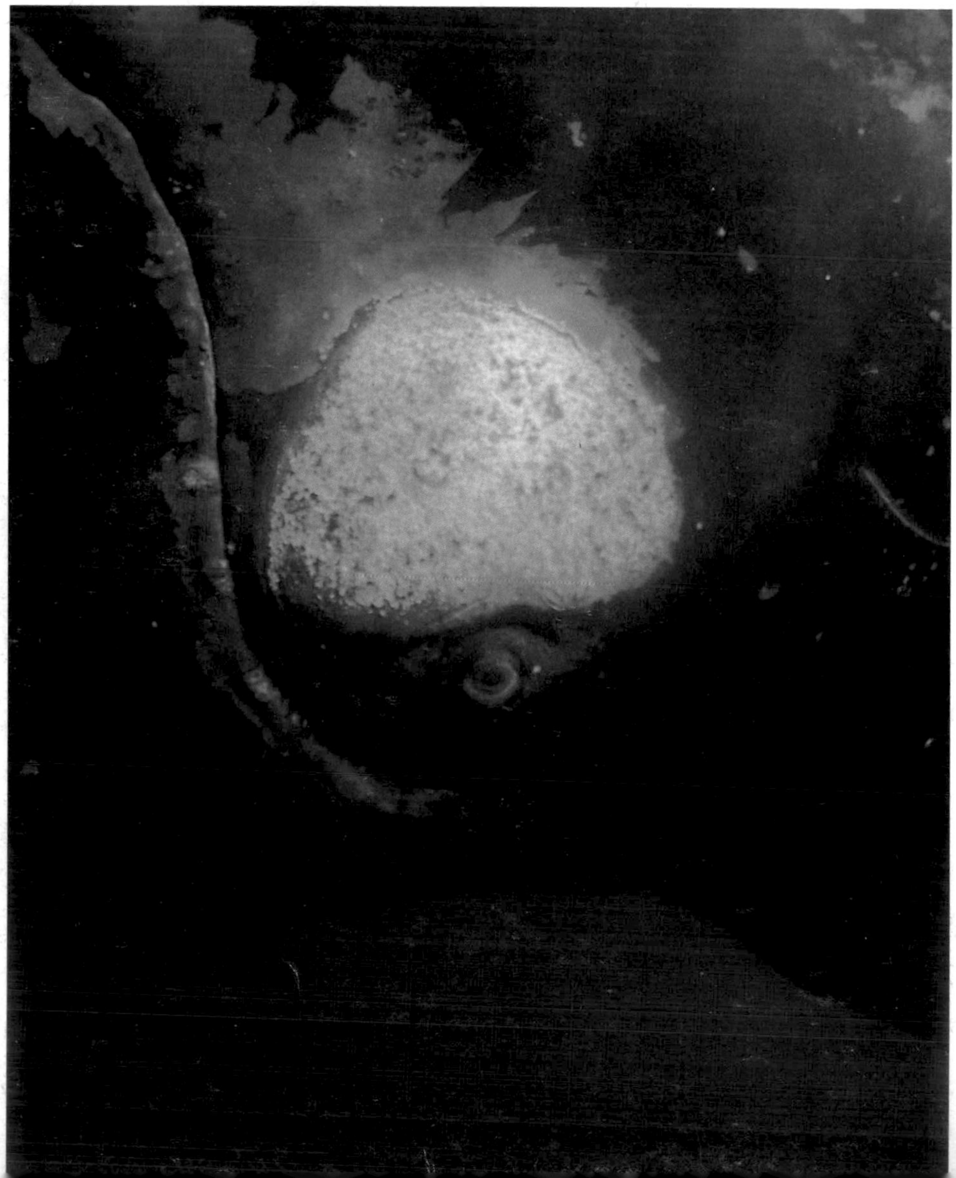

Cetaceans are sound-oriented animals. Their sense of hearing is paramount. However, there is no external ear as such: only a minuscule opening a few centimeters behind the eye. The auditory canal, only 1 to 2 millimeters in diameter, is partially obstructed. Below: Cross section of the hearing apparatus of a rorqual; the auditory meatus is at the left. Above: Although it appears to be sleeping, this California gray whale in Magdalena Bay, Baja California, is "all ears."

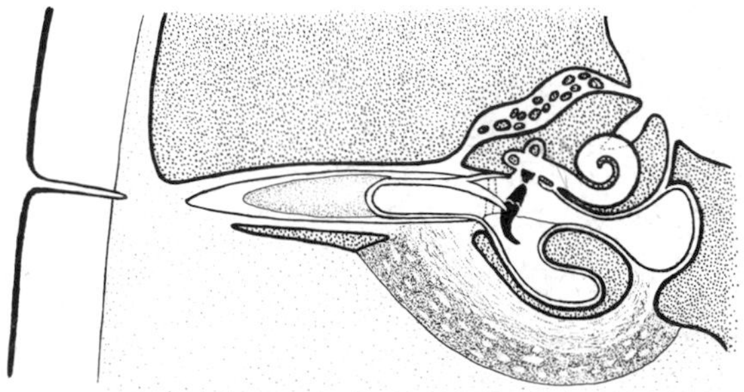

pooned individuals as a rough indicator of age. The ear plugs of baleen whales are comparatively bigger than those of toothed whales.

The auditory canal ends in a peculiar eardrum that looks like a glove finger pointing outward. It is about 3 inches long and far more rigid than the human eardrum.

The bones of the middle ear, although fused to each other, are not directly connected to the rest of the skull; they are suspended from it by means of ligaments. All around them is a complex network of cavities and sinuses filled with a foamy mucus that further insulates the ear from the skull and provides yet another means by which whales filter out all but essential sounds.

Close examination of the inner ear indicates that "whales, especially toothed whales, hear with a versatility that is probably without equal in the animal kingdom" (Van Heel, 1974), which ability has been demonstrated by other scientists.

The auditory nerve looks like a length of thick cable. It is not only much thicker than any other sensory nerve in the whale, but comparatively much larger than the auditory nerve of other mammals. The corresponding lobes in the brain are highly developed, as are the pathways connecting the acoustic centers to other parts of the brain.

Although toothed whales seem to hear better than baleen whales, large cetaceans in general have excellent hearing and can pick up sound far better than humans. They are particularly sensitive to high-frequency sound, and Van Heel (1974) notes that "in odontocetes the auditory center that decodes high frequencies is particularly well developed." The range of human hearing is about 30 to 16,000 hertz (cycles per second). In dolphins, the range is an amazing 100 to 150,000 hertz (W. Schevill and B. Lawrence, 1953; Scott Johnson, 1968). The susus—river dolphins of South America—and the bottlenosed dolphin can tune in to even higher frequencies.

Whales rely on sharp hearing to detect the presence of prey, ships, and possible predators. Never is that dependency greater than when they have to find their way through turbid or murky waters. It is an established fact that some odontocetes use the structures associated with the "forehead" region to send out sequences of sounds, then analyze the vibrations any objects in the vicinity bounce back. This process of echolocation—one of the wonders of evolution—makes it possible for whales to piece together a minutely detailed acoustical "picture" of their surroundings. They rely on echolocation to get their bearings, wend their way between reefs, recognize their own kind, identify foes, and locate schools of fish or shoals of invertebrates. How else could sperm whales detect giant squid in the pitch-black abyssal zone? The "resolving power" of large whales has not yet been determined, but research with dolphins showed that small odontocetes can "see," from a distance of eight inches, a copper wire 0.2 mm (0.008 inch) thick—blindfolded (R.-G. Busnel). Baleen whales lack all structures that are associated with echolocation in toothed whales; baleen whales do produce sounds, but apparently only for communicating with each other.

## GLUTTONS OF THE SEA

A whale feeding is a phenomenal sight that has inspired many a tall tale. Dumbfounded travelers and naturalists claim to have seen, with their own two eyes, sperm whales gulp down entire ships, crew and all. According to Cuvier (1835), sperm whales have been known to attack seals, sharks, dolphins, small whales, "even men, although this has yet to be confirmed."

In fact, man-eating whales are a figment of the imagination. The story of Jonah has never been "confirmed," to quote Cuvier. Only one such incident has been reported in the corpus of whaling literature. A man fell into the sea and was supposedly swallowed (no doubt inadvertently) by a fairly large sperm whale. When the whale was opened, the man was found "badly crushed and partially digested" (Dr. E. Y. Davis, *Natural History*, 1947).

Aside from this case, there is no reliable firsthand account of man-eating on the part of whales. Yet artists the world over depicted whales with their mouths agape, gulping down fish, seals, terror-stricken fishermen, ships with crews, even entire islands—houses and all. What unreasoning terror, what transferences prompted them to do so? The verbal and pictorial flights of fancy inspired by the sinister myth of Jonah shall be discussed in the final chapter of our book. Meanwhile, let's stick to the facts.

The feeding behavior patterns of the sperm whale will be discussed separately from those of other whales because it is the only large cetacean with teeth, and its diet consists primarily of cephalopods. No one has ever seen a sperm whale feeding, and with good reason: These creatures usually stalk their prey hundreds of yards below the surface, sometimes venturing more than a thousand yards down, in the fearsome abyss.

We know considerably more about mysticetes. The scores of horny baleen plates in their capacious mouths act as a sieve, trapping small fish or planktonic

*Like all cetaceans, rorquals have a phenomenally keen sense of hearing. Do rorquals use biosonar to echolocate the way dolphins, killer whales, sperm whales, and other odontocetes do? Some cetologists believe that mysticetes (baleen whales) do not echolocate at all; others maintain that their sonar is simply less sophisticated than that of toothed whales. There is not enough data from the field to settle the matter one way or the other.*

*Overleaf: Baleen whales, such as the humpbacks in this photograph, eat very little when they are wintering in warm tropical waters, but they make up for it in the summer, when they migrate to polar or subpolar feeding grounds. For sheer intensity and wild grandeur, few sights can match that of whales feasting on plankton or small schooling fish.*

crustaceans, especially krill. Although some species of baleen whales feed underwater at certain times of the day, others are basically skimmer feeders. Right whales, bowheads, and sei whales have a habit of tilting a bit to the side as they zigzag at the surface. As they take in mouthfuls of water and food, the movement of the jaws creates turbulence that "breaks" hydrodynamic flow and slows the whale down. As a result, their "feeding speed" is a lethargic 2 to 4 mph. Here is how Van Beneden describes these orgies at sea: "A whale that encounters a shoal of food proceeds slowly and swims with its mouth open. The water surges in, the lower jaw opens wide, and the tongue is raised, leaving food collected inside the mouth to form a bolus that enters the esophagus."

Baleen plates are cornified skin growths akin to the superficial body growth of other vertebrates—nails, hair, claws, feathers, scales. (Some naturalists, such as Grassé [1955], have suggested that baleen plates are more closely related to the palatine sutures, or *rugae palatinae*—transverse ridges on the roof of the mouth—found in other mammals.) Be that as it may, baleen plates are pieces of epithelial tissue, hardened with keratin, and encased in a cortex of hollow tubules. They vary in size, color, and number, depending on the species. The texture and density of

## *SKIMMERS AND GULPERS*

*Baleen whales fall into one of three groups, depending on feeding technique (Nemoto, 1969). "Skimmers" swim very slowly with their mouths open, "filtering constantly until enough food has accumulated on the baleen to be scraped off and swallowed." This category includes right whales, bowheads, and sei whales. No data are available for the pygmy right whale.*

*"Gulpers"—blue whales, fin whales, Bryde's whales, minkes, humpbacks, and, infrequently, sei whales—swim a bit faster and must feed more intensely to satisfy their food requirements. A meal consists of a series of separate mouthfuls; each time the animal takes in a huge amount of water along with the plankton or fish, then forcefully expels the water through the baleen.*

the bristles that fringe the plates vary with the size of the whale's favorite prey. Each slatlike plate looks like a right triangle with a slightly curved base, but only the curved "hypotenuse" facing the inside of the mouth has the filtering bristles.

Whales have huge tongues. The tongue of a blue whale is thought to weigh as much as an elephant. Melville likened its tender outer skin to "a rug of the softest Turkey." Although the tongues of rorquals are comparatively smaller, more muscular, and more tapered than those of right whales, none of them is able to move it freely: It cleaves to the floor of the mouth from base to tip. The characteristic distension observed in feeding whales is controlled by powerful levators that raise the tongue until it fills practically the entire space between the jaws, expelling the water inside the mouth through the baleen. The living organisms trapped behind the mat of bristles proceed to the pharynx and into the esophagus.

Like latter-day Jonahs, let us tour the alimentary canal. In mysticetes, the pharynx is narrow; in toothed whales, somewhat more capacious. A sperm whale can swallow a shark; an orca can manage a sea lion. Since swallowing and breathing are anatomically separate procedures, food passes into the esophagus and never "goes down the wrong way" into pulmonary passages, even during a dive. Whales swallow their food without masticating it: in mysticetes, the cumbersome baleen plates make it all but impossible to chew. Odontocetes can use their conical, peglike teeth to grasp prey, but they cannot grind once a victim has been caught. The esophagus is narrow across in balaenopterids. The gullet of a large sperm whale, however, is just wide enough to accommodate a human being.

As early as 1680, Edward Tyson described the elaborate stomach of a dissected

*A whale gives a staggering performance every time it feeds. As it propels itself through the water, powerfully, majestically, it spreads its jaws, catching phenomenal amounts of water, krill, and small fish in its dilatable mouth. Then it shuts its jaws and lifts its enormous tongue, pushing water out through the baleen plates and trapping scores of wriggling organisms, ready to be swallowed. Opposite: California gray whales occasionally swallow algae and mollusks along with their favorite crustaceans.*

porpoise. In 1787, however, John Hunter noted that a multichambered stomach was common to all cetaceans. Since this anatomical characteristic was also shared by animals that chew the cud, Hunter concluded that whales were distant relatives of sheep and cows. Actually, this is a case of divergent evolution. The primitive cetacean archaeocetes developed from condylarths, which also produced the line that became ungulates.

The stomach of a typical whale (H. Hosokawa and T. Kamiya, 1971) consists of four compartments in succession. The first, a dilatable saclike extension of the esophagus, has a thick lining and powerful striated muscles. Although it has no digestive glands, it is highly contractible and probably grinds food the way a bird's gizzard does. The second chamber has a generous supply of peptic glands. The third sac may be described as the pyloric part of the stomach; in mature baleen whales, it is the largest of the four (about 2 feet 8 inches across and 3 feet 7 inches long in a sei whale measuring about 52 feet). The fourth and last compartment, an enormous bulge in the intestine, is slightly smaller than the third. It receives a combined bile and pancreatic duct that serves other digestive glands as well. The first and second chambers are separated by a constriction, but there are two semilunar valves between the second and third and a pyloric sphincter between the third and fourth. In sperm whales, the compartments are even more clearly differentiated than in mysticetes, and the first two are larger than the second two. The stomach capacity of a 38-foot sperm whale weighing 18.9 tons is about 220 gallons; a 52-foot individual weighing 45 tons can hold almost 500 gallons.

Why do whales have to have a multichambered stomach? They do not masticate, tear, or grind their prey, and their salivary glands are poorly developed. Therefore the bolus has to be prepared physically and chemically at the very start of the stomach before it proceeds farther along the digestive tract. The four-chambered configuration divides the swallowed food into manageable portions for more effective enzymatic action. (Enzymes help break down huge amounts of hard and durable substances, such as the calcium carbonate and chitin in the carapaces of planktonic crustaceans.)

Structurally, a whale's intestine is a uniform organ. In sperm whales and most other odontocetes, there is no cecum or large intestine as such; the small intestine looks the same all the way to the rectum. In mysticetes, the cecum and colon are similar to those of land mammals. Regardless of the species, the intestine is always extremely long: on average, five to six times the length of a baleen whale (400–550 feet for a 80-foot blue whale) and up to fifteen times the length of a sperm whale (750 feet for a 50-foot individual!). The liver, which is small relative to total length, is roughly divided into two lobes; there is no gallbladder. The elongated pancreas discharges its fluid through a duct that empties into the common bile duct instead of directly into the duodenum. There is an abundance of Lieberkuhn's glands, but very few Brunner's glands.

*A whale's kidney is made up of a large number of renculi ("little kidneys") that excrete a highly concentrated urine. Below: A drawing of part of a sperm whale kidney.*

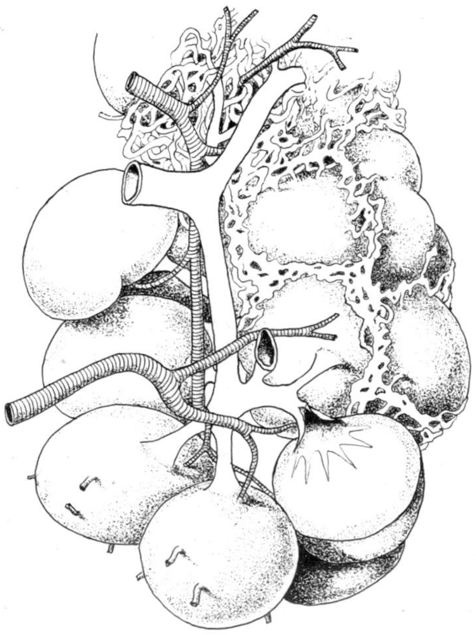

## BANQUETS AT SEA

Just what do these gluttons feast upon? Right whales are partial to zooplankton—minute sea creatures. In the northern hemisphere these whales gorge themselves

*A whale's stomach consists of four chambers, each of which plays a particular part in the digestive process. Many species of rorquals on polar summering grounds feed primarily on small, shrimplike euphausiid crustaceans (krill). Right: The stomach of a blue whale, cut open on the deck of a whaler in the Antarctic, disgorges its undigested load of krill.*

on copepods and, to a lesser extent, euphausiids. South of the equator, their summertime staple is *Euphausia superba*, the shrimplike euphausiid crustacean commonly known as krill.

The essentially planktonic diet of bowheads consists of copepods, krill, and assorted pteropods, or "sea butterflies," creatures so abundant that they sometimes turn acres of the Arctic Sea pink in summer. Named for the winglike growths on their feet, pteropods can constitute the bowhead's main course for weeks at a time. But the whale will not turn its nose up at benthic organisms to round out its menu.

We know no more about the diet of the pygmy right whale than we do about any other aspect of the species—which is to say very little. In 1970, "Soviet whalers killed a few specimens for scientific purposes in the South Atlantic, from which we

### *OUT WITH THE BAD*

*Paradoxical though it may seem, whales do very little drinking; they make do with the fluid produced by the biochemical breakdown of their food. Since they have no sweat glands and do not depend on perspiration to regulate internal body temperature, they require less water than does a land mammal of comparable size.*

*Like all ocean-dwelling creatures, however, whales must deal with osmosis: the water in their bodies contains less salt than ambient seawater, and therefore tries to pass through cell membranes and into the urine. In other words, their bodies wage a never-ending battle against dehydration from the day they are born to the day they die.*

*Evolution came to the rescue and endowed them with enormous kidneys. Those of the fin whale are about a yard long, 8 inches across, and 4 inches thick; each weighs between 130 and 155 pounds. According to E. J. Slijper (1958), they account for 0.44 percent of a fin whale's total weight and as much as 1.1 percent of a dolphin's (compared with 0.37 percent of a human's). The kidneys of most mammals have a smooth outer surface; a whale's are composite organs made up of a great many discrete "renculi" or "little kidneys." There are 40 such units in a beluga whale's kidney, 450 in that of a common dolphin. Krill-eating baleen whales, faced with a serious salt elimination problem, have even more. The bowhead has 1,350 renculi, the fin whale as many as 6,350 (Ommaney, quoted in P.-P. Grassé, 1955).*

*Each renculus is a self-contained filtering system. Collectively, the renculi comprise a large filtering surface and allow the whale to excrete highly concentrated urine. After the water in its body has been relieved of its excess salt, most of it is reabsorbed into the deep layers of the renal cortex and returned to the bloodstream.*

have learned little more than their stomachs contained unidentified species of the tiny crustacean *Calanus*."

Although gray whales consume their share of planktonic organisms on polar feeding grounds, they seem to specialize in bottom feeding. The species' feeding habits earned it the nickname "mussel-digger." The whale probably also uses its huge snout to stir up the bottom; it then strains the sediment-laden water for edible organisms. Gray whales have short baleen with coarse bristles, so the prey they catch inside the mouth must be fairly large. Quick straining action makes up for a relatively meager filtering surface.

Actually, gray whales seem capable of switching from one feeding technique to another. During the summer months in the Arctic, they gobble up huge amounts of amphipods and other planktonic crustaceans. But their muddy snouts and trailing mud plumes are evidence of bottom-feeding. In winter, they chiefly fast.

The gray whale is a living patchwork of barnacles and other parasites, yet the right side of its rostrum is usually free of these irksome organisms. Some naturalists, including Watson (1981), speculate that gray whales may feed on the right side, scraping against the bottom and dislodging parasites in the process. Bottom-feeding grays fill up on anything that happens along, including small fish and squid. Gigi, the immature female gray whale held in captivity for a while at Sea World in San Diego, polished off a ton of squid a day.

The feeding behavior of gray whales in the lagoons of Baja California has been the subject of fascinating research. In January, February, and March of 1980, S. L.

With acres of "crops" to graze on and tons of food to gulp down, a feeding whale is the very picture of gluttony. Left: A group of humpbacks feasting on capelin, a small schooling fish, off Newfoundland. Below: A minke whale, mouth agape, exposes white baleen that contrast sharply with its dusky skin.

## *THE BALEEN OF MYSTICETES*

| Species | Average Number of Pairs | Approximate Maximum Length (inches) | Approximate Maximum Width (inches) | Color of Plates and Fringe |
|---|---|---|---|---|
| *Right whale* | 260 | 105 | 12 | *Gray; bristles greenish* |
| *Bowhead* | 350 | 175.5 | 14 | *Black; bristles silvery* |
| *Pygmy right whale* | 230 | 27 | 4 | *White; bristles blackish* |
| *Gray whale* | 160 | 15 | 10 | *Grayish to cream-colored; bristles yellowish* |
| *Blue whale* | 320 | 39 | 21.5 | *Black; bristles dark gray* |
| *Fin whale* | 360 | 30 | 12 | *Smoky gray; bristles mustard-colored or white* |
| *Sei whale* | 340 | 19 | 15.5 | *Glossy black; bristles white* |
| *Bryde's whale* | 300 | 17.5 | 10 | *Gray; bristles dark gray* |
| *Minke whale* | 300 | 12 | 5 | *Cream or white; bristles white* |
| *Humpback* | 330 | 25 | 13.5 | *Dark gray; bristles clear gray* |

*In* The Origin of Species *(1859), Charles Darwin attempts to explain the process by which mysticetes acquired baleen plates through natural selection. "It may be asked, why should not the early progenitors of the whales with baleen plates have possessed a mouth constructed something like the lamellated beak of a duck? Ducks, like whales, subsist by sifting the mud and water; and the family has sometimes been called* Criblatores, *or sifters. I hope that I may not be misconstrued into saying that the progenitors of whales did actually possess mouths lamellated like the beak of the duck. I wish only to show that this is not incredible, and that the immense plates of baleen in the Greenland whale might have been developed from such lamellae by finely graduated steps, . . ."*

*Controversy still surrounds the origins of baleen plates. We do know that they are unrelated to the teeth of baleen whales, which atrophy before birth. During fetal development, the edges of the hard palate thicken, probably at the tips of the palatine sutures common to all mammals. Cell activity in the Malpighian layer causes these rudiments to grow.*

*"Generally speaking, the baleen plate may be thought of as a horny casing of skin, frayed at the tip, which overlays a huge dermal papilla rich in blood vessels" (P.-P. Grassé, 1955). The plates vary in length, but each is shaped like a right triangle. The smallest side hangs from the upper jaw. The hypotenuse, which faces the inside of the mouth, is frayed out into a great many bristles of varying coarseness.*

*A scant one-quarter to one-half inch separates these slatlike plates of baleen. There are many secondary plates, too; but usually only the primary (that is, outermost) ones are ever counted. If every single plate were included, the figures would be much higher. According to Delage (1885), a fin whale actually has 6,390 pairs of baleen plates in all: 430 primary, 430 secondary, 430 tertiary, 860 fourth-level, and 4,300 fifth-level plates—not to mention some 10,000 epidermal ridges that abet filtering action.*

Swartz observed six whales in Laguna San Ignacio methodically feeding on "mats of eel grass (*Zostera marina*) for period ranging from ten minutes to two and a half hours. . . . On closer inspection, the laminae of the plants were found to be encrusted with invertebrates, and there were shoals of fish larvae beneath the floating mats." Swartz also had a chance to watch a classic feeding pattern in action. Mixed groups of mature and juvenile grays would congregate at places in the lagoon where currents were strongest and position themselves against the flow so that the water would rush into their mouths. Once their mouths were filled with sediment and their throat pleats fully distended, they expelled the water, letting their baleen trap minute marine organisms. Nursing females in particular depend on these amphipods and mollusks as a source of protein in winter.

For most rorquals feeding in polar waters, especially Antarctica, the main course consists of krill, the Norwegian name for *Euphausia superba* and other euphausiid crustaceans. Krill swarm in the billions come spring, forming immense pinkish blooms 30 feet thick at the surface and sometimes swelling to megashoals covering hundreds of square miles. In this colossal plate of food famished whales roll about, cavort, and eat to their heart's content.

Let us take a closer look at the diet of individual balaenopterids. The blue whale is a much more finicky (stenophagous) eater than its polyphagous cousin, the fin whale. Its menu is limited mainly to a few kinds of euphausiids, complemented by copepods, amphipods, and sometimes tiny "red crabs." Squid and small fish have been taken, but probably more by accident than design.

Fin whales are eclectic feeders. We have already touched on their diet in the Antarctic; in the North Atlantic they feed on other planktonic crustaceans, as they do in the North Pacific. The species is also fond of an occasional fish. If neither plankton nor fish is available, the fin whale and many other rorquals will feed on jellyfish and cephalopods, especially pelagic squid.

Fin whales have been observed feeding on the right side, holding the left flipper above the surface of the water. Water and food organisms rush into the open

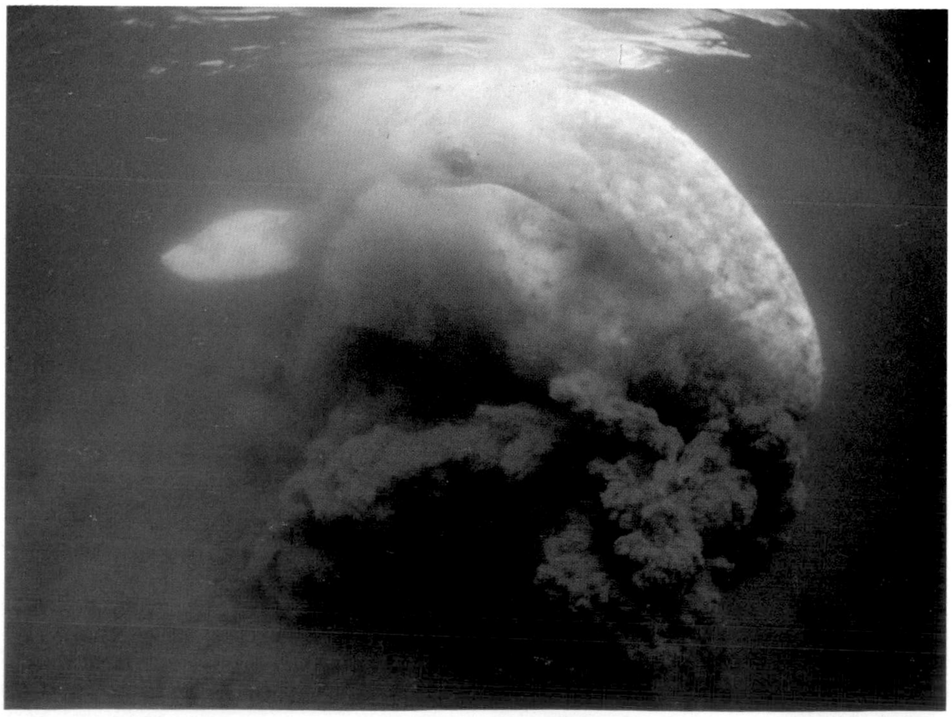

*The fearsome maw of the whale has inspired many a tall tale. Sailors' yarns found their way into the writings of historians, philosophers, and poets. Witness this quote from the* Moralia *of Plutarch (A.D. 46–120), as quoted in* Moby-Dick: *"And what thing soever besides cometh within the chaos of this monster's mouth, be it beast, boat, or stone, down it goes all incontinently that foul great swallow of his, and perisheth in the bottomless gulf of his paunch." Opposite: This photograph shows two humpback whales feeding, baleen and jaws clearly visible. Left: A California gray whale "bottom feeding" in a lagoon. Living up to its nickname of "mussel-digger"—a misnomer, for grays almost never eat mollusks—it plows through the sediment with its curved snout, raising a thick cloud of food-laden sand that is sucked in and strained.*

mouth, swelling the throat grooves. The tongue and baleen finish the job, after which the whale makes a quarter-turn and resumes an upright position. This procedure may explain why the right side of a fin whale's head is a lighter gray than the left side. A fin whale turned on its right side exemplifies the same kind of camouflage seen among sharks and other marine predators, which is known as countershading. The animal is darker above and lighter below, making it more difficult to spot from either vantage point. If correct, this hypothesis suggests that fin whales hunt sharp-sighted prey (such as fish) more often than we suspect—since planktonic organisms are incapable of distinguishing shades of gray.

When it comes to feeding, sei whales are as opportunistic as "finners." More than twenty kinds of planktonic crustaceans have been found in the stomachs of sei whales, which also take sardines, capelin, anchovies, tomcod, and herring. A sei whale in peak form is believed to ingest an estimated 2,000 pounds of assorted organisms a day, mainly at dawn and dusk. The sei is a "skimmer-swallower": at times it feeds like a right whale (though its skimming is less methodical, less impulsive, less assiduous), at times like a fin whale, turned on its side to dine.

Of all rorquals, the least selective species is Bryde's whale, which stays closest to the equator and is therefore the least dependent on the plankton-rich feeding grounds of polar regions. Bryde's whales do eat their share of plankton, but their bill of fare includes warm-water pelagic crustaceans, especially those that swarm in areas of upwelling, where nutrient-rich waters from greater depths are drawn to the surface. The widely spaced baleen plates of these whales are poor sieves for minute organisms but effective filters for huge quantities of herring, anchovies, sprats, sardines, and mackerel—or even small sharks up to about 2 feet long. Bryde's whales feed on lantern fish in the North Pacific and South Atlantic, pilchard off South Africa, mullet off New Zealand, and anchovies in the North Pacific. The stomach of one Bryde's whale contained penguins that the creature must have swallowed by accident; whales and sea birds often feed on the same shoals.

In summer, minke whales gorge themselves on the same concentrations of polar zooplankton as blue whales. Consequently, the dramatic drop in the blue whale population has worked to the minke's advantage, at least as far as food is concerned. In addition to krill, minke whales feast on sardines, anchovies, herring, cod, and capelin. This trusting species readily cavorts near trawlers, swimming back and forth beneath the hull and snatching any fish that slip through the nets (and occasionally getting entangled in the process). In general, minkes exhibit predatory behavior toward fish. They swim rapidly all around a school of fish near the surface. Once the victims have been corralled into a tight cluster, the feast begins.

With their thick baleen and coarse bristles, humpbacks cannot rely solely on planktonic crustaceans, either. In addition to krill, they require substantial quantities of capelin, anchovy, cod, herring, mackerel, and other small schooling fish. They have been known to venture near trawlers in hopes of freeloading a meal. A humpback swallows its prey at the surface, often after lunging at a school of fish from below, mouth agape. As soon as it breaks surface, with throat grooves fully distended, it shuts its powerful jaws tight. At this moment it is not unusual for an overly adventurous cormorant or gull to get swallowed—inadvertently, of course. But the humpback's real claim to fame is its use of a "bubble-net" to trap its prey. Apparently no other species of whale has mastered this astonishing feeding behavior pattern of surrounding prey with a "net" of escaping air bubbles, forcing the fish into a small area where they can be easily taken.

Baleen whales are primarily seasonal feeders that head toward polar waters in summer to build up energy reserves. Long winter fasts or near-fasts result in significant weight loss, sometimes more than one-third of total weight. In summer, however, they make up for their winter diet by consuming staggering amounts of food. During the krill season, a blue whale ingests an estimated 9,000 pounds of these shrimplike euphausiids a day. Since each crustacean weighs about a gram, the blue whale's intake is an astounding 4 million a day.

The humpback and fin whale consume 4,400 pounds and 5,500 pounds of food a day, respectively, during the "high season" in the polar krill grounds. They usually feed twice daily, and although the schedule depends upon the upward migration of plankton, the heavier of the meals normally takes place at dawn. Sei whales spend only a hundred days near the pack ice. Their daily intake of 2,200 to 3,300 pounds of plankton is spread out over five mealtimes, with the heartiest at dawn and the four others from early afternoon to dusk, as appetite dictates.

Although the gluttonous rorquals have colossal bodies to feed, they do not abuse the prodigious mouth that nature gave them. As their low basal metabolic

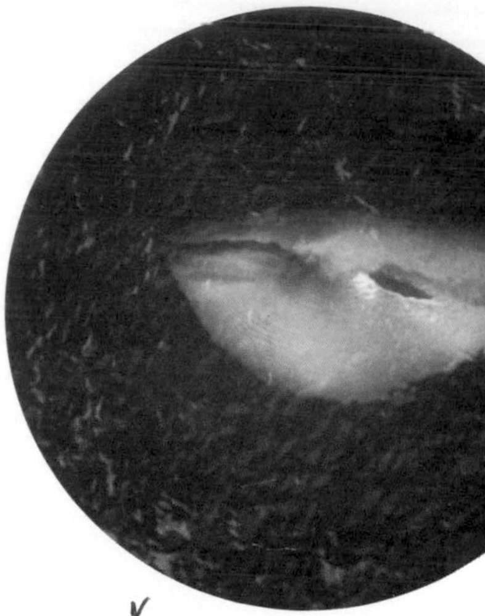

*Of the many species of shrimplike, translucent euphausiid crustaceans the Norwegians collectively refer to as krill, the best known are* Euphausia pellucida *and* Euphausia superba. *They have a life span of four to five years, breed two and one-half years after birth, and cluster in colossal shoals in polar waters come summer. There may be as many as 60,000 individuals in 35 cubic feet of water. Krill populations make up an estimated biomass of between 250 million and 6.5 billion metric tons in the Antarctic Ocean alone. Though only about 2 inches long, these orange to pink organisms swarm in shoals so dense and so profuse that they can turn the sea reddish-brown for several miles around. Most of them have photophores (light-emitting organs) that glow blue-green, making for a fantastically beautiful sight at night.*

*Krill is the staple of many species of mysticetes in the Antarctic during the 120-day summer feeding season. A blue whale polishes off 4 tons (approximately 4 million individuals) a day; a fin whale eats only 2.5 tons. Today, baleen whales in the Antarctic consume nearly 50 million tons of krill annually; in the early 1900s, when whales were still abundant, the yearly intake was on the order of 200 million tons. Other types of marine life—seals, penguins, fish, cephalopods (squid, octopus)—depend upon krill for survival.*

*Above: Throat distended, a blue whale is about to strain krill through its sievelike mat of baleen bristles.*

*Below:* Euphausia superba, *chief food item of many baleen whales.*

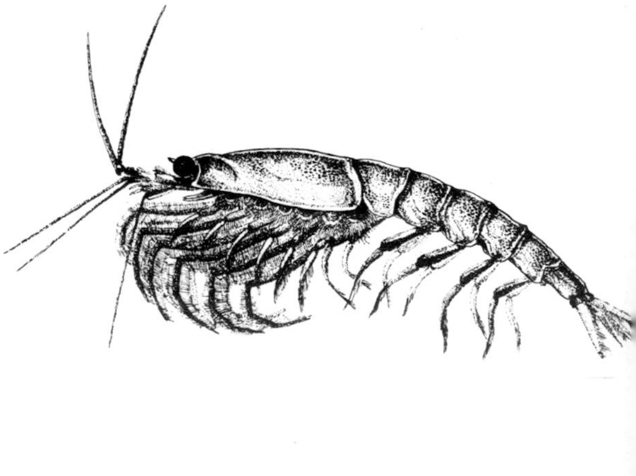

rate would lead us to expect, these whales are actually fairly skimpy eaters, relative to their weight. Assuming a blue whale ingests about 9,000 pounds of plankton a day for 120 days, its total intake for the season would be 1,080,000 pounds of plankton. Yet it will put on only about an ounce or two of weight a day. Here is another way of looking at it: a 120-ton blue whale that ingests 480 tons of plankton a year consumes only four times its weight in food. People eat fifteen or sixteen times their weight a year without even trying, and some sparrows consume nearly their own weight in food each and every day.

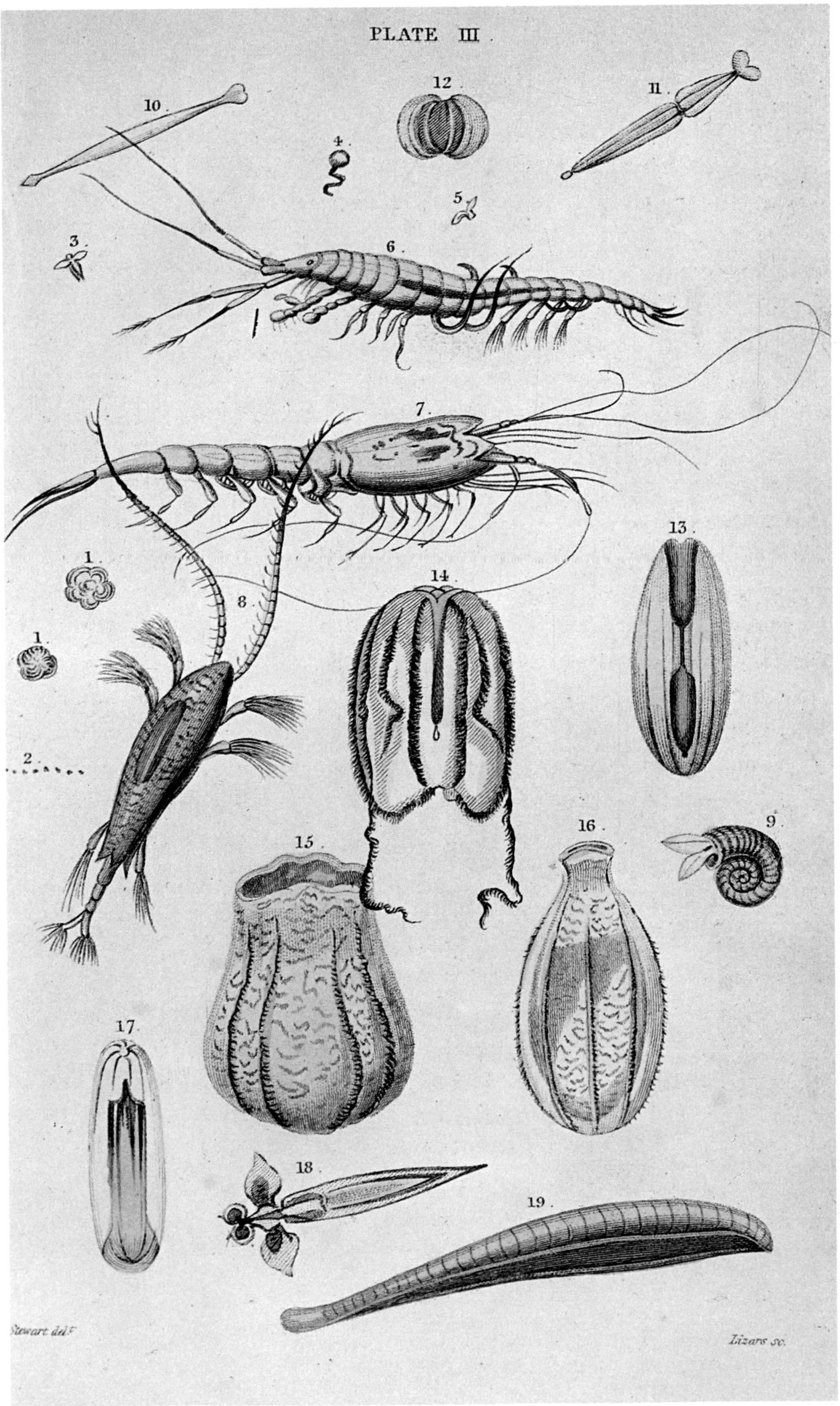


*Baleen whales have a varied diet. Their stomachs have been found to contain fish (herring, sardines, capelin, anchovies), birds (probably swallowed inadvertently), and enormous quantities of plankton.*

*Right: A sampling of the planktonic organisms baleen whales feast on during the summer feeding seasons (from an engraving at the Library of La Rochelle): diatoms (1),* Natantia *(6, 7, 8), mollusks (9), ctenophores (14, 15, 16, 17), chaetognaths (10, 11). To our way of thinking, whales are not choosy—although in fact some are finicky eaters.*

## *BUBBLE-NET FEEDING*

*Humpback whales have perfected an ingenious technique for catching krill or small fish: they literally "blow" nets made of air bubbles. Whalers reported this feeding method as far back as 1928, but no one believed them. The first scientists actually to witness this behavior were Virginia and Charles Jurasz, who saw it off the coast of Alaska.*

*"Like a giant undersea spider spinning its web," writes Roger Payne (1979), "the humpback begins perhaps 50 feet deep, forcing bursts of air through its blowholes while swimming in an upward spiral. Big bubbles, followed by a mist of tiny ones, rise to create a cylindrical screen that concentrates krill and small fish. Bubbles and food pop to the surface, followed by the gaping mouth of the whale as it emerges in the center of its net."*

*According to Charles and Virginia Jurasz, there are times when two whales work together on a net that can stretch as much as 100 feet across (although the diameter usually does not exceed 10 to 15 feet). While working with the Juraszes, Dr. Payne recorded sound sequences produced while the whales blow their bubble nets. "Whales can select the size of the bubbles," he notes. "They can make their nets any size 'mesh' they want." Unlike the spider, which is guided solely by instinct and spins the same web over and over again, whales adapt their traps to the size of prospective prey. On the one hand, a genetically programmed automaton; on the other, an intelligent mammal.*

*Humpbacks avail themselves of other techniques to "corral" shoals of plankton or schools of fish. They have been known to herd their prey together with their huge flippers. In addition, "an alternate tactic called 'flick feeding' has been observed, during which the whales splash water over their heads with their flukes so that it lands in front of them as they swim. The impact of the water startles krill long enough for a quick gulp."*

*Like most baleen whales, humpbacks travel to tropical breeding grounds to calve, then backtrack to subpolar or polar waters in the summer to build up fat reserves. Whale migration has long fueled speculation, but one explanation seems more persuasive than most. Whales are so well insulated by their protective layer of blubber that they must adapt their diet to the climate of the region they are in. If they gorged themselves in temperate or tropical waters the way they do in higher latitudes, they would die of fever. That is one of the reasons they fast most of the winter. Their young, however, which are at a disadvantage because of their lower surface-to-body weight ratio, must be delivered in warm waters and feed on extremely rich milk. Hence, the giants of the sea are compelled to undertake their staggering journeys year after year.*

## BATTLES ROYAL IN THE ABYSS

Now we turn to the amazing feeding habits of the sperm whale—which may well be the most staggering and spectacular sight that nature—even in all it's amazing diversity—has to offer.

In terms of both intake and technique, sperm whales have more in common with land carnivores than with baleen whales. Daniel Eschricht, the Dane who did so much pioneering work in this field, coined the word "teutophagous" (from *teuthos*, Greek for "squid") to describe all cetaceans that, like the sperm whale, feed primarily on cephalopods.

It is estimated that a mature sperm whale consumes 3 percent of its weight daily; for a 50-ton male, this would mean a ton to a ton and a half of squid a day. It spends a great deal of its time in tropical waters, where most species of cephalopods live. All told, sperm whales worldwide polish off approximately 100 million tons of squid a year (M. Clarke, quoted by Kanwisher and Ridgway, 1983). Compare that with man's paltry total annual catch of about 70 million tons of fish and shellfish.

Sperm whales feed on squid of every size and shape—more than forty species in all. If the prey are small, the whale wolfs them down by the thousand: one individual was discovered to have 28,000 of them in its stomach (Akimuskine, 1955), and it can even take in scores of large squid at a time. In 1984, Hal Whitehead and his crew aboard the *Tulip* examined the feces of several sperm whales in the waters off Sri Lanka. Most of the squid beaks they found were about a half-inch long, indicating that the ingested squid were 1 to 2 feet long and weighed between 2 and 5 pounds each.

Sperm whales are known to descend to the abyssal zone to stalk giant squid of the genus *Architeuthis*. These colossal invertebrates, measuring 40 feet, may have inspired the monstrous *kraken* of Scandinavian mythology.

Before proceeding to these furious and awe-inspiring hunts in the ocean depths, we ought to mention that a sperm whale will eat just about anything that moves. Squid may be its favorite dish, but it still has to ingest 2.5–3.5 percent of its weight each and every day. Therefore, it comes as no surprise that these whales welcome any source of calories that comes within reach: crustaceans (crayfish, lobsters, crabs), primitive invertebrates (sponges, jellyfish), tunicates, or schooling fish. Sperm whales have also been known to eat seals or small cetaceans (porpoises, dolphins).

A list of some of the objects sperm whale's bellies have turned up makes for entertaining reading: large rocks, a gallon of sand, a coconut, a buoy, an apple, a piece of wood, a chunk of whale flesh, a branch of coral, sea fans, deep sea sponges, plastic bags, a pail, and even a few odd shoes! However, this array should not be considered proof that sperm whales feed randomly on anything that comes their way; they swallow these things inadvertently along with their usual prey. Indeed, their ability to echolocate is so accurate and so sophisticated that on several occasions whalemen have caught blind individuals that were nonetheless in excellent physical condition (until harpooned, that is) with full stomachs.

Some naturalists were unwilling to admit that titanic battles pitting sperm whales against giant squid actually took place. The conclusive evidence came when a giant squid, measuring about 37 feet and weighing nearly 450 pounds, was found in the stomach of a 45-foot sperm whale taken in the Azores. We have indirect proof, too. The heads of sperm whales, especially those of large bulls that dive the deepest, are studded with scratches and scars left by the suckers and beaks of giant squid. It is not unusual for some of these enormous beaks (as well as squid "pens," the skeletal stiffening of a cephalopod's body) to turn up in the stomach of a sperm whale.

No human being, however, has ever witnessed a standoff between a giant squid and a sperm whale, and with good reason. This tumultuous drama is played out hundreds of yards below the surface, where only bathyscaphs (and whales and giant squid) dare to venture.

The huge cephalopod is no pushover for an odontocete. Apart from its daunting size, it wields tentacles bristling with suckers as big as dishes, beaklike jaws, poisonous saliva, an ink sac, efficient sense organs, and, above all, a highly developed brain—the largest, most complex, and most responsive brain of any invertebrate.

From indirect evidence we can get a general idea of how a sperm whale stalks its prey. Assuming (L. Watson, 1981) that it descends at an estimated 4 to 5 mph and comes back to the surface at about 6 mph, and assuming a depth of about a thousand yards, the roundtrip would take about fifteen minutes. Since a dive can last up

## *THE TEETH OF THE SPERM WHALE*

*The conical teeth of* Physeter macrocephalus *are nearly 8 inches long and weigh more than 2 pounds each. There are between 24 and 30 of them on each side, but they grow in the lower jaw only. When the whale closes its mouth, each tooth fits into a socket in the upper jaw. The teeth are made of ivory, have no enamel, and are uniform in shape.*

*The dentition of odontocetes has sparked considerable debate. Some experts hold that their milk teeth fall out very quickly to make room for permanent ones. In 1888–93, however, Kükenthal (quoted in P.-P. Grassé, 1955) demonstrated that precisely the opposite is true. Drawing on anatomical observation as well as examination of teeth from archaeocete fossils, he argued that cetacean teeth are, in fact, "extended" milk teeth and that the growth of adult teeth is arrested before they ever erupt.*

*Sperm whales must wait ten years before a full set of mature teeth is in place. In the interim, they seem to have no difficulty making do without them. To be sure, teeth come in handy for grasping the squid or other slippery creatures that make up the bulk of a sperm whale's diet. But they are not designed for tearing or chewing. A juvenile will not try to take on a large squid; it makes do with more manageable mollusks. Actually, when not battling giant squid, sperm whales make so little use of their teeth that some cetologists wonder if they might be a secondary sexual characteristic designed to keep rival males at bay.*

*In general, sperm whales are haplodont—that is, their teeth have simple crowns with a single root. The fact that they are also homodont raises the question of how their teeth evolved. Archaeocetes were equipped with clearly differentiated teeth, a hallmark of placental mammals. For example,* Pappocetus lugardi, *which lived in the Eocene, had the following dentition: incisors 3/3, canines 1/1, bicuspids 4/4, molars 3/3. Its molars were of the "classic" carnivorous variety. As the group evolved, their teeth became simpler, molars lost their multiple roots (*Basilosaurus*), and the addition of teeth increased the total number (notably in* Neosqualodon, *a Miocene odontocete: P.-P. Grassé, 1955). There is an obvious connection between the extremely simplified dentition of modern odontocetes and their diet. Catching fish or mollusks calls for teeth that bite and grasp instead of ones designed to tear and chew.*

*As this photograph clearly shows, the uniform teeth of the sperm whale's lower jaw fit like dowels into corresponding sockets in the upper jaw. Once in a great while, stumps of teeth may erupt in the sockets.*

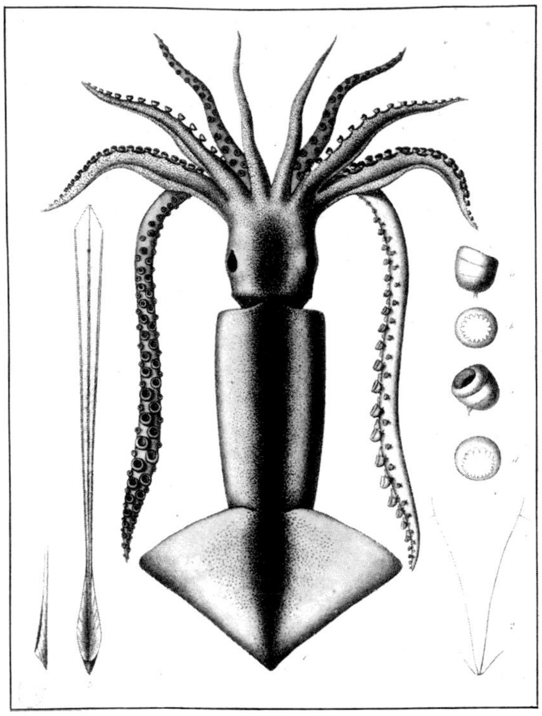

*Like other toothed whales, the sperm whale is teuthophagous, meaning that it feeds primarily on squid (Greek,* teuthos*) and other cephalopods. Above: Some odontocetes are not fussy about the type of cephalopod they eat, but the average-sized genus* Loligo *(shown in engraving, above), which live in large schools, is a favorite. Sperm whales consume an estimated 100 million tons of squid a year.*

to an hour, assume that the whale spends the other forty-five minutes at the bottom. At first it was thought that sperm whales roamed the ocean floor in search of food. But whalemen and scientists alike have seen them surface close to the spot where they sounded. There is another hypothesis that makes sense: once the whale has reached the bottom, it might wait in ambush, motionless, until its prey ventured into reach.

The whale would use up little oxygen and few calories resting on the ocean floor. Malcolm Clarke has speculated that the spermaceti organ, about whose function nothing is really known, may come into play in a scenario such as ours. According to his theory, the sperm whale circulates seawater through the nasal passage on the way down, cooling the surrounding spermaceti until it very gradually solidifies. This process would increase the average density of the whale's body and make it less bouyant. Sam Ridgway, however, notes that when a sperm whale dives, it becomes negatively bouyant, simply because, with the increase in water pressure, the lungs have collapsed—therefore precluding the use of the spermaceti organ.

A sperm whale on the prowl might use echolocation to detect any squids that may happen by. Since many deep-sea cephalopods have light-emitting organs (photophores), the whale may also rely on its eyesight, albeit strictly as a back-up sensing device. The foes come face to face, and there ensues a pitched battle that only an epic poet could describe. No one has ever seen what takes place down there. One moonlit night in the tropics, however, Frank Bullen, an American whaleman, witnessed what must have been the conclusion of one such contest. He wrote about it in *The Cruise of the Cachalot* (1899).

"I was perfectly satisfied by a short examination that neither volcano nor earthquake had anything to do with what was going on; yet so vast were the forces engaged that I might well have been excused for my first supposition.

"A very large sperm whale was locked in deadly conflict with a cuttle-fish, or squid, almost as large as himself, whose interminable tentacles seemed to enlace the whole of his great body. The head of the whale especially seemed a perfect network of writhing arms—naturally, I suppose, for it appeared as if the whale had the tail part of the mollusc in his jaws, and, in a business-like, methodical way, was sawing through it. By the side of the black columnar head of the whale appeared the head of the giant squid, as awful an object as one could well imagine even in a fevered dream. Judging as carefully as possible, I estimated it to be at least as large as one of our pipes, which contained three hundred and fifty gallons; but it may have been and probably was, a good deal larger. The eyes were very remarkable from their size and blackness, which, contrasted with the livid whiteness of the head, made their appearance all the more striking. They were, at least, a foot in diameter, and, seen under such conditions, looked decidedly eerie and hobgoblin-like. All around the combatants were numerous sharks, like jackals round a lion, ready to share the feast, and apparently assisting in the destruction of the huge cephalopod. . . .

"The conflict ceased, and the sea resumed its placid calm, and nothing remained to tell of the fight but a strong odor of fish, as of a bank of seaweed left by the tide in the blazing sun."

## MINIATURE JAPANESE GARDENS

Inhabitants of ancient Iceland showed their analytical bent when they divided the right whales in their waters into a parasite-ridden southern species and a northern species (bowheads) that was practically free from these unbecoming guests. This was first-rate ecology centuries before ecologists as such ever existed.

Whales depend on crustaceans, mollusks, fish, and other groups of marine life for survival. It was only a matter of time before these very classes or phyla reciprocated by "inventing" species specially adapted to "exploiting" the body of the whale.

In this respect, there is some truth to the myth of whales as floating islands, for they are the host organisms of assorted flora and fauna. Mind you, the plants that flourish on their bodies are not grasses or palm trees, but *Cocconeis ceticola* and other varieties of yellowish or silvery diatoms. The growth period of these unicellular algae reaches its peak in the Antarctic from November to March, at which time they spread over the skin of right whales, sperm whales, and blue whales like

*The epic battles between sperm whales and giant squid in the pitch-black abyss have set many an imagination spinning. What titanic standoffs they must be! For many years, the scientific community was skeptical about gigantic deep-sea cephalopods, despite reports from sailors who had seen pieces of the creatures floating on the ocean's surface. These battles are today as enigmatic as ever, but at least no one doubts their occurrence. The best known member of the genus* Architeuthis *is* A. princeps. *The largest specimen ever to be duly examined was found at Thimble Tickle, on the coast of Newfoundland, on November 2, 1978. Its head and body measured 20 feet long, its tentacles 35 feet, its eyes almost 16 inches across, its beak 88 inches long, and each sucker almost 4 inches across. Other carcasses have since been identified in Norway, Iceland, Canada, and New Zealand. The most mind-boggling account (which is unfortunately unconfirmed) involves a squid stranded on the beach at St. Augustine, Florida, in 1896. Its body was reportedly nearly 20 feet thick and its tentacles, albeit incomplete, measured almost a foot and a half across at the base. The total length of this monster would have to have been between 130 and 165 feet!*

a gelatinous film. Come winter, they vanish in the warm waters of tropical seas (Omura, 1950). This is how the blue whale got its seasonal nicknames of "sulfur bottom" and "silver bottom."

The huge bodies of these leviathans are the life-support system for scores of animal species, too: internal and external parasites, sea birds and other opportunistic cleaners, and commensals such as remoras and dolphins.

Every animal alive must put up with internal parasites, and whales are no exception. When archaeocetes returned to the water, they may have brought these unwelcome guests along with them; it is possible that present-day whales nourish the offspring of the organisms that exploited their forebears. A number of parasites gravitate to the digestive system, the sinuses, and hearing passages: roundworms, particularly filariae, nematodes that proliferate in the intestines; *Acanthocephala* (worms related to roundworms); and flatworms, especially tapeworms and related cestodes. According to Lockyer (1976), most nursing calves in the Antarctic are free from parasites; a few short weeks after weaning, however, 94 percent of all juveniles have already been infested. (The infestation rate among adults is 95 percent.) Van Beneden reported that the liver of minke whales is often infested with a trematode similar to the liver flukes in land mammals, while the encysted larval form of the *Omiseus* fluke burrows deep into the skin of sperm whales. A number of scientists, among them Prescott and Geraci (1973), maintain that the "suicide" of some whales is in fact caused by small roundworms (akin to the threadworms and pinworms in human children) that infest the inner ear and interfere with their biosonar navigational system.

The most spectacular parasites are external. The largest of them, the lampreys, use a sucking disk to attach themselves to the whale's mouth corners, anal and genital zones, and other tender areas of the skin.

A smaller but more common type of external parasite proliferates into miniature "Japanese gardens" on the head, around the lips, above the eyes, and on the chin. Commonly known as acorn barnacles or sea acorns, these cirripedial crustaceans (balanoids) "hitch" rides on the host organism and feed on microplankton; they do not suck its blood. They must cause the helpless whale considerable discomfort, however, because they attach themselves by burrowing headfirst into the skin. Acorn barnacles will cling more readily to slow-moving species, such as the right whale and humpback, than to the swifter rorquals or the sperm whale. Their numbers are subject to seasonal fluctuations: they proliferate on the whale's skin in cold polar waters during the summer, then loosen and fall off in the temperate or warm waters of wintering grounds. Some individuals carry tens of thousands of them about, and one humpback was reportedly covered with nearly a thousand pounds of them (L. Watson, 1981).

The most prevalent kind of acorn barnacles belong to the genus *Coronula*. The bowhead is practically free from them, but right whales attract several different species, including one that is "host-specific"—that is, it attaches only to the right whale. Other balanoids also attach themselves to the head, lips, snout, and flippers of humpbacks and grays. One variety of barnacle is host-specific to the gray whale.

Some barnacles have a muscular, stalklike protuberance that "boosts" them up from the skin surface for better access to the plankton on which they feed. They

*Sperm whales detect their prey by echolocation, meaning they emit click trains that are bounced back by surrounding obstacles. With phenomenal sensitivity the animal's brain analyzes the time between emission and reception (probably making adjustments for sound wave distortion, too), and pieces together a highly accurate "sonic picture" of the world around it. On several occasions blind sperm whales have been seen maneuvering freely in the sea. They do not look underfed or debilitated; presumably they relied solely on sonar to locate food. However, sperm whales may use echolocation for more than just detection. According to one astonishing hypothesis, they actually kill their prey with sound! Although the technique might not work on a giant squid (like the one shown above), a sperm whale approaching a school of small cephalopods could conceivably "beam" click trains with such intensity that the shock waves would immobilize and incapacitate the mollusks. Then it would just be a matter of gobbling up the meal. An underwater "death ray."*

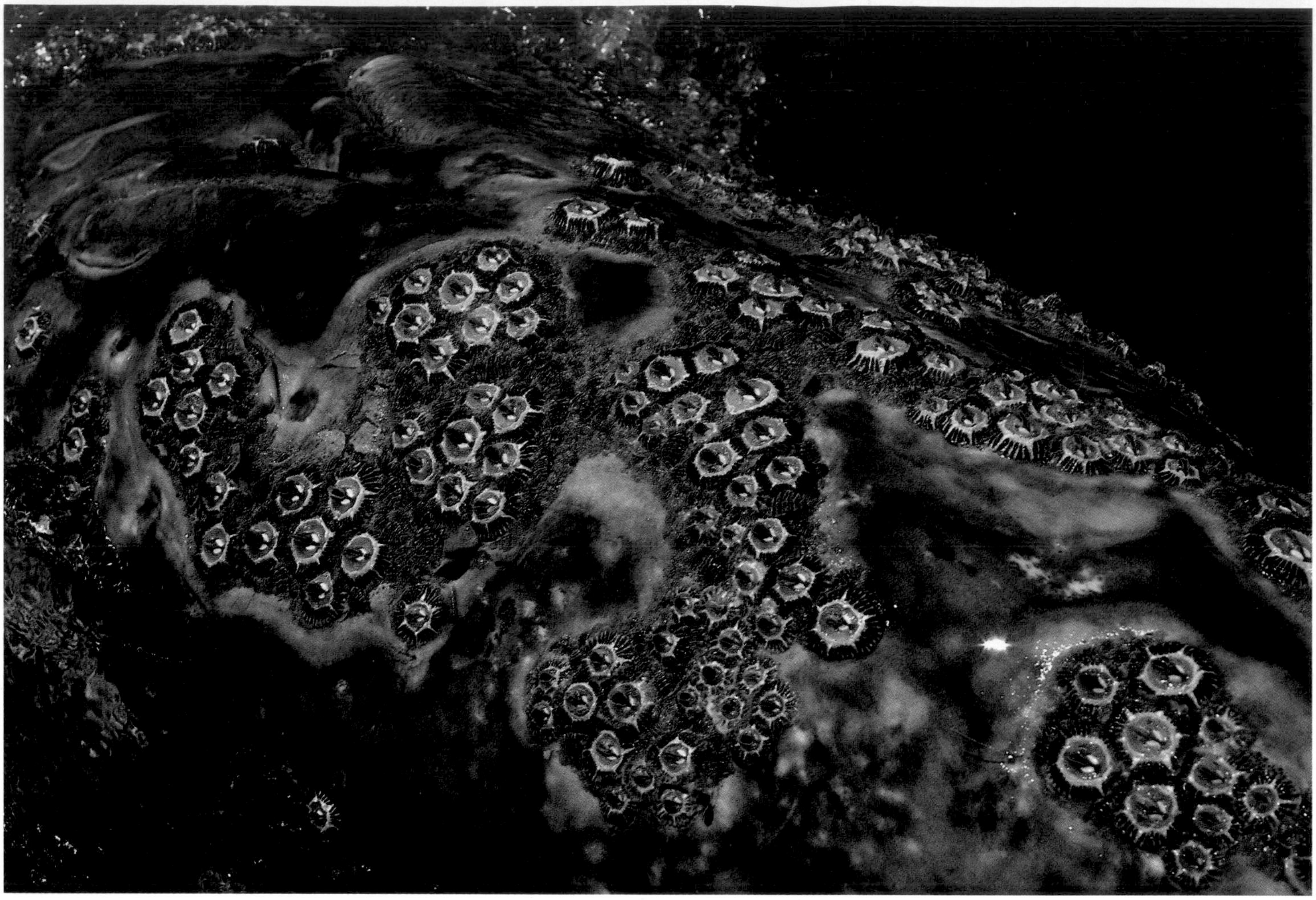

usually make their homes on rocks, ship hulls, and other inorganic supports. When they choose a whale as their host, they gravitate toward the baleen or other sheltered location. They also have a habit of attaching themselves to established barnacles, forming peculiar-looking double-decker growths. The commonest organisms in this category belong to the genus *Conchoderma*.

Some pseudostalked barnacles burrow deep inside body tissues. The species that make up the genus *Xenobalanus* (especially *X. globicipitis*, a parasite found on many-toothed whales and the fin whale) is a case in point. Another group of burrowers belongs to the genus *Tubicinella*; they secrete an enzyme that digests skin but does not derive nutrients from the host's blood.

Still another group of crustaceans, the copepods, includes quite a few parasitic species, some of which live at the expense of whales. Commonly known as water fleas, these animals use their oversized, oarlike antennules to "row" toward the victim. After they settle on the skin, they start to burrow headfirst. Water fleas are true parasites; unlike acorn barnacles, they do feed on the blood of the host organism. The ones belonging to the genus *Penella*, which are partial to rorquals, look like strange algae or convoluted worms embedded in the whale's blubber. Fully developed females grow to be a foot long, but males are smaller. The females burrow into the whale, where they live until they have released their eggs into the sea, when they drop off and die.

Another type of copepod, *Balaenophilus*, is less aggressive. Although these creatures can spend their entire life swimming freely in the sea, they prefer to conceal themselves among the hairy fringes of baleen plates. Rorquals are a favorite of *B. unicetus*.

Unlike the external parasites that bedevil birds and land mammals, the amphipod crustaceans known as "whale lice" are not insects. Stealing into crevices left by barnacles, or onto the naturally formed cornifications, they swarm—sometimes hundreds of thousands at a time—in the callosities of gray whales and humpbacks or in the bonnets and "Japanese gardens" of right whales.

The commonest whale lice are the ten-legged members of the genus *Cyamus*. There are sixteen known species, ranging up to an inch in length. The legs terminate in strong pincers that grip their traveling meal like a vise. Lacépède described the behavior of these parasites as long ago as 1804.

Every species of whale is infested with cyamids. Even the otherwise unmolested bowhead is a favorite of *C. ceti* (Van Beneden). Northern right whales provide nutrients for *C. biscayensis*, while their counterparts south of the equator are plagued by *C. ovalis* and *C. erraticus*. Southern right whales are also the host organisms for *C. catadontis*, a species that usually infests sperm whales. This had led some observers to speculate that right whales and sperm whales occasionally frequent the same waters.

Gray whales harbor *C. scammoni* and *C. kessleri*, both of which swarm by the hundreds of thousands on the blowholes, eyelids, lip corners, cheeks, throat grooves, genital slit, and anus.

No balaenopterid is more popular among whale lice than the humpback, which unwittingly ensures the survival of *C. boopis*. The blue whale and other rorquals attract the less bothersome *C. balaenopterae*. Sperm whales provide nutrients for

*Whales are huge vehicles that attract all kinds of opportunists. Some of these parasites are satisfied with hitching a ride from one part of the world to another. Most barnacles—the genus* Coronula *in particular—fall into this category. Opposite: The cirripedial crustaceans visible on this California gray whale belong to* Cryptolepas rhachianecti, *a host-specific barnacle.*

*Other parasites feed directly on their host. "Whale lice," for example, albeit every bit as unpleasant as their namesake in the insect world, are actually isopod crustaceans. Right: The California gray whale harbors barnacles (right) as well as large numbers of cyamid crustaceans, particularly* Cyamus scammoni.

two cyamid species, *C. catodontis* and *Neocyamus physeteris*. The former (which, as we mentioned, also infests right whales) is partial to bulls; the latter is usually found on females and juveniles.

## FRIEND AND FOE

In addition to these irritating parasitic organisms, whales travel with commensals (organisms that derive nutrients from a host, but do it no harm), and these include escorts that cling to the whales for free rides across the sea. No creature is literally more attached to whales than remoras ("whalesuckers"), which use a modified dorsal fin as a suction disk. One remora, *Remilegia australis*, has been found with fin whales on several occasions (R. Payne, 1981). Pilotfish (*Naucrates ductor*) are known to hitch energy-saving rides with sharks and large whales alike. As they ride their host's bow wave, they salvage food scraps from its meals.

Large whales rely on squads of "cleaners" to rid themselves of external parasites. We know that some types of shrimp and fish specialize in cleaning other animals in the marine ecosystem, but little is known about their interaction with whales.

More opportunists than commensals, sea birds sometimes associate with feeding whales, picking up scattered tidbits. "Long before the whales could be seen from the coast, instinct had told the phalaropes of [their] approach," writes Georges Blond. "When they see the whales surfacing they settle on their backs and begin a search for the delicacies in question. Each time the whales dive the phalaropes fly away till the animals emerge again. When the whales go deep down, the birds rise a little higher in the air and continue to fly in the direction taken by the whales. They fly in leisurely fashion, wheeling, retreating a short distance and then returning, like dogs following their master on a walk. When [the] whales emerged, the phalaropes were all there to receive them and immediately settled on their backs again."

External parasites, commensals, cleaners: whales endure the first, tolerate the second, and welcome the third. Surely these are not the only relationships whales have formed with other sea creatures. Like all large mammals, whales harbor symbiotic bacteria in their intestines, but no one has yet looked closely at this phenomenon, as far as we know. On the other hand, much has been written about whales as victims of predation. Unbelievable though it may seem, these mammoth, powerful animals are by no means immune to attack.

Needless to say, their deadliest foe is man, that superpredator who kills not only to satisfy hunger but for inessential commodities and for the "sport" of it. Aside from this primate of questionable intelligence, only a few adversaries pose any real threat to these giants of the seas.

The sperm whale fears no animal species. Juveniles are protected by the pod, and when full-grown they wield a daunting mouth, head, and tail. To be sure, infirm individuals unable to keep up with the group have been attacked and killed by sharks, swordfish, or killer whales. And sperm whales that take on giant deep-sea squid sometimes become the victims. An intriguing footnote: according to several accounts (Bennett, 1840; Murphy, 1947, in K. S. Norris, 1966), sperm whales

*Above: Two varieties of whale lice that infest the cheeks, throat pleats, snout, blowholes, lips, eyelids, genital slit, and anus of the gray whale. These crustaceans are a source of great discomfort, and whales often attempt to dislodge them or shake them loose by rubbing against rocky surfaces or by breaching.*

*Aside from ourselves, large whales have few enemies. The most ruthless foe of right whales, sperm whales, and rorquals alike is the killer whale, a remarkably intelligent "super-dolphin" that measures 25 to 30 feet long and weighs between 7 and 10 tons. Rarely has a species more richly deserved its popular name. Hunting in pods, these swift swimmers prey on disabled, isolated stragglers or immature strays. Once a victim has been targeted and surrounded, they lunge at it from all directions and sink their teeth into its tongue, lips, and belly. Below: Killer whales attacking a right whale, by American engraver Charles L. Bull.*

## *WOLF OF THE SEA*

*It is nothing short of ironic that the killer whale (Orcinus orca), beloved performer at a dozen marine life stadiums throughout the world, is also one of the most fearsome predators of the deep. The nature of this creature excited comment as long ago as 1725; in an essay published in the Philosophical Transactions of the Royal Society, the Hon. Paul Dudley described the orcas "that prey upon the whales, and often kill the young ones, for they will not venture upon an old one, unless much wounded."*

> *They go in company by Dozens, [he wrote] and set upon a young whale, and will bait him like so many Bull-dogs; some will lay hold of his Tail to keep him from threshing, while others lay hold of his Head, and bite and thresh him, till the poor Creature, being thus heated, lolls out his Tongue, and then some of the Killers catch hold of his Lips, and if possible of his Tongue; and after they have killed him, they feed chiefly upon his tongue and Head, but when he begins to putrefy, they leave him."* (cited in Matthews, 1978).

*The only creatures that orcas need to worry about are humans; otherwise, these cetaceans go virtually unchallenged. Although they seem most often to prey on fish, orcas have been known to attack the giant of giants—the blue whale. Here is an account of an attack, recounted by Les Line:*

> *The blue whale (Balaenoptera musculus) is the largest animal ever to inhabit this planet. But size does not necessarily equal might. A young blue whale was at the mercy of its tormentors when attacked by a pod of 29 killer whales (Orcinus orca) in the Gulf of California. For five hours, over a distance of 20 miles, marine researchers watched a bloody, one-sided battle that had begun before they arrived on the scene. Like bees swarming on a bear, but with deadlier intent, the killer whales completely surrounded the 60-foot-long blue whale, preventing its escape. They tore off its dorsal fin, shredded its flukes, and gouged a gaping hole, 6 feet square, in its side. Then, inexplicably, they swam away, leaving the leviathan mortally wounded."*

*Like other predators, the orca is fairly gregarious. The animals form large social units of up to about thirty members; occasionally several pods join together to form larger temporary herds of up to a hundred.*

*The male killer whale is larger than the female (up to about 28 feet long and weighing in at 8 tons); in both male and female, the most distinguishing characteristic is the dorsal fin, which in males grows to 6 feet, and slices through the water's surface as the cetacean swims smoothly along. The flippers and tail are also fairly large, especially in comparison to the overall size.*

> *This sleek predator is distinguished by its handsome black-and-white pattern (black above and white or cream below, with a pale patch on the back, just behind the dorsal fin). This pattern of sharp contrasts, a type of disruptive coloration, may help orcas to recognize each other visually, and to perceive different forms of behavior. What is more, the confusing patterns may disorient prey.*

*There have been suggestions from a number of researchers and scientists that orcas engage in fairly sophisticated cooperative hunting, and accounts such as the one above tend to bear out this hypothesis. Like North America's wolves and the lions of the African savannas, which are known to hunt in pairs, trios, or even larger numbers, the orcas probably stand a better chance of succeeding when they hunt in groups—effectively cornering their prey, even though it may be much larger than they are. Such strategies keep these predators at the top in their respective territories.*

will scatter at the sound of a group of clicking dolphins—even if it is only a recording. Why a marine giant should dread these small-fry under certain conditions remains a mystery.

It is unusual for rorquals, humpbacks, or grays to be attacked when traveling in groups. Obviously, the larger they are, the more intimidating their presence. But if they are very young or very old, or cut off from the group, or enfeebled, they may fall victim to killer whales, false killer whales, and several types of large predatory fish. Right whales seem to have been singled out for this unenviable fate. The sight of bloodthirsty killer whales clustered about a right whale, devouring their quivering quarry, has inspired many an impassioned account. Pliny the Elder described just such an attack in the first century A.D. Philemon Holland made a translation of Pliny's observations in 1601: "Monstrous fishes . . . armed with the most terrible, sharpe, & cutting teeth. These being ware that the whales are there, break into their secret creek, seeke them out, & if they meet either with the young ones, or the dammes that have newly spawned, or yet great with spawne, they all to cut and hacke them with their trenchant teeth."

In 1804, Lacépède outlined the attack strategy of an animal he variously referred to as orcas, killer whales, and gladiators: "Gladiator dolphins congregate and form a large herd and will bear down as a single unit on a right whale, besieging it from every direction, biting, harrassing, wearing it down, forcing it to open its mouth. They will lunge at the tongue (accounted one of their favorite dishes) and tear it to

*Above: This photograph was taken the instant a pod of killer whales began stalking a right whale in preparation for an all-out attack. Ruthless though this behavior may seem, we should bear in mind that killer whales, unlike man, attack very rarely and only to satisfy hunger. Opposite: An artist's visualization of a scene that has never been captured on film: a marlin attacking a rorqual. Although swordfish (unlike killer whales and sharks) do not attack whales to eat them, they are irascible creatures that routinely charge intruders. Broken swordfish bills have been found in the belly or side of a whale on several occasions.*

shreds. Vastly outnumbered, the bloodied whale endures unbearable pain as they inflict one mortal wound after another." The same technique of forcing the whale to open its mouth and expose its tongue was described by Steller (1841). In another graphic account, Blond (1953) tells of how a group of ravenous killer whales set upon a pod of rorquals.

There is some truth to all of these sensational stories. No doubt fierce attacks by killer whales on right whales, blue whales, and humpbacks have occurred and probably still do. However, killer whales, like all predators, kill only when they are hungry and will choose the weaker of two animals for prey. They dread the tail of large whales and will not initiate an attack unless there is no alternative. A right whale under attack by a killer whale reportedly sent its assailant ten yards into the air with a single slap of the tail. But recent observations suggest that small and large cetaceans get along better than we suspect. The most intriguing evidence concerns not *Orcinus orca* but the smaller pygmy killer whale, *Feresa attenuata*. "Throughout the day we observed the humpbacks and pygmy killer whales swimming together in a rare commingling of these two quite different species," writes Sylvia Earle (1979) of her discovery in Hawaiian waters. "Both seemed to enjoy the high seas, riding the waves, playing with the water." In short, they acted like anything but predator and prey.

Sharks (white sharks, in particular) are the fish most inclined to show aggressive behavior toward whales. Most classical authorities also mention sawfish, as does Lacépède (1804). However, recent findings indicate that swordfish and marlin are a more common peril. In 1969, a sword from the head of a swordfish was found stuck deep in the throat of a sei whale taken in the Antarctic (L. Watson, 1981). But let us note in passing that it was man, not the fish, that proved to be the whale's undoing.

Swordfish and related species are a testy lot. They will charge any competitor that encroaches on their feeding grounds or territory; presumably whales are no exception. They do not attack whales to eat them, but their irascibility can cost them dearly just the same. After all, being struck by the tail of a rorqual or a gray whale is like having a small mountain come crashing down on you!

CHAPTER 5

# The Nature of the Beast

*Whales are capable of showing an easygoing affection, be it between individuals within a herd, male and female, or a female and her suckling, on which she lavishes the tenderest of care, rears with concern, protects with solicitude, and defends with courage. This behavior, which stems from keen sensitivity, sustains, nurtures, and motivates her young. Instinct—the inevitable product of experience and sense perception—is developed, broadened, and refined. The two of them get used to being together and sharing pleasure, danger, and fear. This bonds mothers to offspring, females to males, and whales in a group to one another. No doubt this elevated animal instinct to a higher level and somehow transformed it into intelligent behavior.*

**Lacépède (1804)**

The more we learn about cetacean behavior, the more astonished we become at the complexity of their relationships. Their mating, play, and stratified group structure absorb and baffle us. Do these mighty nomads of the sea have their own traveling cities, perhaps even their own nations? They court, form families, carefully raise their young. The oceans reverberate with their whistles, grunts, songs, and conversations. Their pulsating calls are hymns to animal intelligence.

Of course, there are as many stands on the issue of cetacean intelligence as there are cetologists. A number of them dismiss the possibility outright and scoff at those who embrace it. Undaunted, their "anthropomorphist" colleagues go right on collecting data (some more judiciously than others) in hopes of buttressing their arguments.

We lean toward the latter view and shall attempt to show that whales are intelligent creatures. We are fully aware of the obstacles before us. Observations are open to debate; field work is out of the question. The few "scientific" studies currently available involve experiments with killer whales, dolphins, or porpoises in captivity. Such a stressful situation is obviously not suited to producing manifestations of natural intelligence or sociability—nor would we expect persons imprisoned against their wills to provide the best subjects for evaluating the intelligence and sociability of human beings.

## TRANSOCEANIC COMMUNICATION

Assuming that we can discuss the social interaction of whales in the same terms we use for land-dwelling animals, we could say that most baleen whales tend to live in small family units, while sperm whales prefer to associate in larger groups, such as harem schools and bachelor schools. Right whales usually form clusters of fewer than ten; so do bowheads, which used to often be seen feeding in herds of fifty to over a hundred before whaling decimated the species. Apparently pygmy right whales always pair off, although there are sightings of five to eight individuals together. Gray whales are not particularly social animals, typically migrating in pods of two to five, but they do mass seasonally on cold-water feeding grounds and in the tropical lagoons where they bear their young. Blue whales travel in close-knit groups of two, three, or four that coalesce into larger herds when they reach feeding grounds. For the more gregarious fin whale, the usual social unit seems to be a pod of three to ten or twenty; it is still not unusual to see concentrations of a hundred or more feeding on shoals of krill.

In winter, sei whales can be found in small families of two to five or six that form larger concentrations in polar waters during the summer feeding season. Bryde's whales also associate in groups of two to five, although there is one report of "30 to 40 together off the southern coast of Madagascar" (L. Watson, 1981). Minke whales roam singly or in pairs, but up to a thousand have been known to congregate at the edge of the pack ice to "harvest" nutrient-rich shoals of plankton. Pods of two or three are the norm for humpback whales. In their sophisticated, shifting groups, sperm whales form harem schools (a mixed group of mature cows and juveniles of both sexes, presided over temporarily by a large, dominant proprietor bull) or clusters of sexually inactive young bulls known as bachelor schools. Except during breeding season, mature males may form small bull schools or, travel alone.

Informative though the observations of whalers or naturalists may be, they yield nothing conclusive about social interaction. As the astute Dr. Payne once pointed out (1971), the very notion of a "herd" may be totally inappropriate for animals that are predominantly acoustic.

Like other mammals, whales interrelate by means of vocalizations, physical contact, and special positions or body language. What sets them apart from land animals, aside from their inability to exchange olfactory cues, is the fact that they can transmit sounds through the ocean across phenomenal distances.

The speed of sound in water varies with the temperature, salinity, and density of the layers through which the sound waves pass. But low-frequency "broadcasts" travel great distances regardless of conditions. For example, a signal transmitted at a frequency of 20 hertz (cycles per second) loses practically no energy when bounced off the ocean floor, and loses a scant 3 decibels over 5,500 miles! Some ocean layers conduct sound better than others; one such layer is a band of warmer water, "which in polar waters may occur near the surface but in low latitudes is most often found at depths of around 1,100 meters" (L. Watson, 1981). Given exactly the right conditions, it is possible that individuals hundreds of miles apart could pinpoint each other's position and perhaps exchange messages through these long-distance "speaking tubes."

From this point of view, the conventional concept of a herd loses all relevance. Far-flung whales can "socialize" by "tuning in" to one another with their highly developed sense of hearing. Blue whales, for example, keep track of each other's whereabouts in the oceans across dozens of miles.

## THE FACTS OF LIFE

The love life of the whale is an unlikely combination of disproportionate size and consummate poise. We shall preface this chapter with a brief discussion of the male and female reproductive organs.

It is hard to tell the sexes apart on the high seas. Female baleen whales are larger than males; sperm whale bulls are bigger than cows. Apart from size, however, there are almost no secondary sexual characteristics to go by. If a whale is seen

*Man has wiped out whales by the tens of thousands, lighted his lamps with whale oil, fashioned objects from baleen, fed whale meat to livestock and household pets. But what do we really know about the amazing creatures we have brought to the brink of extinction? Practically nothing. To this day, cetology is a little island of knowledge in a sea of ignorance. What little we do know about their language, intelligence, and social interaction is based on sketchy observations. Pages 190–91: A humpback calf stays close to its watchful mother as it explores the vast, watery world around it.*

*By and large, the social behavior of whales remains a mystery because its backdrop is the vast, featureless sea. We humans are essentially visual creatures; no matter what we do, we invariably reason like terrestrial animals. Whales, however, live in the water and rely primarily on their sense of hearing. Between these differences lies an irreducible gulf. Of course, there are times when whales send out unambiguous signals even we can understand. Above: This California gray whale, its penis extruded, is making its feelings known in no uncertain terms.*

*And they rock, and they rock, through the*
*sensual ageless ages*
*on the depths of the seven seas,*
*and through the salt they reel with drunk*
*delight*
*and in the tropics tremble they with love . . .*
*(D. H. Lawrence, from "Whales Weep Not!"*
*in* Selected Poems, *1932)*

swimming belly up at the surface or breaching, and its genital slit comes into view, one would have to know that the male's is farther forward than the female's. The penile slit is about midway between the umbilicus and the anus, the vulvular cleft, along with its flanking mammary glands, is located just forward of the anus.

The testicles of male whales, regardless of species, lie completely inside the body wall, tailward of the kidneys. They look like shiny, elongated cylinders. The fact that there is no external scrotum to interrupt body contours certainly aids streamlining, an advantage for locomotion and protection in sperm production.

The testicles of a mature blue whale are about 18 inches long and weigh about 100 pounds; those of the fin, sei, and sperm whale are about 10 inches long and weigh between 22 and 26 pounds. In the mature northern right whale, they can be over 6 feet long and weigh, together, up to a ton. Sizeable though these organs may be, there is nothing unusual about the sperm they produce. They closely resemble those produced by artiodactyls (ruminants and swine) and are shorter than man's.

For years it seemed impossible for anyone to comment on the size of a whale's penis without a salacious wink of the eye. Here is what Guillaume Rondelet, that worthy contemporary of Rabelais, had to say about it in 1568: "Since mating whales cannot unite at close quarters due to their huge bodies, their membrum virile is 13 cubits long. Once I saw a whale organ that size slung over the shoulder of a tall man, with both ends dragging on the ground. You can imagine how big it must get when whales anxious to mate are in pursuit of females."

Actually, the length of the male organ, albeit stupendous, does not come close to "13 cubits" (21 feet). Even in the largest species, it is no more than 10 feet long—about one-tenth total body length—and 10 to 12 inches across at the base. More-

*Above: This engraving of a stranded sperm whale, from* Theatrum animalium *(1718), is one of many dating from the eighteenth century. The artist's rendering of the external genitalia is fairly accurate. A fibroelastic organ similar to that of ruminants, the penis is usually withdrawn in an S-curve when relaxed. In stranded individuals, however, it is always extruded as a result of being distended by the gases of decomposition.*

*Opposite, bottom: The spermatozoa of the sperm whale are similar in shape to human sperm but smaller—40.6 microns against 55 microns.*

over, it is not extensible. When relaxed it is drawn into an S-curve and usually lodged in an internal penile sac. When erection begins, this invaginated fold of skin opens out to a penile slit just tailward of the navel. No more than two-thirds of the penis can ever protrude beyond this slit. In terms of position, structure, and operation, it is a fibroelastic organ similar to those of pigs, camels, and giraffes, not the vascular kind seen in horses, rhinos, carnivores, and primates. Generally speaking, it is designed for sudden erection and rapid copulation. Dissection has shown that there is no os penis. The tip is enclosed in a very tender preputial membrane; the retractor muscles that hold the relaxed penis inside its sheath lose their elasticity when the whale dies, and the gases associated with decomposition force the penis outside the carcass of a stranded male.

The inconspicuous vulva of female whales, located just forward of the anus, has labia majora and minora as well as a short, curved clitoris. Female whales that have never had intercourse have a hymenlike band of fibrous connective tissue that survives as a shred of flesh after their first sexual encounter. In most species, a cervix separates the vagina from the uterus, but right whales have seven or eight well-defined circular folds instead of a cervix. The uterus proper is bicornuate, as it is in most mammals. "In odontocetes," E. J. Slijper (1949) tells us, "the fertilized ovum is almost invariably attached to the wall of the left horn. In mysticetes the fetus is found in either horn, with a slight prevalence of the right horn (about 60%)." Twin births are rare.

The nonlobulate ovaries open onto slender, convoluted fallopian tubes. In fin whales, each ovary is 2 to 8 feet long, and its weight varies with the condition of the female: 2 pounds in nonpregnant fin whales to 57 pounds in pregnant females and about 17 to 64 pounds for nonpregnant and pregnant blue whales, respectively (E. J. Slijper, in K. S. Norris, 1966). The ovum is no bigger than that of a human. As with females of all species, ovulation is triggered by a combination of hormonal factors, controlled by internal stimuli (sexual maturity) and external cues (length of day).

Right: The external genitalia of a female whale, as depicted in an engraving from J. Dubar's Ostéographie de la baleine échouée a l'est du port d'Ostende le 4 november 1827 (1828). The Belgian scientist's account includes a detailed description of the specimen's external sex organs. "Even a cursory inspection of the vulva reveals striking similarities to the genitalia of the human female."

Most whales ovulate in winter or early spring, but for sperm and Bryde's whales, estrus is much less season-specific. The minke whale is the only species that ovulates twice a year.

In general, birth and lactation hold ovulation in check for quite a few months. Postpartum estrus and fertilization are rare, but two species—the gray whale and the humpback—are capable of bearing a calf two years in a row, although this happens rarely. Female minke whales have a short lactation period and can conceive every eighteen months. But for right whales and all the other rorquals, the interval between births is at best two years. Most females of these species bear young only once every three years. A gestation period of over sixteen months, combined with a lactation period of two years or longer, brings the entire reproductive cycle of the sperm whale to between three and four years. A cow that gives birth for the first time at ten years and lives to be forty can bear no more than seven

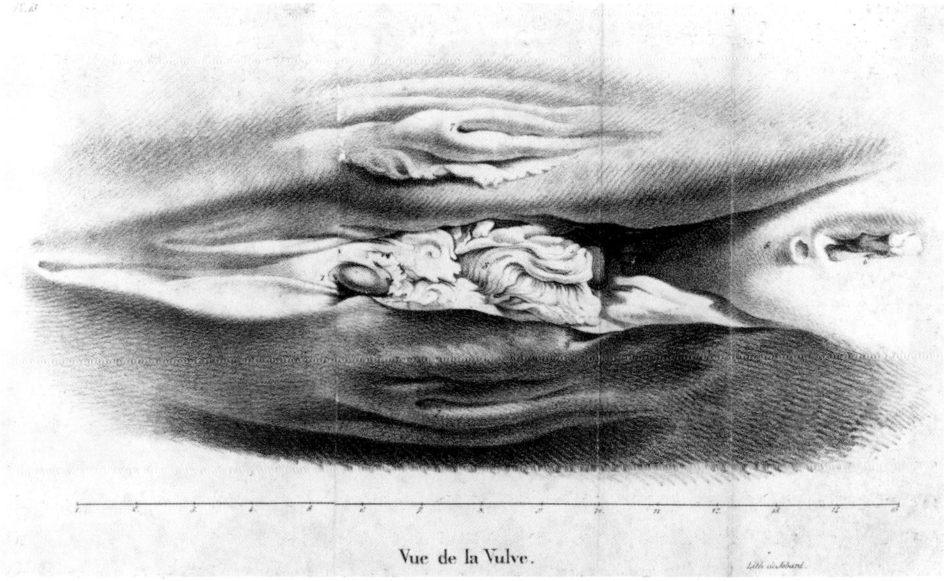


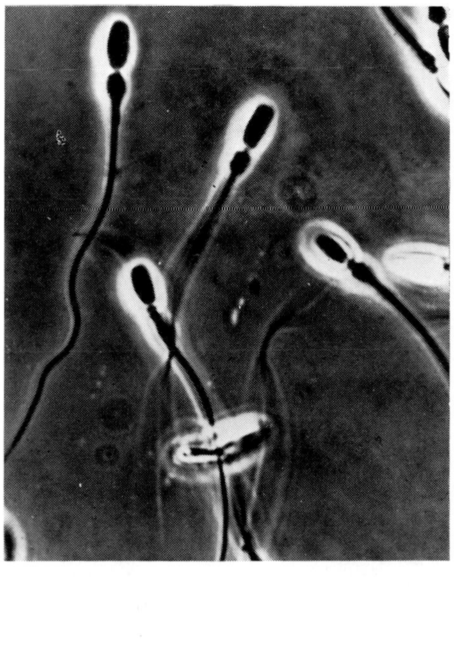

to ten calves. These low birth rates are one reason that overfished species take so long to replenish their original stocks.

## WEIGHTY WOOING

Most baleen whales mate in the dead of winter or in early spring, when they are in temperate or subtropical waters (southward migration in the northern hemisphere, northward migration in the southern hemisphere). There and only there does the mighty concerto of courtship and conquest get under way. December and January mark the onset of the mating season for blue whales north of the equator, June and July for their southern counterparts. The rut gets off to a somewhat earlier start (November–December or May–June) for fin and sei whales. Bryde's whales do not stray much beyond warm-water zones and are far less constrained by seasonal factors. Apparently the sedentary near-shore variety can breed throughout the year, while the migrating pelagic variety mates primarily in the fall. We know nothing about the breeding habits of the pygmy right whale.

Although sperm whales mate at various times of the year, there is a more favorable period for breeding in each hemisphere: January to July (peaking in March, April, and May) north of the equator, August to December (peaking in October) south of the equator. Naturalists have been aware of this as far back as the nineteenth century. According to Toussenel (1862) and Van Beneden (1867–92), the local stock off Mexico, Panama, and Peru congregated every spring around the Galápagos Islands to begin their subtle yet lively mating rituals. The sperm whales that Jonathan Gordon and the crew aboard the *Tulip* studied east of Sri Lanka in 1984 breed en masse from April to June. March is the peak month of the mating season for the stock around Japan (Mizue and Jimbo, 1950). The less eager group off the coast of California waits until April, May, and June. The breeding range of the species appears to be generally confined to the 40th parallel on either side of the equator, but there is a great deal of variation, and much remains unknown.

The rutting season sends up clouds of spray, for courtship is a playful, boisterous activity punctuated by breaching, thrashing about, lobtailing, smacking of flukes against the water, and gentle "love taps" with both flippers. Males of many animal species respond to sex-attractant substances—pheromones—secreted by females. Such is not the case with whales. Their sense of smell is absent or severely limited, so male and female must signal readiness to mate by means of body language, water acrobatics, and vocalizations. The mating imperative may be partly why humpback whales have developed the ability to "sing." We do not venture to say that massive Romeos woo spouting Juliets with cetacean serenades, but some degree of vocal cueing does take place.

However, whales do not make particularly faithful lovers. The rorquals seem to form stronger male-female bonds than other species and may even be monogamous, but most experts hold that mating pairs are only exclusive for the breeding season. As for sperm whales, we had long thought that the jealous "schoolmaster" enjoyed sole rights to his harem and defended the privilege with all the energy his tail, head, and jaws could muster. Recent studies suggest that the harem master is not so tenacious and that his reign is temporary. At the first sign of abdication, other mature bulls stand ready to compete for his place.

Experts are divided about the extent to which rival mysticetes engage in aggressive behavior. In any event, the scuffles between male baleen whales are never as violent as those between sperm whale bulls. Divers with the Cousteau team were

*The sight of whales mating conjures up visions of prehistoric times: moving islands uniting in primeval seas, locked in embraces both monstrous and sublime. Philippe Cousteau and the crew of the* Calypso *had ample opportunity to observe the courtship and mating behavior of southern right whales off Peninsula Valdés, Argentina. Opposite, below: A launch approaches a threesome (two males and a female) while mating is in progress.*

*Females are not always receptive to the advances of would-be partners. When they are not "in the mood," they roll over onto their backs (above), thereby exposing the belly and vulva at the surface and making it impossible for males to get into the proper position for mating. But aroused males are not easily deterred. They patiently wait for the female to roll back onto her belly to breathe and immediately press their advantage. If a female is determined to give a suitor the brush-off, she may sprint toward an underwater shoal and simply let the pursuing male crash into it.*

struck by the comparatively peaceful attitudes of rival suitors; at the very most, their displays of strength took the form of shoving matches or raps on the nose. Others, however, have witnessed less innocuous acts of aggression. According to Dr. Mandojana (1982, 1983), male right whales do not stop at powerful head butts and intimidation (smacking of the flukes against the water). They use their rock-like, barnacle-studded callosities to wound their rivals. These slashing matches can inflict serious harm, for the skin of these whales is tender and easily bruised.

This view is shared by Sylvia Earle, who has spent a great deal of time watching the mating behavior of humpbacks in Hawaiian waters. Males competing for females in heat are often more brutal than was previously thought. They will swim headlong into rival males, and the scars they all bear attest to the violence of previous battles. As with other animals, opponents do not get down to really serious fighting unless the symbolic battle of intimidation ends in a draw. Earle suspects that some of the songs humpbacks sing may be a form of sexual display. She also believes that males "weave" bubble nets not only to corral shrimp or fish at mealtime, but to put up a "symbolic screen" between the desired female and other males (Earle, 1979).

Just because a female has been chosen does not necessarily mean she is receptive. She may not have the slightest intention of responding to a male's advances. At such times, the easiest ploy is to lie belly-up at the surface, a maneuver that puts her genital slit out of the suitor's reach. But males eager to mate are not put off so quickly. Some of them will lie patiently beneath the female and wait for her to run out of air. As soon as she rolls over to take a breath, they press their advantage.

When a female is determined not to mate, she heads toward water too shallow for males to maneuver beneath her. Frustrated suitors have no alternative but to give up. One female on the open sea was seen attempting to spurn the advances of a pursuing male by hanging vertically, head-downward, in the water, with her tail and lower abdomen thrust high in the air, revolving and presenting just her torso to the hapless male (R. Payne, 1976).

For sheer heartlessness, however, no rebuff can match another reported by Dr. Payne (1976). An exasperated female was seen swimming at full tilt at the surface, heading toward a sandbank. The excited male kept pace directly beneath her, attempting copulation along the way. Just when victory seemed within his grasp, they reached the sandbank, and the lout went crashing into it!

## THE CETACEAN KAMA SUTRA

Just before male and female copulate, the titanic creatures break into a wonderful courtship dance. Few sights can equal those beautiful aquatic arabesques, the graceful gliding and rolling over, the contact of bellies and flippers, the sublime moments of swimming side by side, the sudden release of sexual tension that ends in tender nuzzling.

The act of intercourse proper is acrobatic and very brief. The fibroelastic penis of the male is designed for quick coitus. Whales have to join their massive bodies, yet there is nothing to use for leverage. They usually mate at the surface and apparently rarely avail themselves of their extraordinary breath-holding ability. Erection is sudden, and copulation lasts less than a minute, depending on the position. Whales often mate early in the morning; the poetically inclined might think they greet the first rays of the sunrise with a reaffirmation of life.

Captive dolphins have been seen copulating repeatedly for more than a half-hour at one- to eight-minute intervals. While it is true that some whales mate several times in a row, they do not display the compulsive behavior of male dolphins in captivity, which often masturbate with ropes, oars, inflow water jets, and even fish given to them at mealtime. Captive dolphins have been known to attempt copulation with anything that crosses their path, including other males, mothers, daughters, sharks, and turtles.

Discrepancies among accounts of mating behavior suggest that whales can mate in any number of ways. Actually, if cetaceans had a Kama Sutra of their own, it would make for a slim volume. There are three basic positions: with both rolled over on the side, belly to belly; with the female on her belly at the surface and the male beneath her, belly up; and with both partners upright in the water, at the surface.

Aristotle was the first to observe and describe the belly-to-belly position. "The technique for dolphins and all whales is the same: The male and female mate while they lie side by side. Copulation lasts for neither too long nor too short a time." This was confirmed centuries later by Cuvier (1836): "In all likelihood, they mate while both of them are on their side." Van Beneden (1867–92) referred to Guldberg's account: "A male and female, both on their side, were seen edging towards each other, then lying belly to belly." (That was back in whaling days, and the story had a violent ending. "The boat fired at the male, which let go of the female and escaped uninjured. The following day, a 78-foot female was taken. When she was cut open, the vaginal mucosa was found to be red and inflamed.")

The side position seems to be a favorite of several whale species, especially rorquals, although few have ever actually been seen mating. It is also popular among

*Opposite: Gray whales mating off Baja California. Philippe Cousteau had a chance to observe and film right whales mating underwater off Peninsula Valdés, Argentina, and the scene was somewhat similar to this one. He described what he saw in his log. "A few meters from our launch a female raced past with, not two, but three males in pursuit. There wasn't any air left in my tank, but I grabbed my camera and jumped into the water anyway. I went swimming after that quartet of whales like a man possessed. All of a sudden the female sounded, followed by her trio of suitors. I dived behind them, straight down. At the end of this desperate descent I beheld an extraordinary* fleur géante*: the female and her suitors, all gently undulating, head down and bodies tilted, like the petals of some huge underwater corolla. The entire scene was suffused in an otherworldly glow. The smallest male, probably too young and too ungainly, withdrew from the competition; that got the other two all the more excited. . . . Each of the remaining suitors positioned himself on either side of the female and took aim with an erect, yet pliant penis. . . . At long last one of them managed to find the proffered vagina and slipped inside."*

gray whales, whose winter mating in the lagoons of Baja California has inspired a number of accounts (L. Watson, 1981, etc.).

Some males mate with the female on top and male on the bottom. Dudley (1725) was one of the few to mention it, and his account was later mentioned, in turn, by Cuvier (1836): "Dudley, however, reports that they lie belly to belly, one above and the other below." This is a favorite position of right whales, and Dr. Mandojana (1982) has observed them many times off Peninsula Valdés, Argentina.

## *THE "PAS DE TROIS" OF MATING GRAY WHALES*

*Captain Cousteau's crew and Dr. Ted Walker have watched 40-ton gray whales mate in the lagoons of Baja California. "In the shallow lagoons of Baja California," writes Lyall Watson (1981), "sometimes 50 kilometers (30 miles) from the ocean, mature adults congregate in January. In the early morning there is much spyhopping and circling, intensified around midday as the whales break up into trios composed of two males and a single female.*

*"Only one male is involved in actual mating. He can usually be identified by a single flipper which is held up motionless above the surface of the water, presumably as a signal. The female approaches with a delicate touch display, caressing the male with her flippers until they come to lie belly-to-belly in very shallow water. The other male remains in close attendance, taking an upright position on the far side of the female and apparently forms a prop or wedge. There they stay for up to an hour, copulating several times, with each contact lasting about two minutes. . . ."*

*Here is part of Philippe Cousteau's account. "The female clearly uses her flippers to clasp the male. It is a moving sight, but not devoid of less romantic moments. The male's sex organ, a gigantic spar 2 meters long, comes into view. . . . We witnessed one mating session in its entirety. The preliminaries and foreplay lasted nearly an hour; the animals copulated, or attempted copulation, about ten times. At one point, we noticed a large patch of froth some 35 meters long floating on the surface. It was semen the male had ejaculated after an unsuccessful attempt at coitus. With cetaceans, there is no obvious way to tell whether or not the sex act has been successfully completed."*

*Whales do not have an extensive repertory of mating positions, and each species seems to prefer certain ones over others. One of the most acrobatic—upright in the water at the surface (left)—is believed to be a favorite of bowheads and humpbacks.*

*Opposite, top to bottom: The fetus of a California gray whale, from Scammon (1874); an unborn sperm whale calf after removal from a harpooned female; intrauterine position of the fetus of a right whale.*

*Below: As this painting shows, calves usually emerge from the uterus tailfirst. The umbilical cord has built-in weak points and breaks automatically after birth. Then the mother nudges her calf to the surface for its first breath.*

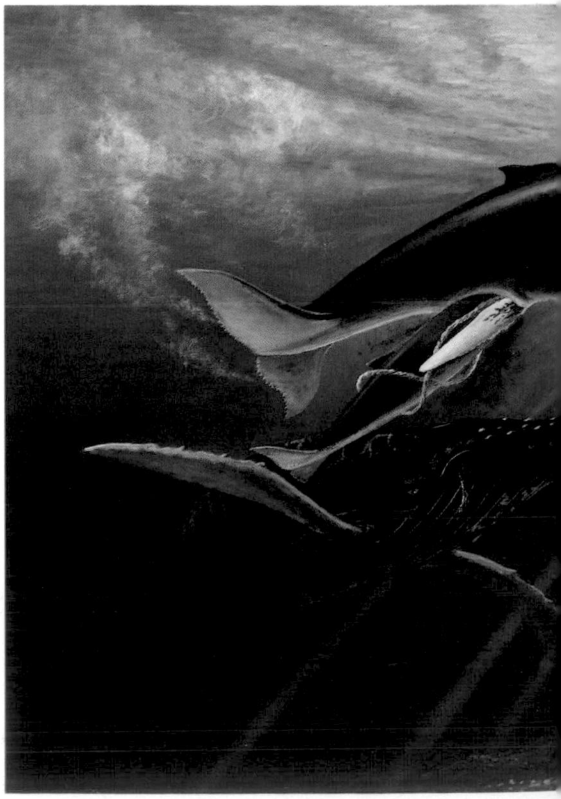

"When right whales are mating, there is commotion in the bay. The act of love involves a great deal of shoving, sparring, and acrobatic stunts. Usually several males pursue a female. During the free-for-all she will often head towards the suitor of her choice, which puts him at a definite advantage. Copulation takes place while the female swims on her belly, with the male belly up beneath her. As they swim or drift in passionate surrender, she keeps her huge partner in place by hugging his slippery body with her broad flippers. This is followed by gentle nudges, love pats, caresses, and other signs of tenderness."

The third position—upright in the water, belly to belly, with heads raised above the surface—is the one Lacépède (1804) described in his discussion of the bowhead whale. "Comparing and weighing statements made by whalers and other eyewitnesses, it would appear that when they mate the male and female stand up, as it were, against each other, tail down, lift the fore part of their bodies, thrust their heads high in the air, and hold this position while clasping each other with their flippers." Actually, a number of species include the acrobatic leaping-in-tandem technique in their mating repertoire. Cuvier (1836) quotes Anderson's report that "mating whales hold each other while upright in the water." According

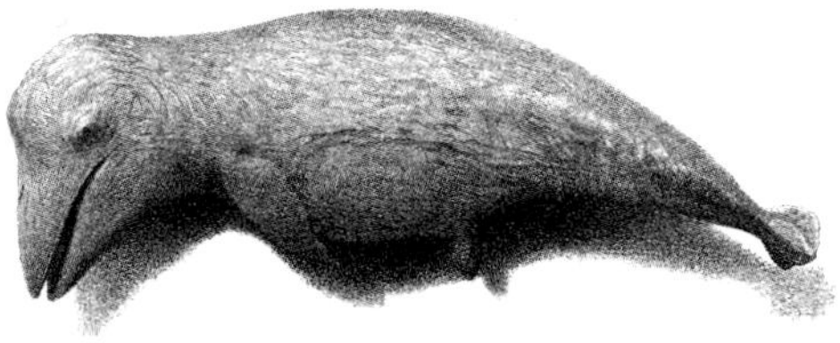

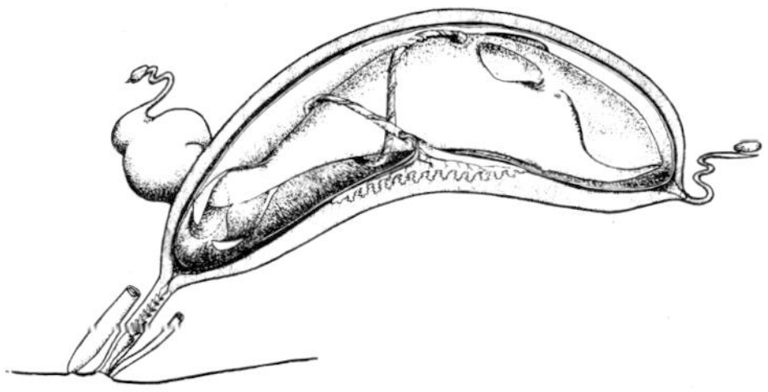

to Nishiwaki and Hayashi (1951), humpback whales copulate belly to belly just as they emerge from the water at high speed. In 1962, E. J. Slijper described the mating antics of the sperm whale in much the same way. "Courtship is playful and splashy," writes Lyall Watson (1981), "often involving an energetic group that races along the surface at breakneck speed, churning the water up into turbulent knots of breaching, slapping whales. Sometimes the confusion ends in a single pair rising, with their flippers interlaced, belly-to-belly above the surface, clasping each other and holding that position for thirty seconds or more until they shudder and subside again."

## TWENTY-FIVE-FOOT INFANTS

Whales are slow breeders; on average, they give birth to one calf every other year. Harpooned females have provided experts with additional data about this crucial demographic factor. The average ovulation rate of the gray whale, for example, is 0.52, the pregnancy rate 0.46. The corresponding figures for Bryde's whale are 0.45 and 0.41. The pregnancy rate of the sei whale is 0.50, but only 0.20 to 0.25 for sperm whale cows.

The percentage of twin fetuses is consistently low (about 1 percent) for all species. It seems to be slightly higher for sei and right whales, but extremely low (0.39 percent) for humpbacks (E. J. Slijper, in K. S. Norris, 1966). There are no records of a mother with two calves.

Relative to their size, the gestation period of whales is surprisingly short. As a rule, the bigger the mammal, the longer the term of pregnancy: nine months for humans, eleven for horses, eighteen for rhinoceroses, and twenty-two for elephants. One would expect whales to have a gestation period of thirty months or more; in fact, it only takes about a year from conception to birth (right whales, ten months; bowheads, twelve or thirteen; gray whales, more than thirteen; blue whales and humpbacks, eleven to twelve; fin and sei whales, eleven; Bryde's whales, twelve; and minke whales, ten). The short pregnancy is dictated by ecological imperatives. Baleen whales spend summers on cold-water feeding grounds; winters are for mating and calving. This immutable annual cycle necessitates a gestation period of about a year.

Odontocetes are not primarily seasonal feeders, so their breeding period is not limited to any particular time of year. Moreover, the gestation period of the sperm whale is more in line with what its size would lead one to expect: from fourteen and a half months to at least sixteen and a half, and perhaps more than eighteen, from conception to birth. Still, compared with the rhinoceros or elephant, that is not a very long time.

Calving almost always occurs in coastal waters, shallow lagoons, or warm-water inlets, except in the case of rorquals. Writing in the first century A.D., in his description of the northern (Biscayan) right whale, Pliny the Elder noted this behavior: "They do not appear in the Ocean of Cadiz until winter, and for a fixed period of time they hide in an open, peaceful bay and there deliver their young." Both Lacépède (1804) and Cuvier (1836) made the same comment about the bowhead. The observant Charles Scammon witnessed the birth of many a gray whale in the lagoons of Baja California, and the slaughter that ensued made him a wealthy man.

Today, southern right whales deliver their young off Peninsula Valdés, Argentina; blue whales, in the Sea of Cortez; humpbacks, in the waters off Maui and the Bahamas; sperm whales, in the vicinity of the Galápagos Islands, the Azores, and the western coast of Sri Lanka. That is only a partial list of the most frequently mentioned calving grounds. Many others have yet to be discovered or confirmed—and given the fullest possible protection.

Little is known about the actual process of giving birth. As the contractions begin, there is an increase in the female's respiratory rate and the number of defecations. (In fact, defecation may be almost continuous with the onset of labor.) She stays near the surface the whole time. The amniotic membrane ruptures, expelling copious amounts of fluid. Whalers that have seen it spill onto the bridge of a factory ship liken it to a "waterfall."

Almost all uniparous land mammals (mammals that produce one offspring at a time) deliver their young headfirst. Whales, however, had to adapt the birth process to the water; they bring calves into the world tailfirst, a crucial advantage for a newborn suddenly thrust into an airless environment. The umbilical cord is short (only 40–50 percent as long as the newborn), quite thick, and fairly rigid. It is connected midway along the body of the fetus. To prevent obstruction as the calf is expelled, the dorsal fin and flippers lie flat in special depressions in the body wall until just after delivery. The mother does not bite off the umbilical cord, but the cord has built-in weak spots and will snap spontaneously when pulled taut. Labor lasts about thirty to sixty minutes, but a difficult birth may take up to four hours. The placenta and accessory parts are not expelled until some ten hours after delivery (S. R. Riedman and E. T. Gustafson, 1966). A newborn baby whale, with no air in its lungs, tends to sink, but instinctively swims toward the surface; the mother helps it, catching it on one of her flippers or with her snout and nudging it upward. (She will do this even if the calf is stillborn.) The neonate takes its first breath less than ten seconds after it has emerged from the womb, and about a half-hour later it has learned to swim well.

Dolphins invariably deliver their young tailfirst, and unborn fetuses found in harpooned pregnant females have always been found in this position (Riedman and Gustafson, 1966). It was long assumed that all cetaceans are born this way, but apparently there are exceptions to the rule. Two American biologists witnessed the birth of a gray whale in a lagoon along the Baja California coast in 1975. As the moment of birth neared, the mother rolled over on her back at the surface. To the onlookers' astonishment, the calf was literally ejected headfirst into the air, and it had little trouble taking its first breath on its own. The mother turned over on her belly and used one of her flippers to help keep the newborn afloat (H. Bertini, 1982).

The fact that cetaceans give birth tailfirst—a reversal of what is considered "normal" procedure in mammals—baffled unenlightened observers and inspired legends as farfetched as they are entertaining. Old seafarers used to say that dolphin calves seek shelter in their mother's womb when threatened. Others maintained that the flippers and tail of newborn whales stay soft and limp several days after birth, so they are unable to swim on their own. Eskimos in Greenland thought just the opposite: according to their stories, baby narwhals, belugas, and bowheads stick their tails out of the womb a few weeks *before* delivery so that they can practice swimming and be ready to keep up with their mother the very day they are born.

Female whales do not calve unassisted. One or more of the mother's congeners—variously termed "aunties," "godmothers," or "midwives"—supervise the proceedings. Possibly attracted by the release of the amniotic fluid into the water, these assistants have been seen looking after the calf, nudging it to the surface for

### *THE BIRTH OF A SPERM WHALE*

*A sizable stock of sperm whales plies the Indian Ocean west of Sri Lanka. With the support of the Netherlands World Wildlife Fund and the International Union for the Conservation of Nature, a team of naturalists led by Hal Whitehead sailed to the region aboard the* Tulip. *In 1983 and 1984 they observed and identified more than two hundred individuals. In the course of their expedition, the scientists also had the good fortune to witness the birth of a sperm whale. Whitehead described what he saw in* National Geographic *(December 1984).*

*"It was in the autumn of 1983 that we witnessed an actual sperm whale birth. . . . Early on the second morning an adult whale, whose callus on the dorsal fin identified it as a female, suddenly surfaced 30 yards off* Tulip*'s bow, flexing her body so that at times both her head and flukes were out of the water. Moments later she rolled over, presenting her belly to us, as a torrent of blood gushed from her genital area. A dark object followed, materializing within seconds into a tiny sperm whale calf with curled flukes and a bent dorsal, bobbing alongside its mother.*

*"Lindy [Weilgart] was instantly overboard with a mask and snorkel, and I was up the mast. We watched in amazement as the calf separated itself from its mother and approached closer and closer to Lindy.*

*" 'I could see the umbilicus attached to the calf,' Lindy said later, 'as well as the afterbirth protruding from the mother. I was astonished that the calf had bright blue eyes.'*

*"Soon the calf was put through a rigorous ordeal. Four adults gathered to inspect the newcomer, pushing and squeezing it among themselves as though to get closest to it. At one point the calf was lifted bodily out of the water. Finally the visitors retired. . . ."*

its first breath, and teaching it how to swim. A newborn whale is weak and unsteady; it does not float well at first and requires constant attention. The mother will lavish care on her calf, but others are there to assist her. There is no nest, no den, no secure refuge, so the assistance of the aunties might be critical.

*LITTLE GIANTS*

*The weight of a rorqual calf at birth is equivalent to 5 or 6 percent of its mother's weight; for grays, right whales, and sperm whales the figure is 8 to 12 percent (compared with 10 to 15 percent for dolphins, 8 to 10 percent for ungulates and phocids, 5 to 6 percent for humans, and 0.5 to 3 percent for rodents and carnivores). The length ratio of calf to mother at birth is about 1 : 4 for rorquals and 1 : 3 for the others.*

*Thus whale calves have the following approximate weight and size at birth:*
*Right whale: 16 feet, 4 to 5 tons*
*Bowhead: 17 feet, 5 to 6 tons*
*Pygmy right whale: 6 feet, 0.5 ton*
*Gray whale: 15 feet, 1 to 1.5 tons*
*Blue whale: 23 to 25 feet, 6 to 8 tons*
*Fin whale: 20 feet, 4 tons*
*Sei whale: 15 feet, 1.2 tons*
*Bryde's whale: 13 feet, 1 ton*
*Minke whale: 9 feet, 0.5 ton*
*Humpback: 14 feet, 2.5 tons*
*Sperm whale: 13 feet, 1 ton*

The humpback mother attracts another sort of attendant. On one occasion, however, a third party swimming with a humpback and her calf in Hawaiian waters turned out to be a large adult male! But he was not helping the little one to breathe or swim; he was too busy trying to mate with the new mother! (S. A. Earle, 1979).

*Like all cetaceans, a humpback calf wastes no time learning how to swim. It is a matter of life and death. But its watchful mother is never far away. She not only produces an extraordinarily rich milk that puts weight on her young at a phenomenal rate, but protects, nuzzles, coaxes, and "talks" to her offspring. Mother and calf stay together for at least a year, often longer, while she schools it in the pleasures and perils of the sea. This constant intimacy fosters a bond of affection that has moved even merciless harpooners.*

## MONSTROUS MEALS

The old belief that calves stay with their mother for several years has proved incorrect, but they do spend quite a few months together. Generally speaking, right whales are weaned within a year after birth, gray whales in eight months, blue whales in seven months, fin whales in seven months, sei and Bryde's whales in six months, minke whales in four months, humpbacks in eleven months, and sperm whales in two years or more.

The female's nipples are located on either side of the vulva. As far back as the sixteenth century it was known that "not only dolphins but whales and sea calves have no protruding teats, for nature has seen to it that no body part whatsoever should impede swimming or other movements in the water" (Rondelet, 1568). Cuvier (1836) gave a reasonably accurate account of how feeding is accomplished: "The muscles above the mammaries are so arranged that they may be squeezed, and apparently mothers are capable of squirting their milk into the calf's mouth. This has yet to be confirmed."

It has since been confirmed. The mammary glands of whales are two elongated internal organs (7 feet 10 inches long and 19 to 20 inches wide in blue whales, about 6 feet long and 17 to 18 inches wide in humpbacks); they are embedded in the subcutaneous tissue on each side of the ventromedial line and tailward of the umbilicus. They terminate in nipples (3.5 inches long in blue whales) that are retracted in clefts on either side of the genital slit. Males have rudimentary nipples at about the same location, forward of the anus.

Feedings of infants are short and frequent, especially at the start of lactation. The suckling takes its first meal less than an hour after birth. Nursing takes place underwater and close to the surface. As the calf approaches from behind, the mother turns a bit to the side to give it easier access to the nipples. The calf catches the teat between its tongue and palate either in the middle or at the corner of its mouth. Because of its underslung jaw, however, a baby sperm whale is forced to suckle out of the corner of its mouth. This was confirmed by Frank Bullen (1899): "The mother lay on her side, with the breast nearly out of the water's edge; while the calf, lying parallel to the parent with the head in the same direction held the teat sideways in the angle of the jaw with its snout protruding from the surface."

Powerful simultaneous contractions squirt the thick, creamy milk into the calf's mouth. When the calf lets go of the nipple the milk continues to spurt into the water for five or six seconds. If exposed at the surface or on the deck of a whaling vessel, the teat can shoot milk up to two yards into the air (Zenkovich, 1938).

The composition of whale milk varies with species and the season; the type of food the female ingests is probably a key factor. The milk is extraordinarily rich: the milk of the fin whale, for example, contains ten times the fat, twice the protein, at least five times the calories, and up to twice the calcium and phosphorus as cow's milk. The sugar content is very low, while the amounts of vitamins A and B, potassium, magnesium, and chlorine are about the same as those in the milk of terrestrial mammals.

This rich, concentrated milk is obviously why calves grow at such a phenomenal rate. For Lacépède (1804), it "stood to reason" that a creature as gigantic as a whale would require a prolonged growth period, perhaps dozens of years. This was one of the times the Frenchman's logic steered him wrong. Sucklings grow to an impressive size after only twelve months at their mother's breast. But they have to gorge themselves if they are to build up the strength needed for the summer migration toward the poles. It takes a whale calf only seven days to double its birth weight—about the same time needed by rats, rabbits, and dogs; human babies require half a year, and cows a month and a half. This rate of growth is remarkable.

During the seven months that blue whales suckle their young, the calf consumes nearly 200 pounds of milk a day; it will have ingested 18 to 19 tons of the precious fluid before it is weaned. It grows almost 2 inches a day and gains, on the

*A mother about to deliver her young is often assisted by another female from her group. According to several reliable accounts, this so-called auntie or godmother seems to give the mother encouragement, helps the calf get its first breath, and, if nothing else, stands guard against potential enemies. Mutual assistance among females continues after birth. Opposite: Two adults seem to be "baby-sitting" a humpback calf that is already several weeks old. Recently some cetologists have challenged the hypothesis that "aunties" are actively involved in the birth and care of young. While observing humpbacks off Hawaii, Sylvia Earle (1979) noted that one individual she had taken for an "auntie" turned out to be a large, self-centered bull attempting to copulate with the mother-to-be while she was actually giving birth!*

average, nearly 200 pounds (that comes to more than 7 pounds an hour!). Assuming an average composition of 49 percent water, 36 percent fat, 13 percent protein, and 1 percent sugar, whale milk has a total calorific value of almost 1,900 kilocalories per pound (kcal/lb). By comparison, cow's milk contains only 1,639 kcal/lb. If the calf gulps down this super-rich milk at the rate of 200 pounds a day, its daily caloric intake is 380,000 kilocalories—more than a hundred times that of an adult man. Moreover, the calf assimilates its food (that is, converts it into useful weight, or into the protoplasm) at the astonishing rate of 90 percent.

During its six-month lactation period, a baby fin whale drinks 143 pounds of milk a day; in a twenty-four-hour period it puts on 125 pounds (5 pounds an hour!) and grows more than an inch. Its assimilation rate can be as high as 92 percent. At the end of the six months, when it is about to swim toward its first meal of krill, it will be 11 to 12 tons heavier than when it was born.

The daily milk intake of the gray whale calf is between 80 and 84 pounds; humpback calves ingest about 100 pounds of food a day. The young of the blue, fin, gray, and humpback whales are irrevocably weaned when they reach the nutrient-rich feeding grounds of the polar seas. They proceed to break their own records for gluttony, for if they are to survive their first winter they have to return from the cold-water plankton shoals with a blubber reserve equivalent to 40 to 50 percent of their total body weight.

The stomach of a newborn sperm whale has a total capacity of about 4.5 gallons, but the first chamber can only hold a gallon or so at a time. Therefore, it takes four or five feedings for the calf to ingest its daily ration of 45 pounds of milk. The milk is slightly less rich than that of rorquals, and since the growth rate of a baby sperm whale is considerably lower than that of its blue or fin whale counterparts, it gains "only" 6 or 7 pounds a day, or about a ton a year. Calves not only spend more time in their mother's womb than rorquals do, but rely on them longer after birth. Small wonder sperm whales are inclined to be more "sociable" than mysticetes.

## NOT BY MILK ALONE

Whales nourish their young as much with care as with their super-rich milk, and the bond between mother and calf is but one example of higher social interaction among whales.

*COMPOSITION OF WHALE MILK AND COW'S MILK*

*(Takemura, 1927; Heyerdahl, 1930; Zenković, 1938; C. Lockyer, 1976)*

*(per 100 grams)*

| | *Water* | *Fats* | *Solids* |
|---|---|---|---|
| *Blue whale* | 41–51 | 34–37 | 14–22 (*) |
| *Fin whale* | 53–55 | 31–33 | 13–14(**) |
| *Sperm whale* | 53–54 | 35–37 | 7–8 |
| *Cow* | 90–91 | 3–4 | 4–5 |

* *includes 11.5–14.1 percent protein (casein, albumin), 1 percent sugar (lactose), and 1 percent vitamins and minerals.*

***includes 11.9–13.3 percent protein (casein, albumin), 0.2–1.8 percent sugar (lactose), and 1 percent vitamins and minerals.*

*A blue whale calf ingests nearly 200 pounds of milk a day! Smaller species take less—a fin whale calf about 150 pounds, a California gray calf 80, a humpback calf 100, and a sperm whale calf 44. Phenomenal though these rations may seem, calves need all they can get. They must put on weight quickly if they are to endure the upcoming migration and brave the perils of the sea. Whales have a low birth rate. At best they calve once every two years, and some only once every three to five years. Assuming that a female can bear young for thirty years, her progeny will consist of about fifteen offspring at the most. (Whales can expect to have roughly the same number that young women used to have before birth control and contraception.) Above: An engraving from Scammon's* Marine Mammals of the North-western Coast of North America *(1874) shows the rarest of sights: a fin whale nursing twin calves. Right: An adult humpback and its calf, as pictured in an eighteenth-century Chinese manuscript. Note the dangling umbilical cord.*

*CONCISE GROWTH CHART FOR WHALES*

| *Species* | *Age* | *Length* | *Weight (metric tons)* |
|---|---|---|---|
| *Bowhead* | | | |
| Puberty | 6 years | | |
| *Right whale* | | | |
| Puberty | 6 years | | |
| *Pygmy right whale* | | | |
| Puberty | 4 years | | |
| *Gray whale* | | | |
| Puberty | 8 years | 30–33 feet | |
| *Blue whale* | | | |
| Puberty: male | 5 years | 72 feet | 72 tons |
| female | 5 years | 75 feet | 87 tons |
| Physical maturity: male | 15 years | 79 feet | 97 tons |
| female | 15 years | 84 feet | 114 tons |
| *Fin whale* | | | |
| Puberty: male | 6 years | 62 feet | 43.5 tons |
| female | 6 years | 64 feet | 47.5 tons |
| Physical maturity: male | 15 years | 65 feet | 51.5 tons |
| female | 15 years | 70 feet | 62 tons |
| *Sei whale* | | | |
| Puberty: male | 3 years | 44 feet | |
| female | 3.5 years | 47 feet | |
| *Bryde's whale* | | | |
| Puberty: male | 2–3 years | | |
| female | 2–4 years | | |
| *Minke whale* | | | |
| Puberty | 2 years | | |
| *Humpback* | | | |
| Puberty | 7–8 years | 36–40 feet | |
| *Sperm whale* | | | |
| Puberty: male | 8–10 years | 30–33 feet | 10 tons |
| female | 8–9 years | 26–30 feet | 6.5 tons |
| Sexual maturity: male | 18–19 years | 36–40 feet | 18 tons |
| female | 9–10 years | 30–33 feet | 13.5 tons |
| Social maturity: male (harem) | 25–27 years | 42–46 feet | 27–28 tons |
| Physical maturity: male | 35–50 years | 49–52 feet | 43–45 tons |
| female | 30–40 years | 33–36 feet | 13.5 tons |

Mothers dote on their offspring in countless ways, clasping them with their flippers and defending them when need be. Aristotle tells of a dolphin that carried maternal love to the point of keeping her dead calf afloat at the surface for hours, presumably in the hope that it might start breathing again. He credited all cetaceans with this type of behavior. One detailed account of a right whale protecting its young dates back to Rondelet (1568): "She has two large flippers at her sides which she uses to swim and to conceal her young when they are frightened. . . . Males are taken with great difficulty, but females can be more easily caught when they are accompanied by their calf. For while they are busy coming to its rescue their own chances of escape fade." Ambroise Paré (1582) agreed. "Females are easier to take than males, because they endeavor to save their young. Their sole concern is to conceal them, not to escape."

These observations have been confirmed countless times since, and whalers have been known to aim deliberately at calves in order to catch their mothers. In the 1800s, for example, Basque whalers struck a right whale calf in the Bay of San Sebastian in northern Spain. "Eventually she [the mother] broke the line and carried the young away. The following day the body of the calf was found floating out at sea and was towed back to the village. The cow followed the towing boat into the harbor and remained there with her dead calf for six hours in spite of the shots

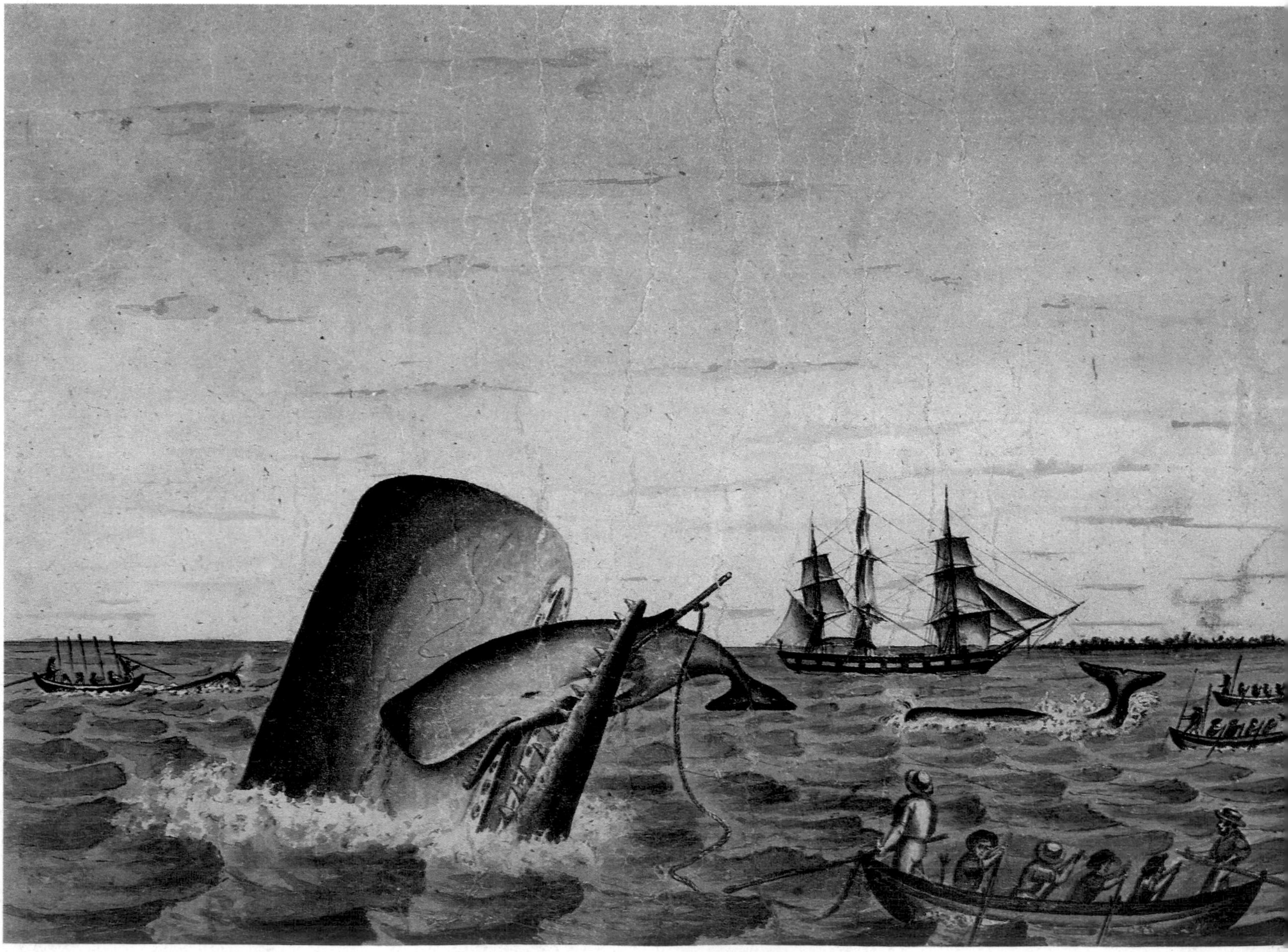

that were fired at her" (M. C. Caldwell and D. K. Caldwell, in K. S. Norris, 1966).

The bond between female bowheads and their calves is just as intense and lasting. Linnaeus (1766) noted that cows drag endangered young away with a flipper when they seem to be stricken or weary. Scoresby (1823) concurred, writing that when a calf lags behind or is in distress, its mother "encourages it to swim off, assists its flight by taking it under her fin, and seldom deserts it while life remains." The whaler-explorer adds that he once saw a whale take six harpoons before it began to move away from its dead calf.

Yankee whalers nicknamed gray whales "devilfish" largely because of their aggressive behavior in defending distressed calves. The mother gray whale will actually slap its young to discourage it from getting too close to danger—spare the rod and spoil the child! But should the reckless calf ignore the warning and end up in harm's way, the mother will rush to its rescue with both brain and brawn.

There are many accounts of how rorquals perform deeds of valor in the face of ill-intentioned forces. According to Rondelet (1568), females defend their young "by shielding them with their flippers." Here is what Lacépède (1804) had to say about the fin whale: "Compared with other species, the females seem more deeply attached to their young, more attentive, more diligent about supporting them with their fins, more concerned about protecting them from foes and rough seas, braver when it comes time to defend them." No other cetacean love, however, is as unswerving, as unstinting, one could even say as human, as that of the humpback. M. C. Caldwell and D. K. Caldwell (in K. S. Norris, 1966) started taking a count of all the times a female humpback warned a calf of danger, took her young under a flipper, shoved it away with her rostrum, placed herself between an enemy and her young, or buoyed up dead young for hours or even days on end. The accounts numbered in the dozens.

The crew of the *Calypso* had a chance to study this behavior off Bermuda, where the local humpback stock breeds in winter. To test the response of mothers to distressed young, some divers approached a calf in a motor launch and circled it very quickly for a while, as if to corral it. Philippe Cousteau tells us what happened next. "The calf inside our 'magic circle' was gripped in fear and seemed numbed by the noise of the engine. Its mother was just as terrified, but she refused to abandon it. Instead, she did everything she could to protect it, to shield it from danger. We dived, bringing to an end the brief torture to which we had subjected these gentle, peaceful whales. Underwater, we witnessed a sight of unbelievable beauty, majesty, and grace. The female had stretched out one of her huge, white, winglike flippers and tucked the calf under it. She seemed to be reassuring it and telling it that everything was going to be all right. The calf rubbed against its mother's side, and the soothing effect of contact with her big, friendly body was plain to see. The two creatures then broke into a kind of pas de deux. The female literally hoisted the calf and supported it at the surface; the more tired it seemed, the more she held him up. Then the calf positioned itself just behind her back to hitch a ride on the bow wave she created as she swam. Their movements were perfectly coordinated. It turned when she turned, dived when she dived, surfaced to spout when she did. It was an amazing display of love between mother and offspring. The sight was . . . beautiful to behold. . . ."

Female whales have what seems to be an inexhaustible store of patience when it comes to their young. Day in, day out, these long-suffering mothers resign themselves to raps on the nose, tail slapping, head butts, and countless other forms of unintentional harrassment. Calves are rambunctious; they are forever squirming

*Whalers were well aware of the mother-calf bond and took advantage of it in order to catch adult right whales (above). They would harpoon the calf first, knowing full well that the alarmed female, instead of fleeing, would try to rescue her young and sacrifice herself if need be.*

*Opposite: In this whaling scene by an unknown nineteenth-century artist, we see the technique of harpooning a calf to catch the adult. Sperm whale mothers vigorously defend their young. Moreover, when danger threatens, the dominant bull (or "schoolmaster") makes it his business to get involved. Here, a bull has taken hold of a calf in its jaws so that the whalers cannot get to it. This extreme form of succorant behavior, virtually unknown elsewhere in the animal kingdom, has been reported by whalers on several occasions. There is nothing exaggerated about this painting.*

and fidgeting. They demand a great deal of attention from their mothers, who nurture them with a constant care that few mammals—with the possible exception of monkeys and humans—are capable of giving.

And in fact, whale calves are insufferable little brats. The observations of Dr. Payne (1976) and Dr. Mandojana (1982, 1983) confirm what the crews of the *Calypso* have witnessed off Peninsula Valdés, Argentina. "The young of right whales are extremely boisterous," writes Philippe Cousteau. "A calf will constantly pester its mother for attention, even if she is resting. It darts about, wriggling up onto her back five, six, ten times in a row. It pokes its snout into her belly or jaws. It slides off her tail, much to its amusement. It covers her blowholes with its tail. It races about its mother's body like a wild puppy. Not once during these high jinks did the mother show the slightest sign of irritation. When the little brat goes too far, she simply rolls over on her back, catches the calf with one of her flippers, and holds it close to her until it calms down. We should mention that calves annoy not just their own mothers, but other adult members of the herd, which, albeit provoked, show commendable forbearance."

## *THE LIFE EXPECTANCY OF WHALES*

*Scientists use a number of techniques to estimate the age of whales. One way is to count the annual laminal accretions of an individual's earplugs. Another is to examine the annual striations of baleen plates (Ruud, 1940, 1945) or, in sperm whales, of teeth. Since the process of ovulation leaves a permanent scar, the ovaries provide useful information about the age of female specimens. Obviously, the more findings that can be correlated and compared, the more accurate the estimate.*

*Like his contemporaries, Lacépède (1804) assumed that the life span of animals was in direct proportion to their size. Right whales were believed to be up to 100 yards long, so he reasoned that they could live to be a thousand. ("Since large cetaceans conceivably have lived more than a millennium, it may be said that they are as much the sovereigns of time as of space.")*

*Clearly that is a gross overstatement. "The greatest age so far discovered by any method," notes Lyall Watson (1981), "is that of a Sperm Whale killed in the Pacific whose teeth contained seventy concentric rings." However, because the animal was killed there is no way of knowing how long it might have lived. Sperm whale teeth do not erupt until the age of ten, but the rings are deposited even prior to eruption.*

*In general, mammals reach sexual maturity when they have lived out 15 percent of their life expectancy. If that rule holds for whales—and that has yet to be confirmed—we come up with the following life-expectancy chart:*

| | |
|---|---|
| *Right whale:* | *40 years* |
| *Bowhead:* | *40 years* |
| *Pygmy right whale:* | *25 years* |
| *Gray whale:* | *50–60 years* |
| *Blue whale:* | *35–40 years (or more)* |
| *Fin whale:* | *40–45 years (or more)* |
| *Sei whale:* | *20–25 years (or much more)* |
| *Bryde's whale:* | *20–25 years (or much more)* |
| *Minke whale:* | *20 years (or much more)* |
| *Humpback:* | *45–50 years* |
| *Sperm whale:* | *70 years (or more)* |

*Calves behave like insufferable brats. They climb onto the mother's back, wake her out of a sound sleep, and constantly pester her for attention. But female whales are paragons of forbearance. Now and again a mother will chastise her calf with a smack, but only if it has acted recklessly. Above: A gray whale calf resting its head halfway across its mother's back—one of the species' favorite positions. Opposite: A humpback calf learns the fine points of diving.*

## MUTUAL AID

When an animal warns others of danger or comes to the rescue of its congeners, ethologists refer to its behavior as epimeletic, or care-giving. In the case of whales, responses such as these are apparently not limited to situations involving mothers and calves. Males and females help each other spontaneously, and members of a group take concerted action when threatened. (Bear in mind, however, the possibility that human bias colors these accounts.)

Conjectures of the bond between male and female blue whales date at least as far back as the nineteenth century. Whalers used to say that if you killed one, its mate was as good as taken. Van Beneden (1867–92) cites several instances of a male helping a mate in distress, as well as the despair they show when one of them dies. "A dead female," he notes, "was found on the coast near Plymouth in September 1881. The following 2nd of November a male was seen beaching itself at the same spot along the coast." Suicide? Epidemic? Coincidence? Or do we romanticize these things?

Here, too, the strongest bond is between humpback whales. Duhamel tells the story of "two humpbacks, probably male and female, drifting together when they were taken" in 1723. The first to be wounded "cried out in pain and made straight for the boat, and with a single slap of its tail battered [the boat] and hurled three men into the sea." The whales refused to part, and "when one of them was killed, the other stretched out over it and let out terrible, doleful moans." So impressed are we by what seems like conjugal affection in whales that it has even occasioned remarks that can only be labeled sexist. "A male will hang around his dead mate," noted Mielche in 1952, "but the fickle feminine sex is off at a sign of trouble."

According to Paul Budker (1959), "If the bull is the first to be harpooned, the cow shows both the timidity of her sex and her indifference to accidents in making off as fast as she can."

Whales often pair off, but they also cluster in small groups or form vast seasonal concentrations, spouting to their heart's content in sheltered lagoons or plankton-rich feeding grounds. At such times mutual assistance can and does occur, not just between mother and calf but also between mates or even between apparently unrelated individuals. At first, epimeletic behavior is aimed at instructing the young, then it is extended to any individual in difficulty—behavior that seems designed to help protect the species.

References to whales helping other whales in distress date back to Aristotle. Of the blue whale's behavior, Van Beneden noted, "Males and females, as well as individuals within herds, assist one another in dangerous situations. Whalers have often seen rorquals come to the rescue of stricken individuals, swimming round and round a carcass as it is being towed until the threat to their own lives becomes too great." According to accounts given by Zenkovich (1956), "Two bulls supported an injured female at the surface. Conrad Limbaugh was given a detailed report on four gray whales that he observed supporting one another at the surface" (K. S. Norris, 1966).

The crews of the *Calypso* have seen firsthand that California gray whales are capable of devising devilishly clever gambits. "As soon as they sensed they were being followed," writes Philippe Cousteau, "the gray whales all sounded at the same time. But while the group made a 90-degree turn, a lone whale surfaced in front of the boat and continued swimming for quite some distance in the original direction." The Cousteau team felt that this move suggested "an extraordinary degree of understanding among members of the group."

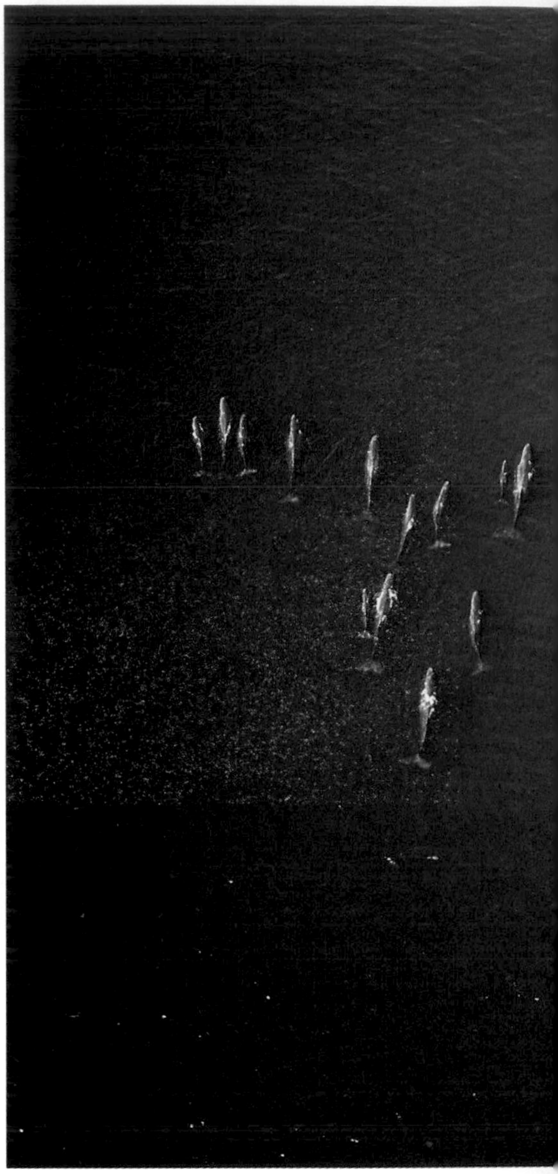

## SPERM WHALES: THE JOYS OF SOCIAL LIVING

Compared to sperm whales, baleen whales act like confirmed individualists. Mysticete clusters are haphazard, temporary, and changeable. Sperm whales, however, live in structured, close-knit communities for which mutual assistance is the rule, not the exception. Eyewitnesses have often been struck by the way an entire pod will take intelligent, concerted action when threatened.

Lacépède (1804) was one of the first to describe in any detail the tendency of sperm whales to display care-giving behavior. "The mother's love for her calf is greater [among sperm whales] than practically any other species of cetaceans. When a herd of them is under attack, whalers have far less to fear from those already taken than from their comrades that are still on the loose. Instead of diving into the sea or trying to escape, they boldly snap the lines still holding the others hostage, drive back or destroy the aggressors, and set them free."

Epimeletic behavior aimed at helping females is particularly well developed. "While giving birth," notes Lyall Watson (1981), "the mother often stands vertically in the water with her head exposed while other adult females gather round her in a supportive group. We once came across such a 'maternity ward' in the Indian Ocean and watched for two hours while the 'midwife' whales in the harem formed a tight protective ring around the central female, eventually taking turns to nudge the newborn calf to the surface to breathe.

"Such supportive behavior is common in harem herds and is something that whalers have ruthlessly exploited. Members of a herd will often gather round an injured whale, all facing inwards toward the stricken individual, tails hanging out and down; they stay as long as the central whale remains alive, while the hunters circle round and pick them off one by one."

Small wonder that Herman Melville gave an albino sperm whale the leading role in his most acclaimed book. As he saw it, consummate intelligence went hand in hand with the consummate monstrousness essential to romantic fiction. Moby-Dick's stratagems would have been less plausible had he been a right whale or a gray whale. "Nor was it his unwonted magnitude, nor his remarkable hue, nor yet his deformed lower jaw, that so much invested the whale with natural terror, as that unexampled, intelligent malignity which, according to specific accounts, he had over and over again evinced in his assaults."

"Intelligent malignity" is precisely the quality sperm whales show, according to hundreds of accounts. "Sperm whales," writes Cuvier (1836), "warn each other of the presence of an enemy six or seven miles away." When the aggressor closes in, a leader takes the initiative, noisily spouts and slaps its tail to distract them, and almost always succeeds in diverting them to where it wishes them to go. Meanwhile, the rest of the pod heads in the opposite direction, out of harm's way.

Sperm whale mothers invariably help their young to escape (Beale, 1839), and "the mother may be seen assisting it to escape by partially supporting it on one of her pectorals" (Scammon, 1874). The rest of the pod either gets directly involved to distract the whalers or stands by at close range, as if to encourage and coach those in mortal danger. Males and females alike have been known to risk their lives to rescue a distressed individual.

The commonly found "harem school" consists of ten to forty mature cows and juveniles of both sexes, joined by a commanding and aggressive bull for the breeding season. Younger adult bulls challenge his breeding prerogatives as soon as they can muster the courage to do so. As with most harem-style animal societies, the fights that determine rank or pecking order within the group are usually symbolic contests and draw little blood. Rival males intimidate one another by breaching repeatedly, smacking their tails on the surface of the water, and clattering their jaws. The pulse streams and "click trains" that they beam at each other at such times may be sonic "curses" or "war cries."

Sometimes, however, confrontation degenerates into warfare; a battle between rivals is joined and violence breaks out. It makes for a hellish, unforgettable sight. D. K. Caldwell and M. C. Caldwell (in K. S. Norris, 1966) quote W. J. Hopkins's account of one such contest. "When the approaching bull attempted to join the herd, he was attacked by one of the established bulls, which rolled over on its back and attacked with its jaw, with the jaw protruding from the surface. Large pieces of blubber and flesh were taken out. Both bulls then withdrew and again charged at full tilt. They locked jaws and wrestled, each seeming to try to break the other's jaw. Great pieces of flesh were again torn from the animals' heads. . . . The charge and withdrawal were repeated two or three times . . . and then for a few seconds the two could be seen lying head to head. The smaller bull then swam away and did not attempt to rejoin the cows. He was allowed to withdraw without further evidence of aggression by the victor."

Neither opponent died, but the winner suffered a broken jaw.

Sperm whales do not limit their social activity to harem schools; far from it.

*Like most odontocetes, sperm whales are social creatures. They live in pods of varying size that may include dozens of individuals. The composition of a pod can vary, too. Often it is a harem school of juveniles and mature females accompanied by a large dominant bull ("schoolmaster"). Bachelor schools consist solely of sexually inactive males eager to take over a harem, but not strong enough to challenge an established schoolmaster. Above: An aerial photograph of a pod of twenty-one sperm whales, including two young individuals, in Japanese waters.*

There have been occasional sightings of as many as five adult males with a large cluster of cows. Although no more than one bull is required for breeding purposes, the number of males in a pod, on average, is 1.48 (C. Lockyer, 1976). We do not know whether such aggregations relate to reproduction cycles, maturation rates, defense strategies, or another factor not yet considered.

At certain times of the year, especially when bulls have done their reproductive duty and break away to embark on their lone journeys northward, pods may consist of nothing but mature cows and juveniles of both sexes. All things considered, these "nursery schools" come closest to being the standard social unit of the species. Strictly speaking, harem schools do not take shape until the onset of the breeding season, and the dominant bull goes off on his own as soon as it is over. Probably an older cow then takes over as "leader" and may even exercise certain prerogatives if the bull returns to breed again. (This is typical of wolves and African elephants.) As the most experienced individual, she would supervise the search for food, choose migratory routes, make sure the pod sticks together, cool flaring tempers, and coordinate group action in dangerous situations. When a calf is attacked, she would rush to rescue it; that is why whalers and other observers always had so much trouble locating a baby sperm whale's real mother. If there is a harpoon to be wrenched free from a stricken individual or a ploy to be devised to discomfit the enemy, she would take the initiative.

When whalers came across a pod of cows, they always used to kill the biggest and oldest one first. This was a disastrous mistake. As soon as a leader is eliminated, the group falls apart, loses its identity as a unit, and finds itself deprived of its

*We know practically nothing about the social life of sperm whales. Eavesdropping with hydrophones, we have learned that they emit an incessant stream of echolocation clicks and other underwater sounds, not to mention actual "phrases" during what appear to be question-and-answer sessions. We have good reason to believe that they are indeed "conversing"—but what about?*

*After studying sperm whales near Sri Lanka, Dr. Hal Whitehead and his associates observed sperm whales off the Galápagos Islands in February and March 1985. They were intrigued by one group of two females or juveniles, an adult bull, and one very large bull. Sometimes they would be seen lying motionless at the surface "like twelve branchless tree trunks"; at other times they would dive in search of squid, or caress one another with their flippers, or indulge in nuzzling, "love bites," and other forms of body contact just beneath the surface.*

*Another local stock some fifty strong treated filmmaker Dieter Plage and naturalist Godfrey Merlen to an unforgettable sight. As though on cue, the whales clustered into "monstrous columns," and formed "several pyramids of gigantic bodies, all with the tips of their open jaws touching." A large bull swam round this breathtaking underwater formation, while all the whales in the pod clattered their jaws as loud as they could. Opposite: A small sperm whale "pyramid" off Sri Lanka. Below: Two adults and a calf at the surface.*

"culture"—the irreplaceable cumulative knowledge stored in the brain of the oldest member of the group. No one is there to tell the pod where and when to migrate, what decisions to make in trying situations, what the nature of the threat is, or how they should go about dealing with it. A nursery school without its matriarch is nothing more than a collection of maladjusted, diffident, unsociable survivors, constantly attacking each other without provocation, fleeing helter-skelter at the first sign of danger, unable to locate food. Some groups have been known to disband after a tragically short period of time. Herds of African elephants have been known to suffer a similar fate a few weeks after the death of the oldest and strongest female.

In addition to harem schools and nursery schools, immature whales of both sexes may form so-called juvenile schools. Sexually inactive 33- to 46-foot males banned from the harem when they reach puberty may team together in bachelor schools to increase their chances of survival in the ocean. These young bulls want to procreate, but it may be years before they are able to do so. Quite a few never will.

Now and again, mature bulls will form a pod, but only one such group has been observed (off the Faeroe Islands). As a rule, mature bulls prefer to ply the seas in solitude. Of course, their priorities shift radically as the breeding season approaches.

Before whaling took its grievous toll, it was not unusual to encounter crowds of sperm whales on the richest feeding grounds. Beale (1839) mentioned concentrations of five to six hundred, while Boyer (1946) claimed to have seen regiments of a thousand. However, these were temporary gatherings of usually discrete families or pods; once the feeding season was over, they unerringly broke up into smaller groups.

## "A DEAD WHALE OR A STOVE BOAT?"

*For centuries, whaling lore made the sperm whale out to be a fearsome killer, a ruthless monster that routinely bore down on whalers and smashed them to pieces with its head or tail.*

*Stories about the whale's combative disposition are legion. As far back as 1668, Richard Stafford wrote that the sperm whale was much to be feared, "such is his fierceness and swiftness"* (Letter from the Bermudas). *Thomas Beale kept the myth alive in* The Natural History of the Sperm Whale *(1839): "Mad with the agonies he endures from these fresh attacks, the infuriated Sperm Whale rolls over and over; he rears his enormous head, and with wide expanded jaw snaps at everything around him; he rushes at the boats with his head; they are propelled before him with vast swiftness, and sometimes utterly destroyed." This was echoed by F. D. Bennett (1840): "The Cachalot [Sperm Whale] is not only better armed than the True Whale [Greenland or Right Whale] in possessing a formidable weapon at either extremity of its body, but also more frequently displays a disposition to employ those weapons offensively, and in a manner at once so artful, bold, and mischievous, as to lead to its being regarded as the most dangerous to attack of all the known species of the whale tribe"* (Whaling Voyage Round the Globe).

*First- or secondhand accounts of such attacks abound. Now, no one disputes the fact that a sperm whale will defend itself when attacked and, if sufficiently provoked, may be capable of capsizing a whaleboat and a crew of ten with a blow of its head or tail. Who, except the hunters, would find such behavior surprising or excessive?*

*However, there is not one bona fide report of any whale charging a boat that did not mean it harm. When it comes to the human race, whales are accommodating to a fault, unfailingly peaceable and forbearing.*

*Let us turn to the question of whether or not an incensed sperm whale is indeed capable of sinking a large ship—the way Moby-Dick was supposed to have staved in Captain Ahab's* Pequod.

*Such mishaps must have occurred from time to time. Melville himself knew about the most famous incident of them all: the shipwreck of the* Essex *as told by the ship's mate, Owen Chase, and published the year after the disaster (1821).*

*On November 13, 1820, the* Essex, *a whaler out of Nantucket under the command of Captain Pollard, encountered a "school" of sperm whales in the South Pacific at 47° S latitude. The whaleboats were lowered and the chase got under way. No sooner had one of the harpoons found its mark than the strongest of the whales broke away from the pod and bore down on the ship. The first collision shattered the false keel. The crew looked on as the whale opened its maw and tried to smash pieces of the quickwork with its jaws. This tactic did not destroy the ship right away, so the big whale swam about two cables (two-tenths of a mile) away, turned around, and charged again. The impact jolted the* Essex *from stem to stern. Water rushed in through the portholes aft. The vessel listed and went under, drowning Captain Pollard and any hands unfortunate enough not to be in the whaleboats. One of the two surviving boats was found a few days later. The other had six men at the start, but only three remained at the end of its three-month odyssey at sea. The survivors had clung to life by eating their fellow crewmen.*

*That was not the only time a whale reportedly staved in a ship. In 1820, the year of the* Essex *disaster, the* Albatross *was rammed west of the Marquesas Islands by a whale that had just been harpooned. The hole the animal made in the hull was big enough to sink the vessel. In 1870 the* Sorensen *went down after a fin whale charged it in the North Atlantic. In 1894 the whaler* Garcia, *sturdy hull and all, sank after a blue whale rammed it in the Varanger Fjord, in Norway.*

*These and other accounts involved small or average-sized whalers with wooden hulls. It is obvious that a sperm whale or a rorqual is no match for an iron-hulled whaler equipped with a harpoon gun, no matter how large or angry the whale.*

*Right whales are unaggressive, even toward whalers; rorquals are nearly as unbelligerent. The California gray whale, however, is more high-strung. The Yankee whalers responsible for nicknaming the species "devilfish" used to say that it was "a cross between a snake and an alligator." But no species can match the sperm whale for willingness to defend itself and come to the rescue of its congeners. Left: Many a hapless whaler met the fate of those depicted in this nineteenth-century American painting by S. Raleigh.*

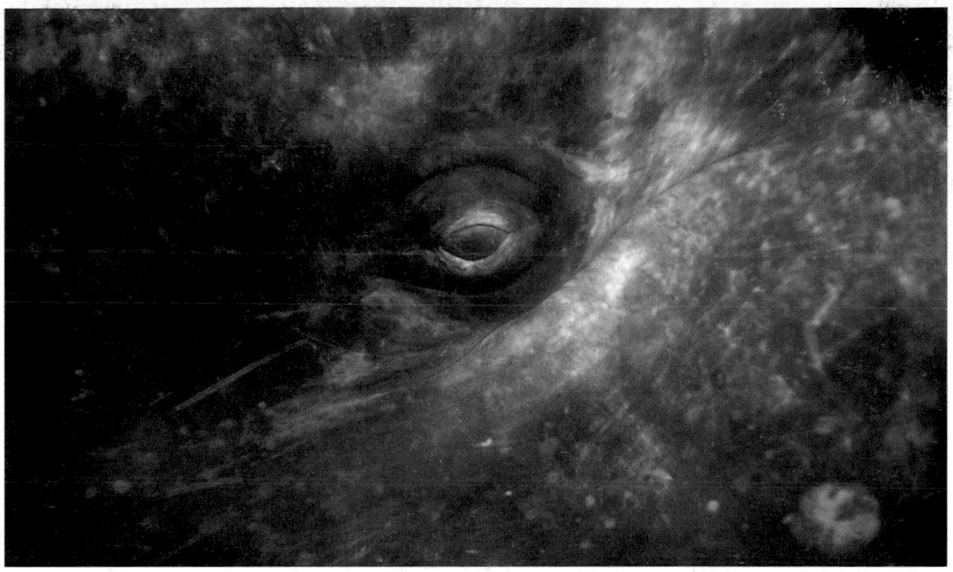

*What does the eye of a California gray whale tell us? Whales have large brains—those of odontocetes being comparatively bigger than those of mysticetes—as well as a highly developed cerebral cortex. At times they behave in ways that seem anything but instinctive, if not actually "intelligent." They communicate with one another by means of body language and, more importantly, by emitting sounds and structuring them in a way that inevitably brings the word "language" to mind. Although it seems a long way off, perhaps we will break the code one day and listen to conversations in "whale."*

*"If you wish, let's make a bet: Whales are higher and extraordinarily well-adapted forms of life, and, assuming they can be compared to us at all, live on a continent that is geographically much bigger than all the ones we live on put together. Let's lay odds, shall we, that whales represent our hope on Earth!"*
*(Hugo Verlomme, French. From the preface to* A l'écoute des baleines, *1978)*

## THE INTELLIGENCE ISSUE

Whales are sociable, affectionate, devoted, gentle, captivating, high-spirited creatures. The entire ocean is their empire—and their playground. Theirs is a "leisure society" that predates ours by some forty million years. They spend less than a tenth of their lives looking for food and feeding. The rest of the time they spend swimming, frolicking in the waves, conversing with each other, wooing the opposite sex, and rearing their young—an inoffensive agenda if ever there was one! Apart from the harpoons of man, they have little to fear on the vast, featureless sea. An upward turn of the mouth gives us the impression they are smiling with pleasure. Call us anthropomorphic if you will, but we would like to see this expression as symbolic of their blissful lifestyle.

Are whales an intelligent form of life? That is a ticklish and fascinating question. No one disputes the fact that whales have large brains (in absolute terms for the largest species, relative to body size for the smallest). Yet, there seems to be no end to the controversy surrounding their mental ability. In fact, the more questions we ask—the more we attempt to gauge their capacity to grasp and adapt their behavior to new situations—the more questions there are to answer.

Whales cavort, protect their young, execute group maneuvers to escape danger, exchange messages, and do countless other things on a daily basis that have led some to characterize them as intelligent. But are these behavior patterns more highly developed than those of elephants, bears, dogs, or monkeys—all known for their superior responses to the changing world around them?

The only cetaceans used thus far in intelligence tests (at least those worthy of the name) have been captive dolphins. The results of those experiments, albeit inconsistent, suggest that the intelligence of odontocetes lies somewhere between that of dogs and chimpanzees. A number of doubts, however, persist. Were the tests themselves intelligently designed? How can highly social creatures like dolphins be accurately tested for reasoning ability when they are in captivity?

Anatomical data are of little help. Whales have large, spherical, high, broad brains. Some areas have drifted backward considerably, probably due to progressive streamlining of the skull. Olfactory lobes are missing or atrophied. The visual lobes are of average size, but those that control hearing are highly developed. The cerebellum is quite large and probably varies in size with the motor ability of individual whales.

The sperm whale has the biggest brain in the animal kingdom; it weighs about 22 pounds. The blue whale's weighs up to about 15 pounds, the fin whale's between 11 and 13 pounds, the right whale's about 7, and the bottlenose dolphin's a little over 3 pounds. (The human brain weighs between 2.2 and 3.3 pounds, a chimpanzee's between 10 and 14 ounces.) Of course, brain size alone does not determine intelligence. Cows have bigger brains than people do, but Bossie would have a hard time proving that she can outwit her keeper.

A different, more accurate ranking emerges if we examine the raw data in a different context:

| | *Brain weight (lb)* | *Body weight (lb)* | *Brain weight as a percentage of body weight* |
|---|---|---|---|
| Man | 2.86 | 154 | 1.8 |
| Dolphin | 3.3 | 440 | 0.75 |
| Chimpanzee | 0.66 | 88 | 0.75 |
| Sperm Whale | 22.0 | 88,000 | 0.025 |
| Blue Whale | 15.4 | 220,000 | 0.007 |

The ratio of brain weight to body weight is the same for dolphins and chimpanzees, but there is a huge gap between small and large odontocetes. If we take the above table at face value, dolphins have more than a hundred times more gray matter for their size than blue whales and more than thirty times more than sperm whales. Even to say that a bottlenose dolphin is a hundred times smarter than a blue whale strains credibility—but to say that it is thirty times smarter than the talkative, resourceful, and crafty sperm whale flies in the face of facts. One hypothesis holds that the ratio of brain to body surface area gives a more valid comparison between species. The size, absolute or relative, of the brain does not tell us how it is used. Therefore, we need more conclusive evidence, such as the size of the cerebral hemispheres.

Whales in general, and toothed whales in particular, have well-developed frontal lobes, the presumed seats of consciousness and conceptual intelligence. Variations are wide, but typically, these lobes have many convolutions, an extensive, thick cortex, and a high degree of neocortical differentiation—more so than do large apes.

By and large, the evolution of cetaceans (especially odontocetes) has been characterized by an increase in the relative size of the "higher" areas of the brain. In archaeocetes, "the cerebral hemispheres were quite small, low, with few grooves or fissures, whereas the cerebellum was comparatively well developed" (P.-P. Grassé, 1955). One cannot help contemplating the possibility that nature set mammals on two different paths toward intelligence: primates on land, cetaceans in the sea.

Whatever the relative intelligence of whales and humans may be, we must not lose sight of the one crucial difference between us: they are acoustic creatures, and we are primarily visual ones. As P.-P. Grassé notes, "The large size of the cerebral hemispheres is due to projections of the auditory nerve" and "there are sizeable associative areas in the cortex around the auditory region." If cetaceans are intelligent, the mental ability differs from ours, not so much in terms of overall performance or range as in the ways they apply it.

Our reasoning abilities depend chiefly on information from our eyes, and an elaborate neural network connects them to our hands and brain. The human mind operates in terms of spatial relationships and physical manipulation of things around us. We think in an analytical, linear manner.

*"Whale in his sleep is like dead men dreaming," writes poet Susan Musgrave (Canadian, b. 1951). Opposite: This napping rorqual makes for a wonderful poem, too! As civilization enters the postindustrial era, why is a segment of humankind still bent on flouting moratoriums and slaughtering the giants of the sea? Why this heartless obstinacy? All kinds of reasons have been given, but we have a hypothesis of our own. Could it be that people, those superants that spend twelve hours a day slaving away in factories or fields and commuting to and from work, are insanely jealous of animals that spend only a small part of their lives looking for food and most of their time frolicking, making love, doting on their young, or conversing for hours on end? Remember: Few motives for crimes are as universal as jealousy!*

*Overleaf: Whales (humpbacks in particular) sometimes bring their tails down flat against the surface with a tremendous slap that sounds like a rifle shot. But what does this mean? Is it a display of anger? A way of making a point? Perhaps it is simply a way to signal a location to other whales. We still do not know for sure.*

Whales react primarily to sounds transmitted through a liquid medium that amplifies and "broadcasts" waves in all directions. There is no reason to assume that they share our turn of mind. For example, they may find it easier than we do to get a complete picture of their surroundings. If they reason, they may do it in a less linear, less analytical fashion. They are as sociable as people (if not more so); but do they exchange information as we do? The odds are that we shall never know whether or not the sperm whale, blue whale, or killer whale is aware of its own existence, or if these creatures stop and think before acting. But it is fascinating to speculate on the possibility that whales have developed an "oral culture" based entirely on sound.

*SLEEPING GIANTS*

*A day in the life of a whale: feeding, swimming, mating in summer, tending its young when the time comes, playing (a great deal), conversing with other whales, lazing at the surface—and sleeping.*

*As Aristotle noted centuries ago, "Dolphins, right whales, and all other animals with blowholes gently move their flippers to and fro while they sleep to keep their breathing orifices above the surface," adding that "there are even people who have heard a dolphin snore." A sleeping whale stretches out flush with the surface; its tail gently "treads water," allowing it to stay afloat even in rough seas. Occasionally a whale may slip just below the surface, but a reflex reaction shuts the blowhole at once. The animal spouts and takes a breath as soon as it clears the surface, unaware that anything has happened. The eyelids of captive dolphins are closed most of the time the animal is asleep, but an involuntary reaction causes them to reopen every thirty to thirty-five seconds.*

*Charles Scammon (1874) was surprised that whales slept so soundly, but noted that they do not limit their dozing to nighttime hours. The lives of most mammals are regulated by the sleeping-waking cycle of circadian rhythm. Not so with whales, or so it seems. Some pilot whales observed by A. G. Tomilin (1951) slept for two hours at a time. Captain Cousteau's crew noted that migrating gray whales take a half-hour snooze six or seven times a day. On two occasions, J. Gray (1927) crossed paths with bowheads sleeping so soundly a few meters from the pack ice that they did not even react to his approaching boat. E. J. Slijper (1962) watched a right whale sleeping somewhere in the South Atlantic, slowly and rhythmically moving its tail and flippers to keep its balance in the water.*

*Although there are reports of collisions between ships and sleeping sperm whales or rorquals, many should be taken with a grain of salt. Seasoned whalers used to say, however, that the gargantuan meals that whales consume in polar waters invariably had a soporific effect on these animals. According to some reports, gray whales have been "observed" sleeping in Arctic waters in summertime, their heads propped up on ice-floe "pillows." Such accounts are as unreliable as they are touching.*

Play—which has been defined as "behavior that appears to bring no material benefit, and is not concerned either with the capture of food or sex relations" (Matthews, 1968)—enables a child to learn through repetition. But play is also a way for adults to release pent-up aggression toward other individuals within a group or elements alien to the group. At first blush, behavior not essential to survival strikes the observer as completely gratuitous. At any rate, whales have been seen breaching (and occasionally turning near-somersaults), lobtailing, sailing, surfing, and spyhopping—at least, those are the types of cetacean play to which experts have given official recognition.

When a whale breaches, it dives for a few minutes, then hurls itself upward with all its might, breaks the surface like a rocket, soars straight up as high as it can, and lands on its side or back with a tremendous splash. Although most large whales seem to enjoy breaching, oddly enough the "clumsiest" species (right, gray, and humpback whales) are the ones most often seen doing it.

Cuvier (1836) was one of the first to describe breaching right whales. "They can be seen moving about in what appears to be a highly confused manner, lifting themselves almost clear of the water, and when they land their massive hulk sends up mighty walls of water that look like breakers crashing against an enormous reef." The southern right whales off Peninsula Valdés are enthusiastic breachers. "The dark hulk of a whale breaking the calm, slick surface and hurling itself almost completely out of the water is quite a sight to behold," Dr. Mandojana (1982) tells us. "It rolls slightly as it breaches, showering spray with its dancing flippers, then lands with a thunderous explosion." Dr. Mandojana, Dr. Payne, and the crew of the *Calypso* have all noticed that juveniles of the species breach more than adults do and are capable of consecutive leaps. In addition, rough or stormy seas seem to bring out their urge to breach, as if they delight in flouting the fury of the elements.

Descriptions of breaching gray whales date as far back as Scammon (1874), and their performances off the coast of California impressed the Cousteau team. Lyall Watson (1981) reports "38 consecutive leaps in a manic sequence by a large male."

For all their power and swiftness, the rorquals do not breach nearly as often, but when they do it makes for a majestic sight. Just picture a 150-ton blue whale rocketing through the surface and crashing down like a clap of thunder. Fin, sei, and Bryde's whales are undemonstrative, but for sheer acrobatic prowess, the humpback and the sperm whale are champs.

The frisky, high-spirited, irrepressible humpback does not limit its breaching to any one style. It bolts through the surface, pirouettes as it lifts itself out of the water, can easily vault a yard or two into the air, and lands in a flurry of spray.

The sight of a sperm whale breaching impressed Melville (1851) and even Charles Darwin, who was not one to marvel awestruck at the vagaries of nature. When the creature lands, the naturalist noted, it "reverberates like a broadside of guns" (1882). Beale (1839) claims to have seen sperm whales leaping completely clear of the water, a feat confirmed by Bennett (1842), who wrote that sperm whales "seemed to suspend several meters above the water." Another report comes from Ashley (1926), who allegedly saw "an 85-barrel sperm leap clear out of the water so that the afternoon sun was framed for an instant under its hurtling form."

Attempts to explain the phenomenon of breaching have resulted in quite a few

*"He is the most gamesome and light-hearted of all the whales, making more gay foam and white water than any other of them" (Melville). "He" is the humpback whale. No species breaches more often, or with greater enthusiasm and zest. Right: This individual looks as though it is trying to vault over a little forested island near its Alaskan feeding grounds.*

*"If rorquals are the Nureyevs of the sea," quips Dr. R. Mandojana (1982), "then right whales are the Oliver Hardys." That may be true in terms of girth and overall bearing, but right whales share with humpbacks and grays the distinction of being among the most robust and frenzied breachers of them all. Below: A right whale rockets through the surface in the Gulf of San José, off Peninsula Valdés, Argentina.*

mechanistic theories. As for the tremendous strength it requires, some have suggested that the whales brace themselves against the ocean bottom when they start their ascent. Actually, neither whales nor dolphins has any need for additional leverage; the speed they build up on their own is sufficient. But nothing has elicited as much comment as the possible motives for these acrobatics.

One school of thought holds that whales breach to loosen parasites, stubborn remoras, or trailing algae. Others think it is a way to frighten and corral krill or fish at mealtime. Quite a few cetologists are of the opinion that breaching has social significance. It may be a way for whales to signal their locations to one another, or a form of sexual display among rival males, or a type of "foreplay" before mating. There is probably some truth to all of these hypotheses, and any one of them may apply for a particular set of circumstances. But why not assume that, in some cases, whales breach out of sheer exuberance and for no other reason except that they enjoy it?

Another important form of play is lobtailing, which is even harder to explain in purely mechanistic terms than breaching. Many whales lobtail, but none more frequently than right whales, humpbacks, and sperm whales. Without warning the animal will literally pitch itself into the water, with head pointed down and flukes

*IS BREACHING A FORM OF COMMUNICATION?*

*Breaching requires a tremendous output of energy. First the animal has to swim horizontally until it reaches maximum speed. Then, as Dr. Roger Payne has noted during his research with right whales near Peninsula Valdés, it lifts its head and straightens out its tail. Horizontal propulsion is turned into upward thrust.*

*The species that breach most often are right whales, grays, humpbacks, and sperm whales. Basically, there are two "styles." One time out of five (according to Hal Whitehead, 1985), humpbacks do a "belly flop"—that is, they emerge while still in a swimming position, back up. This is not unlike "porpoising," the rapid succession of quick leaps used by dolphins, porpoises, and other small cetaceans to minimize water friction. Yet, larger cetaceans have no such need. Belly-flops are not one of their favorite maneuvers. They are usually accompanied by a violent exhalation and seem to hurt the whale.*

*"True" breaching at its most spectacular occurs when the animal lands on its back. During this stunt, the whale emerges sideways, does a half-turn while twirling its flippers, and lands on its back amid an explosion of spray. Apparently this is something whales truly relish. Eighty percent of all breaching falls into this category; while the leap is in progress, the angle between the ocean's surface and the whale's body can range anywhere between 0 and 70 degrees. During one-fourth of all breaching, Hal Whitehead observed on one excursion to the Caribbean, humpbacks lifted more than 70 percent of their bodies out of the water. Once in a while, they managed to clear the surface completely.*

*Whales also seem to enjoy leaping several times in a row. In the group Whitehead observed, each individual breached every 30 to 40 seconds. On average, humpbacks in the western Atlantic breach 9.4 times per "session." Now and again, a whale may go on a breaching "binge": The record (observed) thus far is 130 leaps in an hour and a quarter (Whitehead, 1975).*

*Every time it breaches, a whale the size of a humpback burns about 2,500 kilocalories—the daily caloric intake of an adult man (Whitehead, 1985). Since the basal metabolism of a whale is approximately 300,000 kcal./day, a single leap equals less*

*than one one-hundredth of the animal's daily caloric expenditure.*

*Turning to the question of why whales breach, Whitehead suggests that, at least among adults, it may be a form of communication. Juveniles breach more frequently than do mature individuals; undoubtedly much of this activity is play that is not related to specific situations. They vault through the surface for the fun of it (and, of course, to exercise muscles and improve neuromuscular coordination).*

*Other observations, however, suggest that in many instances adults breach in order to get a message across to other whales. To begin with, whales breach less frequently in summer, when they are busy gorging themselves in polar waters, than in winter, the season of sexual standoffs, courtship, and mating. Moreover, whales that belong to species with structured societies have a greater tendency to breach. In certain situations, breaching may simply be a way of saying to any whales in the vicinity, "Here I am! Just listen to the racket I'm making as I land!" This would be especially useful when high winds or rough seas interfere with their ability to locate one another by underwater sound emission.*

*In other cases, more complex forms of social interaction may be involved. Breaching could conceivably mean "I'm challenging you" or "I'm stronger than you." During courtship, rival males may hold "breaching matches" to decide which one will mate with a female. This hypothesis is borne out by two observations: there is a high incidence of spirited breaching during the mating season, and these sessions are punctuated by another form of strength display, tail-slapping. As often occurs in similar situations, challenge breaching contests among competing males may easily become courtship breaching on the part of the winning suitor.*

*In all likelihood, breaching has no inherent meaning outside of particular contexts. Either it is a message or a way to give a message added weight (40 or 100 tons of it, to be exact!). Whitehead (1985) believes that breaching may often be a way to emphasize other visual or auditory cues—a physical exclamation point, as it were. He says that whales may rocket through the surface the way people raise their voices, gesticulate, or move their bodies to give their remarks greater impact.*

*Gigantic, restless, expressive, graceful, awe-some—a whale's tail is as vital to play, communication, and other forms of social interaction as it is to propulsion. Poets are better at sensing this kind of thing than are scientists. "The more I consider this mighty tail," writes Melville (1851), "the more do I deplore my inability to express it. At times there are gestures in it, which, though they would well grace the hand of man, remain wholly inexplicable. In an extensive herd, so remarkable, occasionally, are these mystic gestures, that I have heard hunters who have declared them akin to Free-Mason signs and symbols; that the whale, indeed, by these methods intelligently conversed with the world."*

*Opposite, top: The tail of a bowhead whale in the Arctic Ocean; bottom: A blue whale sounding in the Sea of Cortez. Above, top: a humpback "lobtailing"; bottom: A right whale "sailing" across waters off Peninsula Valdés, Argentina.*

in the air. It swings its tail to and fro several times, then brings it down flat against the surface with a tremendous slap. The report can be heard for miles around; by all accounts it sounds like a "great gun" (Millet, 1924; Ashley, 1926). The tip of the tail can sometimes hover as much as 15 feet or more above the surface. (How does a 75-foot sperm whale manage to thrust the rear half of its body clear out of the water?) Ashley (1926) mentions the time "an entire school [of sperm whales] simultaneously engaged in lobtailing," as though on cue. Right whales and humpbacks lobtail frequently and punctuate the position with increasingly violent slaps against the surface (R. Payne, 1976; R. Mandojana, 1982, 1983). They are especially fond of lobtailing in stormy, windswept seas.

According to some experts, lobtailing may be a response to a disturbance, or a warning signal to other whales within the group. Perhaps they resort to it when wave motion interferes with effective transmission and reception of vocalizations. (That might explain breaching, too.) It could be a way for a whale to intimidate a rival (would-be suitors) or an enemy (killer whales, a school of sharks). Again, the gamut of theories is itself proof that no single explanation can account for a complex behavior pattern.

The denizens of the deep do not stop at leaping into the air or lifting their tails up among the wheeling gulls. They indulge in other types of activity that have been variously described as odd, mischievous, acrobatic, preposterous, and comical. For example, southern right whales relaxing in waters off Patagonia show their athletic bent by "sailing" (R. Mandojana, 1982). Dr. Payne and the Cousteau team have seen this unusual game firsthand. "The whales unfurl their tail flukes high above the surface to catch the seabreeze or the winds that come howling off the coast of Patagonia and which drive them to the other side of the bay. When they have nearly beached themselves on shore, they turn around, swim upwind to their starting point, and sail back again" (R. Mandojana, 1982). Dr. Payne (1976) noted that "when it comes to this sport, young whales frequently have a lot of trouble attaining the proper set of their tails. What starts as an apparent effort to sail can end in . . . the calf throwing its tail into the air and bringing it down with a thunderous slap."

Another favorite sport of southern right whales is riding currents. At Peninsula Valdés, R. Mandojana (1982) watched a group of them maneuver into the Caleta Valdés, a narrow channel where the tidal flow is especially strong. The whales struggled upstream with all their might until they reached the spot where the current was swiftest. Suddenly they would stop swimming and let the rushing water carry them along for several hundred yards. Then they headed back upstream for another ride on their "water-toboggan." What could possibly be the reason for these antics, if not sheer pleasure?

Still another recurrent activity among whales (especially gray whales, humpbacks, and right whales) is spyhopping. Now and again, a whale will poke its head out of the water in a vertical position and remain there, motionless, for thirty seconds or more. Then it may dunk itself and repeat the process. To keep itself upright, a spyhopping whale is, of course, forced to scull vigorously with its tail. It may even "turn deliberately through a full circle" (L. Watson, 1981), as though to greet the four points of the compass.

It has been suggested that whales spyhop in order to get a better look at their surroundings or to keep an eye out for other members of a group until they feel it is safe to press on alone.

Yet whales have often been seen spyhopping as they migrate near shore, possibly to get their bearings by sighting out of the water. Perhaps they carry with them a kind of internal map, a kind of geographic "culture" that is passed on from generation to generation. In other words, they may know the way. By mimicking adults, juveniles familiarize themselves with migration routes the species has been following since time immemorial.

Humpbacks and rorquals also enjoy swaying the dorsal fin from side to side and then slapping it against the surface with a sudden twist of the body. Could "finning" or "fin-flapping" be an outward manifestation of pleasure? Anger? Intimidation? Its possible social meaning has yet to be discovered.

Right whales, humpbacks, and rorquals are also known to roll onto the side and hoist one of their flippers into the air, then wave it majestically as if to greet the onlooker. A humpback swinging its enormous white or mottled forelimb above the surface ranks among the most sublime sights nature has to offer.

Whales love to play. Sometimes they roll over at the surface like huge torpedos; they seem to revel in intense sensations and appear to go out of their way to find them. On one occasion in the Bahamas, the helicopter from the *Calypso* was hovering at low altitude over a humpback. Not only did the whale not sound to escape the noisy contraption overhead, but it rolled over on its back and exposed its belly to the cool breeze created by the spinning rotor blades. It swam about unconcernedly beneath the aircraft for quite some time, slapping one flipper and then the other on the ocean surface.

One difference between the games people and whales play is that whales generally dispense with the paraphernalia we refer to as toys. Cetaceans play with nothing but their own bodies: skin, senses, muscles.

We know of one instance when a sperm whale played with a floating plank. The animal was diving back and forth under the plank, and not relinquishing it even though a ship was approaching (E. J. Slijper, 1962). Nishiwaki (1962) presents another illustration of a sperm whale playing with a piece of timber while five others, in a kind of game, gave chase.

*For juveniles, play provides exercise and a way to learn through repetition; for adults, it is a way to show pleasure or symbolically release pent-up aggression. To the casual observer, this behavior seems utterly gratuitous—which is not to say, however, that play serves no useful purpose. Is breaching a form of play? Yes, at least some of the time. The same can be said for lobtailing, riding waves ("surfing"), and tail-smacking. Spyhopping may be nothing more than a way for a whale to find its way or scout its surroundings. On this page are photographs of three commonly observed types of behavior; it is not yet known whether they are messages, forms of play, or instances of purely "utilitarian" conduct. Left: A humpback hoists a flipper above the surface. Above: A gray whale mother and calf spyhopping. Opposite: A humpback whale lobtailing.*

Our discussion of cetacean play would not be complete if we failed to mention the joys of surfing. Dolphins can keep it up for hours at a time, either among waves along the coast or in the bow wave of big ships. Although sperm whales and swift rorquals rarely venture near shore, there is good reason to believe that they also indulge in much the same kind of exhilarating fun. Gray whales have been seen "surfing" (D. K. Caldwell and M. C. Caldwell, 1963); and so have right whales, according to Haley's account (quoted in K. S. Norris, 1966). Near Three Kings Islands, New Zealand, he reported "we could see twenty or thirty good-sized whales tumbling about when the big seas would catch them and almost turn them over. Sometimes one could be seen on the crest of a wave. As it broke he would shoot down its side with such speed a streak of white could be seen in the wake he made through the water."

Future research will shed more light on the possible meaning of the now gratuitous, now purposeful behavior patterns of cetaceans. But one thing is certain—the body language of whales is both subtle and complex. Every position, every gesture has a particular meaning that we do not even suspect most of the time. For example, what are we to make of two rorquals swimming side by side for quite some time, tail-flapping and spouting in unison but touching flippers only once in a while and for just a moment? This could be a game, a sexual display, a way of getting acquainted, a token of affection, a conversation, or an act of "pleasuring." How about when two adults (or an adult and a juvenile), side to side and flipper to flipper, engage in prolonged, nonsexual rubbing sessions, or simply pat each other with their flippers?

All animal species have some form of body language. The more highly developed the species, the more complex the language. Animal behaviorists are just now starting to translate into specific words some of the characteristic gestures—of submission, aggression, anger, pleasure, and the like—used by dogs, cats, birds, and chimpanzees. The radically different conditions of an aquatic habitat, however, make the behavior of the sperm whale and the humpback immeasurably more alien and difficult to decipher.

We know that cetaceans of every size and shape use their bodies to convey messages. But what about "real" language, the kind that involves the ears, not the eyes?

Borne on pressure waves, sequences of sounds (phonemes) form words that are grouped into sentences. We link sentences together to describe, reason, argue, and make deductions; in short, we use them to convey information. People are under the impression that language is a uniquely human characteristic. We consider it one of our essential prerogatives. Yet there is no reason why we should rule out the possibility that whales have a form of speech, however rudimentary, that they use language on a daily basis, and that some of them make enough noise to be labeled "chatterboxes."

Everyone has long acknowledged that whales make sounds, and speech of one sort or another has been attributed to them as far back as Aristotle. "Dolphins have a voice, for they have lungs and a trachea; only, since their tongue is not supple and they have no lips, they cannot utter articulate sounds." Rondelet (1568) claims to have heard "rorqual calls" with his own ears. "When they are quite excited these creatures cry out so loud and with such strength they can be heard a mile away."

Right whales, Lacépède (1804) points out, make "a muffled bellowing that expresses both suffering and anger," and adds that "a sperm whale once let out a terrible cry that reverberated in the distance like a mighty tremor."

The bellowing of right whales described by Scoresby (1823) was confirmed by Cuvier (1836), Gray (1846), van Beneden (1867–92), and many others. Toussenel (1862) made the amusing if not altogether accurate observation that "according to Pacific whalers the whistling of the sperm whale sounds for all the world like that of a locomotive."

Maritime literature is replete with stories of inexplicable noises and eerie underwater sounds. For lack of a better explanation, seafarers used to attribute them to sirens and all sorts of fanciful creatures. Back in the days of sailing ships, on a calm night crewmen could hear powerful calls through the hulls of their vessels. Some whalers, according to H. L. Aldrich (1889), were able to tell the voice of a right whale from that of a bowhead, a humpback from a gray whale, a beluga from a pilot whale.

Motor-propelled vessels create noise that makes it difficult to hear whales with the "naked ear." Today we have hydrophones and recording devices that are far more accurate, reliable, and discriminating than our paltry ears. We have been eavesdropping on free-swimming and captive dolphins since the end of World War II. In 1957, Schevill and Worthington were the first to record prolonged sequences of sounds emitted by sperm whales. Schevill's pioneering research paved the way for R.-G. Busnel, R. H. Backus, J. J. Dreher, J. C. Lilly, K. S. Norris, R. Payne, S. Earle, and many others.

Schevill and Worthington (1957) described the three principal types of underwater sounds produced by the sperm whale as a "muffled smashing noise," a "low-pitched groan or rusty-hinge creaking," and more frequent series of "sharp clicks." Schevill and Watkins (1962) later refined these observations, noting that the groaning and creaking sounds were apparently nothing more than distortions of clicks.

We know that sperm whales emit bursts of rapid-fire clicks, but how are these so-called click trains actually produced? As we have seen, whales have a function-

The sperm whale's long, narrow jaw appears to play only a secondary role in catching prey. The teeth do not erupt until about the age of ten, and individuals that have lost their lower jaw accidentally or in battle have been found in perfect health, stomachs full of squid. According to Hal Whitehead (1984), "the lower jaw of the sperm whale is primarily used for social purposes"; most cetologists agree. Sometimes they use the jaw to gently grasp their young, or nibble at each other's mouth, or "kiss" by touching snouts. At other times they clatter them above or below the surface to intimidate rivals, a display that occasionally erupts into battle.

*Above: A sperm whale breathing its last. What kind of cry does a dying giant utter?*

ing larynx, but no vocal chords. In addition, H. Haas (1959) noted that these mammals can speak equally well with the mouth open or closed. It seems highly unlikely that the clicks originate in the lungs themselves, as some experts have suggested. We have since learned that sound waves are created by the vibrations of structures associated with the air sacs and diverticula of the nasal passages, "filtered" through the ultrafine oil in the spermaceti organ, reamplified through the bones of the upper jaw, focused into "beams" as diffuse or as concentrated as the situation warrants, and projected through the tip of the snout. Although many aspects of the process remain unclear, certainly head shape is involved in projecting echolocatory sounds.

Click frequency is known to range from 200 to 30,000 hertz (R. H. Backus and W. E. Schevill, in K. S. Norris, 1966), but higher frequencies are not uncommon. By way of comparison, bear in mind that the thresholds of human hearing are 30 and 16,000 hertz and that a dolphin can "broadcast" on frequencies from 100 to 150,000 hertz.

The repetition rate, or pulse pattern, of clicks also varies among all odontocetes. The interval between clicks ranges from 0.0025 to 1.25 seconds (that is, 1 to 40 clicks per second), but the average is 15 and upper limit is about 50. The average speed of a sperm whale's click trains is equivalent to the speed of the slowest click trains emitted by the bottlenose dolphin (*Tursiops truncatus*).

The duration of a single click can vary, too. In emergency situations, clicks can become extremely brief—no more than 2 milliseconds. Under normal conditions, however, each lasts about 24 milliseconds. Spectrographic analysis reveals that a 24-millisecond click actually consists of six pulses of 2 milliseconds each, separated by five intervals of 2 to 4 milliseconds each (R. H. Backus and W. E. Schevill, in K. S. Norris, 1966).

Naturally, the purpose of these vocalizations has generated intense interest and fueled speculation. Certainly they are used for echolocation. The wave trains a sperm whale "beams" through its head bounce off objects in its path and back to the whale, an "acoustical creature" that listens not just with its tiny auditory canal, but with its entire head. The bones in its skull and the oil in its spermaceti organ may play a part in both transmitting and receiving waves. The highly developed hearing center in its brain instantaneously analyzes the time between transmission and reception, deduces the distance of targets, and pieces together a "sonic landscape" of its surroundings. Research with dolphins has shown that cetaceans have phenomenally acute hearing. A blindfolded dolphin had no trouble detecting and dodging a copper wire 0.2 millimeters thick and could tell from several yards' distance the difference between a real (dead) fish and a plastic lure of the same size and shape (R.-G. Busnel). Of course, sperm whales do not lend themselves to experiments of this kind. But how else could they hunt for prey at depths of up to a mile, in total darkness, unless they make use of sophisticated biosonar? As Lyall Watson (1981) points out, "There is at least one report of a completely blind adult in good condition captured alive with a well-filled stomach."

Let us proceed from discussing the use of clicks for echolocation to the far more controversial issue of whale vocalizations as possible units of language. Lacépède's thoughts on the subject show astonishing foresight: "Strictly speaking, we cannot rule out the possibility that the time whales spend in each other's company, combined with the irresistible effect of powerful sensations, recurrent impressions, and enduring feelings, may provide them with the rudiments of an imperfect, yet discernible language." Does Lacépède's intuition have any basis in fact?

The same echolocatory apparatus that sperm whales use to detect prey or possible enemies may be involved in social interaction. By literally bombarding an approaching individual with beams of clicks, a sperm whale can "see" it coming long before it comes into view. It is reasonably safe to assume that members of a pod quickly learn to identify others by recognizing acoustic "silhouettes." Sperm whales also emit individual patterns of clicks—"codas"—that are identifying, signature signals.

It has been known for some time that sperm whales miles apart exchange information—at least warnings and danger signals—by transmitting and receiving underwater sounds. "Sperm whales become apprised of the near approach of danger," wrote Beale in 1823, "although the distance may be very considerable between them, sometimes amounting to four, five, or even seven miles."

The Cousteau team had occasion to study this aspect of sperm whale behavior in the Indian Ocean. Using hydrophones, the crew was able to correlate wave trains with certain types of group activity. "As we closed in on a harem school," notes Albert Falco, "we first heard all kinds of clicks from various individuals, followed by a few very strong wave trains from the 'schoolmaster.' The cows and juveniles fell silent. The dominant bull swam fairly close to us and started spouting for all to see. As he conspicuously spouted at the surface, he led us in the direction he had decided upon. Meanwhile, the rest of the school stole away underwater without saying a word. . . . The sperm whales had taken concerted action on a cue from the bull. They had followed instructions, that is, they had grasped the meaning of a message and reacted accordingly." It would be hard not to concede the possibility that this was an instance of collective strategy involving language. Now, some birds know how to distract a predator threatening the nest by making obvious visual or sound displays or by pretending to be wounded. But the instinctive behavior of the parent does not involve any complex communication with the young, which do not budge from the nest, are oblivious to the danger they are in, and must rely solely on camouflage for protection. In the world of sperm whales, however, it is all for one and one for all, and every individual seems to know what it is doing.

Some naturalists dismiss the notion of cetacean language as anthropomorphic hogwash, and their views should be given due consideration. But some unsettling observations remain unaccounted for:

1. It is easy to recognize an individual by its clicks, and they comprise a kind of acoustic signature. Every whale's vocalizations have a distinctive timbre and pitch, delivery, perhaps even pronunciation (although that has not been confirmed). "Accents" may vary from one ocean to another. The "ID card" of individual whales, vocal signatures would be instrumental in recognizing the leader (be it dominant bull or cow), following its orders, maintaining group discipline, coordinating group response in dangerous situations, and helping juveniles gradually absorb the group's knowledge or culture. Skeptics point out that alleged differences in tonality, accent, and timbre picked up by hydrophones are due to extraneous factors, the conditions of the experiment itself—particularly since the speed of sound varies through water layers of different salinity, temperature, and density. Their claims may not be totally unfounded.

2. Sperm whales click a great deal when they are traveling and looking for food; at such times they are probably using sound to echolocate. However, they get even

*Whales rarely release air when emitting underwater sounds, although the sperm whale has been known to do so. Most of the time, however, the process of sending out calls or rapid-fire clicks does not require air bubbles.*

*As things now stand, cetologists are not in a position to state positively that whales actually talk to one another, that they use "words" and "phrases" to express feelings or convey information. However, all research carried out to date strongly suggests that they are capable of transmitting certain kinds of messages at a distance. We need a reference system that would serve as a basis for translation. Until we find this Rosetta Stone, deciphering "whale talk" will remain a distant dream.*

*"The whales surfaced close by.*
*Their foreheads were huge,*
*and the doors of their faces were closed"*
*(Mark Strand, American, b. 1934)*

more "talkative" when, relieved of the necessity to find their way or detect prey, they gather simply to relax. An individual may "take the floor," after which there will be a "question-and-answer session" followed by stormy or relaxed discussion. The word "conversation" inevitably comes to mind. Then again, disbelievers retort, lots of social animals make noise, and their racket could also be interpreted as exchanges of information.

3. The pattern of sperm whale "chatter" does not appear to be either an electronic artifact or the result of an erroneous or anthropomorphic reading of the data. Every recording made thus far reveals well-defined themes at regular intervals, recurrent rhythms, periodic reprises of sequences, and signals of the types that experts refer to as U, V, and W (for the way they show up on echograms). Could these repeated signals be the equivalent of words and sentences?

At this point, skeptics counter that the only way to make a convincing case for cetacean language would be to break the code and get at the things behind the words, the ideas behind the symbols. But most people will agree that actual translation of even the most rudimentary and nonabstract language is a long way off. Our only hope is to increase our contact with whales until the accumulated data involving sounds and simultaneous behavior yield demonstrable links between utterances and deeds, between words and things. It is a tall order, to say the least.

This exciting field of inquiry is not unlike the research that has already been done with human whistled language. This phenomenon is known to exist in at least three places: Mazateco, Mexico (G. M. Cowen, 1948); Silbo Gomero in the Canary Islands (A. Class, 1957); and Aas, a small village in the French Pyrenees (R.-G. Busnel, in K. S. Norris, 1966). Sonographic analysis of this unusual form of communication indicates that mountain shepherds are capable of "conversing"—giving descriptions, exchanging information, issuing instructions—at great distances. Each whistle is very loud (108–110 decibels about 1 yard from the source) and carries more than a mile. The whistlers use not only frequency and amplitude modulation, but also special inflections and stresses that encode the information content in the way that consonants do in normal speech. Furthermore, varying harmonics give each voice a distinctive (hence, readily identifiable) quality of tone or timbre.

The vocalizations of the sperm whale are analogous to human whistled language, but in all conscience that is all we can say about it for now. After all, the "sentences" sperm whales utter may not be much more abstract than those of a dog or cat. Just the same, it would not surprise us if, as some cetologists maintain, the crafty sperm whale—that sovereign of the seas with the gleaming, "malevolent" eyes—turned out to have more common sense in his enormous head than an alley cat or suburban lapdog.

## THE SINGING WHALE

Sperm whales and other odontocetes avail themselves of what may be called, with all due caution, a language. Ancient authors aside, however, few cetologists have ventured to make the same claim for mysticetes. Years after dolphins were found to use sonar, some experts insist that baleen whales have nothing comparable, either to echolocate or communicate.

Right whales are quite talkative, however, and the Cousteau team recorded some of their sounds off Peninsula Valdés, Argentina. "The whales make all sorts of cracking and crashing sounds, belchlike utterances, and variations on a single tone," writes sound engineer Guy Jouas. "Although the overall pattern is much less elaborate than that of humpback whales—which are the sirens of the sea—the fact that there is phrasing, rhythm, and melodic line suggests that these sounds are not produced randomly." According to R. Payne (1976) and L. Watson (1981), "the most common sound is a belch which lasts about a second at a frequency of 500 Hz. Moans have also been recorded between 160 and 235 Hz. Occasionally there are pulsed sounds with a duration of 0.6 second at 2,100 Hz." Northern right whales in the Bay of Fundy have been heard "broadcasting" at low frequencies when members of the herd are scattered, and at higher frequencies as they close ranks. We cannot rule out the possibility that some of this chatter may, as Lyall Watson (1981) once reported, turn out to be "nothing more than the noise of the flexible plates of baleen bumping into each other as a stream of water passed between them."

Sad to say, bowhead whales have become rare, and recording them is difficult at best. Like right whales, they produce bellows, strange cries, and powerful "belches," some of which probably involve some form of social interaction.

Nothing whatever is known about the vocalizations of the pygmy right whale, but research with gray whales has yielded a considerable amount of data. Gray whales utter series of repeated grunts and grumbles (Eberhardt and Evans, 1962); each grunt consists of four to nine pulses of about 11 milliseconds each (Painter, 1963). They also emit assorted whistling sounds ranging from 700 to 2,200 hertz, and perhaps click trains (Asa-Dorian and Perkins, 1967). In 1966 and 1967, William C. Cummings, Paul O. Thompson, and Richard Cook lowered hydrophones near Point Loma and Point La Jolla during the annual migration of gray whales along the coast of California. In the course of the thirteen days and nights that the experiment was in progress, they recorded 231 vocalizations (108 of which were pinpointed to individuals), for the most part consisting of moans (1.5 seconds each at 20–200 hertz), blow sounds, and occasional bubble sounds accompanied by sharper "knocking." The scientists noted that the whales vocalized both night and day, but could not explain why they did not pick up any of the high-frequency "beams" at 2,000 hertz (up to 32,000 hertz, by some accounts) that researchers before them had detected.

The blue and fin whales "take the floor" with ultra-low-frequency sounds that travel great distances. Several reliable recordings have been made of blue whale vocalizations, and the ones W. C. Cummings and P. O. Thompson recorded in May 1970 off the coast of Chile make for the most fascinating listening. Blue whales, they discovered, utter low-frequency moans that are phenomenally loud—in fact, "the most powerful sustained utterances from whales or any other living source." One such sound was measured at 188 decibels; remember that the noise of a jet plane taking off measures between 150 and 170 decibels. According to Cummings's and Thompson's report (1971), each "call" lasts, on average, 36.5 seconds, is broken into three distinct segments, ranges from 12.5 to 200 hertz, and reveals use of amplitude modulation (possibly "deliberate" inflections and changes in pitch). Their utterances follow a repetitive, structured pattern interrupted only when the whales surface to breathe.

What might be the purpose of transmitting such powerful signals at such low frequencies? If they were used for echolocation, their extremely low resolving power would not enable the whales to detect anything smaller than, say, a shoal of

*The humpback whale—the singing whale. Right: This one is spyhopping, that is, poking its head above the surface to have a look around. When singing their eerie, captivating melodies, humpbacks place their heads down in the water and tilt their bodies at a 45-degree angle. What does this music of the deep mean? Do whales sing for the pleasure of it? To keep a rival at bay? To woo the opposite sex? No one can say.*

*"Deep in the maternal womb*
*The humpback whale begins to sing*
*A song without mankind"*
*(Vagn Lundbye, Danish, b. 1939)*

*"Only the sea can answer their voices, only*
*The song of the sea can return their chant"*
*(Ron Riddell, New Zealander, b. 1952)*

*"... Oh*
*Wailing whale ululating underocean's sonic roar of Despair!"*
*(Allen Ginsberg, American, b. 1926)*

*Humpback whale, humpback whale! What are you singing about us?*

plankton blanketing a few square miles. It seems logical to assume that blue whales do indeed avail themselves of biosonar to home in on concentrations of krill from a distance. But if that were the case, why do they need to repeat them so often? And why use them in winter, in regions blue whales hardly ever feed in? Once again, the great temptation is to conclude that language is somehow involved. If blue whales do not use their tremendously powerful vocalizations to "converse," at least these noises may act as a social bond that enables members of a far-flung herd to monitor each others' locations.

The fin whale has been identified as the source of a mysterious recurrent bellow that hydrophones have picked up in temperate waters virtually worldwide (W. E. Schevill, 1964). "During the 1960s a network of underwater listening posts was set up around the world, . . . and there was concern about a pattern of intense, high-level, low-frequency sounds. These were repetitive bursts of pulsed sound . . . and the military believed they were threatening. They were the normal vocalizations of fin whales" (L. Watson, 1981). Aside from these "broadcasts" (possibly augmented by blue whale sounds), fin whales produce a variety of muffled noises, short bangs, grunts (less than 200 hertz), chirps, whistles (1,000–5,000 hertz), and click trains at frequencies as high as 32,000 hertz.

Nor do the other rorquals move about in silence, either. "The only confirmed recording of sei whale voices features a train of metallic pulsed sounds at a frequency of 3,000 hertz" (L. Watson, 1981). As for the Bryde's whale, "the only known recording of the voice of this whale is of a pop lasting 0.4 second at a frequency of 124 hertz" (L. Watson, 1981). The minke whale, however, is a veritable treasure trove of sonic material. The species may be diminutive, but that does not prevent it from letting out unbelievably loud, powerful utterances up to 152 decibels, or as loud as a jet fighter taking off! (P. Beamish and E. Mitchell, 1973.) "The voice of the Piked (minke) whale," notes Lyall Watson (1981), "has been described as a series of low-frequency grunts, thumps, and ratchets. Most are trains of sound at 100–200 Hz which seem to make the call of each individual unique. They also produce pure-frequency pulsed sounds at 48 kilohertz involving series of clicks for 6–8 seconds at a time, possibly used for echolocation." The elaborate speech patterns of the minke whale suggest that it conveys messages, information, instructions to its young, warning signals for the herd, and—why not?—protestations of love between mates or mother and calf.

Of all whale species, by far the noisiest, chattiest, most exuberant, and most imaginative is the humpback. It is the noisemaker and the Caruso of the deep, now grating like an old hinge, now as melodious as an operatic tenor. The cetacean with the long, white flippers boasts a complex, extensive, changing repertory that is replete with unearthly tones and compositions of baffling virtuosity. Humpbacks sing prolonged, slow-paced recitatives interspersed with identifiable "tunes" or themes. Voice interaction takes place as members of a group close ranks. Each whale has its own timbre and register. They have been known to break into wonderful nighttime choruses. "On certain nights in Bermuda, when it was unusually calm, the songs of the humpback whales sounded to us like choruses from another world" (Philippe Cousteau).

Humpback whales have performed for many an audience, and the three most listened-to stocks have been the Bermuda group that heads northward in the spring to Newfoundland and the Arctic by way of Nantucket and Cape Cod; the Hawaiian group (especially near Lahaina Roadstead) that migrates to summer

*It is generally acknowledged that whales (like this fin whale, below) are capable of remembering, learning, speaking, and reasoning. To a certain extent, it's a question of semantics. But even if there is disagreement about degree of sophistication, there is not a single cetologist unwilling to credit them with at least rudimentary skills of communication and comprehension. Hundreds of millions of years ago, evolution set in motion a first "ascent toward intelligence" by providing cephalopods like the octopus and squid with large brains. It started over with mammals: primates on land, cetaceans in the sea. Did it endow whales with intelligence? Probably. Did it do the same for man? Debatable. As Loren Eiseley pointed out, we may have "something to learn from creatures that do not know how to fling harpoons into living flesh."*

feeding grounds near Alaska, particularly Glacier Bay; and the Tonga Island population that summers in Antarctica.

"When one dives near a group of singing humpbacks," writes Philippe Cousteau, "there is a rather unpleasant feeling of compression. It is as if one were right next to a set of huge organ pipes. The powerful sounds they make can travel across hundreds or even thousands of kilometers. For the human ear underwater, it makes for rather painful listening. . . ." Lyall Watson agrees. "On one occasion near Tonga we found ourselves surrounded by underwater Leviathans that made the blue breeding lagoon thrum almost painfully despite the fact that there was not a whale in sight."

All singing humpbacks observed thus far have been males, and they seem to position themselves a special way to sing: body tilted head down at a 45-degree angle a few meters below the surface, with the snow-white flippers extended and occasionally raised and lowered in time with the "music" (S. A. Earle, 1979). No matter how long the song lasts—and it can go on for half an hour or more—the whale will take only one breath from beginning to end, gently tilting its body upward to spout without ever interrupting the performance.

As Sylvia Earle points out, "The expulsion of air is not necessarily a part of sound production," and the fact that a whale does not have to blow bubbles to sing has been confirmed by divers from the *Calypso* and R. and K. Payne (1981). The tones are produced, not with vocal chords, but by bursts of air from the lungs, trachea, and pharynx.

Anyone listening to the songs of humpback whales for the first time is immediately struck by the incredible variety of sounds. For one thing, humpbacks have a wider frequency range than other baleen whales: between 20 and 9,000 hertz, sometimes higher. Spectrographic analysis of these modulated, plaintive calls reveals series of notes combined into recognizable sequences. Each note, itself made up of several very rapid pulses, is one of the sound units that the whale arranges into a phrase, and phrases form the patterns or themes that make up a song. Several whales may take part in a "session." In general, the song of an individual can last from seven to thirty minutes. Each sequence combines three different sound patterns: repeated high-speed pulse trains alternating with pure-frequency tones held for long periods of time; a series of high-frequency sound units, each with a rising modulation at the end; and long, deep, monotonous tones, repeated over and over, with a falling modulation at the end.

Further research with humpbacks (R. and K. Payne, 1981) revealed that they sing their themes in a set order (a, b, c, d, e, f) and that there are usually six themes per song. If one of the themes is dropped—say, "c"—the rest of the song will be sung a, b, d, e, f. Apparently humpbacks sometimes abridge a theme, as if they were "swallowing" part of their musical phrases. At other times, they seem to tire of certain themes and stop singing them. But they are not forgotten and reappear the following season. Conversely, some themes are "smash hits" that humpbacks sing year after year, adding new phrases as they go along.

Detailed analysis of the humpback's repertoire shows that the rules of composition are the same everywhere, but that every stock works out particular variations. Experts can tell where a humpback song was recorded just by listening to it.

Humpbacks do not sing when they migrate or once they have reached cold-water feeding grounds. They may groan or make scraping sounds, but their wonderful choruses are reserved for the warmer waters of the winter breeding season.

Since singing seems to be a male prerogative, it was naturally (and logically) assumed that they broke into these serenades to woo their lady loves, or to challenge rival males. Humpbacks are widely considered the troubadours of the seas, singing plaintively of their jealous longing.

Yet, it is difficult for us to believe that humpback whales sing for no other reason except to keep rival males at bay or to break down a female's resistance, as robins or nightingales do. The way they join in choruses, interlace arias and recitatives, revive old leitmotifs, improve and refine established melodies—in short, their originality—suggests a degree of artistic sensitivity. The songs birds sing are innate, uniform, unchanging; an individual that ad-libs is doomed to exclusion from the group because no other individual will understand it. But the vocalizations of the humpback whale are clearly learned, changeable, creative. The messages their musical phrases convey can mean different things precisely because they change. And what shall we call this elaborate process of conveying information, if not language?

## ACCIDENT OR SUICIDE?

It is one thing for an animal to store information in order to adapt its behavior to the changing world around it. Self-awareness is quite another matter. Those who maintain that whales are conscious of their own existence note that on occasion they "decide" to perish and therefore "know" that they are mortal. A great deal has been written and said about alleged suicide in whales. Every time a whale or dolphin beaches itself, sensation-seekers describe the event as a suicide. Their assertions, made in the absence of scientific proof, do nonetheless call attention to a provocative issue that deserves closer examination.

All kinds of animals have been known to "die of a broken heart" after losing a companion or mate to which they have become deeply attached. This is particularly true of dogs, cats, and other household pets. Such a death is not suicide, but the result of devastating stress that, according to some neurologists, may be related to destabilization of the central nervous system. If an animal is suddenly deprived of an essential compensating factor, stress builds up unrelieved until its cumulative effect becomes irreversible.

On the surface, at least, cetaceans seem to fall into a different category. Captive dolphins cannot bear to be left alone and seem to pine away when cut off from other dolphins. Whalers report many instances of deliberate self-sacrifice; whaling literature abounds with stories of how mothers sacrifice themselves to harpooners to protect their young, or when their calves have been captured. It must be noted, however, that people who relate these tales may not have distinguished suicide from panic, defense tactics gone sour, or pure coincidence.

Until the nineteenth century, there were also reports of whale graveyards. One was known to exist just off the coast of Brazil, another off South Africa, another off the coast of southern Australia, another in the vicinity of the Galápagos. "The bay of Howard Town, Tasmania, is nothing less than a graveyard for whales," notes Van Beneden (1867–92). Nowadays, whales have become too scarce for even groups of carcasses to look anything like a mass grave. The "graveyards" may well have simply been beaches to which cetacean carcasses were brought by the actions of currents. However, if there is any truth to the stories about these now-legendary

*Whale strandings are awesome, baffling events. Why do these sea mammals risk death by swimming toward shore? Some are already dead and have simply been washed ashore by ocean currents. Others perish on the beach after falling prey to disease, parasitic infection, or pollution.*

*In many cases, however, there is no logical explanation—hence the tendency to refer to this behavior as "suicidal," an ambiguous word if ever there was one. Above: When these sperm whales swam en masse toward a beach near Florence, Oregon, in June 1979, were they deliberately trying to do away with themselves?*

sites, which are not unlike the storied elephant graveyards, then it is just possible that these marine giants, sensing that death was near, summoned their last ounce of strength to cross thousands of miles and breathe their last on ancestral burial grounds.

The perplexing thing about the stranding question is that these events probably cannot be attributed to any one factor. Strandings have been reported since ancient times, and beached dolphins provided Aristotle with a ready supply of specimens for his work on cetacean anatomy. "It is not known why they sometimes rush headlong toward the coast," the philosopher writes, "but the fact remains that they do so spontaneously and for no apparent reason." In his *Natural History*, Pliny the Elder tells of the orca (possibly a killer whale, possibly a sperm whale) that burst into the port of Ostia in the first century A.D.

One of the most famous mass strandings reported by naturalists in recent times occurred in 1783, when eighteen sperm whales beached themselves at the mouth of the Elbe, in the North Sea. According to eyewitnesses, the whales thrashed about and "let out frightful roars and bellows." The locals chopped to pieces two individuals that had the misfortune not to be swept out to sea with the rising tide.

Since then, the beaching phenomenon has fueled considerable debate. There is as much speculation about whale strandings as there is about the sudden disappearance of the dinosaurs during the Late Cretaceous. (For the record, let us state that a few imaginative souls claim that the beaching of whales and dolphins is somehow tied in with U.F.O. sightings, comets, or impending calamity.) And now we can move on to serious hypotheses:

1. Some strandings (perhaps most of the ones involving mysticetes) are of animals that have already died at sea of old age, illness, or accidental causes and have been washed ashore by currents.

2. Some of the whales that reach shore dead or dying have succumbed to lethal doses of contaminants. Denise Viale (1976) suggested a link between the dumping of toxic waste by Montedison (an Italian firm) in the Tyrrhenian Sea and the incidence of sperm whale strandings along the coast of Liguria and Corsica. Surely this is not the only instance of pollution-related poisoning.

3. A number of autopsies suggest that whales may suffer from the ill-effects of parasites. S. H. Ridgway and M. Daily (1972) discovered flatworms in the brains of some dolphins that had beached themselves en masse along the coast of southern California. These long, slender platyhelminths usually gravitate to the host's head sinuses without causing too much trouble. But when they proliferate and invade the brain to burrow and lay hundreds of tiny triangular eggs, they can cause irreversible damage. Infested whales may experience loss of coordination, making it impossible for them to swim properly. Some may drown at sea, others may die on shore.

4. J. Maigret (1979) has studied the recurrent mass strandings of dolphins and pilot whales off Yoff, on the Cape Verde peninsula (Senegal). He stresses that these strandings could be caused by any number of factors, including the local (and illegal) practice of fishing with dynamite. However, most strandings in this area happen to occur in late spring, when the arrival of warm water along the coast triggers an enormous "bloom" of plankton. The swarming species that form this natural "red tide" include Dinophyceae, and some of these algae, such as *Gonyaulax*, are toxic. Cetaceans could become poisoned, Maigret notes, "either by swimming through these waters or by eating fish that have themselves ingested toxins"—just as seems to have happened in the humpback strandings in New England in 1987.

5. We know that toothed whales form well-organized groups with rigidly defined hierarchies. If for any reason a leader should head toward the coast, the entire pod will follow suit (possibly to assist it) and end up on the beach.

6. That still leaves us wondering *why* a leader should suddenly lose its way and swim toward shallow waters and certain entrapment. Since cetaceans echolocate, experts speculate that sandy or muddy bottoms may interfere with the sound waves they emit. But this theory seems tenuous, and R.-G. Busnel (in Maigret, 1979), for one, does not subscribe to it. In Florida, the Cousteau team studied dolphins that force fish to jump into muddy shallows, then leap halfway out of the water themselves to get at their prey. The ease with which they execute this maneuver suggests that their biosonar is in no way hampered by mud or sand.

7. Another variation on the disorientation theory: W. H. Dudok van Heel (1962), a Dutch cetologist, maintains that "gently sloping beaches or extensive shallow areas may lead to mistakes in navigation," especially if the seas are churned by stormy weather.

8. Internal factors still loom large in the stranding issue. Hearing disorders—a death warrant for acoustic creatures—can be traced to any number of causes, including congenital malformation or bacterial or viral infection. For some years, however, researchers have been focusing on parasitic worms. In 1973, Profs. Geraci and Orescott noted that the middle ears and auditory sinuses of some

*This much we do know about strandings: They have been recorded since the beginning of history. The Greek poet Antye wrote an "Epitaph on a Dolphin" in the fourth century B.C.:*

*No more in delightful chase through*
*buoyant seas*
*Shall I toss up my throat from the depths, . . .*
*But the sea's*
*Glittering blue has thronged*
*me out of the moist element:*
*I lie stretched out on a narrow space of dry*
*land.*

*(translated by John Heath-Stubbs and Carol A. Whiteside)*

*Beached cetaceans provided Aristotle with specimens for anatomy research. "It is not known why they sometimes rush headlong toward the coast," he writes, "but the fact remains that they do so spontaneously and for no apparent reason." Twenty-three centuries later, the phenomenon remains largely unexplained.*

*Opposite: An early nineteenth-century engraving of a stranded bowhead whale. Below: The carcass of a beached whale is a moving sight.*

beached dolphins were infested with nemathelminths (roundworms) and nematodes related to the threadworms and pinworms that have been known to infest human children. About an inch long and slightly thicker than a pin, these invertebrates can proliferate in sufficient quantities to interfere with an animal's ability to locate food or maneuver around deadly shoals. As far back as 1913, R. C. Murphy wrote in *Logbook for Grace* that "every blackfish [pilot whale] I dissected in the West Indies last summer had clusters of roundworms in the ear passages" (quoted in Geraci, 1978). In 1955, S. L. Delyamure heard about "deaf porpoises" (or *azovka*, as Crimean fishermen called them) that had a habit of stranding en masse. The Russian scientist suspected that parasites were the culprit, and, sure enough, roundworm infestation of the middle ear turned up in 100 percent of the specimens he examined. No doubt the roundworm theory accounts for quite a few strandings. Moreover, it dovetails with the follow-the-leader theory, namely, that if a leader suffers from an ear disorder and beaches itself, the rest of the pod will do likewise.

9. It has been suggested that stranded whales may have been trying to negotiate once-clear channels they had instinctively "remembered" from eons past, now obstructed by geological upheaval.

10. F. G. Wood (1978) has proposed an even more startling theory. Cetaceans, he argues, are descended from amphibious mammals whose greatest fear was that of drowning; they would instinctively head for terra firma whenever they were wounded, ill, or threatened in the hostile environment of the water. A case in point is illustrated by the marine iguanas of the Galápagos, shore-dwelling descendants of land reptiles. The strandings we see today may be a throwback to this ancestral evasive action. The moment dolphins and whales feel stressed, a reflex reaction induces them to head toward their archetypal habitat—the shallows. If this is so, cetaceans would seek safety near land whenever they feel sick, or if they are suffering from a hearing disorder, and most of all when there are sharks, killer whales, or other predators about. F. G. Wood (1978) himself concedes that his argument is not airtight. First, how is it that a creature as intelligent as a cetacean does not realize that heading toward the coast means almost certain death? Wood explains that panic responses are subcortically controlled and bypass the "higher" centers of the cortex. Whenever a learned, "reasonable" solution no longer seems appropriate to a predicament, age-old behavior patterns resurface and take over. (In this respect, man is no different from other animals.) The second objection is that a panic-induced blind urge to self-destruct is maladaptive. However, what appears to be a suicidal response may tie in with highly favorable evolutionary factors, such as the tendency to seek shallow water in order to calve or escape predators.

We shall refrain from commenting on the validity or plausibility of these theories and simply point out that some conflict and others dovetail. To quote Lyall Watson (1981), "we do not even begin to understand why it is that so many mass strandings are connected with electrical storm activity, or why they tend to occur on the days directly before or after a full moon."

Let us hasten to add that the death-wish theory cannot be summarily brushed aside with a wave of the scientist's hand—given what we know, or do not know, at the present time. For years we refused to admit that cetaceans were intelligent on the grounds that we wanted to avoid the pitfall of anthropomorphism. Surely we can wait a little longer before deciding whether or not to credit them with awareness of their existence and the corollary inclination to bring it to an end.

CHAPTER 6

# Thou Shalt Bring Forth Monsters from the Depths of the Sea

Incipit ionas propheta.

*A tremendous indictment rose from that strip of beach, from that gelatinous, prostrate mass—an indictment that settled over the whole world. Men and animals: We had a common enemy, a common knowledge, a common defense. We were in league. An immeasurable sense of pity, which we could not keep from falling back on ourselves, welled up inside us as we beheld the preposterous remains of that stranded leviathan, the biblical beast. Before us lay what seemed to be the last whale on earth, just as every dying man seems to be the last man on earth. Seeing it transported us out of time, out of this senseless world of ours which, amid the din of exploding bombs, seemed to be rushing headlong toward its final adventure. We thought it was just another stranded creature, but we were actually looking at a lifeless planet.* **Paul Gadenne, *Baleine***

*Mythology, religion, and folklore the world over teem with dragons, giant snakes, krakens, bloodthirsty hydras, murderous sirens, and countless other maleficent creatures loosed on land and sea for no other purpose than to terrorize a helpless world. Chief among the animals that roam this fearsome bestiary is the whale. By virtue of its size, enormous mouth, and cavernous gullet, it has long been considered monstrousness incarnate.*

*Above: "Horrible monsters along the coast of Norway," as pictured in an engraving from* Historia de gentibus septentrionalibus *(1555) by Olaus Magnus.*

*Opposite: The story of Jonah—the prophet swallowed and regurgitated by a whale—has inspired countless works of art. This is from the so-called* Bible of John XXII, *a fifteenth-century illuminated manuscript produced in the Palais des Papes, Avignon.*

Fantasy provides uncomprehending minds with a cure for ignorance and anxiety; that is why civilizations start off with a mythological age. When man—that strange assemblage of molecules crowned with a dream-filled brain—first beheld the sea, the waters came alive with imagined monsters.

So, Poseidon brandished his trident and sired Tritons and Cyclopes. Six-headed Scylla devoured hapless sailors from passing ships, while Charybdis sucked in and spewed out the sea three times a day. Sirens with vulture's wings or scaly tails sang from a rocky island strewn with sun-bleached bones. Valiant Beowulf stalked the horrible sea wolf and her son, the monstrous Grendel. The Germans had their water sprites, the Philistines had gruesome Dagon (revived by H. P. Lovecraft), and medieval Europe had sea bishops, sea monks, and *Homo aquaticus*, a web-footed man that could breathe underwater.

Of all the fabulous creatures that roam this marine bestiary, none was considered more bizarre than the whale. For the paltry human mind, it was the embodiment of absolute monstrosity. This reaction goes beyond the mere fact that the whale is the biggest animal on earth. The creature seemed consubstantial with its habitat, the water—most mysterious of the four elements. It enjoyed the privilege of belonging to both the murky realm of the ocean depths and the light-drenched realm of the air. It seemed to die every time it slipped beneath the surface, only to be reborn in triumph with a mighty, liberating blow—the breath of life. For all these reasons, people through the ages have looked upon the whale as a living compendium of everything that symbolizes the unfamiliar and the unknown.

## BALAENUS COSMOPHORUS

Little wonder, then, that so many whales or whale-like monsters roamed the primordial waters of so many primitive, Mediterranean, Eastern, African, and Scandinavian cosmogonies.

In Akkadian mythology, the four-eyed, four-eared Tiamat (Bel above and Ninlil below) is sometimes depicted as a deformed or humpbacked fetus of tremendous size. Islamic texts tell of a whale that was believed to support the world. When the Earth was created, the myth goes, it swayed on the sea. Allah sent an angel down from heaven, and the angel lifted it onto his shoulders. But it needed something solid to stand on, so Allah created a green rock and perched it on the horns of ar-Rayyum, a hundred-thousand-headed bull, which, in turn, stood on the whale Hut (or al-Bahmut). So enormous was this whale that "if all the water in the sea were gathered in one of its nostrils, it would be as a mustard seed in the desert" (quoted in J. Chevalier and A. Gheerbrandt, 1969). The whale had to keep perfectly still; if it lurched or made any sudden movements, there would be earthquakes. Of course, the devil Iblis tried to tempt the whale to shake off its burden. That would have sealed the fate of Creation had not Allah come to the rescue. He dispatched a little creature that entered one of the whale's nostrils and burrowed to its brain. "The great fish moaned and prayed to Allah, and Allah allowed the creature to escape. But from that time forth it stood in front of the whale, threatening to go back in every time the whale was tempted to budge."

The dreaded "daughters of the whale" are still a part of Arab tradition. These celestial signs—eclipses, comets, shooting stars—are thought to warn that the stability of the world is giving way and that humankind must prepare for the disasters that mark the end of a cosmic cycle.

## THE DIVINE WHALE

Not all myths and religions assign whales the vitally important task of holding up the universe. For many peoples, however, the sovereign of the seas is the incarnation of a divine being that plays an irreplaceable part in the general scheme of things.

For example, the ancient Chinese believed that a strange mythological figure, Yu-kiang, held sway over the sea. This dragon-riding water deity had the body of a fish but the hands and feet of a human being. It was not a true fish, however, but a *kuan*, a huge whale several thousand *li* long that came from the Northern Sea. Sometimes the monstrous *kuan* got angry, and when it did it turned into a gigantic bird *(p'eng)*, whipping up terrible storms as it emerged above the ocean surface (M. Soymié, in P. Grimal, 1963).

"The fishermen of Viet-Nam," notes L. H. Matthews (1968), "believe that whales are sent by the 'God of the Waters' to protect sailors and to carry shipwrecked mariners on their backs to safety. . . . When they find a dead whale or dolphin they bring it to shore, and the person who has found it is counted as the eldest son of the animal. He wears a mourning turban for three months and six days, and then the turban is burnt and the bones of the animal are dug up and deposited in a sanctuary bearing the name only given to the tombs of royalty or high officials. Every time a whale or dolphin dies the rain pours and the wind rages without stopping for three days; consequently when wind and rain persist for several days it must be because one of these animals is dead. It must at once be searched for and, if it is found, given solemn burial, whereupon the bad weather at once stops."

The Japanese, too, honor dead whales with religious services, chants, and shrines. "In the grounds of the Koganji temple," writes Matthews (1968), "there is a shrine called Seigetsu-an, and near it stands a tomb and a granite monument 7½ feet high. The whale embryos taken from mother whales during flensing were carried there and buried wrapped in straw mats. . . . A necrology was kept in which every whale buried, having been given a posthumous Buddhist name, was registered with the exact date of capture."

In Africa, too, the death of a whale was cause for sorrow. People in the Missili region of Angola believed that whales were the ruling spirits of the sea. Whenever

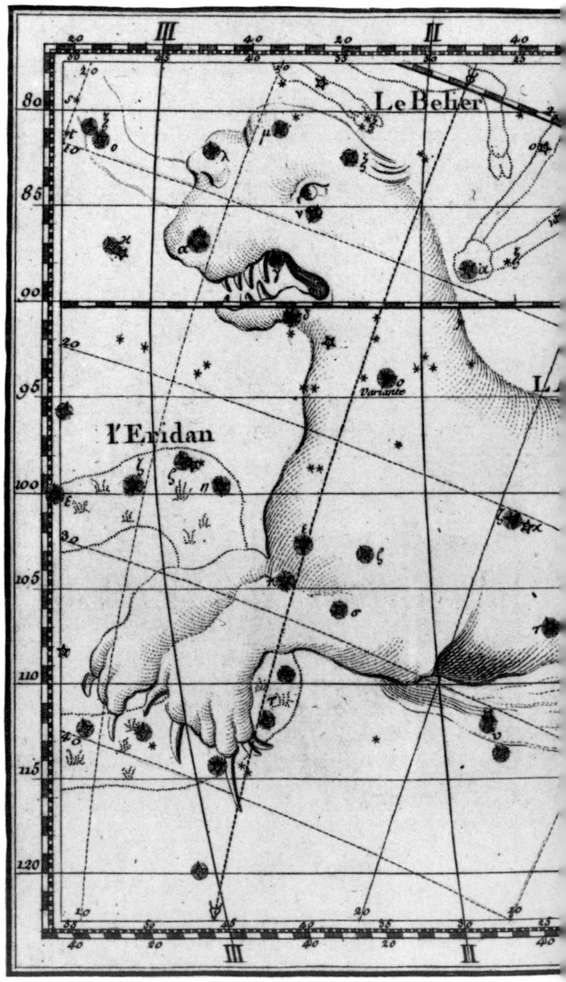

*How could a creature so enormous fail to influence the lives of men? Below: As shown in this engraving from the celestial atlas of British astronomer royal John Flamsteed (1646–1719), the whale has its very own constellation in the heavens. Whales were believed to have an astrological influence on human events; they portended catastrophe. In the year 1000, all Christendom thought the end of the world was at hand. What were the signs of the coming Apocalypse? Comets, of course—and whales, which presaged disaster. "A whale of astonishing size was seen slicing through the waves. . . . No sooner did this omen from the sea appear than the clash of arms was heard across the length and breadth of the western world, not only in Gaul but on the overseas islands of the Angles, the Bretons, and the Scots."*

*In the Far East, stranded whales were looked upon as gods. The montagnards of Vietnam believed that a child destined to redeem the world and deliver it from evil would be borne on a fabulous whale. This tradition had deep roots in Indonesia, the Philippines, China, Korea, and Japan, as well as Indochina. Right: A pilot whale, from* Twenty-Three Types of Whales, *an anonymous Japanese scroll painting from 1798.*

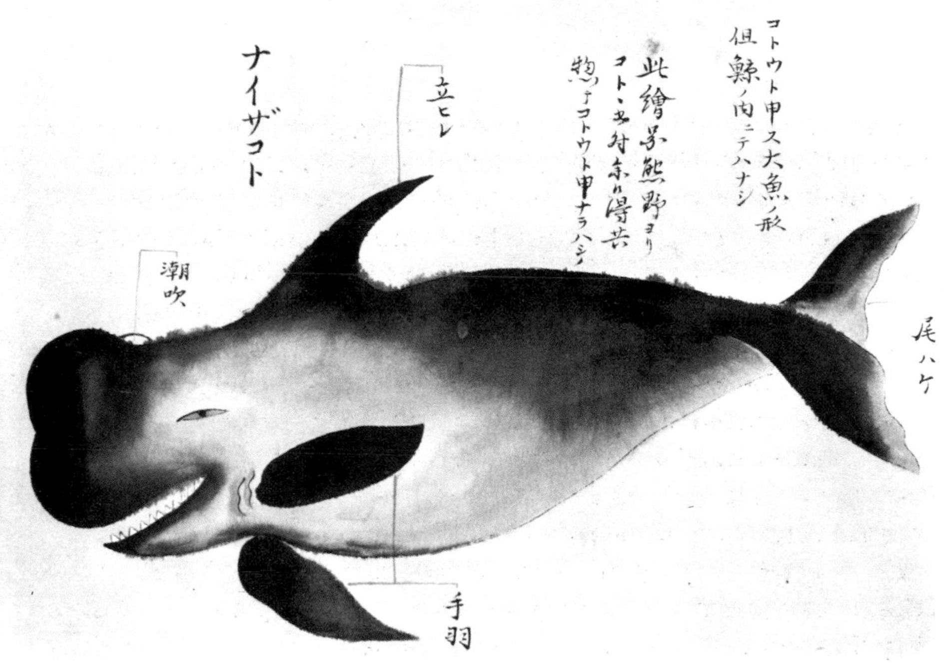


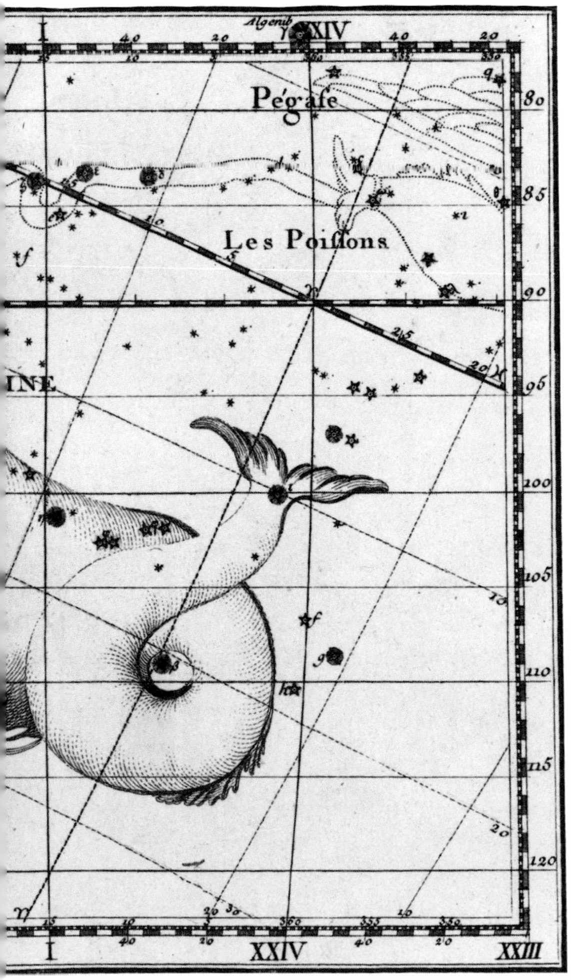


a fisherman found a stranded whale on the beach, the entire populace assembled in the palace courtyard to the incessant beating of drums. The chief, grieving and dejected, would appear and call for silence. Then the court messenger told the story of the Missili, reminding one and all that their destiny had always been bound up with the sea. The speech would end with a proclamation that everyone in the land wear mourning, for a monarch of the sea had perished on the beach.

## THE PEOPLE OF THE WHALE

In Inuit mythology, Sedna was the goddess of the sea and the whale was her most magnificent subject. Sedna was a winsome girl who had spurned all of her suitors and married a bird. Outraged, her father killed her husband and took her home in a boat. On the way back he threw her overboard. She clung to the umiak, so he had to chop off her fingers, one by one. Sedna turned into the huge, voracious deity of the Lower World and ruled over all creatures that dwell in the sea. Each of her severed fingers turned into a different animal: a right whale, a narwhal, a beluga, a seal, and so forth.

The whale also appears in Inuit myths about the beginning of the world. One of the chief characters in their creation myths is Big Raven, a deity in human form. One day, Big Raven came upon a stranded whale and asked the Great Spirit to help him get the creature back out to sea. The Great Spirit told him of a place in the forest where moonlight fell a special way. There he would find mushrooms that, if eaten, would give him the strength to drag the whale into the water unassisted. Big Raven did as he was told, rescued the whale, and thereby safeguarded the order of the world.

The multifaceted relationship between the Inuit and the whale has been the subject of considerable anthropological research. According to R. M. Swiderski (1982), the Eskimos of Alaska give a strange and elaborate performance before every whaling expedition. They bring out whale figurines made of wood, bone, or ivory, with twigs for the spout. Then they break into a ritualistic dance that mimics swimming whales. For added realism they tint some water red, take it in their mouths, and spit it out to reenact the death throes of a mortally wounded whale.

While preparations for the hunt are under way, the Eskimos sing two kinds of ceremonial songs. One is a collective prayer that everyone knows. They call out to the whales, imploring them to let themselves be taken, promise them fish in return, swear that they will have an easy death, and assure them that their sacrifice will not be in vain because it will support families in the village. They also ask them to bring along some seals and other animals for the hunters to catch.

The other song is secret. Every harpooner has his very own, revealed to him in a dream by an animal spirit. Only whales, with their keen sense of hearing, can hear it.

Naturally, changes in whaling techniques and the encroachment of modern civilization on the Arctic have diluted these rituals considerably. But the cult of the whale is still very much alive. Among the Koryak people of Siberia, masked dancers still beckon the whale by invoking spirits. They also hold astonishing meetings during which they confess to whales any sins they have committed, any taboos they have broken, any evil thoughts they may have had (Swiderski, 1982). According to E. Mitchell and R. R. Reeves (1980), most Eskimo villages along the coast of Alaska are still very much "whale cultures." "The whale is the focal point of our life and culture," the Inuit mayor of North Slope Borough, Eben Hopson, stated in 1979. "We are the People of the Whale. Catching and distributing whale is our Eucharist and our Passover. The feast of the whale is our Easter and Christmas—an ancestral celebration of the mysteries of life."

## THE WHALE AND THE POTLATCH

Like the Eskimos, the Nootka Indians of Vancouver Island in western Canada consider the whale the focal point of social, cultural, and religious life. R. L. Webb (1981) has given a detailed account of their whaling rituals.

The bravest and highest-ranking men in the tribe go off into the forest to purify themselves. Their leader dives into a sacred pond and swims and spouts like a whale. Then the Indians return to their hunting camp, where they pray for the whales to come and mutter chants that sound like spouting whales.

When the long-awaited spouts appear on the horizon, the men push their canoes out onto the water and enthusiastically pull away at the oars. Leading the fleet is the chief, who sings songs to the whales, talks to them, tells them he loves them, hails them as "chiefs" and "rulers of the world." "Make haste to the shore!"

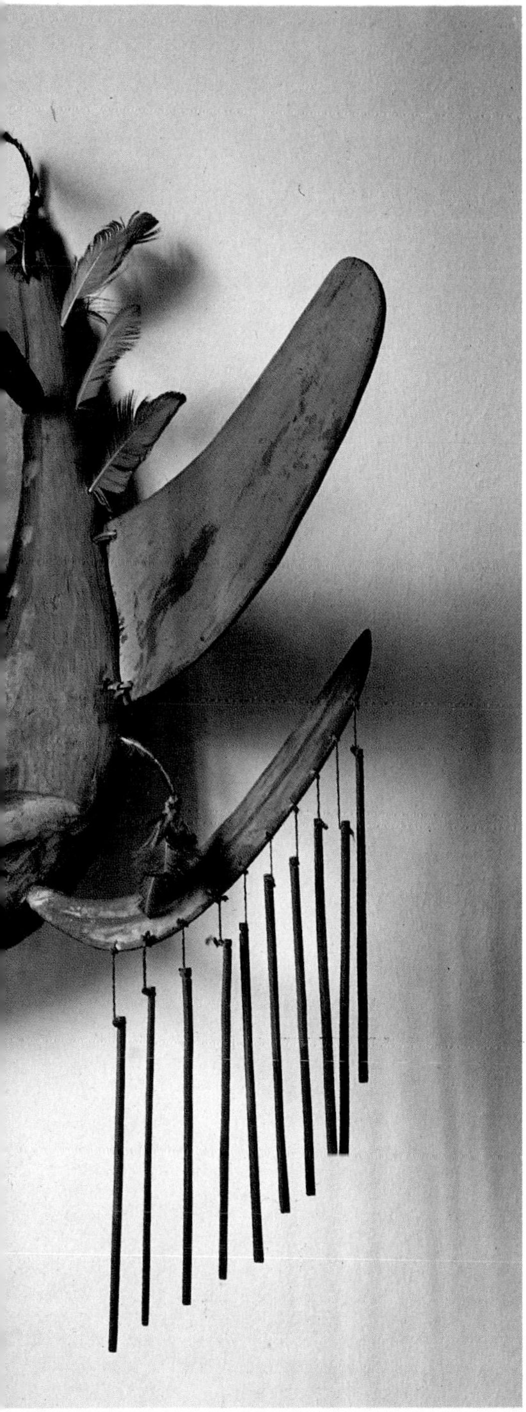

*Strong yet ambivalent ties to the whale link the Indians of northwestern North America and the Inuit (Eskimo). To this day, whaling is the mainstay of their social life, the cement of human interaction, and a vital part of child-rearing.*

*Above: A ritual ceremonial mask from the late nineteenth century, representing a benevolent spirit believed to lead whales to hunters. Feathers and painted wood, height 72 cm. Collection André Breton, Paris.*

*Opposite: Indian blanket with stylized figures of the Whale and Thunder-Bird, woven by the Nitinat people (a subdivision of the Nootka), Vancouver Island, Canada, c. 1860–70.*

he shouts at any whale he spots. "My people await thee! Come closer, that they may marvel at thee and sing thy praises!"

When the canoes are within striking distance, everyone falls silent. The leader stands up in his boat and flings the first harpoon. The others follow suit. The stricken whale spins out the line, spouts blood, and dies. The carcass is towed back to shore; the distribution begins. The size of the piece each hunter receives is determined by his rank in the tribe and his part in catching the whale. Flensing provides an opportunity for a potlatch, a ceremonial distribution of wealth during which it is customary for those who receive to give the host an even bigger gift.

The hunt concludes with songs and dances of thanksgiving. The little ones gather round the elders to hear the ancestral legends of the tribe. They hear of Wasgo, the white wolf of the forest that can turn himself into a killer whale. They hear of Tlu-Kluts the Thunder-Bird, whose wings conceal snakes that create bolts of lightning when they shoot out their tongues. When Tlu-Kluts is hungry, he eats a whale. But another great spirit, Kwatyaht, comes to the whales' defense. He disguises himself as a whale to trick Tlu-Kluts, and the mighty confrontation that ensues causes both land and sea to tremble.

## LEGENDS FROM THE OPPOSITE ENDS OF THE EARTH

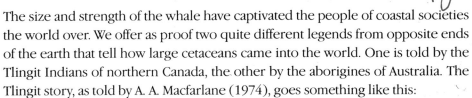

The size and strength of the whale have captivated the people of coastal societies the world over. We offer as proof two quite different legends from opposite ends of the earth that tell how large cetaceans came into the world. One is told by the Tlingit Indians of northern Canada, the other by the aborigines of Australia. The Tlingit story, as told by A. A. Macfarlane (1974), goes something like this:

Natsihlane was a good hunter, and his brother-in-law was jealous of him. One day, the two of them went ashore on a far distant land, but the brother-in-law went off and left him behind. Natsihlane fell asleep and was awakened by a big gull. He heard it say that the sea lion chief wished to see him and that he had been sent to fetch him. Knowing that there was strong medicine at work, Natsihlane climbed on the back of a sea lion that swam until it reached a great rock beside a cliff. The rock opened, and the Tlingit hunter found himself inside a great house in which the sea lions were assembled.

"This is my son," the chief of the sea lions said to him. "He has been wounded by a harpoon. Help him, and I will help you get back to your homeland." Natsihlane removed the harpoon and tended to his wounds. The chief thanked him and gave him a magic sea-lion stomach filled with air to use as a boat.

When the hunter woke up on the beach, he heard an inner voice speaking to him. He went into the forest and carved eight big fish from spruce branches. He said some medicine words over them and ordered them to jump into the water. They sprang into the sea at his command, but lay lifeless on the surface. Natsihlane then cut eight more fish from red cedar, but they would not live, either.

Then he carved eight fish from yellow cedar and painted each fish with a white stripe across the head and a circle on the dorsal fin. He sang his most powerful spirit song and commanded the fish to leap into the water. They did so and soon grew into great black whales. They obeyed his orders. He asked them to swim out and see to it that his brother-in-law was drowned. They did as he requested, after which he called them out of the water. They formed a line on the shore. "I made you to get revenge," he told them. "That was a bad thing to do. From now on, you must never again harm any human being."

PISCE SVPER CVRVO VECTVS CANTABAT ARION

The aborigine legend, as told by Charles P. Mountford (1969), comes from the southern coast of Australia near Encounter Bay. The story goes something like this:

In ancient times performers had no means of providing light for evening rituals. Kondole was the sole owner of fire and he hid it in the bush. He was mean and disagreeable, as well as a large, powerful man, and no one was brave enough to force him to bring his fire to the ceremonial grounds.

Finally, one of the performers, completely losing his temper over Kondole's mean behavior, crept up behind him and threw a spear that penetrated his skull. Suddenly, the people of the ceremony were transformed into creatures. Some became kangaroos, some opossums, others the smaller creatures. Some rose into the air as birds, while others, entering the sea, were changed into fish in their many forms. Kondole, the largest of them all, became the whale which has spouted water from the spear wound in his head ever since.

## THE CONSUMMATE MONSTER

Probably the first alarming description of a whale comes to us from Nearchus of Crete, who chronicled Alexander the Great's conquests in India. The following incident took place during his expedition along the coast of Asia in the fourth century B.C.

"The sea early in the morning was observed to be blown up into the air as if by the force of a whirlwind. The men, greatly alarmed, enquired of the pilot the nature and cause of this phenomenon, and they were informed that it proceeded from the blowing of whales as they sported in the sea. This report did not quiet their alarm, and they let the oars drop from their hands."

Poets—and an occasional naturalist—embroidered on these early accounts, and one of the monsters they created was given a place of honor in the story of Andromeda. It is mentioned by two Latin authors from the first century A.D. Pliny the Elder wrote of the phenomenon with clinical detachment. "The skeleton of the monster to which Andromeda was said to have been exposed was brought

*To our minds, there is something quintessentially unfathomable about the whale. Imagine how dumbfounded our ancestors must have been when they stumbled upon their first stranded rorqual, their astonishment when they saw that cavernous mouth, that mountain of swarthy flesh on a beach. We can only get a faint idea of the awesome monsters that must have haunted their dreams.*

*Opposite: Albrecht Dürer (1471–1528) based his version of* Arion Riding a Dolphin *on drawings of whales circulating throughout Europe at the time, and which resurfaced in the books of Conrad Gesner and Guillaume Rondelet. Here, Arion sits astride a monster known as a "boar whale." 1514. Brown ink, heightened with watercolor, 14 x 23 cm. Kunsthistorisches Museum, Vienna.*

*Below: Equally redolent of Greco-Roman mythology is this* Rescue of Andromeda *by Florentine painter Piero di Cosimo (1462–1521), c. 1515. Oil on panel, 70 x 123 cm. Uffizi, Florence.*

from the city of Jaffa in Judaea and displayed in Rome. . . . Its bones were forty feet long. Its ribs were higher than those of the elephants of India. Its spinal column was a foot and a half thick" (*Historia Naturalis*, IX, 11).

At the fantastic end of the literary spectrum, Ovid (43 B.C.–A.D. 17 or 18) turned Andromeda's monster into a loathsome beast and described it with all the epic grandeur his poetic genius could summon. Andromeda was the daughter of Cepheus, king of Ethiopia, and Cassiopeia, who had the temerity to boast that she was lovelier than the Nereids. Angered, Poseidon (father of the Nereids) sent a sea monster to ravage the coast. The oracle was consulted. The Nereids had fastened the virgin Andromeda to a rock on the seashore, and she had to be rescued. Just as the princess was about to be devoured, who should come along but Perseus, the hero with the winged sandals, who had just beheaded the sinister Medusa.

. . . So Perseus came plunging
In his steep dive down air, attacked the monster
That roared as the right shoulder took the sword-blade
Up to the hilt. The wound hurt deeply, the sea-beast
Reared, lashed, and dived, and thrashed, as a wild-boar does
When the hounds bay round him. Perseus rose
When the fang struck, he poised, he sought for openings
Along the barnacled back, along the sides,
At tapering fishy tail; the monster's vomit
Was blood and salty water.

*(translated by Rolfe Humphries)*

Andromeda's monster, fury incarnate, had a number of literary predecessors and successors. Few were as baroque as the one that killed Theseus' son, the young Hippolytus. Phaedra, his father's wife, fell madly in love with Hippolytus—to his misfortune—and a gruesome monster emerged from the sea to attack him.

The first to relate this horrible scene was Euripides (480–406 B.C.), whose *Hippolytus* won first prize in 428 B.C. at the competition for tragedy in Athens.

As we gazed toward the wave-beat shore, a wave tremendous we beheld towering to the skies, so that from our view the cliffs of Sciron vanished, . . . then swelling and frothing with a crest of foam, the sea discharged it . . . and in the moment that it broke, that mighty wall of water, there issued from the waves a monstrous bull, whose bellowing filled the land with fearsome echoes, a sight too awful as it seemed to us who witnessed it.

*(translated by E. S. Coleridge)*

Seneca (4 B.C.–A.D. 65), the Latin playwright and philosopher, made this scene the dramatic zenith of *Phaedra*, as did French playwright Jean Racine in the climactic fifth scene of the last act of *Phèdre,* which was first performed in 1677. Here is an excerpt from one of the monuments of French literature:

Meanwhile surged from the sea a mountainous wave
With wild sea horses lashed to furious spray;
The flood approached us through the quivering spume. . . .
His long-drawn bellows set the seashore trembling,
The sky with horror viewed his monstrous rumbling,
The earth was all a-quiver, air infected,
The waves that spewed him forth drew back deflected.

*(translated by Samuel Solomon)*

## THE RED-HEADS

The people of ancient Iceland were no strangers to real live whales—right whales, rorquals, what have you—but that did not stop them from telling stories about horse whales, boar whales, or the vicious and cunning "Red-Heads."

The fearsome Red-Headed Whales, which roamed the seas in mighty, belligerent herds, were the bane of mankind. They seemed to revel in tracking people down and destroying them. Icelandic seamen sailing the Atlantic dreaded crossing paths with these fiendish cetaceans, which had a taste for human flesh and regularly returned to scenes of earlier meals for fresh victims. The Vikings were careful to steer clear of any spot where whales had destroyed ships. The Icelandic legend of how the Red-Heads came to appear in the sea is a fantastic fable, complete with a moral.

One day some men from Sudurnes rowed out to the Geirfugla Skerry to trap auks; when they wanted to set off for home once more, one man was missing. Some elves had lured the man to them by magic and kept him among them because an elf-woman was with child by him. The man got permission to leave the skerry on the condition that he promised to arrange for the child to be baptized. He swore he would and sailed back to the mainland.

One Sunday when people came to Hvalnes for the service, there was a cradle standing outside the church door, and a small baby was in it. Over the cradle lay a coverlet, very beautiful and delicately worked, and woven of some unknown cloth; and at the foot of the cradle was a slip of paper with these words written on it: "He who is the father of this child will see to it that it is baptized." No one would acknowledge that he was the father or claim the child as his. The priest had his suspicions about the man who had been missing for a whole year, but the man replied gruffly that he was not the child's father and did not care in the least what became of it.

*No one knew more about whales than the Vikings—witness the following quotation from* The Saga of Erik the Red, *an epic poem from the ninth century: "May our sturdy craft explore measureless expanses of sea and our intrepid warriors sing of newfound lands as they pitch camp and cook whales!"*

*Above: Anonymous engraving of a whale, possibly a sperm whale, spouting a single column of spray. French, c. 1600.*

*The monsters that the ocean occasionally cast forth on shore inspired a mixture of terror and fascination the world over. Opposite: This illustration, painted for a new edition of André Thevet's* Cosmographie universelle, *dates from the latter part of the eighteenth century.*

While they were still arguing, up came a tall, stately woman. She was extremely angry, and snatching the coverlet from the cradle she flung it through the church door, saying: "The church must not lose its dues!" Then she turned to the man and said: "This do I say and this curse do I lay: you shall turn into the most vicious whale in the sea, and shall destroy many ships!"

After which the woman disappeared, and so did the cradle with the baby in it. But soon after the woman vanished, the man she had cursed went mad and went rushing off. He ran to the sea and jumped over the cliff called Stakksgnypa, which is between Keflavik and Leira. Then all at once he turned into the most vicious whale, and was known as Red-Head from then on. He was very evil and destructive, and drowned boatloads of men (Jacqueline Simpson, 1972).

In Iceland, fishermen feared the Red-Headed whales that capsized boats and fed on human flesh. Other species, however, were considered friendly to man, even though he had to kill them now and then in order to survive. The following examples from Icelandic lore were retold in *The Whale*, by L. H. Matthews (1968).

Once a poor fisherman had nothing left to eat. "Seeking help from the blessed Thorlákur he took a rope and laid it down on the shore; the next morning a whale as long as the rope was found caught by it."

"The best-known whale in Icelandic legend is the one said in Snorri Sturluson's 'Heimskringla' to have been sent there by a Danish king, who was angry because the Icelanders had made libelous verse about him. He considered sending an army to Iceland, but first he sent a magician disguised as a whale to spy for him. The journey was fruitless because everywhere the magician went he was frustrated by the country's guardian spirits."

According to another legend, "a man threw a stone at a fin whale and hit the blowhole, causing the whale to burst. This deed was condemned and the man was told not to go to sea for twenty years. In the nineteenth year he could no longer resist the desire to return to sea. He went fishing—and a whale came and killed him." Whales could forgive a crime, but only if it had been properly atoned for.

Throughout Scandinavia, "the fin whale especially was thought to drive herring shoals toward the shore." Along came Svend Foyn and his harpoon gun. "The fishermen were very angry when this whaling started, as they considered it endangered their future livelihood," Matthews reports. The age-old belief in benevolent whales was alive and well even in the nineteenth century.

## HE MAKETH A PATH TO SHINE AFTER HIM . . .

All the literature of whales makes it clear that God invested the huge, monstrous whale with tremendous power, including the power to strike fear into the hearts and minds of men. Nowhere does the whale's terrifying presence inspire more lyricism and hyperbole than in the Holy Scriptures.

In the Genesis, the first creature God releases into the waters is the whale. "And God said, Let the waters bring forth abundantly the moving creature that hath life . . . And God created great whales, and every living creature that moveth."

The biblical whale par excellence is the stupendous Leviathan—symbol of evil, focal point of all human fears, embodiment of unmitigated power—that the Lord created on the fifth day of Creation as a warning to mankind. From then on "Leviathan maketh a path to shine after him," wherever pride and the temptation to sin well up in the sons of Adam. Its gaping mouth is terrible to behold; nothing can equal its strength; its heart is harder than the hardest stone. What man could contemplate this horrible beast and dare to disobey the Lord? Leviathan is mentioned in a number of places in the Bible, including the Book of Job, the Psalms, and the Book of Revelation. Here are a few excerpts from the Book of Job:

Canst thou draw out Leviathan with a hook? or his tongue with a cord which thou lettest down?
Canst thou fill his skin with barbed irons? or his head with fish spears?
I will not conceal his parts, nor his power, nor his comely proportion.
Who can discover the face of his garment? or who can come to him with his double bridle?
Who can open the doors of his face? His teeth are terrible round about.
His scales are his pride, shut up together as with a close seal.
By his neesings a light doth shine, and his eyes are like the eyelids of the morning.
Out of his mouth go burning lamps, and sparks of fire leap out.
Out of his nostrils goeth smoke, as out of a seething pot or cauldron.
In his neck remaineth strength, and sorrow is turned into joy before him.
He maketh a path to shine after him; one would think the deep to be hoary.

*The terrible Leviathan, sent by the Lord to inspire a salutary fear in mankind, was a source of endless fascination for painters, illustrators, and poets alike. Above: An engraving from the illustrated Bible by Gustave Doré (1832–83) and H. Pisan.*

*"The huge leviathan, dame Nature's wonder,*
*Making his sport, that many makes to weep."*
*(Edmund Spenser, 1552–99;*
*from* Visions of the World's Vanity*)*

*"This is the black sea-brute bulling through*
*wave-wrack*
*. . . He is called Leviathan . . .*
*And he waits for the world to begin"*
*(W. S. Merwin, American, b. 1927)*

This terrifying symbol of the Lord's omnipotence was a source of poetic and mystical inspiration for centuries. It is mentioned in Fourth Esdras, a Jewish apocalyptic work usually included in the Apocrypha.

On the fifth day thou didst command the seventh part, where the water had been gathered together, to bring forth living creatures, birds, and fishes . . .
Then thou didst keep in existence two living creatures; the name of one thou didst call Behemoth and the name of the other Leviathan . . .
But to Leviathan thou didst give the seventh part, the watery part.

The beast rears its loathsome head centuries later in Canto I of *Paradise Lost* (1677). Here, John Milton (1608–74) turns Leviathan into a horrible symbol of the Tempter, the Evil One: Satan himself.

. . . That Sea-Beast
Leviathan, which God of all his works
Created hugest that swim th'Oceän stream:
Him haply slumb'ring on the Norway foam
The Pilot of some small night-founder'd skiff,
Deeming some Island, oft, as Sea-men tell,
With fixed Anchor in his scaly rind . . .
So stretcht out huge in length the Arch-fiend lay.

Later, in Canto VII:

. . . there Leviathan
Hugest of the living Creatures, on the Deep
Stretcht like a Promontory sleeps or swims,
And seems a moving Land, and at his Gills
Draws in, and at his Trunk spouts out a Sea.

## THE WHALE-ISLAND

Chroniclers did not stint when it came to details about the wonders of the sea. If anything, they tended to embroider on the facts. One of their favorite imaginings was the living island, the animal island, the whale-island. The notion of a sleeping whale, with its dark, rocklike back, being mistaken for an uncharted land is as old as maritime literature itself. A number of ancient authors mention it with varying degrees of exaggeration. Aelian, Roman rhetorician and author of the third century A.D., claimed that one such whale-island measured fully one-half the length of a stadium, or more than 250 feet.

Another early reference occurs in the *Physiologus* (Greek, second century), a collection of anecdotes dealing mainly with natural history. Gatenby (1983) recounted:

There is a certain whale in the sea called the aspidoceleon, that is exceedingly large like an island. . . . Ignorant sailors tie their ships to the beast as to an island and plant their anchors and stakes in it. They light their cooking fires on the whale, but when it feels the heat it urinates and plunges into the depths, sinking all the ships.

Al-Jahiz (or al-Djahidj), an Arab zoologist who lived in the ninth century, had a name for this imaginary monster (*zaratan*) but was skeptical about its existence. "I know of no one who ever claimed to have seen the *zaratan* with his own eyes. A few sailors report that occasionally they ventured near islands in the sea, with forests and valleys and ravines thereupon, and they lighted a great fire. But when the heat reached the back of the *zaratan*, it started to glide across the water, taking with it all of them and all the vegetation thereon, until only those who contrived to escape were spared. Even the most fabulous stories are more plausible than this one."

Stories about whales as big as islands were especially popular during the Middle Ages. One of the oldest works from this period, *The Voyage of Saint Brendan*, recounts the fabulous adventures of St. Brendan, an Irish abbot, and his crew during a seven-year journey in search of the Promised Land of the Saints, or *Terra Repromissionis Sanctorum*. (The historical Saint Brendan was a bishop of Kerry in the sixth century, but little is known of his ministry.) Based on Irish oral tradition, the tale was translated into Latin in the ninth century and given the title *Navigatio sancti Brendani Abbatis*. An Anglo-Norman monk named Benedeit rendered the text into the French of William the Conqueror in the twelfth century.

A messenger of the Lord with "yellow eyes" and "white hair" sends Brendan and his monks to an island (Gatenby, 1983).

> While the brothers spent the night outside in prayers and vigils, the man of God remained sitting inside the boat. . . . While Saint Brendan himself was singing his Mass in the boat, the brothers began to carry the raw meat out of the boat. When they had done this they put a pot over the fire. When, however, they were plying the fire with wood and the pot began to boil, the island began to be in motion like a wave. The brothers rushed to the boat, crying out for protection to the holy father. He drew each one of them into the boat by his hand. Having left everything they had had on the island behind, they began to sail. Then the island moved out to sea. The lighted fire could be seen over two miles away. Saint Brendan told the brothers what it really was, saying: "My sons, do not be afraid. God revealed to me during the night in a vision the secret of this affair: Where we were was not an island, but a fish—the foremost of all that swim in the ocean."
>
> *(translated by John O'Meara)*

Many a sailor has followed Saint Brendan's little boat and stumbled upon just such an island—at least in his mind's eye. It crops up time and again in popular, occasionally even in scientific, literature from the Middle Ages to the nineteenth century. In *Orlando Furioso* by Ariosto (1474–1533), one of the poem's heroes,

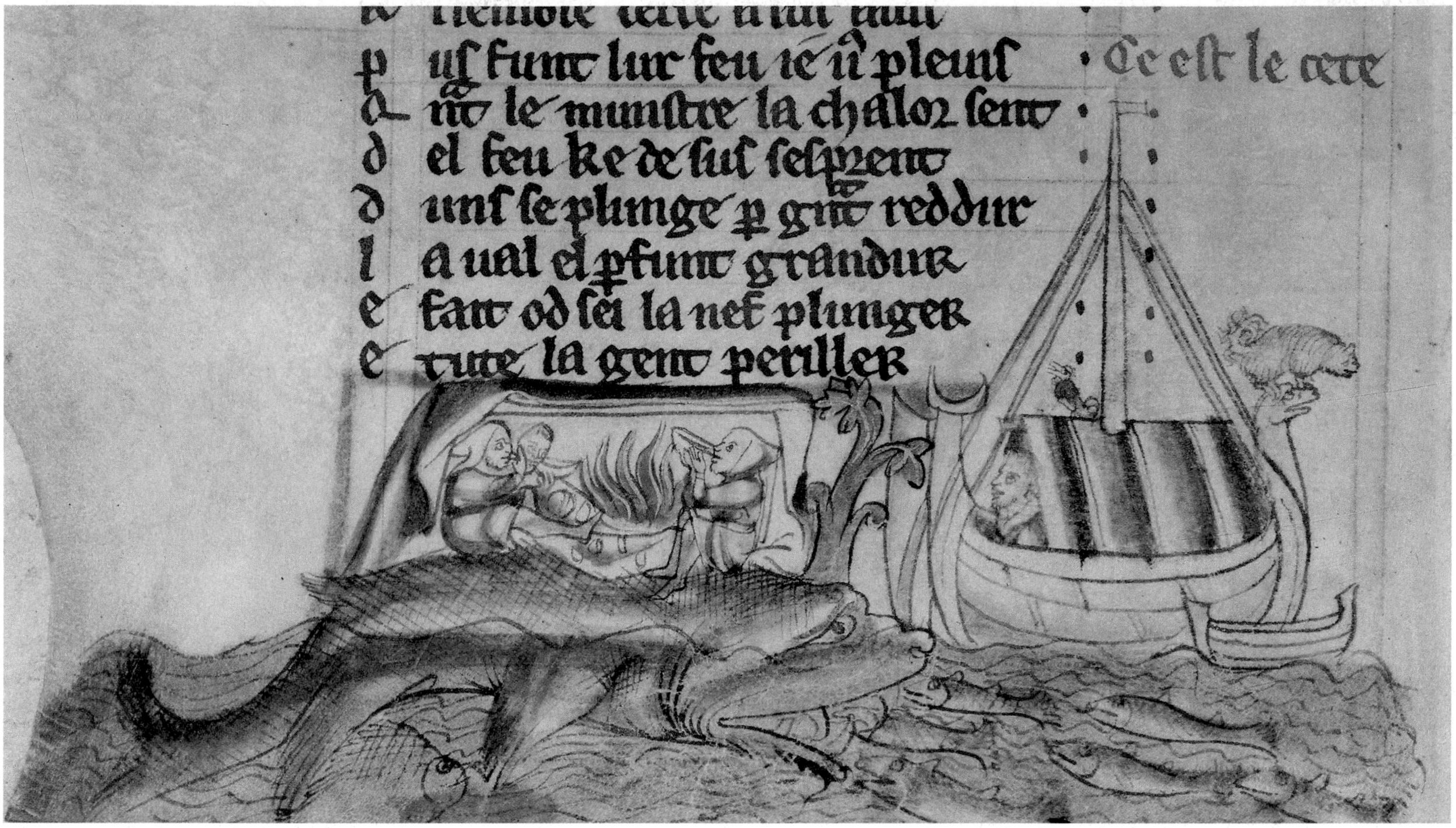

*The theme of the whale as a living island has been a fixture in literature and folklore since ancient times. In their mind's eye, the sailors, writers, and illustrators of centuries gone by made these giants of the sea out to be bigger than they already were. Many a story tells of how sailors dropped anchor at a massive, heavily forested rock and lighted a cooking fire, whereupon the whale suddenly woke up and dived, sucking the ship and crew down to the bottom of the sea.*

*The "whale island" was grist for many an artist's mill, as the illustrations on these pages attest. Opposite, top: Illuminated manuscript from a twelfth-century English bestiary. Bodleian Library, Oxford (MS Ashmole 1511, fol. 86v). Opposite, bottom: A sixteenth-century engraving of the "Miracle of St. Malo," a "remake" of the Legend of Saint Brendan.*

*Above: Yet another "whale island," as pictured in the* Bestiary *of Guillaume le Clerc. French, late thirteenth century. Bibliothèque Nationale, Paris.*

Astolfo, tells how he came under the spell of Alcina and how the sorceress "kept" him (the euphemism is delectable) "all that day and through the night" on an island that turned out to be a whale.

Hard, spiteful Fate traced our path which brought us out, one morning, onto a lovely beach on which stood a castle of the potent Alcina. . . . Swift-moving dolphins hastened to her, and ponderous tunny, open-mouthed; the sperm whales and sea lions were disturbed out of their indolent sleep. . . . We descried a whale, the largest one ever to be seen in the ocean: its vast shoulders protruded eleven cubits and more above the briny waves. All of us fell into the same deception—we took it for an island, it lay so still with never even a ripple, and its two extremities were at so great a distance apart.

With a cheerful smile [Alcina] came to meet us and showed easy courtesy as she addressed us. . . . She pointed to the vast whale which, as I said, looked like a small island. I who have always (to my regret) been too impetuous, stepped onto that fish. . . . All that day and through the night she kept me in the midst of the sea on the monster's back.

(*translated by Guido Waldman*)

Saint Brendan, Orlando Furioso—many other names could be added to the ranks of those who have set foot on these living islands. Olaus Magnus and Conrad Gesner are two such. John Milton likened his Leviathan to "some Island" into which a Pilot might fix "Anchor in his scaly rind." In *The Seasons*, Jean-François de Saint Lambert (1716–1803), French poet and intimate of the Encyclopedists, described winter as follows:

Neptune he subdues, enchaining fast
That murky sea where whales great and vast
Appear in autumn before sailors' eyes,
Seeming reefs stretched out 'gainst the skies.

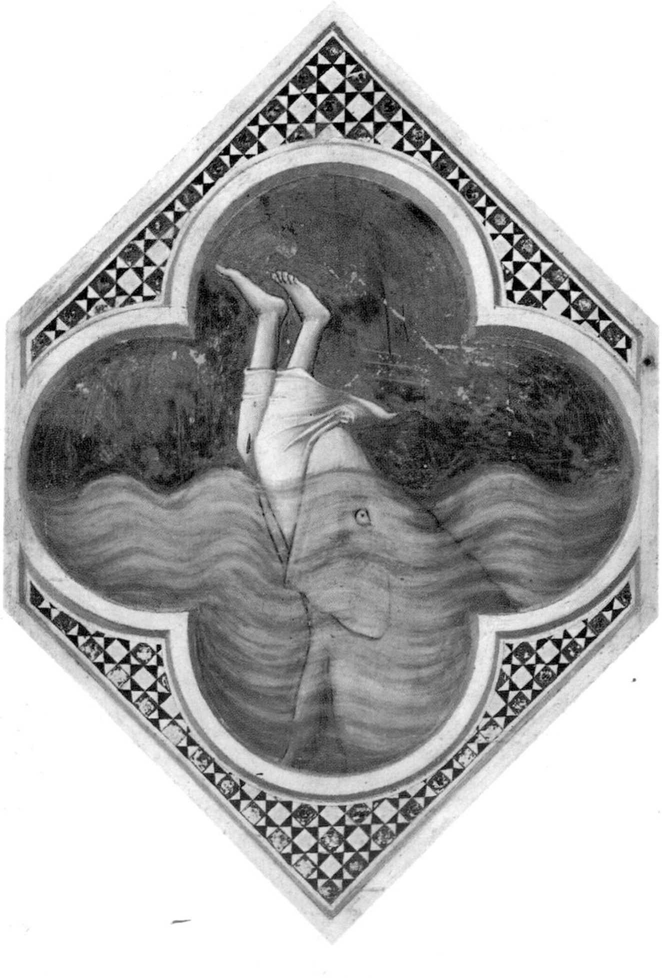

*The story of Jonah fired the imagination of exegetes, storytellers, novelists, poets, painters, engravers, illuminators, and watercolorists throughout the Judeo-Christian and Moslem worlds. The illustrations on these pages are but a sampling; we could easily add many other works of the same caliber.*

*Opposite, top: An Iranian version of Jonah and the Whale, from the* Jāmi at-tawarīkh *of Rashīd ad-Dīn, a universal history. c. 1400. Gouache on paper, 32 x 47 cm. The Metropolitan Museum of Art, New York.*

*Bottom, left:* Jonah Cast into the Sea, *from the* Mirror of Human Salvation. *Flemish, fifteenth century. Musée de Chantilly.*

*Bottom, right:* Jonah and the Whale, *quatrefoil fresco by Giotto (1266–1337). Arena Chapel, Padua.*

*Above:* Jonah Cast upon the Dry Land, *historiated initial from a thirteenth-century French manuscript. Bibliothèque d'Amiens.*

*Right:* Jonah Cast into the Sea. *Anonymous, sixteenth century. Klosterneuburg Abbey, near Vienna.*

Our lesson in fanciful geography would not be complete without the voyages of Sinbad. Here is an episode, translated from the Arabic by N. J. Dawood, and as recounted in Gatenby (1983):

We came at length to a little island as fair as the Garden of Eden. The passengers went ashore and set to work to light a fire. Some busied themselves with cooking and washing, some fell to eating and drinking and making merry. . . .

Whilst we were thus engaged we suddenly heard the captain cry out to us from the ship: 'All aboard, quickly! Abandon everything and run for your lives! The mercy of Allah be upon you, for this is no island but a gigantic whale floating on the bosom of the sea, on whose back the sands have settled and trees have grown since the world was young! When you lit the fire, it felt the heat and stirred. Make haste, I say, or soon the whale will plunge into the sea and you will all be lost!'

Some reached the ship in safety, but others did not; for suddenly the island shook beneath our feet and, submerged by mountainous waves, sank with all that stood upon it to the bottom of the roaring ocean.

## IN THE BELLY OF THE FISH

Riddles based on biblical subjects were a popular pastime of olden days:

A coffin living,
A man inside trembling;
A coffin devouring,
A man inside praying.

Everyone knows the answer: Jonah in the whale. Stories about a whale swallowing and then regurgitating a man have long been a part of religious and fictional literature the world over. We begin our journey through this theme with the version told in the Bible.

The Almighty instructed Jonah (from the Hebrew for "dove") to prophesy against the wickedness of the city of Nineveh. Fearing the reaction of the lewd, luxury-loving Assyrians, he balked at the mission, rushed to Joppa, and stole away on a boat bound for Tarshish. But he had spoken ill of the Lord and doubted his Infinite Wisdom, so he never reached his destination. The ship ran into a terrific storm. Believing it to be a sign from the Almighty, the crew threw Jonah overboard at the prophet's request. As the water swirled round him and death seemed at hand, Jonah asked God to have mercy on him. The Lord, hearing His name uttered in prayer, sent a Great Fish from the depths to swallow him. After three days and three nights the whale "vomited out Jonah upon the dry land." The prophet had been taught a lesson in unconditional obedience.

An anonymous thirteenth-century text tells the Arabic version of how Divine Wisdom dealt with a recalcitrant prophet:

Allah heard his prayer and rescued him from the belly of the fish. There is disagreement about the length of time he spent inside the creature. Ikrima says three days; Ibn-Mas'ud, three hours; Qatada, forty days; Muqatil, a single day. When Jonah cried out, 'Glory to Thee, Allah! There is no other God but Thee! I have sinned in Thy sight,' Allah ordered the fish to cast him out onto dry land. He found himself at a place seven parasangs above Mossul, on the Euphrates, that is now called *Balt*, which means Castaway.

Regardless of the language in which it is told, the story of Jonah can be interpreted a number of ways. From a psychoanalyst's point of view, this unwilling jour-

*Whales figure prominently in Islamic cosmology. It was believed that a whale called* Hut *or* al-Bahmut *carried the world on its back. The twenty-ninth letter in the Arabic alphabet,* nun, *has a numerical value of fifty, but also means "fish" or "whale." The intriguing thing about its shape, philosopher René Guénon points out, is that it looks like the lower half of a circle with a dot in the middle. Some see this as representing the embryo in the womb; others, Noah's ark. The myth of Jonah (in Arabic,* Yunus *or* Dhun-Nun*) can also be tied in with this symbolism: Jonah inside the whale is not unlike the dot of immortality and knowledge in the "belly" of the letter* nun. *Above: An initiatory scene inspired by the story of Jonah, from an anonymous illuminated manuscript. Turkish, c. 1595.*

ney in the warm belly of a sea monster may symbolize the wish we all have to revert to the fetal stage.

The temporary disappearance of the prophet in the stomach of the beast may also be read as a rite of passage. The hero withdraws completely from the world, reaches some higher religious or magical truth through suffering, fear, solitude, and symbolic death, after which he returns to the world changed or reborn. The whale stands for death, for the self-effacement that must precede the attainment of True Life. Jonah emerges from the cavelike belly of the whale and into the light of the knowledge of the Lord.

## CHILDREN OF THE PROPHET

The myth of Jonah swallowed up and "vomited out" by a whale has flourished in literature and folklore as well as in religious writings. Today the children of the prophet make up a large family indeed.

Mihály Babits (1883–1941) wrote *The Book of Jonah*, a high point in Hungarian poetry, when he knew he was suffering from an incurable disease. In this subtle, probing psychoanalytical work—an "inner biography," as it were—the poet draws on the theme of a disobedient prophet who vanishes in a whale and returns to earth as an allegory and counterpoint for his own spiritual development.

Curiously, the French poet Jean-Paul de Dadelsen (1913–57), like Babits, wrote his collection *Jonah* (1962) when he knew that he was going to die. "They dwelled with us in the maw of the whale," we read in the Introductory Invocation. Here, the whale symbolizes not just the death of one man, but the dark disorder of world war.

In a poem entitled "Jonah," British poet D. J. Enright (b. 1920) writes,

The whale is a gigantic supermarket
Crammed from top to bottom with desirable commodities . . .
Inside you may also find an unforgiving prophet.

*The cavernous maw of the whale has inspired many a tale, some dramatic, philosophical, and moralizing, others droll or highly graphic. Carlo Collodi's* The Adventures of Pinocchio *is both entertaining and didactic. The marionette shows his mettle by rescuing the shoemaker from the belly of a whale, thereby earning the right to become a real live boy. Right: Illustration from an early edition of* Pinocchio, *by C. Chiostri.*

Another variation on the theme, "Holy Week," was written by Mexican poet Gabriel Zaïd (b. 1934):

Something profound is
rising up through the waters
to breathe, Jonah,
with great jets of grief.

There waits for you
the whale of melancholy.

*(translated by Margaret Cullen)*

Yes, Jonah had many children, but few as popular or as endearing as Pinocchio, the wooden marionette turned little boy. The serialized story Carlo Collodi (pseudonym of Carlo Lorenzini, 1826–90) published in Florence's *Giornale dei Bambini* ("Children's Magazine") appeared in book form in 1883. The adventures of Pinocchio inspired Walt Disney's feature-length cartoon, which in its turn has found an enduring place in modern popular culture.

One of the key episodes in *The Adventures of Pinocchio* takes place in the belly of a sea monster, a creature Collodi describes as a "gigantic Dog-fish," an "Attila of fish and fishermen" that is "more than a kilometer long, not counting its tail." Readers soon realize that it must be a whale, as the creature breathes through its lungs . . . and suffers from asthma!

The Dog-fish "sucked Pinocchio in as he would have sucked a hen's egg." When the marionette reaches the monster's stomach, he meets up with a philosophical tuna that assures him, "When one is born a Tunny it is more dignified to die in the water than in oil." Then Pinocchio thinks he sees a light. It is the glow of a candle held by—can it be?—Gepetto, his father! The old carpenter had survived inside the whale "for almost two years," living on supplies from a ship the beast had inadvertently swallowed. Dragging, then carrying his father, Pinocchio makes his way to the tongue of the Dog-fish, which one would mistake for "a lane in a large park." They manage to get past the giant fish's "three rows of teeth" because it "suffered very much from asthma" and had to sleep with its mouth open.

## THE MORALIZING AND PHILOSOPHICAL WHALE

When Pinocchio finds himself in the belly of the gigantic Dog-fish, he is given the opportunity to rescue his father, gain wisdom, and earn the right to become a real live boy. In this manner, Collodi teaches children a lesson in an entertaining way.

This was not the only time moralists pressed the whale into service. Whales are massive, powerful, persuasive creatures. They make a point. They have that smiling steadfastness of purpose, that unshakable benevolence people associate with confessors.

In one East African legend, recounted in Gatenby (1983), a whale teaches a king a lesson in humility:

One day, when all people, spirits and animals in his kingdom had eaten their fill, Sulemani prayed to God that He might permit him to feed *all* the created beings on earth. . . . But God wished to show him that all human enterprise must have an end in the very size of the encounter it has sought so fervently to face. It pleased God to raise to the surface of the sea a fish such as fishermen had never seen. In the learned books it is described as a whale, but it was much bigger. It rose up from the water like an island, like a mountain. It ate and

*Below: Frontispiece from the 1877 edition of Jules Verne's* Twenty Thousand Leagues Under the Sea *(1869), one of the most famous maritime novels in literature. More than once during their amazing underwater adventure, Captain Nemo, Professor Aronnax, and harpooner Ned Land meet up with whales (among other assorted monsters), which at one point provide the author with a chance to inject some humor into their discussions.*

*"But what you undoubtedly don't know, Monsieur Aronnax, is that in the beginning of time whales could swim even faster than they do now." "Oh, really, Ned! And why was that?" "Because at that time their tails were crosswise, just like fish. . . . When the Lord realized that they were swimming too fast, he twisted their tails, and from then on they have had to beat the waves up and down and, of course, they lost some of their speed."*

*In* Hamlet *(Act III, Scene 2), Shakespeare compared a cloud to a whale. J.M.W. Turner (1775–1851) also seemed intent on turning whales into clouds. The connection between these two giants of English culture is rather unsettling. Turner painted four whaling scenes. Two date from 1845:* Whalers *and* The Whale Ship. *The other two are from 1846:* Hurrah! for the Whaler Erebus! Another Fish! *and* Whalers (boiling blubber), entangled in flax ice, endeavouring to extricate themselves. *Right:* The Whale Ship. *Oil and watercolor on canvas, 91.8 x 122.6 cm. The Metropolitan Museum of Art, New York.*

*John Huston directed a film version of Herman Melville's celebrated novel* Moby-Dick *(1851). Below: The final moments of the obsessed Captain Ahab (Gregory Peck) and the white whale.*

ate, until there was not a single bag of corn left. The whale raised its voice and roared: 'Oh king, I am still hungry. Feed me!' Sulemani asked the big fish if there were more fishes of its size in the sea, to which the sea-monster replied: 'Of my tribe there are seventy thousand.' At these words, King Sulemani prostrated himself upon the ground and prayed to God: 'Forgive me, Lord, for my foolish desire to feed Thy creation.' King Sulemani thanked the creature for teaching him a lesson. From then on, he no longer tried to take over God's job of feeding all His creatures.

*(translated from the Swahili by Jan Knappert)*

Before long, whales had broadened their involvement in human affairs from moralizing to philosophy. And no wonder: their very size forces people to ponder the insignificance of their own species.

Never did whales appear so frequently in philosophical treatises than in seventeenth- and eighteenth-century England and France. One of the first to tap its potential as a cogent vehicle was Thomas Hobbes (1588–1679), author of *Leviathan, Or the Matter, Forme and Power of a Commonwealth Ecclesiasticall and Civil* (1651). As the pessimistic and mechanistic Hobbes saw it, "every man is Enemy to every man." The only way to end "this warre of every man against every man" is to establish a commonwealth that can safeguard the lives and property of individuals within it. In return, however, the commonwealth exacts absolute obedience. This man-made totalitarian state Hobbes refers to as Leviathan.

Voltaire (1694–1778) also pointed up his philosophical tales with whales, but in a different way. In *Micromégas* (1752), whales serve as living proof of man's colossal conceit. When Micromégas, the super-giant from Sirius, and an average-sized giant from Saturn reach Earth, they assume that a planet so ridiculously small could not possibly harbor living things. Then, using diamonds as magnifying glasses, they manage to spot a whale. Later, they have to squint and strain their eyes to make out a boatload of philosophers.

After a long time, the inhabitant of Saturn saw something almost imperceptible in the Baltic Sea: it was a whale. Very adroitly he picked it up with his little finger and, placing it on his thumbnail, showed it to the Sirian, who started laughing at the extreme smallness of the inhabitants of our globe. The Saturnian, satisfied that our world was inhabited after all, assumed immediately that all the inhabitants were whales.

大漁
鯨の

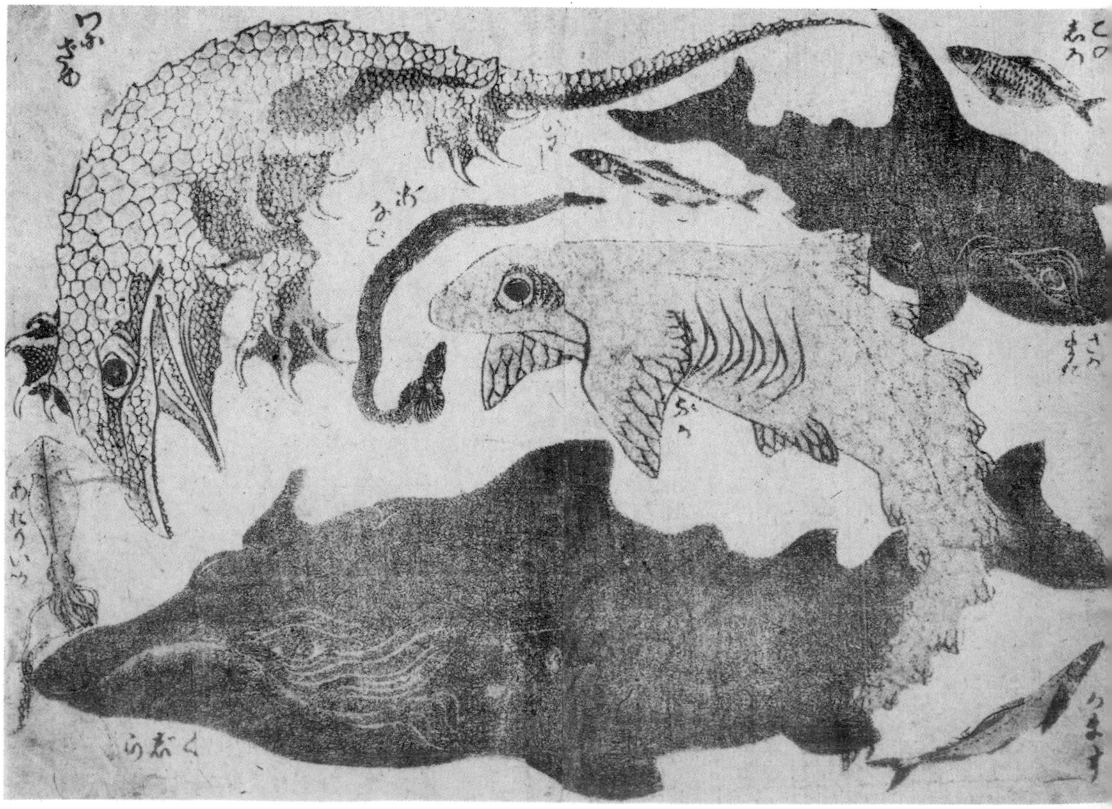

*Whales have inspired artists the world over. From India comes this quote from the epic poem* Mahābhārata *(Adi Parva, XXI):*

*"Along the way they saw the ocean turn into a windswept, bellowing reservoir of choppy waves: an ocean of whales . . ."*

*The Japanese waxed lyrical about whales, too—and not just the ones in the sea. Witness this haiku by Buson (1716–84):*

*"Fresh-killed whale meat is*
*offered for sale. The clash*
*of market knives resounds."*
*(translated by Greg Gatenby)*

*Japanese painters and engravers took turns depicting the wondrous whale. Left:* Dignitaries in Boats Beholding a Great Whale, *a triptych print by Kuniyoshi (1798–1861). 1847–52. 35 x 75 cm. Opposite, left: A whale, a crocodile and a carp, by Hokusai (1760–1849). 16.5 x 23.5 cm. Below: Another print by Kuniyoshi, c. 1848–52, illustrates a famous episode in Japanese history: The samurai Miyamoto Husashi slays a huge whale with his sword.*

## THE WHALE IN LITERATURE

Whales have appeared in more tall tales, religious parables, moralizing fables, and philosophical treatises than any other animal. They also hold a place of honor in masterpieces of literature.

Not all literary inventions involving whales, however, have been masterpieces. Most were simply embroidered rewrites of whaling accounts. The best example of this genre in English is *Peter the Whaler* (London, 1851) by W. H. G. Kingston; and in French, *Les Baleiniers* (1858) by Alexandre Dumas, in which the author of *The Three Musketeers* trades in his swords for harpoons and sends his heroes off into the Arctic to hunt whales. Frank Bullen's *The Cruise of the Cachalot* (New York, 1899) is in much the same vein.

All of these efforts pale next to Herman Melville's *Moby-Dick* (1851), one of the masterpieces of world literature. In 1840, Melville went to sea aboard the whaler *Acushnet* (prototype of the *Pequod*). He wrote about his South Seas adventures in *Typee* (1846) and *Omoo* (1847) and began writing *Moby-Dick* "in a kind of mesmeric trance." He finished the first version of his magnum opus in the middle of 1850, met Nathaniel Hawthorne, rewrote the entire book, and, in 1851, published it almost simultaneously in London (as *The Whale*) and New York (as *Moby-Dick; or, The Whale*).

Running the gamut of literary styles from the comic to the epic, *Moby-Dick* tells the story of Ahab, captain of the *Pequod*, Queequeg the harpooner, and a crew persuaded to hunt the biggest and most majestic sperm whale of them all. The narrator is young, impressionable Ishmael, sole survivor of the *Pequod's* deadly confrontation with the white monster. The novel weaves at least three different levels of meaning into a richly textured symphony.

In encyclopedic documentary fashion, the author describes in mind-boggling detail whale species, whaling ships, harpooning techniques, and flensing procedures. It is a magisterial feat of research. The character of Moby-Dick is based on two sperm whales that actually existed. The first attacked and sank the whaler *Essex*, under the command of Captain Pollard, in the Pacific in 1820. The second was a whale "white as wool" that was sighted in 1810 off the coase of Chile, near Mocha Island, and which J. N. Reynolds, a writer for *The Knickerbocker* magazine, christened "Mocha Dick."

Running parallel with this compendium of whaling information is Ishmael's narrative, which starts out as a fairly routine, if picaresque, sea tale. Before long, however, it takes on the sweep of an epic adventure. The obsessive, deranged Captain Ahab—who is half angel, half devil—prevails upon his men to turning their energies from ordinary whales to a white whale in which are concentrated all the forces of nature. And so begins a haunting sea voyage complete with dead calms, raging storms, dramatic turns of events, sensation, the sinking of the *Pequod*, and the incredible death of Ahab himself, lashed to the side of the creature he was bent on destroying.

The whale is a world unto itself. In his attempt to conquer an incarnation of Almighty God, Ahab knows full well he will be damned for the sin of pride.

Not all whales in literature have the cosmic sweep of Melville's. But even in lesser works, the whale's size makes a lasting impact on the reader all but inevitable. Three examples rank with *Moby-Dick* for sheer loftiness of tone. The first is by D. H. Lawrence (1885–1930), the provocative author of *Lady Chatterly's Lover*. One of the works included in *Last Poems* (1932) is "Whales Weep Not!":

*Whales are the stuff dreams are made of. Above: An illustration from the Hetzel edition of* The Adventures of Captain Hatteras *(1878) by Jules Verne. In this scene, a bowhead tries to escape a whaleboat by swimming between two icebergs, but is crushed when they close in.*

*Right: Even more astounding is* The Whale Within the Iceberg, *an 1884 watercolor by George R. Halm. It depicts a sight Captain Ben Pendleton reportedly saw "with his own two eyes" during an Antarctic whaling expedition in 1820. It was probably a figment of the good captain's imagination, although there is one documented instance of a whale on an iceberg—presumably frozen there after death.*

They say the sea is cold, but the sea contains
the hottest blood of all, and the wildest, the most urgent. . . .
Then the great bull lies up against his bride
in the blue deep bed of the sea,
as mountain pressing on mountain, in the zest of life:
and out of the inward roaring of the inner red ocean of whale blood
the long tip reaches strong, intense, like the maelstrom-tip, and comes to rest
in the clasp and the soft, wild clutch of a she-whale's fathomless body.

And over the bridge of the whale's strong phallus, linking the wonder of whales
the burning archangels under the sea keep passing, back and forth . . .

And enormous mother whales lie dreaming suckling their whale-tender young
and dreaming with strange whale eyes wide open in the waters of the beginning and the end.

The second excerpt is from *Baleine* by Paul Gadenne, which appeared in *Empédocle* in 1949. A girl by the name of Odile informs the narrator that a white whale is stranded on the beach. The two of them go down to have a look at the

carcass. The dead whale comes to symbolize the "European cataclysm" and a "universe in chaos."

We had learned nothing from everything anyone had told us about whales or from what science or history had taught us about them. All we wanted to know was that secret, that key to creation it stood for . . . . We thought we were only looking at a stranded animal. We were looking at a lifeless planet.

Our last example, unlike the previous one, is a celebration of life. The whale's beauty, grandeur and movement are a hymn to nature. In *L'Oeil émerveillé, ou la Nature comme spectacle* (1976), writer and illustrator Samivel (Paul Gayet, b. 1907) describes the emotional impact of seeing a blue whale in the Arctic.

A fabulous presence emerged, and the world took on a whole new dimension. Centuries of immobility suddenly unfurled, the granite was moving, swimming, breathing! I can still see the prow of that living Nautilus curling back the sea, the water streaming down its hulk, the peaceable jaws. I can still hear the swish of spray, the mighty, measured panting of its breathing apparatus, . . . For a few seconds, deep in a remote cove in southern Greenland, I had come face to face with the wellsprings of pure beauty and could not help experiencing a broader feeling of cosmic brotherhood. All I know is that, ever since that encounter, nothing has been quite the same. Secretly I've had to date everything as happening before or after that whale.

## THE COMIC WHALE

We say "to laugh oneself silly"; the French say *rire comme une baleine*. You have to expect things like that when you have a jaw-spread of several yards!

The earliest surviving humorous story to mention whales was written by Lucian of Samostata (c. 125–192). Irked by the spate of fantastic tales that were appearing at the time, and in which authors swore to the veracity of far fetched legends and yarns, Lucian came out with a hilarious parody entitled *A True Story*. The following excerpt is the part that features a whale:

Toward sunrise we suddenly saw a number of sea-monsters, whales. One among them, the largest of all, was fully one hundred and fifty miles long. He came at us with open mouth, dashing up the sea far in advance, foam-washed, showing teeth much larger than

*The sight of a whale eating has struck terror in the hearts of men, but it also occasioned an endless stream of far fetched "reports" and hilarious yarns. "When a whale is hungry," we read in the* Physiologus *(Greek, second century), "it opens its mouth, emitting an odor that attracts all kinds of fish." A reference to whales appears in the* Golden Legend *by Jacobus de Voragine (1230–98): "At that time there lived on the banks of the Rhône, in a forest between Avignon and Arles, a dragon that was half-animal, half-fish, bigger than an ox, longer than a horse, with teeth as sharp as horns and wings on either side of its body. This monster killed all passers-by and sank ships. It had come by the Sea of Galatia. Its parents were Leviathan, a snakelike monster that dwells in the sea, and Onagre, a terrible beast from Galatia." Below: a man-eating monster, from Sebastian Münster's* Cosmographia Universalis *(Basel, 1550).*

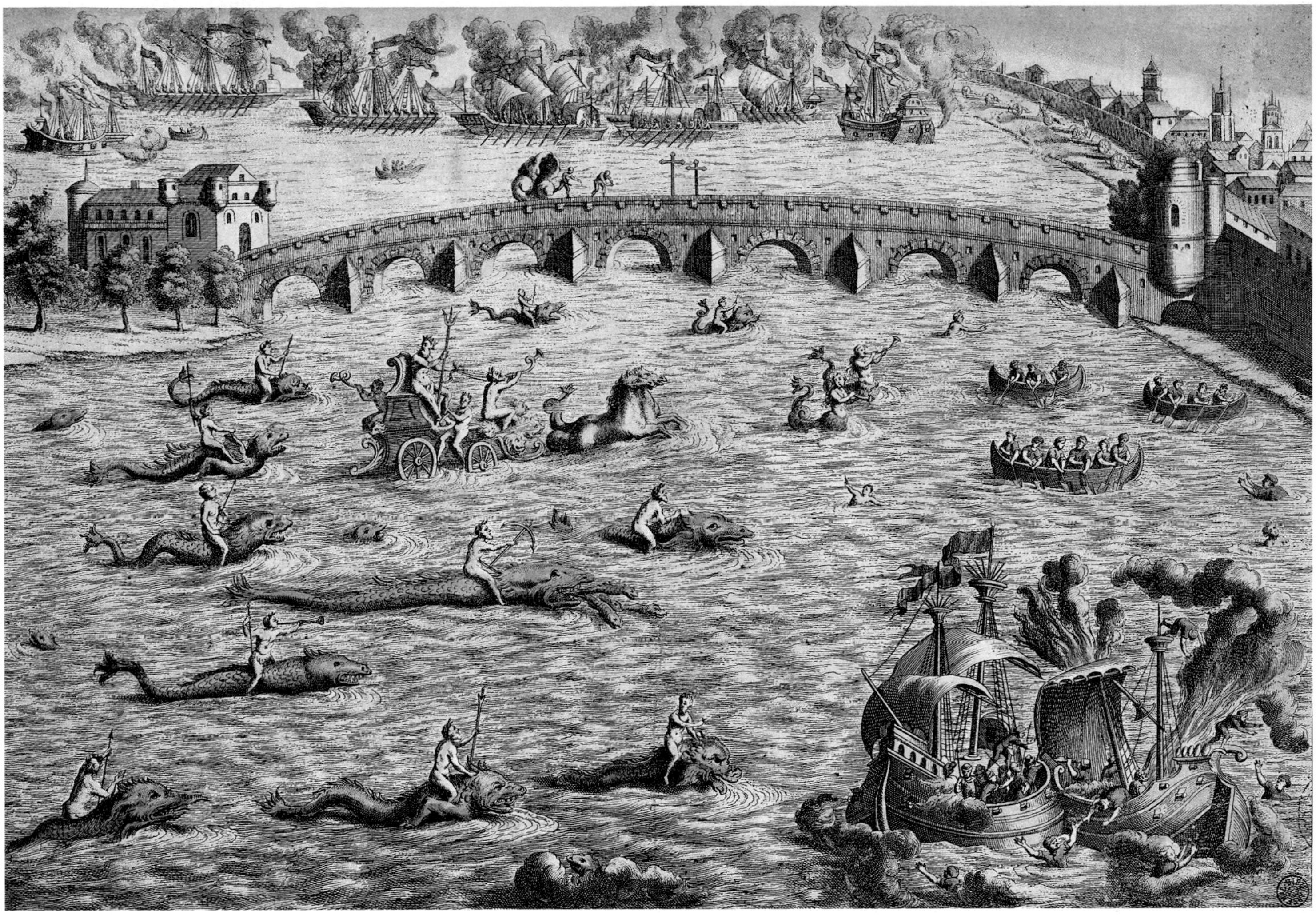

*Whales have also been cause for celebration. Above: Engraving of a* Naumachia on the Seine for the Entrance of Henry II into Rouen, 1550. *The following excerpt from Virgil's* Aeneid *was read during the ceremony: "Monstrous Triton bears him aloft, terrifying the azure waves with his conch. From head to waist his hairy body is that of a swimming man; from the belly down, a whale."*

the emblems of Dionysius in our country, and all sharp as caltrops and white as ivory. We said good-bye to one another, embraced, and waited. He was there in an instant, and with a gulp swallowed us down, ship and all. . . .

When we were inside, it was dark at first, and we could not see anything, but afterwards, when he opened his mouth, we saw a great cavity, flat all over and high, and large enough for the housing of a great city. . . .

On the fifth day of the ninth month, about the second mouth-opening—for the whale did it once an hour, so that we told time by the openings—about the second opening, as I said, much shouting and commotion suddenly made itself heard, and what seemed to be commands and oar-beats. Excitedly we crept up to the very mouth of the animal, and standing inside the teeth we saw the most unparalleled of all the sights that I ever saw—huge men, fully half a furlong in stature, sailing on huge islands as on galleys. Though I know that what I am going to recount savors of the incredible, I shall say it nevertheless. There were islands, long but not very high, and fully a hundred furlongs in circumference, on each of which about a hundred and twenty of those men were cruising, some of whom, sitting along each side of the island one behind the other, were rowing with huge cypress trees for oars—branches, leaves, and all!

*(translated from the Greek by A. M. Harmon, in Gatenby, 1983)*

Lucian rambles on like this, page after page, with unflinching self-assurance. He positively revels in nonsense. His twisted fabrications speak volumes about his zestful, tongue-in-cheek attitude toward life. His parody reaches its climax when he informs us that, incredible though what he says may seem, he fully intends to tell us anyway.

This brand of humor is the hallmark of quite a few eminent writers, including

François Rabelais (1494–1553). In chapters 33 and 34 of the *Fourth Book*, Friar Jean, Panurge, and Pantagruel meet up with a whale. A mock-epic battle ensues.

Toward noon, as we neared Wild Island, Pantagruel spied a monstrous, great *physeter* (Greek for 'blower') or whale. It was still far off, but was heading straight toward us. It was snorting, spurting, swelling, and rising above the waves, high over our maintops; it spouted water aloft in front of it. It looked like a great river flowing down a mountainside. . . .

Panurge began to howl and lament more forlornly than ever.

"Ubbubbughshw!" he moaned. "This is worse than anything that's happened before. Let us flee, I beg you. God's death, this is Leviathan, as described by the noble prophet Moses in the life of the holy Job. That whale will swallow us up like so many pillules: ships, crew, and all the rest of it. We will take up no more room in his infernal, great gullet than a sugarplum in an ass's snout! I vow it is the sea monster sent by Neptune to devour Andromeda because her mother boasted that she was lovelier than the Nereids. We are lost, every one of us! Ah, would there were some valiant Perseus here, to deliver us as he delivered Andromeda!"

"I'll give him Perseus," Pantagruel cried. "Never fear!" . . .

Taking one of those darts (he had plenty aboard), Pantagruel scored a mark with his first shot. It hit the whale downward in the forehead, piercing both jaws and tongue so clean that the beast could not open its mouth to suck out or expel water. With his second shot, Pantagruel put out the monster's right eye; with his third, its left eye. No man but exulted as

*Above:* Storm at Sea, *probably unfinished, was the last painting of Pieter Bruegel the Elder (c. 1525–69). Dating from 1568, it depicts either the boat from which Jonah was cast into the sea, or the belief that sailors could distract a whale by tossing out an empty barrel. Oil on panel, 70.5 x 97 cm. Kunsthistorisches Museum, Vienna. Few scenes can match this one for tragic grandeur: with an ominous reddish-brown sky and ocean as a backdrop, the ship struggles against surging crests that glow a maleficent silvery green.*

*There is something intrinsically dramatic about whales. But reality wavers between tragedy and comedy; these sea giants have also occasioned laughter over the centuries. Below: An illustration from the original edition of* The Adventures of Baron Münchhausen *(London, 1785), by Rudolf Raspe and Gottfried Bürger. Other examples abound. The celebrated Captain Cap, created by Alphonse Allais (1854–1905), was a member of the "General Federation of Whalers of Corrèze." "A corset can be fashioned from what's in its mouth," noted Jules Renard (1864–1910) in* Histoires Naturelles *(1894), tongue firmly in cheek. "But just try and get a waist like that into one!"*

*It would be hard to find a blacker example of black humor than the following explanation of why whaling exists. "Some whales sing off-key. The sour notes cause harpooners with an ear for music to go mad and die. . . . The real reason for this well-intentioned operation (whaling), which some mistake for flensing for pecuniary gain, is to tune their vocal cords" (Gébé and Professor Choron, in the monthly* Hara-kiri*).*

he saw the whale's brow adorned with a trio of horns meeting in an equilateral triangle. The whale veered and whirled, now to the right, now to the left, staggering and swaying like one dazed, blinded, and about to die.

*(translated from the French by Jacques Le Clercq)*

Both Lucian of Samostata and Rabelais had disciples, if not outright imitators, in Rudolf Erich Raspe (1737–94) and Gottfried August Bürger (1747–94), whose *Adventures of Baron Münchhausen* ranks among the high points of literary tall tales. Raspe published the first version in English in 1785; Bürger translated it into German the following year. In his escapades, the braggart Baron has two encounters with whales. The second is event-filled, to say the least.

But our joy was not of long duration, for some hours afterwards we found ourselves surrounded by whales and other fish equally vast in size. There was one of such prodigious length that we could not see the end of him, even with a telescope. By ill luck we did not see the monster till he was close to us; he swallowed at one gulp our ship at full sail.

When we had been some time in his throat, he opened his jaws to take in a great gulp of water. Our vessel, floating on this current, was drawn into the monster's stomach, where we were as quiet as though we had been at anchor in a dead calm. . . . When the monster drank we floated, and when he poured the water out we were left dry. We made an exact estimate of the quantity of water he drank, and found that it would be sufficient to fill the Lake of Geneva, which is thirty miles in circumference. . . .

When the fish opened his mouth again, and poured the water out, we assembled afresh, and I was chosen president. I proposed to them to fasten two of our tallest masts together, end to end, and when the monster opened his jaws, to plant them in such a manner as should prevent his shutting his mouth again. This plan was passed by acclamation, and a hundred of the strongest men among us were selected to put it into execution. The two masts had scarcely been arranged according to my directions, before a favorable moment presented itself. The monster began to yawn; we planted our two masts in such a way that their lower end was fixed in his tongue, while the upper pierced the roof of his palate, so that he would be unable, for ever after, to make his jaws meet. . . .

When everyone had left the vast stomach of the monster, we found we were a fleet of thirty-five ships of all nations.

In dozens of stories like this, whales gulp down people, armies, whole nations at a time solely for our amusement. Jonah had a long line of humorous successors. At one point in *The Little Humpbacked Horse* (1834), Russian writer Piotr Ershov (1815–69) gives a whale center stage:

The Little Horse reared and cried out with all his might: "O wondrous whale-fish, if you suffer it is because you have gone against the will of God. On far-off seas you have swallowed two score and ten splendid ships. If you set them free, the Lord shall put an immediate end to all your suffering."

No survey of humorous whales, however cursory, would be complete without "How the Whale Got His Throat," one of the *Just So Stories* Rudyard Kipling (1865–1936) published in 1902. In it we learn how the whale came to get a grating in his throat, thanks to a "'Stute Fish" and a "Mariner of infinite-resource-and-sagacity."

In the sea, once upon a time, O my Best Beloved, there was a Whale, and he ate fishes. . . . All the fishes he could find in all the sea he ate with his mouth—so! Till at last there was only one small fish left in all the sea, and he was a small 'Stute Fish, and he swam a little behind the Whale's right ear, so as to be out of harm's way. Then the Whale stood up on his tail and said, "I'm hungry." And the small 'Stute Fish said in a small 'stute voice, "Noble and generous Cetacean, have you ever tasted Man?" . . .

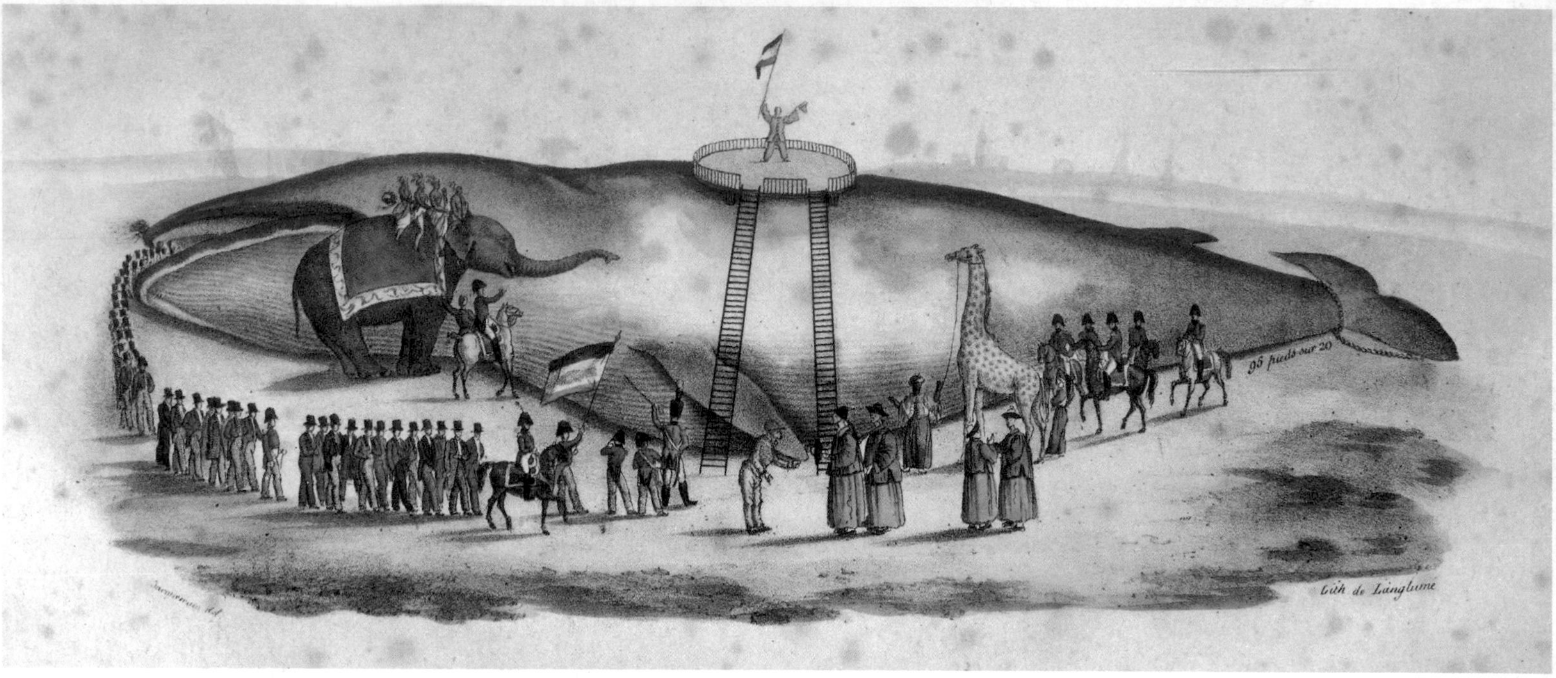


But as soon as the Mariner, who was a man of infinite-resource-and-sagacity, found himself truly inside the Whale's warm, dark, inside cupboards, he stumped and he jumped and he thumped and he bumped, and he pranced and he danced, and he banged and he clanged, and he hit and he bit, and he leaped and he creeped, and he prowled and he howled, and he hopped and he dropped, and he cried and he sighed, and he crawled and he bawled, and he stepped and he lepped, and he danced hornpipes where he shouldn't, and the Whale felt most unhappy indeed. (*Have* you forgotten the suspenders?)

So he said to the 'Stute Fish, "This man is very nubbly, and besides he is making me hiccough. What shall we do?"

"Tell him to come out," said the 'Stute Fish. . . .

. . . and just as he said 'Fitch' the Mariner walked out of his mouth. But while the Whale had been swimming, the Mariner, who was indeed a person of infinite-resource-and-sagacity, had taken his jack-knife and cut up the raft into a little square grating all running criss-cross, and he tied it firm with his suspenders (*now* you know why you were not to forget the suspenders!), and he dragged that grating good and tight into the Whale's throat, and there it stuck! . . .

From that day on, the grating in his throat, which he could neither cough up nor swallow down, prevented him eating anything except very, very small fish; and that is the reason why whales nowadays never eat men or boys or little girls.

This joyous procession of comical whales continues to this day. In *Paroles* (1972), by Jacques Prévert (1903–77), there is a little poem that delights schoolchildren in France even when it is assigned to them as a recitation:

A-whaling we will go, a-whaling we will go,
Said the father in a cross tone of voice
To his son Prosper, stretched out 'neath the cupboard.
A-whaling we will go, a-whaling we will go.
Don't you want to go?
Why on earth not?
Why on earth should I go fishing for a creature
That never did me any harm?
Go catch him yourself, papa,
If that's what you want,
I'd just as soon stay home with my poor mother
And cousin Gaston.

*All Europe was fascinated by the whale that beached itself at Ostende, Belgium, in 1827. Above: In this engraving signed Langlumé, we see it "visited by an elephant, a giraffe, the Osage, and the Chinese."*

*The awesome strength of the whale fired the imagination of Alphonse Toussenel (1803–85), Fourierist, naturalist, and author of* L'Esprit des bêtes, zoologie passionelle *(1862). "Man does not realize the benefits he could have derived from these natural locomotives. It would have taken just a little patience and some training tailored to their monstrous bearing and disposition. When I think that it takes a right whale or a sperm whale no more than a fortnight to circle the globe, I cannot help regretting that people have not yet hankered to make them their partners. Imagine harnessing the strength of a towboat that can race along at 60 knots an hour! What is steam power compared with that?"*

*Domesticate whales, indeed! Just try it! Below: One of a series of illustrations depicting* The World in the Year 2000 *(1900). Here we see a handy-dandy "whale bus" that Toussenel would have approved of.*

## FLORILEGIUM

*THE METAPHYSICAL WHALE*

Whales in the Sea
God's voice obey.

*—New England Primer*
*(quoted in* Moby-Dick, *1851)*

When I was small,
God and a foundered whale were possible.
Whales are rarer, God as invisible.

*—From "The Whale, His Bulwark,"*
*by Derek Walcott (St. Lucian, b. 1930)*

The whale skeleton:
I kneel to pray in it, as
in a cathedral.

*—From "Three Whale Haiku," by Sen Akira*
*(Japanese, b. 1926)*

The Whales are singing . . . through the
water repeating strange verses. Listen,
God, Listen.

*—From "Cetus, a Letter from Jonah,"*
*by Siv Cedering (American, b. 1939)*

Yes, we can still do what we can to preserve not only such rare things as whales and dolphins, but the eternal Mystery of which they are both emblem and incarnate form.

*—From "Whales and Dolphins," by David Gascoyne (British, b. 1916)*

*"The whale," note J. Chevalier and A. Gheerbrandt (1969), "symbolizes a container. It can stand for hidden treasure or lurking misfortune, depending on the contents. Within it lie all the possibilities of the unseen and the unknown. It is the seat of all the opposites that life is capable of spawning. Thus, its ovoid shape has been likened to two circle segments joined together, symbolizing the world above and the world below, Heaven and Earth."*

*Right:* The Travelers, *by Roland Cat (b. 1943, Neuilly, France). 1979. Oil on canvas, 78 x 62.5 cm. Private collection.*

## *THE VISIONARY WHALE*

Whale is a village in Cumbria:
not a huge one, I imagine—
a few farms, a church perhaps,
a Post Office, a pub . . .

*—From "Whale, Cumbria," by Fleur Adcock (British, b. 1934)*

In its great blue whales, hunted even to between houses, an entire people was dreaming of a less silent light.

*—From "Les Grandes Baleines Bleues," by Jean Oriet, 1973.*

Once I had a whale's shape but then I had
only sadness. A devil sucked my spirit out;
now I am a ghost wading inland to die.

*—From "Ghost Song," by Susan Musgrave (Canadian, b. 1951)*

I think of it as a vast city
plunging through the history of our
  dreams
singing its largely inaudible songs —
its highways, its alleys, even its crammed
  slums

*—From "Whale," by Andrew Taylor (Australian, b. 1940)*

Dreamt of
  Moby Dick the Great White Whale
    cruising about
      with a flag flying
        with an inscription on it
"I Am what is left of Wild Nature"
And Ahab pursuing in a jet boat with a ray
  gun and jet harpoons . . .

*—From "The Dream Book," by Lawrence Ferlinghetti (American, b. 1919)*

We are ignorant and strangers in cities of
nature our imagination is watered down
and diluted whales are black roses in the
rivers of our age.

*—From "Black Roses," by Jan Boelens (Dutch, b. 1928)*

The whale came back.
It took off its hat.
It took off its overcoat.
It took off its dark glasses
and put them in its suit pocket.
It looked exhausted. . . .
Next I sneaked back into the back garden
  and buried The History of Genetic
  Possibilities.

*—From "Note from the Laboratory Assistant's Notebook," by Brian Patten (British, b. 1946)*

Envoi
December 26
It is raining on the sea. Leaden sheets of gray sky mingle with the gray of an endless expanse of water: infinity.

I've finished this book on whales. In the distance, the ocean is blanketed with snow; water congeals on the horizon; the pack ice takes shape; before me lies the Arctic Ocean. In my mind's eye I see a right whale, smiling broadly as it swims by amid ice castles, a moving billow of gray flesh in a gray back of beyond, a fantastic spout in the fog. A pair of crescent-flukes lingers on the watery dreamscape.

I go down to the beach. I put my feet in the water. My body swells all over. My legs retract. My hands broaden into flippers. I weigh 10 tons. I stretch out in the maternal sea. I weigh 20 tons. The pink tongue in my cavernous mouth brushes baleen plates five meters long. I weigh 60 tons. I have the urge to move my body back and forth; my huge tail stock goes to work. I swim; I breathe through my two blowholes; I dive. I shudder as the water gently rushes past my skin. I feel the water reverberating with powerful, melodious calls. Wait for me, sisters, I'm coming!

Yves Paccalet
"The Smell of the Sun in the Grass"
*Nature Diary*

*Hiroshige (1797–1858), a master of the Japanese print, was an avid nature lover whose peerless pictures of flowers, birds, insects, shells, and fish are at once impressionistic, lyrical, and scientifically accurate. His interests included whales. Opposite:* Whaling at Goro, Hizen Province, *from* Shakoku Meisho Hyakkei *(One Hundred Famous Sites in the Provinces).*

*"Now, standing on the strand of time,*
*I try to catch the whale with my words . . .*
*With all the weight of his dream*
*the whale dives undersea."*
*(Mokuo Nagayama, Japanese, b. 1934)*

諸國名所百景
肥前
五嶌鯨漁の圖

# BIBLIOGRAPHY


Albert le Grand. *De Animalibus*. Rome, XIII[th] century.
Aldrovandi. *Histoire naturelle*. Bologna, 1615.
Ariosto. *Roland furieux*. Retold by Italo Calvino, transl. by C. Hippeau, Flammarion, Paris, 1982.
Aristotle. *Histoire des animaux*. Transl. by Pierre Louis, Les Belles Lettres, Paris, 1969.
Atassi, M.-Z. "Properties of Components of Myoglobin of the Sperm Whale," *Nature*, Vol. 202, May 2, 1964.
*Aventures de Sindbad le Marin (Les)*. Transl. by René R. Khawam, Phébus, Paris, 1985.
Babits, M. *Le Livre de Jonas*. Transl. by N. Abraham, In *Jonas*, Aubier-Flammarion, Paris, 1980.
Barloy, Jean-Jacques. *Le Bon, la bête et le chasseur*. Paris, 1975.
— "Les Monstres marins, Histoires de la mer." *Éditions Historiques*, no. 26, Paris, April 1982.
Barnes, Lawrence G., and Mitchell, Edward. *Cetacea, in Evolution of African Mammals*. Cambridge, Harvard University Press, 1978.
Bateson, Gregory. *Problems in Cetacean and Other Mammalian Communication*. In K.S. Norris, 1966.
Beale, Thomas. *A Few Observations on the Natural History of the Sperm Whale*. London, 1835.
— *Histoire du cachalot*. London, 1839.
Beddington, John, and May, Robert. "L'exploitation d'espèces interdépendantes dans un écosystème naturel." *Pour la Science*, January 1983.
Belon, Pierre. *Histoire naturelle des poissons marins et étrangers*. Paris, 1551.
Benedeit. *Le Voyage de Saint Brandan*. Text and translation by Ian Short. 10/18, Paris, 1984.
Bennett, F.-D. *Campagne de pêche à la baleine autour du monde*. London, 1840.
Bertini, Hélène. "Le Peuple de la mer." *Greenpeace*, no. 10, spring 1982.
— "Chant des baleines, nouvelle interprétation." *Greenpeace*, no. 13, winter 1983.
Bertino, Serge. *Guide de la Mer mystérieuse*. Tchou/E.M.O.M., Paris, 1970.
Besnard W. *Les Produits d'origine marine et fluviale*. Paris, Payot, 1948.
Best, Peter B. *Status of Bryde's Whale (Balaenoptera edeni or Balaenoptera brydei)*. F.A.O.-A.C.M.R.R., December 1975.
Blond, Georges. *La Grande Aventure des baleines*. Fayard, Paris, 1953.
Bonnemains, Jacky. "Le Cachalot cosmopolite." *Le Monde*, July 24, 1985.
Bonner, W.-N. *Whales*. Blanford Press, Poole, Dorset, United Kingdom, 1980.
Boulle, Pierre. *La Baleine des Malouines*. Julliard, Paris, 1983.
Bret, Corinne. "Japon: les chasseurs de baleines meurent aussi." *Libération*, March 30, 1983.
Brouard, Jean-Yves. *Chasse à la baleine: bas les masques!* Océans, s.d.
Bryant, Peter J., and Lafferty, Susan K. "Photo-identification of Gray Whales." *Whalewatcher*, Vol. 14, no. 4, 1980.
Budker, Paul. *Baleines et baleiniers*. Horizons de France, Paris, 1957.
Buffon, Georges-Louis Leclerc, comte de. *Histoire naturelle, générale et particulière*. Paris, 1749–1789.
Burton, Robert. *The Life and Death of Whales*. London, 1973.
Busnel, René-Guy. *Information in the Human Whistled Language and Sea Mammals Whistling*. In K.S. Norris, 1966.
Caldwell, Melba C., and Caldwell, David K. *Epimeletic (Care-Giving) Behavior in Cetacea*. In K.S. Norris, 1966.
— *Behavior of the Sperm Whale Physeter Catodon L.* In K.S. Norris, 1966.
Camper, Petrus. *Observations anatomiques* . . . Paris, 1820.
Cans, Roger. "Jojoba, huile précieuse." *Le Monde*, July 24, 1985.
Chabert, Pierre. "Un nouveau bestiaire." *Poésie 1*, no. 50-51, Paris, December 1977–February 1978.
Chace, O. *Narrative of the most extraordinary and distressing Shipwreck of the Whaleship "Essex."* London, 1821.
Chevalier, J., et Gheerbrant, A. *Dictionnaire des symboles*. Robert Laffont, Paris, 1969.
Clarke, Malcolm R. "Function of the Spermaceti Organ of the Sperm Whale." *Nature*, Vol. 228, November 1970.
Clarke, Malcolm. "La Tête du cachalot." *Pour la Science*, no. 17, March 1979.
Colnett. *A Voyage to the South Atlantic*. London, 1792.
Collodi, Carlo. *Pinocchio*. Transl. by Madame de Gencé, Le Livre de Poche, Paris, 1983.
Cook, Joseph J., and Wisner, William L. *Blue Whale: Vanishing Leviathan*. Dodd, Mead & Company, New York, 1973.
Cousteau, Jacques-Yves, et al. *Almanach de l'environnement*. Robert Laffont, Paris, 1981.
Coyaud, Maurice. *Fourmis sans ombre, Le Livre du haïku*. Phébus, Paris, 1978.
Cummings, William, Thompson, Paul O. *Sounds of Migrating Gray Whales, Eschrichtius glaucus*. San Diego, 1967.
— *Underwater Sounds from the Blue Whale Balaenoptera musculus*. San Diego, 1971.
Cuvier, Frédéric. *Histoire naturelle des mammifères*. Paris, 1826.
Darwin, Charles. *L'Origine des espèces*. Version of P.-P. Grassé. Verviers, Belgium, 1973.
Dawbin, William H. *The Seasonal Migratory Cycle of Humpback Whales*. In K.S. Norris, 1966.
Diolé, Philippe, and Cousteau, Jacques-Yves. *Nos amies les baleines*. Flammarion, Paris, 1972.
Dorozynski, Alexandre. "L'étrange chant des baleines." *Science et Vie*, no. 758, November 1980.
Duby, Georges. *L'An mil*. Paris, 1967.
Dudok Van Heel, W.-H. *Navigation in Cetacea*. In K.S. Norris, 1966.
Duguy, Raymond, and Robineau, Daniel. *Cétacés et phoques des côtes de France*. Paris, 1973.
— *Guide des Mammifères marins d'Europe*. Delachaux et Niestlé, Neuchâtel-Paris, 1982.
Duhamel. *Traité des pêches*. Paris, 1782.
Durhan Floyd E. "Eskimo Fact and Fiction about the Bowhead Whale." *Whalewatcher*, no. 4, 1981.
Earle, Sylvia A. "Humpbacks: The Gentle Whales." *National Geographic*, Vol. 155, 1979.
Ellis, Richard. *The Book of Whales*. Alfred A. Knopf, New York, 1980.
Esnoul, Anne-Marie, Garelli, Paul, *et al. La Naissance du Monde*. Paris, 1959.
F.A.O.-C.C.R.R.M. *Les Mammifères de la mer*, Groupe *Ad Hoc I* sur les grands cétacés, *Projet de rapport* and *suppléments*. Bergen, 1976.
F.A.O.-C.C.M.R.R. *Cetacean Behavior, Learning and Communication*, June 1976.
— *Mammals in the Seas*, Groupe *Ad Hoc IV, Ecological and General Problems*, and *suppléments*. June 1976.
— *Substitutes for Sperm Oil*. June 1976.
Fabricius, Othon. *Fauna Groenlandica*. Leipzig, 1780.
Fraser, F.-C., and Purves, P.-E. "The 'Blow' of Whales." *Nature*, no. 4495, December 24, 1955.
Gadenne, Paul. *Baleine*. Actes Sud, 1982.
Gambell, Ray. *A Review of Population Assessment of Antarctic Fin Whales*. F.A.O.-A.C.M.R.R., December 1975.
— *A Review of Population Assessment of Southern Minke Whales*. F.A.O.-A.C.M.R.R., December 1975.
— *Population Assessment of Antarctic Sei Whales*. F.A.O.-A.C.M.R.R., December 1975.
— *A Review of Population Assessment of Antarctic Sei Whales*. F.A.O.-A.C.M.R.R., February 1976.
Gatenby, G. *Whales, A Celebration*. Little, Brown & Company, Boston, Toronto, 1983.
Geraci, Joseph R. "The Enigma of Marine Mammal Strandings." *Oceanus*, Vol. 21, 1978.
Gervais, Paul. *Histoire naturelle des mammifères*. Paris, 1843.
Gesner, Conrad. *Historiae animalium*. Zurich, 1551.
Glockner-Ferrari, Deborah A. "Photo-identification of Humpback Whales." *Whalewatcher*, winter 1982.
Gordon, Jonathan. *A Multitude of Whales*. World Wildlife Fund, Monthly Report, May 1984.
Grassé, Pierre-Paul. *Traité de Zoologie*, Book XVII (2 parts): *Les Mammifères*. Masson, Paris, 1955.
— *L'Évolution du vivant*. Paris, 1973.
Gulland, J.-A. *A note on the Abundance of Antarctic Blue Whale*. F.A.O.-A.C.M.R.R., June 1976.
Hageland, Albert Van. *La Mer magique*. André Gérard-Marabout, Verviers, Belgium, 1973.
Hamner, William M. "Krill—Untapped Bounty From the Sea?" *National Geographic*, Vol. 165, no. 5, May 1984.
Harlan. *Fauna Americana*. Philadelphia, 1825.
Holt, S.-J. *Whale Management Policy*. F.A.O.-A.C.M.R.R., June 1976.
— "How Red Herrings and Soft Variables are Killing the Whales." *La Sirène*, no. 24, May 1984.
Hosokawa, Hiroshi, and Kamiya, Toshiro. "Some Observations on the Cetacean Stomachs, with Special Considerations on the Feeding Habits of Whales." *The Scientific Reports of the Whale Research Institute*. Tokyo, no. 23, 1971.
Hoyt, R. Erich. *The Whale Watcher's Handbook*. Doubleday & Company, New York, 1984.
Hunter, John. *Observations on the Structure and Oeconomy of Whales*. London, 1787.
Ichihara, Tadayoshi. *The Pigmy Blue Whale, Balaenoptera musculus brevicauda, a New Subspecies from the Antarctic*. In K.S. Norris, 1966.
— *Review of Pigmy Blue Whale Stock in the Antarctic*. F.A.O.-A.C.M.R.R., December 1975.
*International Whaling Statistics*. The Committee for Whaling Statistics, ed., Sandefjord, Norway.
Jonsgård, Åge. *The Distribution of Balaenopteridae in the North Atlantic Ocean*. In K.S. Norris, 1966.
Jonston, Johan. *Historiae naturalis de piscibus et cetis*. Amsterdam, 1657.
Kanwisher, John, and Ridgway, Sam. "L'écophysiologie des cétacés." *Pour la Science*, no. 70, August 1983.
Kasuya, Toshio. "Caryotype of a Sei Whale." *The Scientific Reports of the Whale Research Institute*, Tokyo, no. 20, 1966.
Kaza, Stephanie. "Recreational Whalewatching in California: A Profile." *Whalewatcher*, Vol. 17, no. 3, 1983.
Kipling, Rudyard. *Histoires comme ça*. Transl. by R. d'Humières, L. Fabulet and P. Gripari. Delagrave, Paris, 1961.
Lacépède, Étienne, comte de. *Histoire naturelle des cétacés*. Paris, 1804.
Lawrence, D.-H. *Poèmes*. Transl. by J.-J. Mayoux, Aubier-Montaigne, Paris, 1976.
Leatherwood, Stephen, and Reeves, Randall R. *The Sierra Club Handbook of Whales and Dolphins*. San Francisco, 1983.
Leblanc, Gérald. "Sur les traces des Basques." *Québec Science*, Vol. 22, no. 11, July 1984.
*Les Mille et Une Nuits*. Transl. by A. Galland, 1704.
Lesson. *Histoire naturelle des cétacés*. Paris, 1828.
Lillo, Samuel A. *Canciones de Arauco*. El Arponero, Santiago, Chili, 1940.
Linné, Carl Von. *Systema Naturae*. 1758.
*Livre des Ruses (Le)*. Transl. by René R. Khawam, Phébus, Paris, 1976.
Lockyer, Christina. *Estimates of Growth and Energy Budget for the Sperm Whale Physeter Catodon*. F.A.O.-A.C.M.R.R., February 1976.
— *Growth and Energy Budget of Large Baleen Whales from the Southern Hemisphere*. F.A.O.-A.C.M.R.R., March 1976.
Macfarlan, A.-A. *The Fireside Book of North American Indian Folktales*. Stackpole Books, Harrisburg, Pennsylvania, 1974.
Machin, D. *A Multivariate Study of External Measurements of the Sperm Whale (Physeter Catodon)*. J. Zool., London, 1974.
Mackintosh, N.A. *The Stock of Whales*. London, 1965.
— *The Distribution of Southern Blue and Fin Whales*. In K.S. Norris, 1966.

Magnus, Olaus. *Historia de gentibus septentrionalibus*. 1555.
Maigret, J. *Les Echouages massifs de cétacés dans la région du Cap-Vert (Sénégal)*. Notes Africaines, Université de Dakar, January 1979.
Mandojana, Ricardo. "The Right Whale to Save." *Oceans*, March-April 1981.
— "A Close-Up Look at Patagonian Right Whales." *Whalewatcher*, winter 1983.
Matthews, L. Harrison. *La Vie des Mammifères*. Rencontre, Lausanne/Bordas, Paris, 1971.
McIntyre, Diana Ryan. "The Wonders of Magdalene Boy." *Whalewatcher*, Vol. 14, no. 4, 1980.
Mearns, Charles. *International Trade in Whale Products, A Review*. R.S.P.C.A., June 1980.
Melville, Herman. *Moby-Dick*. London, New York, 1851. Transl. by L. Jacques, J. Smith and J. Giono, Gallimard, Paris, 1941.
Milton, John. *Le Paradis perdu*. Transl. by de Pongerville, Charpentier, Paris, 1843.
Mitchell, Edward. *Porpoise, Dolphin and Small Whale Fisheries of the World*. Morges (Switzerland), 1975.
Mitchell, Edward, and Reeves, Randall R. "The Alaska Bowhead Problem: A Commentary." *Arctic*, Vol. 33, no. 4, December 1980.
Morzer Bruyns, Captain, W.F.J. *Field Guide of Whales and Dolphins*. Amsterdam, 1971.
Mountford, C.-P. *The Dawn of Time*. Rigby Publishers, Sydney, 1969.
Nayman, Jacqueline. *Whales, Dolphin and Man*. London, 1973.
Nishiwaki, Masaharu. *Distribution and Migration of the Larger Cetaceans in the North Pacific as shown by Japanese Whaling Results*. In K.S. Norris, 1966.
Norris, Kenneth S. *Whales, Dolphins and Porpoises*. University of California Press, Berkeley and Los Angeles, 1966.
Ohsumi, Seiji. *Some Investigations on the School Structure of Sperm Whale*. In K.S. Norris, 1966.
Ommaney, F.-D. *Lost Leviathan*. Dodd, Mead & Company, New York, 1971.
Ovid. *Les Métamorphoses*. Transl. by J. Chamonard, Garnier-Flammarion, Paris, 1966.
Paccalet, Yves, et Cousteau, Jacques-Yves. *La Vie au bout du monde*. Flammarion, Paris, 1979.
— *Du grand large aux Grands Lacs*. Flammarion, Paris, 1985.
Parmentier, Rémi, Dewez, Georges, and Greenpeace. *À l'écoute des baleines*. Le Dernier Terrain Vague, Paris, 1978.
— "La chasse aux baleiniers pirates." *Greenpeace*, no. 11, summer 1982; no. 12, fall 1982.
— "Un pas de plus vers l'application du moratoire." *Greenpeace*, no. 16, fall 1983.
— "Krill: la faim des baleines." *Greenpeace*, no. 17, winter 1984.
Patten, Donald R., *et al.* "Whales, Move Over!" *Whalewatcher*, Vol. 14, no. 4, 1980.
Payne, Roger, and McVay, Scott. "Songs of Humpback Whales." *Science*, Vol. 173, no. 3997, August 1971.
Payne, Kathy and Roger. "At Home With Right Whales." *National Geographic*, Vol. 149, no. 3, March 1976.
Piveteau. *Traité de paléontologie*. Book VI, *Mammifères*. Masson, Paris, 1958.
Pliny the Elder. *Histoire naturelle*. Transl. by E. de Saint-Denis. Les Belles Lettres, Paris, 1955.
Portier, Paul. *Physiologie des animaux marins*. Flammarion, Paris, 1938.
Purves, P.-E. "Locomotion in Whales." *Nature*, Vol. 197, January 26, 1963.
Rabelais, François. *Œuvres complètes*. Garnier, Paris, 1962.
Racine, Jean. *Phèdre*. Nouveaux Classiques Larousse, Paris, 1971.
Raspe, Rudolph Érich, and Bürger, Gottfried. *Les Aventures du baron de Münchhausen*. Transl. by Théophile Gautier fils, Folio junior, Gallimard, Paris, 1977.
Reysenbach De Haan, F.-W. *"Listening Underwater: Thoughts on Sound and Cetacean Hearing."* In K.S. Norris, 1966.
Rice, Dale W. *Status of the Eastern Pacific (California) Stock of the Gray Whale*. F.A.O.-A.C.M.R.R., December 1975.
Riedman, Sarah R., and Gustafson, Elton T. *Home is the Sea: for Whales*. Rand McNally & Company, 1966.
Rondelet, Guillaume. *Histoire entière des poissons*. Lyons, 1568.
Rorvik, Carl Jacob, and Jonsgård, Åge. *Review of Balaenopterids in the North Atlantic Ocean*. F.A.O.-A.C.M.R.R., December 1975.
Ross, G.J.B., Best, P.B. and Donelly. "New Records of the Pigmy Right Whale (Caperea marginata) from South Africa." *Journal of Canadian Fisheries*, March 1975.
Roux, Charles. "Quand les baleines s'amusent." *Geo*, no. 64, June 1984.
Samivel. *L'Œil émerveillé, ou la Nature comme spectacle*. Albin Michel, Paris, 1976.
Scheffer, Victor B. *The Year of the Whale*. Souvenir Press, London, 1969.
Scoresby, William. *An Account of the Arctic Region*. Edinburgh, 1820.
—*Journal of a Voyage to the Northern Whale Fishery*. London, 1823.
Sergeant, D.-E. *Stocks of Fin Whales Balaenoptera physalus L. in the North Atlantic Ocean*. F.A.O.-A.C.M.R.R., June 1976.
Sibbald, R. *Phalainologia nova*... Edinburgh, 1692.
Simpson, J. *Icelandic Folktales and Legends*. B.T. Bastford Ltd, London, 1972.
Slijper, E.-J. *Whales*. Cornell University Press, Ithaca, New York, 1969.
Small, George L. *The Blue Whale*. Columbia University Press, New York, 1971.
Soulaire, Jacques. *À la recherche de Moby Dick*. Hachette, Paris, 1959.
Stenuit, Robert. *Dauphin mon cousin*. Le livre de Poche, Hachette, Paris, 1972.
Stonehouse, Bernard. *A Closer Look at Whales and Dolphins*. Hamilton, London, 1978.
Swartz, Steven L. "Laguna San Ignacio: Abundant Marine Life. . . ." *Whalewatcher*, Vol. 14, 1980.
Swift, Jonathan. *Œuvres*. Bibliothèque de la Pléiade, Gallimard, Paris, 1965.
Thiercelin, Louis. *Journal d'un baleinier*. 1866, Editions Vernoy, Geneva, 1979.
Toussenel, Alphonse. *L'Esprit des bêtes, zoologie passionnelle*. E. Dentu, Paris, 1862.
Triolet, Elsa. *La Poésie russe*. Seghers, Paris, 1965.
True, F.-W. *Whalebone Whales of the Western North Atlantic*. 1904.
Van Beneden, P.-J. *Cétacés, Mélanges* (31 études). Brussells, 1867–1892.
Verne, Jules. *Vingt mille lieues sous les mers*. 1869. Le Livre de Poche, Hachette, Paris, 1966.
Viale, Denise. *Relation entre les échouages de cétacés et la pollution chimique en mers Ligure et Tyrrhénienne*. F.A.O.-C.C.R.R.M., July 1976.
Voltaire. *Romans*. Hachette, Paris, 1961.
Watson, Jane Werner. *Le Livre des baleines*. Éditions des Deux Coqs d'Or, Paris, 1976.
Watson, Lyall. *Sea Guide to Whales of the World*. Hutchinson & Co Ltd, London, 1981.
Whitehead, Hal. *Allô, cachalots*. Géo *Magazine*.
—"Les Sauts des baleines," *Pour la Science*, no. 91, May 1985.
Willoughby, Hugues. *Historiae piscium*. . . . Oxford, 1686.
Winn, Howard E., and Perkins, Paul J. *Sounds of the Humpback Whale*.
Wood, F.-G. *The Cetacean Stranding Phenomenon: An Hypothesis*. Naval Oceans Systems Center, San Diego, 1979.
Zordrager. *Description de la pêche à la baleine*. Amsterdam, 1720.

# INDEX

*Page numbers of illustrations are in italics*

## ILLUSTRATION CREDITS

Altonaermuseum, Hamburg: 22-23. American Cetacean Society: 114-15, 201. Archiv für Kunst und Geschichte, Berlin: 52. Archives, City of Tokyo/Arch. E.R.L.: 18 top and bottom. Archives E.R.L.: 12, 13, 14, 15 bottom, 16, 20, 21 top, 26 bottom, 55, 194, 245, 254, 256, 257, 261, 262, 266, 268, 271. Archives du Nord, Chambre des Comptes, Bayonne: 15 top. Ardea, London (Ph. F. Gohier): 103, 193: Bacon, William: 67. Bancroft Library, Berkeley, California: 29. Bartlett, Jen/©Nat. Geo. Society: 223, 223. Belbeoch, Bruno/Atlas Photos: 186. Bibl. de la Rochelle/Ph. E.R.L.: 89 bottom, 175. Bibl. Nationale, Paris: 56, 269. Bodleian Library, Oxford: 256. British Library, London: 25. British Museum: 260. Bruce Coleman Ltd.: 78, 105 (Ph. Gordon Williamson), 183, 184 top and bottom. Bryant, P.J.: 138, 139. Cahiers du Cinéma, Paris: 263. Cedri, Marina/Ph. Soulaire: 230, 231. Charmet, J.-L.: 272. Compagnie des Reporters/Ph. B. Mathieu: 28, 37. Curto, Paolo: 113, 178. Earthview/Ph. Ken Balcomb: 76, 112; Richard Sears: 174. East Wind Films Ltd.: 43 bottom. Ellis, Graeme: endpapers, 58. Evans, Dr. Wh. E.: 142, 143. Explorer/Ph. M. Moisnard: 10-11, 150. Ferrari, Deborah & Mark: 50-51, 108-09, 126, 155, 188-89, 190-91, 203, 210, 220-21, 224-25. Fondation Cousteau: 33, 46 bottom, 78, 95 bottom, 116, 133, 134 bottom, 152, 154, 196, 198. Gardinier, Alain: 92-93, 154. Giraudon: 54, 258 (bottom of), 259 (top). Gohier, François: 64, 71, 76, 94-95, 106, 124-25, 134, 176, 182, 193, 211, 217, 219, 228-29, 235. Greenpeace: 31, 34, 35, 38, 39, 41 top, 46, 153, 273. di Gregorio, Piero: 119. Hall, Howard: 166. Hobbs, L.: 117. Holford, Michael/Coll. André Breton: 248-49. Jacana/Ph. Carré: 118. Joyce, G.: 158. Kendall Whaling Museum: 24-25, 28, 30, 56, 185, 216, 264, 265, 267, 264 bottom, 281. Kristof, Emory/©Nat. Geo. Society: 47. Kunsthistorisches Museum/Ph. E. Lessing: 250. Lanceau, Yves: 73, 81, 140, 226, 236, 237. Lüden, Walter: 45 top. Magnum: 32; Ph. E. Lessing: 250, 259, 270. Dr. Mandojana: 160, 197, 227, 240. Mansell Collection, London: 27, 209. McSweeney, Dan: 62-63, 135, 136, *222, 227* top. Menil Foundation, Texas: 248. Metropolitan Museum of Art, New York: 258, 263. Minasian, Stan: 132-33. Mol. Thijs: 36. de Muizon, Christian: 60, 61. Museo de Arte, Madrid: 253. Musée de la Marine/Ph. Charmet/©E.R.L.: 31, 247-48. Musée océanographique de Monaco: 129, 159, 179, 195, 201, 206. Musée de La Rochelle/Ph. E.R.L.: 67 right. Mušee d'Histoire Naturelle, Paris/Ph. E.R.L.: 17 top and bottom, 53, 54, 57, 67, 78, 129, 207, 240. New Bedford Whaling Museum: 26, 49. New England Aquarium/Ph. Krauss, Scott: 170 bottom. Nicklin, Flip: 8-9, 85, 87, 96, 130, 144, 148-49, 172, 205, 214, 229, 233. Ocean Images, Inc./Ph. Al Giddings & Rosemary Chastney: 2-3, 4-5, 49, 120-21, 164-65, 170, 173, 228. Old Dartmouth Historical Society, New Bedford: 208. Orti, Dagli: 244. Pitman, R.L.: 239. Port Elisabeth Museum, South Africa/Ph. T. Dicks (Courtesy Mrs. F. Hayes): 69. Rapho/Picture Researchers, Inc.: 118 (Ph. Curtsinger), 122 (Ph. R. Kinné), 147, 147 bottom, 157. Robin des Bois/Ph. Sylvain Solaro: 48. Rogers, Eda: 161, 185. Roger-Viollet: 127 top. Scala: 258; E.R.L.: 251. Schleswig-Holsteinisches Landesmuseum, Schleswig: 21 bottom. Société de Géographie, Paris: 45 bottom. Coll. Soulaire/Ph. Charmet/© E.R.L.: 44 top, 242-43, 252, 272, 275. Swartz, Steve L.: 99 bottom. Suisan Koku Co./ © T. Kasuya: 212-13. Taiyo Fishing Co., Japan: 42. Todd, Frank: 98, 226. Topham Picture Library: 7, 169. The Whale Research Institute, Tokyo: 107, 125 (Omura Hideo), 194. Woods Hole Oceanographic Institution: 110.

Original drawings and paintings by Gabriel Paccalet: 66, 68, 70, 72, 75, 77, 79, 80, 82, 84, 88, 141, 142, 143, 151, 161, 167, 168, 174, 176, 180, 181, 187, 199, 200, 201.

The publishers wish to thank Dr. Soulaire, Thijs Mol, Greenpeace, and the Kendall Whaling Museum for material they graciously made available, as well as the photographers and agencies which provided illustrations for this book. For the English language edition, particular thanks are due to Dr. John Heyning of the Natural History Museum of Los Angeles County for his scientific review of the translation, and much gratitude is owed to Dr. Richard C. Murphy, Pam Stacey, Clark Lee Merriam and Lesley D. High of The Cousteau Society for their invaluable assistance.